Studies in Church History

7

COUNCILS AND ASSEMBLIES

COUNCILS AND ASSEMBLIES

PAPERS READ AT
THE EIGHTH SUMMER MEETING AND
THE NINTH WINTER MEETING
OF THE
ECCLESIASTICAL HISTORY SOCIETY

EDITED BY

G. J. CUMING

AND

DEREK BAKER

CAMBRIDGE
AT THE UNIVERSITY PRESS
1971

Published by the Syndics of the Cambridge University Press
Bentley House, 200 Euston Road, London N.W.1
American Branch: 32 East 57th Street, New York, N.Y.10022

© Cambridge University Press 1971

Library of Congress Catalogue Card Number: 70–132284

ISBN: 0 521 08038 X

Printed in Great Britain
at the University Printing House, Cambridge
(Brooke Crutchley, University Printer)

PREFACE

'Councils and Assemblies' was the theme of the eighth summer meeting (at the University of Kent) and of the ninth winter meeting of the Society. The papers are arranged in chronological order of subject-matter.

Dr Derek Baker has kindly agreed to act as joint editor for the preparation of this and future volumes.

G. J. C.

CONTENTS

Contents

Contents

CONTRIBUTORS

DEREK BAKER, Lecturer in Medieval History, University of Edinburgh

G. V. BENNETT, Fellow of New College, Oxford

A. J. BLACK, Lecturer in Political Science, University of Dundee

BRENDA BOLTON, Lecturer in History, North Western Polytechnic, London

MARGARET GIBSON, Department of History, University of Liverpool

JOSEPH GILL, S.J., Lecturer in Church History, Campion Hall, Oxford

ROY M. HAINES, Department of History, Dalhousie University

E. E. Y. HALES

BASIL HALL, Professor of Ecclesiastical History, University of Manchester

MARGARET HARVEY, Department of History, University of Durham

PETER HINCHLIFF, formerly Professor of Ecclesiastical History, Rhodes University, South Africa

PETER LINEHAN, Fellow of St John's College, Cambridge

STUART P. MEWS, Lecturer in the Sociology of Religion, University of Lancaster

JANET L. NELSON, Newnham College, Cambridge

DONALD M. NICOL, Koraës Professor of Modern Greek and Byzantine History, Language, and Literature, University of London

GEOFFREY F. NUTTALL, Lecturer in Church History, New College, University of London

W. B. PATTERSON, Associate Professor of History, Davidson College, North Carolina

Contributors

ROBERT PETERS, Staff Tutor in Religion, The Open University

A. N. E. D. SCHOFIELD, Department of Manuscripts,
British Museum

EDITH C. TATNALL, Assistant Professor of History,
Metropolitan State College, Denver, Colorado

WALTER ULLMANN, Fellow of Trinity College, Cambridge;
Professor of Medieval Ecclesiastical History, University
of Cambridge

M. J. WILKS, Reader in the History of Political Thought,
Birkbeck College, London

ABBREVIATIONS

AC	Archivo de la Catedral
AHN	Archivo Historico Nacional Madrid (Seccion de Clero)
Ann. Bertin	*Annales Bertiniani*
Annales ESC	*Annales, Economies, Sociétés, Civilisations*
AST	*Analecta Sacra Tarraconensia*
BIHR	*Bulletin of the Institute of Historical Research*
BRAH	*Boletin de la Real Academia de la Historia*
Cal. Reg. Brans.	*A Calendar of the Register of Wolstan de Bransford*
CCR	Calendar of Close Rolls
CQR	*Church Quarterly Review*
C &S	*Councils & Synods 1205–1313*, ed. Powicke & Cheney, 2 vols, Oxford 1904
DNB	*Dictionary of National Biography*
EHR	*English Historical Review*
Germ. Abt.	*Germanische Abteilung*
GR	J. Hales, *Golden Remains* (London 1673)
JEH	*Journal of Ecclesiastical History*
JTS	*Journal of Theological Studies*
Mansi	J. D. Mansi: *Sacrorum Conciliorum nova et amplissima collectio*
MC	*Monumenta Conciliorum Generalium Saec. XV*, 3 vols and index (Vienna 1857–86)
MGH	*Monumenta Germaniae Historica*
AA	*Auctores Antiquissimi*
Capit.	*Capitularia*
Conc.	*Concilia*
Const.	*Constitutiones*
Epist.	*Epistolae*
L de L	*Libelli de Lite*
SS	*Scriptores*
SS rer. Germ.	*Scriptores rerum Germanicarum in usum scholarum*

PG	J. P. Migne: *Patrologia Graeca*
PL	J. P. Migne: *Patrologia Latina*
Reg. Orleton	*Register of Adam Orleton*, Bishop of Winchester
Rot. Parl.	*Rotuli Parliamentorum*
RS	*Rolls Series*
TRHS	*Transactions of the Royal Historical Society*
Wilkins	*Concilia Magnae Britannia et Hiberniae*, 4 vols (London 1737)

PUBLIC WELFARE
AND SOCIAL LEGISLATION IN THE
EARLY MEDIEVAL COUNCILS

by WALTER ULLMANN (*Presidential Address*)

THE reason for singling out the early medieval period is not only because it constituted the age of infancy, puberty, and adolescence of what later became Western Europe, but also because some of the relevant issues stand out much more clearly when they make their first appearance, that is, before they have become overlaid, encrusted, if not suffocated, by subsequent developments. The recognition of these issues is facilitated by the (comparatively speaking) simple social structure and by the low-geared exigencies of society itself. It is only in retrospect that one can appreciate, measure, and assess the achievements—or their lack—of any age, and this truism applies with particular force to the period between the sixth and ninth centuries, for it was in these centuries that the firm foundations of medieval and to a large extent of modern Europe were laid.

The choice of my subject is to express the conviction that some of the great merits of modern welfare institutions and modern social legislative measures have their definite and demonstrable roots, not in antiquity, not in the high Middle Ages, not in the nineteenth century, but roughly speaking in the Frankish age. And here it was the councils which were the chief organs either in initiating legislation or in establishing welfare institutions and making arrangements for the execution of their decrees as far as this lay in their competency. The councils to my mind constitute a vast reservoir of source-material which from the angle of my subject has barely been tapped. As ecclesiastical assemblies they were perhaps the most articulate media through which attempts were made to turn some of the basic tenets of Christianity into socially realizable measures. The councils were not, however, platforms for propounding ethical or religious counsel—there was plenty of this too—but primarily legislative assemblies. And as such they had, I am inclined to think, greater topical influence than the very sparse and oftentimes extremely crude secular royal legislation. Moreover, the synodal legislation is a prime source of social-historical knowledge, and in so far not only supplements, but also surpasses, the annalistic records. The decrees are on the whole extremely well preserved and transmitted, and in their overwhelming majority the councils can be dated to the month and day, the importance of which feature cannot be overrated. This observation does not, however, apply to the Anglo-Saxon councils of the seventh to the ninth centuries: the transmission is poor, and what there is, most certainly cannot compare with the Frankish councils. The Anglo-Saxon decrees show a rather primitive state of affairs during that period, and the decrees are almost wholly of a disciplinary kind.[1]

The feature, however, which makes these early medieval councils first-class witnesses of contemporary society, is that their participants were men who knew conditions from their own observations and experience. We know the names of the participants of most of these early councils: they were almost exclusively bishops, and not only is the frequency of these assemblies and the character of their legislation important, but also, and perhaps of even greater significance, is the high number of those taking part. To mention just a few facts and figures: in the council of Orléans in 511, 32 bishops took part; at Epaon in Burgundy in 517 there were 25 bishops; at Orléans in 549 there took part no fewer than 50 bishops, 10 priests and 9 deacons acting on behalf of absent bishops, and 2 abbots (a total of 71); at Mâcon in 585 there were 78 episcopal participants. Of course, there were also councils at which not more than 12–15 bishops were present. Next to the frequency of meetings and the usually high figure of participants, there is a third feature, that is, their purely clerical, or rather episcopal, character: the educated and adequately informed layman did not exist, a feature which raised the episcopal participants

---

[1] The notable exception is the legatine council of 787, in J. D. Mansi, *Sacrorum conciliorum...collectio* (Florence–Venice 1759 ff.), XII, 943 ff., chapters 11 and 12.

to the level of determinant organs laying down the law for the Christian community represented in the council. In other words, the synodists functioned as actual builders of a Christian society— it is not necessary to remind you how tender a plant Christianity was in sixth-century Gaul in comparison with the Roman empire in the East or, for that matter, in comparison with Italy.

Overwhelmingly concerned as they were with purely practical questions, the synodists had neither the leisure nor the inclination to dabble in theological disputes or to legislate on theological items. All the greater emphasis therefore was laid upon the corporate decision, the conciliar decree, which was arrived at after discussion, debate, and deliberation, a point which I cannot stress strongly enough, for the bishops in the West of Europe assumed the role of an executive instrument of the council, and this despite the full development of the monarchic episcopate in the South of Europe, notably in Italy. The extreme poverty of Italian councils both in quality and quantity forms a striking contrast to the lively Frankish and Visigothic councils: there were councils in Rome, but neither in the quality of legislation nor in frequency or influence can they stand comparison with the Frankish ones, which is not indeed surprising, since the problems debated and resolved in Rome were so largely dictated by Byzantine-Eastern issues which were of an unadulterated theological-canonical nature. The corporateness of the Frankish and Visigothic decisions and laws might well be a remnant of the Germanic past, so recently left behind. Just consider for a moment the situation in Visigothic Spain: between the conversion of Reccared in 589 and the extinction of the kingdom in 711 there were no less than fourteen very large councils held at Toledo; to which must be added in the same period the numerous councils at Braga, Barcelona, Merida, Huesca, Egara, and so on—a very respectable number indeed when put next to those held in the Italian peninsula.[1]

This corporate decision-making fostered a very noticeable social

---

[1] For modern literature on the councils see the standard work by J. Hefele, ed. H. Leclercq, *Histoire des conciles* (Paris 1909–11), III and IV; the illustrative studies by Ch. de Clercq, *La législation religieuse de Clovis à Charlemagne* (Louvain–Paris 1936), and *idem* in *Revue de droit canonique*, IV (1954)–VII (1957).

cohesiveness which in this context meant that the otherwise unbridgeable if not irreconcilable diversities of the various regions could effectively be mitigated, if not eradicated, at least in so far as the basic social concerns came into question. In fact one can say that, not despite of, but because of, the difficulties in communication between the various provinces, the ecclesiastical councils provided by their legislation the virtually only available means to weld these regions together—to make them one whole, one living *corpus Christi*, in a word, one Church. We ought to see this diversity in a proper perspective, in order to appreciate all the more the cohesion which the councils brought into being: we have but to think of the different historical evolutions of the South and the North of Gaul, the linguistic barriers, the diversities of customs and habits and usages prompted by the diverse ethnic and topographical features, and so on, to realize fully the difficulties which faced the bishops in their efforts to weld this mosaic into one consistent and coherent whole.

To this function, nay, this achievement of the early medieval bishops far too little attention is paid: it was they, not as monarchic governors of their dioceses, but in their corporate function as members of the councils, who saturated this society with Christian elements and thus brought about a unity of basic outlook which no sword, no royal measure, no legislation by kings could have attained within so short a span of time. And the synodists were in a position to do this, because they came from that stratum to which the overwhelming part of the population belonged, that is, the agrarian section of the population, and they lived and worked amongst them. It seems rare that legislators have this intimate contact with the population at large. The synodists were not legislators residing far away from those who were directly affected by their legislation. Above all, as legislators they knew on the whole what was, and what was not, feasible, what was and what was not acceptable to the population—they knew better, I am sometimes inclined to think, the mind of their 'constituents' if I may use so anachronistic a term, than those whom we send to Westminster.

This practical side of the legislative work of the synodists can also be further explained by the very task they set themselves. Indubitably, they were the only really educated section of contemporary society, that is, they knew to some extent at least what Cyprian, Jerome, Augustine, and the other patristic luminaries had taught, even if they may have had their knowledge only at second hand, but it is one thing to know and understand a dogma or a theory or doctrine, and quite a different matter to distil this doctrine etc. into a practical legislative measure which appeared sensible, feasible, and, in its tenor, was not to lose anything of the essence of the doctrine itself. What these bishops as synodists were not concerned with was high-falutin' theological speculation or ponderous exhortations which in prevailing circumstances would have entirely failed to succeed. What, on the other hand, they were concerned with was, as far as the scope of my topic goes, the translation of one of the all-pervading Christian virtues, charity, into a social–legislative norm. Looking through this conciliar legislation from the sixth to the ninth centuries, one is, I think, entitled to give it the appellation of legislatively enacted charity: both public welfare and what we call social legislation were nothing more nor less than instances of charity moulded into the law. After all, it was St Augustine who had taught them that charity was the perfect manifestation of justice applicable primarily between the members of society. Certainly, there were some concrete instances of charitable institutions, especially in the East, but these had almost wholly reference to conditions in Byzantium which vastly differed from those in the still rather primitive West and could hardly be adopted without an antecedent adaptation. Let me now turn to the consideration of a few specific conciliar enactments relative to public welfare.

Of the measures decreed by the early medieval councils the most outstanding and also perhaps the socially most beneficial ones were those taken to assist the poor. Now the concept of poverty is and always has been a somewhat flexible one, but it seems that the early medieval idea of poverty included those who were physically unable to earn their livelihood, and this category also included the aged—hence, as far as I can find out there were no special

enactments for those infirm due to old age—as well as those
who through no fault of their own had lost what they had, either as
a result of illegal machinations, for instance, fraud, or who were
made penurious through circumstances beyond their control, such
as losing an inheritance through defective arrangements.[1] Now
the feature that is impressive is that those in a state of poverty
were considered to have a claim, to have a right, to be maintained
by the other members of society. This, I think, should be emphasized, because there was no suggestion that the poor had to rely
on alms: in other words, synodal decrees were enacted with the
view to prevent vagabonds and beggars roaming about the
localities. In this conception of poverty the early Middle Ages
were I think nearer to the gospel teaching than the later Middle
Ages. Differently expressed, there was not the slightest suggestion
in any of the numerous decrees that the poor should be patronized
or pitied: they had a right to sustenance.

One channel by which the councils became conversant with the
Christian idea of poverty was the New Testament itself, which in
some contrast to the Old Testament and especially to the sur-
rounding pagan conceptions of poverty, did not denigrate the
poor. On the contrary, rich and poor had exactly the same
standing. The other channel was the law, that is, the so-called
Apostolic Constitutions of c. 400 which gave precision to the
abstract idea of the New Testament. In them the maintenance of
the poor was squarely put on the shoulders of the bishops[2] who
were to see that sufficient clothing and food was provided for
those in need.[3] This was enacted as early as 511 in the council of
Orléans.[4] And this stipulation was extended by the council of
Tours in 567: the citizens of each and every locality had to be
responsible for providing the necessary means for the maintenance
of the poor, the main reason being that 'ipsi pauperes per civitates

[1] Cf. Mainz (813), c. 6, p. 262. Unless otherwise stated, all references are to the
MGH edition of Concilia, vols. I–II/I–2 (Hanover 1893–1908). The citation
gives the place, followed by the year in brackets, the relevant chapter and
page.
[2] See Const. Apostol., ed. F. X. Funk (Paderborn 1905), III, 4, pp. 186, 188.
[3] Cf. A. Hauck in Realenzyklop. f. prot. Theol. & Kirche, XXI, 441 ff.
[4] See Orléans (511), c. 16: 'Pauperibus vel infirmis...victum et vestitum'.

alienas non vagentur'.[1] These and similar decrees were frequently
re-enacted. The danger of vagrancy and vagabondage was clearly
seen as a social evil and the synodists of the sixth century deserve
credit for having tried to avoid this danger, albeit with perhaps
inadequate means. After all, right down to the threshold of this
century, this social evil was one of the strongest incentives for the
social legislation against poverty. But what the council of Tours
in 567 initiated was also important from another point of view,
that is, that the duty of maintaining the poor was imposed on the
whole local community: it was not a private charity that was
postulated, but a legislative act that foreshadowed the English
development by nearly a thousand years.[2] In other words, the
sustenance of the poor was a public charge,[3] a measure which in
its basic assumptions was perhaps one of the most significant acts
towards translating a fundamental Christian precept into a concrete measure.

Now the question was, of course, where were the means to
come from? Clearly, in the beginning of our period the conciliar
decisions still had in mind urban conditions, but the more Christianity became organized and spread to the countryside, the more
difficult it not only became to enforce these decisions, but also to
make proper provisions in the shape of funds available for the
distribution to the needy. Here we meet—unless I am very badly
mistaken—a very interesting development. The Old Testament
knew the tenth, and as far as I am aware, made its payment a duty,
a point of view which did not apparently meet with the approval
of patristic writers who seemed to have considered that the
voluntary character of the payment was the real sign of charity.
No doubt, the tenth was given, and patristic authors did not cease
to exhort the faithful to contribute. In brief, the payment of the
tenth was really in the nature of giving alms. This was still the
view expressed in the letter which the synodists assembled at

---

[1] Tours (567), c. 5, p. 123; almost the same in Lyons (583), c. 6, p. 154: 'ut illis
per civitates vagandi licentia denegetur'.
[2] Tours (567), c. 5.
[3] Cf. E. Loening, *Kirchenrecht im Reiche der Merowinger* (Strasbourg 1878), II,
242 n. 2 and 243; also G. Grupp, *Kultergeschichte des Mittelalter*, 4th ed. (Paderborn
1932), I, 262.

7

Tours in 567 addressed to their people: here the tenth was explicitly equated with alms, and even the unfree were exhorted to give, if not the ninth, at any rate the tenth.[1]

It was less than twenty years later that the synod of Mâcon in 585 turned the exhortation into a precept so that everyone was compelled to pay the tenth into the chest of the bishop. What is furthermore of interest is the explicit reason prompting the synodists at Mâcon to insist on the payment, namely to provide for the relief of the poor.[2] The step taken at Mâcon was not as abrupt as it might perhaps appear, since the council of Orléans in 511 had already pointed that way: whatever was given to an individual church, was to be used on behalf of the infirm and the poor.[3]

There is every justification for saying that the tenth was considered a kind of income tax, a proportion of which was to be used for the sustenance of the poor. The council of Arles in 813[4] put itself squarely on the Old Testament regulation that the payment of the tenth was a duty to be discharged by a payment to God.[5] The usual proportion to be made over to the penurious was one quarter of the whole received,[6] although there were also proposals that as much as a third should form the contribution, a suggestion made by the council held in Freising in 800 and supported by Charlemagne.[7] In any case, the alimentation of the poor by the bishop from episcopal funds was a charge on the portion of the tenth.[8] If, as sometimes happened, the bishop did not need the quarter for himself, he was at liberty to use it for the poor, in other words, exactly half of the income derived from the tenth.[9]

Next to the tenth the regular income of the episcopal funds for the support of the poor were the alms proper, which I have a strong suspicion differed only in name from the tenth. Thus the

[1] *MGH Conc.* I, 137–8: *Epistola episcoporum prov. Turonensis ad plebem.*
[2] Mâcon (585), c. 5, p. 167, lines 7 ff.
[3] Orléans (511), c. 5, p. 4.   [4] Arles (813), c. 9, p. 251.
[5] Cf. also Aachen (816), c. 28, p. 455: one tenth to be given to nuns for the support of the poor.
[6] For instance, Salzburg (807), p. 234, which was also adopted by the bishops in their *Relatio* preceding the council of Paris (829), in *Capit.* 196, c. 5, p. 32.
[7] Freising (800), c. 13, p. 209; Charlemagne in *Capit.* 36, c. 7, p. 106, anno 802.
[8] Cf. Tours (813), c. 11, p. 288; also Aachen (836), c. 19, p. 709.
[9] Paris (829), c. 31, p. 633.

Frankish council of 779 laid down what amount of alms should be given for the succour of the needy—it was little else but the imposition of a tax for purposes of poor relief: the wealthy bishops and abbots should give one pound of silver, the less wealthy half a pound, and the non-prosperous five shillings annually.[1] This was also endorsed by Charlemagne, who in 780 turned the conciliar decree into a royal law.[2] The ingenuity of some councils for finding means to replenish the episcopal funds for the poor was indeed great: a Bavarian council of 805[3] decreed that on the occasion of the death of a prominent personality, for instance, a bishop, his colleagues should give twenty pounds of silver, and each presbyter for their deceased bishop one shilling, and so forth; one cannot help thinking that this was an adaptation of the Germanic *Wergeld* for charitable-social purposes. In parenthesis it should be mentioned that alms were also given as a means to redeem sins which might possibly be a forerunner of indulgences, for instance, as laid down by the council of Châlons in 813.[4]

I think one can say with every justification that these early medieval councils show a degree of social awareness which is quite remarkable. The significance of their measures is only heightened when one considers that the synodists had no models or patterns on which they could have relied. For the institutionalization of charitable organization for social purposes was wholly alien to the ancient world.[5] But it was not enough to provide the poor with food and clothing: they also had to have a shelter and a roof over their heads. The legislation of Justinian considerably developed some embryonic institutions of the preceding century:[6] the general name for houses or institutes was *xenodochia*, which term in course of time gave way to *hospitium* or *hospitale*. They all designated specific buildings which served different purposes, the common feature of which was the accommodation of those who were destitute or otherwise in need. Here, within the ambit of the care for the poor, the buildings were usually attached to the

---

[1] See *MGH Conc.* II, 109, no. 18. [2] *Capit.* 21, p. 52, anno 780.
[3] *MGH Conc.* I, 233. [4] Châlons (813), c. 16, pp. 280–1.
[5] Cf. A. Hauck, *Realenzyklop.*, XXI, 440–2.
[6] *Cod.* I, ii, 22 and numerous *Novellae*.

cathedral or other church, and they soon also came to serve the needs of the sick. The Merovingian and also the Carolingian kings were very active in founding such *xenodochia* or *hospitalia*: one of the earliest was that founded by Childebert I at Lyons in 540, of which the council of Orléans in 548 makes specific mention. Although these foundations were quite generously endowed by the royal founders, it was left to the councils to provide the proper organization and maintenance of these numerous institutes; and by the ninth century the erection of a *receptaculum*, as the building came to be known, was imposed as a special duty on the bishop.[1] We should also note how keen Charlemagne himself was on the erection of these houses, because thereby a biblical stipulation was fulfilled.[2] But whoever erected the building, it was and remained under the control of the bishop, as the councils made clear. Moreover, these hospices enjoyed a heightened protection: for instance, anyone found stealing in or from them was classified as a murderer of the poor.[3] Since the poor and especially the sick needed attention, these hospices provided a convenient employment for the all too numerous and elderly spinsters who could therefore do useful social service of the most important order—an early medieval equivalent of the W.V.S. That these houses also served the aged and the orphaned children need not be specifically mentioned.

The council of Aachen in 816 went even so far as to decree the erection of a *receptaculum* for destitute travellers as well as for widows and poor girls (which may be a euphemism for the unmarried mothers) in the proximity of nunneries and therefore in the neighbourhood of the *hospitale* for the aged and the sick.[4] The subsequent council of Aachen in 836 extended this provision to all towns and all monasteries,[5] while the large gathering at Meaux-Paris in 845 made the restoration of a number of hospices which had fallen on evil days a royal duty, which was indeed accepted by Charles the Bald.[6] In fact, the collection of laws by

[1] Aachen (816), c. 141, p. 416.
[2] Cf. *Capit.* 33 (anno 802), c. 27, p. 96: Matt. 25. 35.
[3] Cf. Orléans (549), c. 15, p. 105, line 17.
[4] Aachen (816), c. 28, pp. 455–6.   [5] Aachen (836), c. 3, p. 707.
[6] *Capit.* 293, c. 40, p. 408 and *Capit.* 257, c. 7, p. 262 (June 846).

Abbot Ansegisus in the late twenties of the ninth century shows how widespread this social and charitable institution of *hospitia* had been.[1] There is plenty of evidence that a number of bishops, such as Theodulf of Orléans, or the great Alcuin himself, or Adalhard of Corbie founded such hospices. That the monasteries themselves gave splendid examples of this practical welfare, seems self-evident, for instance in St Riquier no fewer than 300 poor and 140 widows received their daily sustenance.[2] On crossing the Great St Bernard a few years ago, my thoughts went back to Frankish times and I could not help remarking how profoundly the travelling public had changed in the meantime.

For obvious reasons, isolation hospitals are nowadays considered a social necessity and the reason for prompting their establishment in the early Middle Ages was not one wit different from that which prevails today, that is, to contain the spread of infection. The paramount case in the early Middle Ages was leprosy, and the councils had ample opportunity of expressing themselves on the social danger which the disease carried. One of the earliest conciliar decrees relating to leprosy was that of Orléans in the year 549 which imposed on each bishop the duty to attend with particular zeal to the victims of this incurable disease, by giving them suitable clothing and food, but there was as yet no suggestion of separating them from other people.[3] This suggestion seems to have been made first in the council of Lyons in 583, which made each bishop responsible for supplying those infected with the disease, whether born in the diocese or merely living in it, with so much nourishment and clothing that they could be reasonably denied visits to other inhabited places.[4] Assuredly in practice this meant that these unfortunate people were confined at the bishop's expense in a *hospitium*. Their segregation and hence their confinement outside inhabited localities was expressly

[1] Ansegisus, II, 29 in *MGH Capit.* I, 420–1, where the nomenclatures are all taken from Justinian.
[2] For this see A. Hauck, *Kirchengeschichte Deutschlands* (4th ed. Leipzig 1922), II, 291 n. 3.   [3] Orléans (549), c. 21, p. 107.
[4] Lyons (583), c. 6, p. 154: 'Placuit etiam universo concilio ut uniuscuiusque civitatis leprosi...ab episcopo ecclesiae ipsius sufficientia alimenta et necessaria vestimenta accipiant, ut illis per alias civitates vagandi licentia denegetur.'

ordered by Charlemagne in one of his early capitularies.[1] The councils always insisted upon the necessary spiritual administration in these hospitals: the victims were to receive communion, though spatially separated from healthy communicants.[2] The final ecclesiastical settlement of these lepra hospitals with their own cemeteries did not come about until the Third Lateran Council, when they were also exempt from paying the tenth from their horticultural and agricultural holdings.[3]

The scourge of leprosy impeded the movements of its victims. The same can be said about those in prisons, and here again, the councils showed themselves keenly aware of the very special care which the inmates required. Thus the council of Orléans in 549 decreed that the archdeacon or other suitably qualified ecclesiastical officer should visit those *in carceribus* at least on Sundays to administer to the spiritual needs of the prisoners, while upon the bishop fell the duty to entrust a reliable person with providing the prisoners with adequate food. What is furthermore of some special interest is that this physical care was a charge on the individual church itself, and probably on the general funds established for the succour of those who could not help themselves.[4] No doubt, the eventual aim was the release of the prisoners—an aim which may not always have been conducive to the promotion of justice, but which in prevailing circumstances when the idea of justice was only in a somewhat rudimentary sense developed, was certainly creditable.[5] Nor would it seem quite beyond doubt that those imprisoned were there as a result of judicial proceedings—one cannot help thinking that some inmates were not so much in

---

[1] *Capit.* 23, c. 23, p. 64 (anno 789): 'ut se (leprosi) non intermisceant alio populo'.

[2] See for instance Gregory II to Boniface in 726: *MGH Epist.* III, 277, lines 1 ff., and council of Worms (868), c. 31, in Mansi, *Sacrorum conciliorum*, XV, 875: 'Leprosis autem si fideles Christi fuerint, domini corporis et sanguinis participatio tribuatur: cum sanis autem eis convivia celebrare non permittatur.'

[3] III Lat., c. 23. For details in the high Middle Ages see F. Merzbacher, 'Die Leprosen im alten kanonischen Recht' in *Savigny Zeitschr., Kan. Abt.*, LIII (1967), 27–45. In general for hospitals in the central medieval period, see now especially Hans Wolter in *Handbuch der Kirchengeschichte*, ed. H. Jedin, III–2 (Freiburg–Basle–Vienna 1968), at pp. 230 ff: 'Das abendländische Spital im hohen Mittelalter.' Here also very full bibliographical details for the high Middle Ages.

[4] Orléans (549), c. 20, p. 107.

[5] Cf. A. Hauck, *Kirchengeschichte*, I, 320 n. 2.

prison as in captivity, and their release had, certainly since the fifth century, been one of the foremost charitable and social tasks of the clergy, in importance in no wise ranking below the succour of the poor with whom they were frequently bracketed. It seems that Frankish councils considered imprisonment at least in cases of sorcery and fortune telling and other superstitious practices, as medicinal measures, to use later technical language: the great council of Riesbach, Salzburg, and Freising in 800 declared that these persons should be kept in strict custody, but their imprisonment should nevertheless be such 'ne vitam perdant, sed ut salventur in carcere'.[1] Obviously, the synodists expected proper instruction and visitation by the chief of the priests in the locality. Ostensibly, the purpose was the re-education of the inmates in the social-religious sense. Here mention should be made of the synodal circular of 796 which drew the attention of the lower clergy to the needs of those in 'angustia carceris circumdati' for the administration of sacraments.[2]

Some of the motives prompting the welfare of prisoners can also be discerned in the protection which the individual church was to give to those who sought refuge in it. Conciliar legislation is especially rich within the ambit of what came to be the right of asylum, though the councils had here developed an institution that had roots in antiquity. In some respects fleeing into a church building by escaping from prison or captivity or, as we might add, from slavedom, was merely the other side of the coin depicting the archpriest or archdeacon visiting the prisons to administer the sacraments and to give instructions. In other words, instead of the priest visiting the prison, the prisoner visited the priest in his own church and for the same purpose: in actual fact the Theodosian Code explicitly referred to the custom of the intervention by the bishop with judicial authority or the imperial court on behalf of an already condemned person. Of course, in order to solicit this ecclesiastical intervention, to which the imperial laws were not particularly favourably inclined, the condemned person fled to the bishop's house or church. To the church as a consecrated building

---

[1] Riesbach, etc., c. 15, p. 209.
[2] Riesbach, p. 173, lines 34 ff.

an increased reverence was paid in any case, which in practice meant that violent abduction of those present in it was universally condemned: this was the origin of ecclesiastical asylum, which was as yet not quite the same as the right of asylum.[1] The exercise of public authority and power in the neighbourhood of ecclesiastical buildings—usually 30 to 50 yards around it, and sometimes also including the outbuildings, though all this varied considerably—was, so to speak, suspended on account of what was called the *reverentia loci*, but it all depended on the good will of the bishop. That by the turn of the fifth and sixth centuries gross abuses had crept in, is understandable—even debtors came in some places to enjoy the sanctuary in the shape of a pseudo-asylum.

Visigothic, Burgundian, Merovingian, and Carolingian councils issued ample legislation concerning asylum. Despite a somewhat bewildering variety, certain features stand out, and it is these which in a most persuasive way show on the one hand a wholesome realism on the part of the synodists, and on the other hand the translation of the virtue of charity into practice in the face of very adverse circumstances. Here I can only give a conspectus of the respective synodal legislation. The one feature of some moment is that the fugitive did not by virtue of seeking asylum enjoy anything approaching amnesty or exemption from punishment; nor did the slave who managed to escape his master gain his freedom—all he achieved was that he was to be spared corporal punishment, as the Burgundian council of Epaon in 517 laid down.[2] Similarly, Visigothic councils decreed that the clergy had a duty to deliver the fugitive culprit, if he was a murderer, provided that the public authorities had promised on oath not to sentence him to death.[3] Violent removal of the fugitive entailed excommunication of the public officers. The Visigothic councils never gave any

[1] P. Hinschius, *Kirchenrecht* (Berlin 1891), IV, 381. For general orientation and modern literature cf. *Lexikon f. Theol. & Kirche*, I, 968; *New Catholic Encyclopedia*, I, 994. The best survey is in P. Timbal Duclaux de Martin, *Le droit d'asile* (Paris 1939); cf. also G. Le Bras in *Dict. d'hist. et géogr. ecclésiastique*, IV (1930), 1035 ff., at 1037–41.

[2] Epaon (517), c. 39, p. 28: 'Servus reatu atrociore culpabilis si ad ecclesiam confugerit, *a corporalibus suppliciis* excusetur.' But his master may still decalvate the slave, *ibid.*

[3] Toledo XII (681), c. 10, in *PL* LXXXIV, 476.

protection to an armed fugitive who had entered the precincts of the church.

The Merovingian councils went further and obviously desired to eliminate ancient and, as it turned out, very entrenched Teutonic principles. Thus the council of Orléans in 511 declared in firm language that a fugitive could only be extradited if the injured man or the relatives of the killed person took an oath not to take revenge on him—blood feud was very widely practised at the time —which meant that murderers, adulterers, and thieves were free from the death penalty or mutilating punishments.[1] Slaves taking refuge in a church were to be handed back to the owner, if he promised freedom from punishment, as this same council of Orléans declared[2] and as it was frequently repeated afterwards.[3] The councils threatened excommunication against those who broke their promises taken on oath. But it does seem, to judge by the frequency of conciliar enactments and re-enactments, that the ecclesiastical legislation, despite its humane and sensible character, was often enough disregarded. The council of Mâcon in 585 is an indication: the synodists referred to 'Seudo-christiani' who treated with contempt the sacred character of churches and dared violently 'fugitivos subtrahere'; when even the secular laws enforced conciliar decrees and held fugitives inviolable, how dare these pseudo-christians raise their hands against the 'patrocinia immortalis regni coelestis'?[4] According to the council of Clichy in 626, fugitives were to be 'securi de vita, tormento et truncatione'.[5] The council of Rheims of *c.* 627 threatened excommunication of those clerics who without adequate guarantees delivered a fugitive so that he was in danger of being sentenced to death or subjected to torture or mutilation of his limbs.[6] The general conclusion that is permissible is that synodal legislation was primarily concerned with humanizing criminal punishment and the alleviation of the lot of slaves: asylum therefore did not mean a general acquisition of freedom. And in parenthesis I may remark that the Carolingian secular legislation did not favour the fugitives who benefited from

[1] Orléans (511), c. 1, p. 2.   [2] Orléans, c. 3, pp. 3–4.
[3] Cf. Orléans (541), c. 22, p. 107.   [4] Mâcon (585), c. 8, p. 68.
[5] Clichy (626), c. 9, p. 198.   [6] Rheims (*c.* 627), c. 7, p. 204.

synodal legislation.[1] It was no doubt the heavy hand of the great Frank which prevented the full application of conciliar legislation in respect of asylum: on the whole during the Carolingian age decrees relative to asylum became diluted and bloodless, as is evidenced by the council of Mainz in 813.[2]

What the synodal decisions reveal in respect of the persons I have enumerated, such as the poor, captives, prisoners, slaves, was a very practical spirit of Christian charity. The synodists had no easy stand in the face of cruelty and prevalent uncivilized customs, particularly in those regions which had only recently been christianized. Yet, an entirely erroneous picture would be conveyed if it were held that the social legislation of the councils was concentrated only on those classes of society whom I have just mentioned. The dividing line between real poverty and exiguity is never clear-cut in any society, and in the early medieval period there were those who were called the *inferiores*, or still more expressively the *minus potentes*, which referred to wealth and power and influence.[3] They were neither poor in wealth nor prosperous nor socially or politically influential, and yet led a somewhat precarious existence, more or less at the whim of the *potentes*. To those classes the attention of the councils was increasingly directed, and this mainly in connexion with preventing them from being exploited. This was, as you may readily appreciate, a somewhat delicate and moot point, because some of the bishops themselves were without difficulty to be found amongst those who exploited the *minus potentes*. For instance, the council

[1] Cf. *Capit.* 20, c. 2, p. 48: 'Ut homicidas aut ceteros reos qui legibus mori debent, si ad ecclesiam confugerint, non excusentur seque eis ibiddem victus detur.' But cf. also Charlemagne in his *Capitulatio de partibus Saxoniae*, c. 2 (= *Capit.* 26, p. 69), forbidding the expulsion of a fugitive from a church.

[2] Rectors of churches should strive to save the peace, life, and limb of the fugitives —'pacem et vitam ac membra eis obtinere studeant' (Mainz (813), c. 39, p. 271).

[3] For some observations pointing in different directions cf. K. Bosl, 'Potens und Pauper' in his *Frühformen der Gesellschaft im mittelalterlichen Europa* (Munich-Vienna 1964), 106 ff. See especially the hardly noticed Edict by the Lombard King Aistulph (*c.* 750), c. 3, in *MGH Leges* IV, 196: 'De illis hominibus qui negotiantes sunt et pecunias non habent: qui sunt *maiores et potentes*, habeant loricam et cavallos, scutum et lanceam; qui sunt sequentes, habeant caballos, scutum et lanceam; et qui sunt *minores*, habeant coccoras cum sagittas [*sic*] et arcum.'

of Paris in 829 made it quite plain that some prelates, clearly in order to keep the poor in good physical condition so as to get the most out of them as labourers, were interested solely in the bodily well-being of their charges and gave them more than was necessary of the *cibus carnalis*, but at the expense of the *cibus spiritualis*.[1] The problem of avoiding the exploitation of the *minus potentes* was rarely absent from the councils: of course, being indigent, illiterate, and in all likelihood frightened of the power of those in whose hands their very livelihood lay, they were an easy prey to oppression and fraud.

It is in this context that some other social measures taken by the councils must be mentioned. Already the council of Frankfurt in 794, presided over by Charlemagne, laid down that bread must have equal weight throughout the Frankish realms,[2] and the council of Arles in 813 decreed that all weights and measures must be equal, a decree which the royal government re-enacted in the same year,[3] in order to prevent fraud. Another Frankish council repeated this decree and invoked Ezekiel 45.10 declaring that through the differences in weights and measures 'in multis pauperes gravantur'.[4] And at exactly the same time the bishops, prior to the great council of Paris in 829, asked Louis I to take effective legislative measures to prevent territorial lords from having two kinds of weights and measures in use, because 'hac occasione multos pauperes affligi in plerisque locis cognovimus'.[5] It is therefore understandable why the council in 829 went to great lengths to castigate the apparent practice whereby the poor and those in lower social status became the victims of deceitful machinations especially in connexion with wrong weights.[6] This was a malpractice which led in the opinion of the synodists (speaking clearly from experience) to *commotio terrae*, that is, social unrest, nay, to the *periclitatio et infirmatio regni*. The eradication of some blatant social injustices was to them clearly the presupposition for the tranquillity and smooth working of the public organism itself. It is necessary to put this on record, because it was the assembled

[1] Paris (829), c. 24, p. 628. [2] Frankfurt (794), c. 4, p. 166.
[3] Arles (813), c. 15, p. 252; *Capit.* 78, c. 13, p. 174.
[4] Frankish council (between 818 and 829), c. 7, p. 595.
[5] *Relatio episcoporum* in *Capit.* 196, c. 54, p. 44, lines 16 ff.
[6] Paris (829), I, 53, pp. 645–7; and III, 3, p. 671.

episcopal wisdom which knew better than the far away central government where the shoe pinched.

Another form of exploitation consisted in bishops, counts, and other prelates forcing their subjects to sell corn at harvest time and wine at vintage time at a fixed price—an early case of monopoly imposed by the great landlords, some of whom went so far as to fix the price for a bushel of wheat at exactly a third of the price they would have had to pay elsewhere, that is, 4 pennies instead of the usual 12 pennies, and for a gallon of wine the selling price was fixed at 6 pennies instead of the usual 20 pennies. The council of Paris in 829 stigmatized this practice as *res plena impietatis et iniustitiae*,[1] a sentiment with which one can but sympathize, though whether the synodal condemnation had any effect I am not in a position to say. One more form of exploitation by the *seniores* practised against the *infirmiores* consisted in the public officers bringing the latter's goods and chattels at a price which only superficially concealed expropriation. All sorts of subterfuges were apparently employed to deprive the less prosperous of their property. Here the council of Arles in 813 spoke a very forthright language and insisted on what I would like to call due process of law. Conveyances of property should not proceed by administrative-executive acts, but 'in publico coram comite et iudicibus et nobilioribus civitatis'.[2] This council is also noteworthy from another standpoint: it laid upon the bishops the duty of annual visitation of their dioceses, so that they could discover the oppression of the weaker members of society by the stronger, and if episcopal admonition to stop oppression should prove unavailing, recourse should be had to the secular power for orderly judicial process—this seems to me a clear instance of a practical application and amplification of the Isidorian doctrine that when the word of the priest was ineffective, it should be supplemented by the sword of the prince,[3] a point of view which in a rudimentary form the Fourth Toledan Council of 633 had already made in a similar context.[4]

---

[1] Paris (829), I, 52, p. 645. [2] Arles (813), c. 23, p. 253.
[3] Arles (813), c. 17, p. 252.
[4] IV Toledo, c. 32, headed: *De cura populorum et pauperum*, in PL LXXXIV, 375: 'ut quos sacerdotalis admonitio non flectit iustitiam regalis potestas ab improbitate coerceat'. This council was presided over by Isidore himself.

Social legislation of the period under review dealt with the condition and the status of men, and even with whole groups of men. That we today do no longer see social legislation in this sense is due to the absence of the very groups or of the status which was so characteristic a feature of medieval society. Of course, today there is legislation concerning juvenile delinquents, the supply of alcohol or tobacco to persons under a certain age, the working conditions of employees, sanitary regulations, protection of children, drug legislation, and so on, but this kind of legislation does not specifically refer to a whole and legally definable social group which, as in the early medieval period, formed its own social status, its own class if you like, its own condition in society. I propose to say a few words concerning conciliar legislation as far as it related to some of the easily definable groups, such as the slaves or the unfree, the Jews, and the clerics, not in their religious-dogmatic function, but in that as members of society. There can be little doubt that these groups were distinct from other members of contemporary society.

Let us begin with the slaves. One preliminary remark: I have not found one statement made in any of the early medieval councils which in any way impugned or attacked the status of slavery or even questioned whether this condition was in any way compatible with Christian principles. It remains true, albeit with some qualification, what has once been said: the Church was not interested in the slave as a person, but interested in the Christianity of the slave.[1] Yet, on the other hand, in the regions in which the councils were held—predominantly Germanic—the Roman slave as a domestic slave could be found only in the scattered Roman families, and not in the households of the indigenous population. The decree passed by the Burgundian council of Epaon in 517 deserves a remark, because it is quite revealing: it said that if the owner of a slave killed him without proper judicial verdict—*sine conscientia iudicis*—the master shall be excommuni-

---

[1] The fullest treatment of medieval slavery is in Ch. Verlinden, *L'esclavage médiévale* (Iberian peninsula) (Brugge 1955), I, pp. 663 ff. (Merovingian period) and 702 ff. (Frankish period). The second and third volumes have not yet appeared. Cf. also *idem* in *New Cath. Encycl.* XIII, 284–5; and D. Herlihy, *ibid.*, 346 f.

cated for two years.[1] Clearly, these synodists did not consider that the killing constituted murder, otherwise the sanction threatened would be difficult to comprehend; it would therefore seem that the slave was not a human being in the full social sense. What is furthermore interesting is that not even this or a similar decree is found in any later conciliar legislation. It is possible—and more one cannot say—that even this penalty was viewed as too stiff for the murder of a slave. This would seem merely an instance of the official ecclesiastical attitude towards slavery. It was not the officers, the ecclesiastical hierarchy, which attempted the full liberation and emancipation of the slaves, but the monks and the monastic settlements, though their pleas went unheeded by the clergymen represented in the councils.[2]

What on the other hand the councils tried to do was to ameliorate the condition of the slaves. I have already mentioned the slaves in connexion with asylum: beginning with the council of Orléans in 511[3] and that of 517[4] the synodists tried to impose such conditions upon the owner of a slave (who had attempted to escape) which did not expose him to the full rigour of his master's wrath. The other point to be made is that slaves whom the individual churches kept were on the whole more humanely treated than those in the hands of private lords, yet at the same time it is noteworthy that the council of Epaon in 517, as well as the councils of Clichy in 626 and of Rheims in 627, in fact forbade monastic institutions to release their slaves, that is, to give them full emancipation; and other councils were far from encouraging the emancipation of slaves in the possession of churches.[5] This prohibition against releasing and emancipating ecclesiastical slaves was based on the idea that they formed an essential part of ecclesiastical property and that ecclesiastical property could not be alienated. The further reason advanced was—and the councils made abundantly clear that the slaves were *res ad ius ecclesiae pertinentes*[6]—the preservation of the interests of the poor and sick, because it was

[1] Epaon (517), c. 34, p. 27.
[2] Cf. E. Dobschütz, in *Realenzykl.*, XVIII, 429, 431.
[3] Orléans (511), c. 3, pp. 3–4.   [4] Epaon (517), c. 39, p. 28.
[5] For instance, Orléans (541), c. 9, p. 89.
[6] Clichy (626), c. 15, p. 199; Rheims (c. 627), c. 13, p. 204.

held that they would be the prime sufferers if ecclesiastical slaves were allowed to be sold and emancipated. A principle upon which all the early councils were unanimous, beginning with Châlons in the mid-sixth century, was the prohibition of any sale or transfer of slaves outside the confines of the Frankish kingdom.[1] Nor was a sale of any slave to a Jewish family permitted under pain of excommunication of the Christian master.[2]

Paradoxically enough the councils almost unceasingly admonished and urged the lay masters of slaves to release them and set them free. This was urged on grounds of mercy, humanity, and charity, because the emancipation contributed to the master's eventual salvation. The result of this emancipation was: (1) the freed slave came under the special protection of the ecclesiastical authorities,[3] which was not an empty gesture, because the freed slave could not be reclaimed by the heirs of the former master: the bishop became the *patronus* of the freed slave; (2) there was a major departure from Roman law and from what the slave himself might reasonably have expected, in that he was still far from being free in the ordinary social sense, whereas in Roman law the freed slave's own descendants were free in every sense. The Frankish slave freed was, I believe, the serf, the one who was attached to the glebe, the man who was neither slave nor freeman. Hence the council of Paris in 614 put these freed private slaves entirely under ecclesiastical jurisdiction.[4]

Where the councils showed enterprise was in the question of ordination of slaves. By the early ninth century a number of real slaves—despite the opposing canon law[5]—were ordained by the bishop without having first been freed by their own masters.

---

[1] Châlons (639), c. 9, p. 210. The reproach of Charlemagne to Hadrian I, that he had sold Roman slaves to the Saracens, is well known; cf. the pope's reply in *MGH Codex Carolinus* no. 59 (anno 776) in *MGH Epist.* III, 584–5.

[2] Clichy (626), c. 13, p. 188; Rome (743), c. 10, p. 16: anathema threatened, if Christians consented to this kind of transaction.

[3] Cf. Orléans (549), c. 7, p. 103.

[4] Paris (614), c. 7, p. 187: whoever tried to circumvent this decree, was to be excommunicated.

[5] Orléans (511), c. 8, p. 5. For conditions in the late Roman empire see J. Gaudement, *L'église dans l'empire romain* (Paris 1959), pp. 136–41. Cf. also *Lex Romana Visigothorum*, ed. G. Haenel (Leipzig 1849), p. 292, §3.

Canonically, this was obviously an irregularity, since Leo I had proclaimed that only slaves freed and fully emancipated could receive valid ordination; in fact, Louis I himself insisted that emancipation should precede ordination.[1] No doubt, despite the conservative and acquiescent attitude of the councils, the lot of slaves in the Germanic lands was far more favourable than it would have been without the palliatives adopted by the councils and individual churchmen.

In marriage, a matter of profound social importance, the councils showed themselves wholly subservient to the owners of slaves. The general practice seems to have been well enough stated by the council of Châlons in 813 that the marriage of slaves belonging to different masters had to be dissolved, though this council tried to mitigate the rigour of this practice by stipulating that the marriage was to continue provided the owners of both spouses had expressed their agreement to the marriage and that the slaves continued to labour for their respective masters.[2] This seems a rather practical instance of the slave being tied to the glebe. There is one more feature worth mentioning in this context, that is, the noble woman marrying a slave, of whose status she was ignorant, or a freeman marrying a woman slave whose status was unknown to him. In the first case the wife assumed the status of her husband—not at all unlike a modern nationality law where similar principles prevail—though she could escape this consequence by dissolving the marriage and in this way regain her freedom;[3] this I think would in later canonistic doctrine be regarded as an *error in persona* which was the reason for the annulment of the marriage. In the other case the woman slave did not become free because of her marriage: the free husband could buy her from her master, but if he was unwilling, the husband was entitled to leave her and marry another woman.[4] The difference is noteworthy and throws significant light on the prevailing social conditions. However, no escape from

[1] Cf. *Capit.* 173, p. 356, lines 21 ff., where Louis I said: 'Statuimus et decrevimus ut abhinc in futurum nulla vilis et servili condicione obnoxia persona ad gradum presbyterii adspirare permittatur.' Cf. also *Capit.* 138, c. 6, p. 276.
[2] Châlons (813), c. 30, p. 279; cf. *Capit.* 105, c. 12, p. 210.
[3] Dingolfing (770), c. 10, p. 95.
[4] Vermeria (between 758 and 768): *Capit.* 16, c. 6, p. 40.

the bonds of marriage appeared possible if the man knew that his fiancée, and hence his wife, was a slave: 'semper permaneat cum ea'.[1] Yet, as we enter the ninth century, a solitary conciliar voice can be heard which revealed—or at least may reveal—the awareness of some synodists (assembled at Châlons) that slaves were not things, but were brothers of their masters, who had a right to be treated in a humane and orderly manner: slavery, the synodists declared, was but one condition of man, just as nobility was—in other words, within the Church there were many diverse conditions of men whose brotherhood was evident, because they had one father in God and one mother in the Church.[2] Here we may well detect the first embryonic glimmerings of the principle of equality before the law, the principle which barely a generation afterwards was stated in classic simplicity by none other than the great Hincmar of Rheims.

In proximity to the slaves, constituting a condition based on economic status, were the Jews, constituting a distinctly religious status. In contrast to conciliar legislation relating to slavery, conciliar decrees relating to the religious status are much more easily accessible to understanding. The Jews were regarded—and this standpoint went right back to the fourth century when the Roman empire had become Christian—as alien elements living within a totally Christianized body public; their religion marked them off far more distinctly from the constitutive part of society than did the economic status of the slaves, and this despite, or perhaps because of, some of the inherent similarities. From this premiss it is comprehensible why within this pronouncedly Christian society Jews could not become public officers, since this would entail their exercising power over Christians. This was a principle of prime constitutional importance and was also enacted in royal law.[3] The reason advanced was, as the council of Mâcon in 583 declared, that Christians must not become subjects of Jews.[4] If a Jew were to

[1] *Capit.* 16, c. 13, p. 41.
[2] See Châlons (813), c. 51, p. 283, pleading for fair and just treatment of nobles, ignobles, slaves, etc., by their superiors and prelates.
[3] Cf., e.g., Clermont (535), c. 9, p. 67; Mâcon (583), c. 13, p. 158; Paris (614), c. 17, p. 190, re-enacted in *Capit.* 9, c. 10, p. 22.
[4] Cf. further Meaux-Paris (845), *Capit.* 293, c. 73, pp. 416 f.

apply for a public office the local bishop had first to baptize him and his family.[1] I have already mentioned that Christian slaves could not be sold to Jews,[2] and the council of Rome in 743 threatened anathema on those Christians who became active in a transaction of this kind, and this council extended the prohibition to Christian maidservants. But there was in contrast to the Justinianean law[3] no general Frankish prohibition against Jews possessing Christian slaves, though this too was prohibited in Visigothic Spain.[4] What was illegal was the sale of Christian slaves to Jews or the attempt to convert Christian slaves to Judaism, in which latter case the Jew not only lost his Christian slave,[5] but also incurred a stiff penalty.

That on the great Christian feast days, especially at Easter time, Jews were prohibited from leaving their homes and mixing with the population, was one more restriction decreed by the councils, and in general Christians were to avoid the company of Jews, and on these occasions no meals could be taken with Jews, an offence which entailed excommunication.[6] Marriages between Jews and Christians were not permitted and were treated in law as fornication.[7] If the children of Jewish parents were baptized, they were to be separated from their parents and to be delivered to monasteries or to be handed over to Christian foster-parents: this was one of the Visigothic decrees of the Fourth Toledan Council in 633.[8] Measured by the standards of the time, Frankish conciliar legislation does not appear unduly oppressive against Jews, and in some respects showed even mitigation in comparison with the late-Roman legislation. These remarks do not, however, refer to the Visigothic legislation (both royal and conciliar), particularly from the just-mentioned Toledan council of 633 onwards: the Twelfth Toledan Council[9] of 681 surpassed in oppressiveness everything

---

[1] Paris (614), c. 17, p. 190.
[2] Clichy (626), c. 13, p. 199; IV Toledo (633), c. 66, in *PL* LXXXIV, 381; Rome (743), c. 10, p. 16.　　　　　[3] *Cod.* I, iii, 56 (3).
[4] IV Toledo, c. 65–6, *PL* LXXXIV, 381.　　　　[5] Mâcon (583), c. 16, p. 159.
[6] Orléans (538), c. 33, p. 83. Further, Mâcon (583), c. 15, p. 159.
[7] Orléans (533), p. 19, p. 64; etc.
[8] IV Toledo, c. 60, *PL* LXXXIV, 380.
[9] XII Toledo (681), c. 9, *PL* LXXXIV, 477 f. and XVII Toledo (694), c. 8, *loc. cit.*, cols. 559–61.

that the ancient and early medieval world had witnessed.[1] It was probably through Agobard of Lyons, who himself wrote a violent anti-Jewish tract (which confers little credit on a Christian prelate), that some Frankish councils became familiar with the Visigothic legislation and felt constrained to adopt at least some of these decrees, as for instance the large council of Meaux-Paris in 845 did, though this was done only on a selective basis.[2]

The third group of men is vocational, that is, the clergy. The proper canonical qualifications and those matters directly arising from the specific functions of the clerics are evidently outside the scope of my topic. What does seem relevant however is the position of the clerics within contemporary society, as seen through the eyes of the councils. Precisely because of their specific charismatic functions and their vocational status, the social life of the clerics was considered by the councils to be in need of special restrictions, partly in order to preserve the personal integrity of the clerics, and partly to conserve their independence vis-à-vis other members of society. It is in this context that the early medieval councils came to draw heavily on the ancient councils.

Leaving out regionally conditioned differences and modifications, there were two major items which in one form or another always made their appearance in the decrees. And these were the repeated emphasis on the need to avoid all unnecessary social engagements and entanglements, and quite especially the company of women and other (from the clerical standpoint) undesirable contacts. In both instances the councils went sometimes into considerable concrete detail which it is not necessary to set forth. There is an abundance of legislation relative to clerical attire and the appropriate personal appearance, though beards were apparently forbidden only in Italy, as nowhere north of the Alps is there a corresponding enactment.[3] The attendance at banquets, feasts, parties, and the like was almost universally frowned upon by the synodists, though with varying degrees of disapproval.

---

[1] See also *Leges Visigothorum*, XII. 3, in *MGH* pp. 427 ff., containing the laws of Erwig, 28 in number.

[2] *Capit.* 293, cc. 57, 58, 59, 73, 75.

[3] Rome (743), c. 8, p. 15: threat of anathema.

While, for instance, the council of Mainz in 852 categorically declared that clerics must leave before the banquet had actually started,[1] the council of Rheims in 813 had advised that they should not linger too long at these occasions.[2] The real reason why the councils looked askance at these festivities was that they provided an occasion for the clerics to lose their sobriety, and that was the main reason for the council of Soissons in 813 to castigate those who attended banquets, because loss of sobriety—it need not amount to drunkenness—leads to what the synodists thought was an *alienatio mentis*. Because on these festive occasions the participants indulged also too much in gastronomical and epicurean delights (what the synodists called *gastrimargia*), it was better for clerics to stay away altogether.[3] No doubt, since clerics occupied a special place in the community, their attendance at some of the local festivities was a pleasure and honour to both sides: after all, this was an almost exclusively agrarian population, which had to work very hard indeed throughout the year, and the cleric was one of them. As we know from the council of Auxerre in 573, the clerics themselves contributed to the entertainment, otherwise the prohibition of this council against clerics singing and dancing on these occasions would be barely comprehensible.

It was similar considerations which made the councils put taverns and inns out of bounds for clerics, though here again we meet with a great variety of respective prohibitions. Some councils only forbade priests to visit a tavern both for drinking and eating, while others limited the purpose of a visit to eating, and still others extended the prohibition right down to the exorcist.[4] The large gathering of Riesbach, Salzburg, and Freising in 800 laid down that not even in their abodes must clerics have meat and wine on Wednesdays and Fridays, though this rule (as so many others) suffered considerable relaxations, such as when entertaining a visiting friend or in time of war or if the cleric was *en*

[1] *Capit.* 249, c. 23, p. 191.
[2] Rheims (813), c. 18: 'Nimis incumbere'.
[3] Soissons (813), c. 10, p. 276.
[4] Cf., e.g., Frankfurt (794), c. 19, p. 168; Châlons (813), c. 44, p. 282; *Capit.* 123, c. 4, p. 243; Rheims (813), c. 26, p. 256; Tours (813), c. 21, p. 289; Aachen (816), c. 60, p. 364; *Capit.* 119, c. 7, p. 237; etc.

voyage or engaged in public business.[1] It is always a sign of legislative statesmanship to provide for such exemptions and contingent allowances which prevent the law from being flouted or
disregarded. Amongst the four main defects of the contemporary
clergy dealt with by the council of Aachen in 836 were indeed the
disregard of the prohibition to visit taverns, and clerical conduct
being indistinguishable from that of peasants and farm labourers:
again, considering the structure of society, this alleged defect
cannot cause much surprise to anyone who in modern times has
an acquaintance with conditions in the countryside,[2] though
neither then nor now did the bishops as synodists like to remember their own past. The other complaint listed by the same council
of Aachen was that as so many clerics were poor, they tried to
supplement their meagre living by taking all sorts of gainful
employment. Indeed, vagabondage of clerics was not an unknown
thing even in the early ninth century, for the council of Mainz in
813 issued a stern decree empowering the arrest of the *clerici vagi*
whom the bishop was to imprison *sine ulla mora*.[3]

For reasons similar to those forbidding visits to taverns and
attendance at banquets, were those which not only prohibited the
bearing of arms by clerics—again we ought to cast our mind back
to conditions of contemporary society which was not known for
its gentleness—but also prevented the clerics of whatever rank,
including the episcopal one, from taking part in the usual recreations, such as hunting, as for instance the council of Soissons in
744 laid down.[4] Consequently, no cleric was allowed to keep dogs
or hawks, though watch-dogs were apparently permitted.[5]
However, one council, that at Mâcon in 585, refused permission
to bishops to keep watch-dogs because they might bite the helpless poor and sick seeking the bishop's hospitality. Since the local
church was the centre of both the religious and social life, its
precincts also became frequently enough the place for popular
amusements, which were in any case rare enough, but then all the
gaudier. By the late sixth century councils began to look upon

[1] Riesbach (800), c. 3, p. 214.   [2] Aachen (836), II, 7–8, pp. 712–13.
[3] Mainz (813), c. 22, p. 267.   [4] Soissons (744), c. 3, p. 34.
[5] Epaon (517), c. 4, p. 20; Mâcon (585), c. 13, p. 170.

these entertainments with disfavour, not so much on account of the recreations themselves, as on account of the clerics taking an active part in them. Later this was extended to all *spectacula* and theatrical performances, thus adopting Justinian's legislation.[1]

While these social restrictions were, as we shall presently see, felt strongly by the clerics, the decrees restricting contact with women were felt even more strongly. This is not the occasion to deal with the problem of celibacy which, as far as I can see, did not cause much opposition. Where however the line was to be drawn at which celibacy was enjoined, was not certain at all. The council of Paris in 614 sternly decreed that all bishops and priests may *nulla ratione* marry,[2] thereby allowing at least by implication the lower orders to indulge in the marital status. Nevertheless, the widows of sub-deacons, exorcists, and acolytes were not allowed to re-marry, and if they did, faced imprisonment.[3] In any case, the sons of clerics did not remain in the power of their father, but came under that of the bishop, as the council of Orléans in 511 had already laid down.[4] What however appeared to have caused some considerable apprehension was the frequently issued decree relating to avoidance of all familiarity with women, because this was held to leave the door wide open to all sorts of vicious gossip. The Fourth Toledan Council in 633 prohibited clerics any *consortia* with women, and if found out, the bishop was to take the women away and sell them as slaves.[5] Moreover, the Ninth Toledan Council decreed that if any cleric from the bishop down to the subdeacon had a connexion with a maidservant or a woman of free birth, which resulted in progeny, these children were to become permanent slaves.[6] Although these somewhat drastic decrees were not repeated in the Frankish domains, even there the clerical restrictions in regard to women were severe enough. Thus, according to the council of Aachen in 816 all familiarity with women was to be shunned by clerics nor should they cast lustful

[1] Cf., e.g., Auxerre (573–604), c. 9, p. 180; Mainz (813), c. 10, p. 263, lines 6 ff.; Aachen (816), c. 83, p. 368.   [2] Paris (614), c. 12, p. 195.
[3] Auxerre (between 573 and 604), c. 22, p. 181; Mâcon (585), c. 16, p. 171.
[4] Orléans (511), c. 4, p. 4.
[5] IV Toledo (633), c. 43, *PL* LXXXIV, 377.
[6] IX Toledo, c. 10, *PL* LXXXIV, 437.

looks at women or make obscene gestures at them in public.[1] Still more severe was the standpoint taken by the council of Rome in 826: if there was mere suspicion of fornication with a woman, and if the cleric after admonition was still found *fabulari*, that is, to chat with her, he was to be subjected to canonical penance.[2] It does not need much historical imagination to visualize what untold damage upon the reputation of a cleric could be inflicted by chit-chat and idle gossip, considering the smallness of the village population. The vocation of a cleric in these circumstances would seem to have been almost an occupational hazard.

A great deal depended on the discretion and practical wisdom of the bishop. It is self-evident that a great many bishops lacked these qualities. And that is why a number of councils were forced to take up the matter of rebellious clerics—in other words, there was no student unrest, but priestly unrest, indeed a curious parallel with most recent developments. Thus the council of Orléans in 538 had occasion to refer to conjurations, formal protests, and signed declarations of defiance against episcopal authority— *diabolo instigante*, as the synodists were sure—with the consequence that these clerical rebels were threatened with canonical sanctions.[3] Similarly the council of Clichy in 626 spoke of a *causa rebellionis* amongst clerics,[4] who were threatened with deprivation of their clerical status, whereas the council of Rheims of 627 made short shrift and deposed the rebels.[5] Once again, Visigothic legislation was the most severe: if on the occasion of a popular revolt a cleric joined in and took up or tried to take up arms, he was to be deposed without further ado and incarcerated in a monastery.[6]

Yet, there were some compensating features for the cleric: he was free from as much public-social responsiblity as possible, thus he was not allowed to assume a tutorship or the *mundeburdium* over minors, which was a great concession and relieved the clerics from a great many personal burdens.[7] At least in theory the

[1] Aachen (816), c. 145, p. 420, lines 24 ff.
[2] Rome (826), c. 15, p. 574; cf. also *Capit.* 249, c. 7, p. 188.
[3] Orléans (538), c. 24, p. 80.   [4] Clichy (626), c. 3, p. 197.
[5] Rheims (c. 627), c. 2, p. 203.   [6] IV Toledo, c. 45, *PL* LXXXIV, 377.
[7] Orléans (541), c. 13, p. 90; Bourges (663), c. 2, p. 215; etc.

councils opposed the ever-growing proprietary church system by declaring that lay persons were not permitted to appoint or dismiss priests without episcopal consent,[1] though all this without much avail. On the other hand, in obtaining his justice for himself, the cleric was by no means free: in order to appeal to the royal court for help in remedying an obviously unjust decision or action by a royal officer, the cleric had to have his bishop's permission,[2] and if he was temerarious enough to proceed without it, he was to be whipped. I do not think that I go far wrong when I say that the vocational status of a cleric entailed as many duties and restrictions and limitations of movement attached to his estate as it contained rights and privileges which, at the time we are considering, had as yet not been conspicuous or in practical evidence. What was in evidence was the vocational status, according to which so many things were denied to the cleric which ordinary mortals took for granted. If the cleric lived and acted as the synods laid down, his was certainly a difficult and onerous vocation dedicated to the service of God—but how many lived and acted *secundum legem* will always be a matter of some speculation.

Let me now turn to a kind of social legislation which too is not unfamiliar to us today. There are the factory acts, the laws regulating the forty-hour week, the detailed laws concerning free time for employees, acts relating to the closing of shops, and the like. However detailed these regulations are, they can be reduced, I think, to the one common feature, that is, to make sure that workmen have sufficient free time and are not exploited through working unduly long hours. In the early medieval period the ecclesiastical councils had not at all dissimilar aims, although their reasons were based on wholly religious grounds. Freedom from work was above all insisted upon for Sundays and mostly also for holidays of obligation: Sunday rest from work was, so to speak, a precondition as well as a consequence of the attendance of divine service. But again there was great variety as to what kind of work was allowed on Sundays as well as the motives prompting the law restricting Sunday work. Some councils, for instance,

[1] Arles (813), c. 4, p. 250; Mainz (813), c. 29, p. 268; etc.
[2] Riesbach (800), c. 26; and *Capit.* 22, c. 10, p. 55; *Capit.* 13, c. 7, p. 32.

the council of Tours in 813, pointed out that the resurrection of the Lord should be kept alive[1] while others modelled the Sunday law on the seventh day in Exodus (20. 8. 11) which imposed a duty on the Christian to rest on Sunday.[2] In any case, rest on Sunday was considered an opportunity, not of having leisure or of being idle in the modern sense, but of recollection and meditation, which is exactly what the expression that Sunday was a 'dies requietionis perpetuus' was meant to convey: the idea behind this was that (as the council of Mâcon in 585 said) man should recollect and recreate himself.[3] This seems to me an application of the idea of renaissance, of a rebirth, which man should experience through Sunday recollection and prayers.

Apparently no domestic work was ever envisaged as falling under the prohibition of Sunday work: in view of the predominantly agricultural character of the households it would have been somewhat impracticable to prohibit any work connected with livestock. In fact, the council of Orléans in 538 made exactly this point and took the opportunity of contrasting the Jewish Sabbath with the Christian Sunday: the former prohibited what was obviously licit on the latter.[4] On the other hand, all the more stress was laid on the work that was not to be carried out in the fields: there was almost universal prohibition against ploughing, weeding, and hoeing in the vine yards, furrowing, or even gathering in the harvest.[5] The council of Auxerre in the late sixth century forbade any work which required the use of two oxen, in other words, heavy field work. It was at this time that Archbishop Martin of Braga in Spain resurrected the hitherto forgotten Jewish term of 'servile work' for the Sabbath and applied it to

[1] Tours (813), c. 37, p. 291; Paris (829), c. 50, p. 643.
[2] Put forward by Rome (826), c. 9, p. 557. The doctrinal and theological background is very well drawn by L. L. McReavy, 'The Sunday repose from labour', in *Ephemerides theol. Lovanienses*, XII (1935), 291–323.
[3] Mâcon (585), c. 1, p. 165: 'Iustum igitur est, ut hanc diem unanimiter celebremus, per quam facti sumus, quod non fuimus; fuimus enim ante servi peccati, sed per cam facti sumus filii iustitiae.'
[4] See Orléans (538), c. 31, p. 82: 'Id statuimus, ut die dominico, quod ante fieri licuit, liceat.'
[5] Orléans (538), c. 31, p. 82; Mâcon (585), c. 1, p. 165; Auxerre (573–603), c. 16, p. 181; Châlons (639), c. 18, p. 212; etc.

Sunday, including herein all work on a Sunday in the fields.[1] And from here the term 'servile work' began its career throughout the medieval period and beyond. It was a 'revolutionary' step, turning the wheel right round.[2] There were some Carolingian councils which adopted the Jewish sabbatarian custom of keeping the Sabbath, that is, now Sunday, from sunset to sunset.[3] Other councils avoided this term of servile work and spoke of *ruralia opera*, which in any case were carried out by serfs. Here the Wessex council in 691 deserves special mention, because it decreed that if upon the order of his master, a slave were to work on a Sunday he was automatically freed, an enactment which was also incorporated into the Anglo-Saxon laws.[4] Moreover, all business transactions and commercial activities, such as holding of fairs and markets, were forbidden.[5] Nor were judicial sittings in criminal proceedings allowed, though apparently civil proceedings could be carried out.[6] I think it must have been a singular, nay, puritanical, standpoint which the council of Friuli in 796 expressed when it imposed abstention from what it called an *opus carnale* or *opus terrenum* in which was also included abstention *a propriis coniugibus*.[7] It was probably similar considerations which prompted the council of Aachen in 836 to forbid the celebration of nuptial ceremonies on Sundays.[8]

What is noteworthy, however, is that, as far as I could ascertain, none of the conciliar decrees make any concessions to pre-

[1] See the quotation in McReavy, *Ephemerides theol. Lovanienses*, XII, pp. 311–12.
[2] Cf. McReavy, *art. cit.* p. 312.
[3] For instance, Aachen (789) in *Capit.* 22, c. 15, p. 55, re-enacting Laodicea (360), c. 29; Friuli (796), c. 13, p. 194. As usual Visigothic legislation was most severe; the royal law extended the prohibition of Sunday work to Jews and Jewesses, and if they were found working in the fields on a Sunday, each was to receive 100 lashes and undergo decalvation: *MGH Leges Visigoth.* III, 12, 3 (6), p. 434; cf. also McReavy, *art. cit.* p. 320. That 'Sunday' lasted from Saturday sun-set to Sunday sun-set or sometimes Monday sun-rise, was the law in later Anglo-Saxon England, cf. F. Liebermann, *Die Gesetze der Angelsachsen*, II (Halle 1906), 656–7.
[4] See Ine's law book in F. Liebermann, *Gesetze, cit.*, c. 3, i, 91.
[5] Rome (826), c. 30, p. 580.
[6] Mainz (813), c. 37, p. 270; Rheims (813), c. 35, p. 256; Rome (826), c. 31, p. 580, mentioning expressly criminal proceedings.
[7] Friuli (796), c. 13, p. 194.   [8] Aachen (836), c. 58, p. 722.

vailing weather conditions. The prohibition of Sunday work in the fields was apparently absolute, a matter of considerable concern to those engaged in agricultural pursuits, because especially at harvest time inclement weather conditions might make it imperative to carry on with the gathering of corn and fruits on any day of the week. I think that it was the unconcern with the actual weather prevailing at certain times by the synodists which made people disregard the prohibition, and on the other hand explains the frequent repetition of this kind of legislation by the councils. We should bear in mind the great number of feast days, in addition to Sundays, to which similar considerations applied. Together with the usual festivals at Christmas, Easter, Whitsun, and the fifteen other general feast days in conjunction with those of local saints, there was quite a respectable number of 'free' days throughout the year.[1] Yet, despite the rigorism adopted by the councils, hunting as a recreational pursuit was not apparently included in the activities prohibited on Sundays.

It was probably in connexion with popular entertainments that there was an escalation of the consumption of both food and drink. Here the English, whether lay or cleric, bishop or priest, did not shine forth as examples to be imitated. When St Boniface informed Cuthbert, the archbishop of Canterbury, of the decrees of the general Frankish council in 747, he took the opportunity to reproach the English bishops with not prohibiting the immoderate consumption of alcohol: they, the bishops themselves, Boniface declared, set a bad example in so far as they 'nimis bibentes inebrientur' and encouraged others to drink more by 'poculis maioribus'.[2] It was this letter which in actual fact led to the synod of Cloveshoe (Abingdon) in 747, though Boniface's grievance found only a very weak echo in its decrees.[3] The council of Tours in 813 was quite clear that according to the testimony of the *physici* severe and serious corporal diseases were the result of drunkenness, which was also the 'causa et origo pene omnium malorum':[4] this same council declared in theological-

---

[1] Mainz (813), c. 36, pp. 269 f., enumerates the general feast days; cf. also *Capit.* i, 179, which has slightly fewer.   [2] *MGH Epist.* III, 355.
[3] In Mansi, c. 3, XII, 395 f.   [4] Tours (813), c. 48, p. 293.

juristic language that the works of the devil, such as homicides and adulteries, were the work of the flesh, for they were first conceived mentally *diabolico instinctu* and then translated into the deed, which meant that drunkenness was no excuse for committing any crime, and the perpetrator acting in a state of drunkenness was considered to act *culpose*, that is, he remained responsible.[1] The synodists assembled at Mainz in the same year 813 also viewed dipsomania as a *magnum malum*, from which *omnia vitia* took their origin and anyone unwilling to give up the habit was to be excommunicated until he showed *congrua emendatio*,[2] which seems to me the ninth-century precursor of present-day measures against those who fail the breathalyser test.

However much society in the early Middle Ages was called Christian, pagan cults, pagan customs and manners were still practised to a large extent. In their function as organs which were to bring about a renaissance of society, the councils had of course to take notice of these remnants and to issue decrees against what must have appeared to them the most objectionable excrescences of these pagan practices. It is perhaps noteworthy in this context that there was very little difference between the Western and Eastern parts of the Frankish realms. Superstition and popular *mores* were sometimes intermingled with Christian elements, and it was therefore all the more difficult to detach the one from the other. The two synods of Orléans in 533 and 541 are quite typical of this early period. The former threatened excommunication against those who despite their baptism nevertheless sacrificed in the old pagan manner,[3] while the latter in two decrees[4] referred to the custom of reverting to the ancient pagan rites almost immediately after people had attended Christian services: after unsuccessful admonition, excommunication followed. It seems that early January was a favoured time for the revival of pagan cults, as the respective decree of the council of Tours in 567 made clear when the synodists referred to Janus as the deity to whom Christians, after having been to mass, sacrificed in their own homes.[5]

[1] Tours (813), c. 18, p. 289.   [2] Mainz (813), c. 46, p. 272.
[3] Orléans (533), c. 20, p. 64.   [4] Orléans (541), cc. 15, 16, p. 90.
[5] Tours (567), c. 23, p. 144.

One might perhaps think that they took out a double insurance policy. In the region of Auxerre by the end of the sixth and early seventh century these pagan rites seem to have been cultivated with undiminished vigour, again in January.[1] Idolatry and pagan feasts were also mentioned by the council of Rheims in 627 as reprehensible to Christianity, and those taking part in them should be gently rebuked.[2] The decrees against superstition are so numerous that one is justified in the assumption that they were general and widespread. In fact, Charlemagne himself had published an *Indiculus superstitionum* in which he listed some thirty particularly prominent superstitious practices,[3] amongst which is the cremation of corpses in accordance with pagan rites, which practice carried the death penalty—the same dire penalty was inflicted upon anyone who, blinded by the devil, believed a woman to be a *striga* (which I take to mean a witch) who eats human beings, and then himself burns this woman or eats her flesh.[4] These practices and still more the steps taken to combat their spread and growth are very interesting indeed—a wide field of enquiry for the historical sociologist if such a species exists.

I do not wish to leave this particular topic without at least mentioning the sorcerers, fortune-tellers, practitioners of divinations, enchanters, and similar folk whose trade briskly flourished in our period, and against whom, for the sake of preserving the mental health of society, the councils were constantly on the watch. On the whole it would seem that conciliar legislation was in this respect far less successful than the corresponding royal legislative measures.[5] As usual, the most severe penalties were threatened against sorcerers and the like by the Visigothic councils: the Fourth Toledan Council in 633 sentenced a cleric, if

[1] Auxerre (between 573 and 604), cc. 1 and 4, pp. 179, 180.
[2] Rheims (*c.* 627), c. 14, p. 205: 'benigna admonitione suaderi'.
[3] *Capit.* 108, pp. 222–3.
[4] *Capitulatio de partibus Saxoniae, cit.*, c. 6, p. 69: 'Si quis diabolo deceptus crediderit secundum morem paganorum virum aliquem aut feminam strigam esse et homines commedere et propter hoc ipsam incenderit vel carnem eius ad commendendum dederit vel ipsam commederit, capitali sententia punietur.' Further c. 7: 'Si quis corpus defuncti hominis secundum ritum paganorum flamma consumi fecerit, et ossa ad cinerem redegerit, capite punietur.'
[5] See Orléans (511), c. 30, p. 9; also Clichy (626), c. 16, p. 199.

found asking the advice of a sorcerer, to life imprisonment,[1] whilst the Sixteenth Council of Toledo in 693 took drastic steps to eradicate practices which the synodists obviously believed to be abominable. They manifested themselves in the veneration of certain trees, sources of rivers, and stones, in the lighting of torches, in witchcraft and other forms of idolatry: anathema was decreed in all these cases, and the wealthy ones were to pay three pounds of gold, whilst those unable to do so, had to receive 100 strokes as well as having to undergo the disgracing decalvation and to hand over half of their property to the fisc.[2] I have mentioned these instances to show that the synodists cared for what may be termed the public health of society, public health understood not in terms of physical well-being, but in terms of protecting and if necessary immunizing and inoculating the mind of the people against infectious diseases of a pandemic kind. This was, I would like to think, a kind of social legislation which was germane and adapted to contemporary society, and which is still of some interest today, even if nomenclatures and issues are slightly different.

The time has come to draw to a close. You have been patient enough to listen to a very sketchy and patchy *exposé* on topics which greatly excited the bishops sitting in the numerous ecclesiastical councils of the early medieval period—that is, topics which, I am sure I need not specifically emphasize before this forum, have considerable relevance to the historian who wishes to find out what we were before we have become what we are. And the distance between what we were and what we are is—within the compass of my topic—certainly great in degree, but is it really also great in kind?

But there is more to be said in conclusion. The subject of public welfare and social legislation would seem to me to need urgent professional treatment. When preparing the material for this paper, I was powerfully struck by the great influence which the decrees of these early councils had upon later works right through

---

[1] IV Toledo, c. 29, *PL* LXXXIV, 375.

[2] XVI Toledo, c. 2, *PL*, 537–8. This has obviously served as the model for Charlemagne's *Capitulatio, cit.*, c. 21, and is further proof that the Visigothic conciliar legislation was known in the Frankish realm in the seventies and eighties of the eighth century.

the subsequent period and culminating in Gratian in the twelfth century. Not that Gratian himself had ferreted out these decrees from the original sources—he was not very original, you know—but the important point is that he had found them in the collections upon which he himself drew and these collections had, in this instance, an ancestry going right back to the ninth century. Through the vehicle of their social legislation the early medieval councils had imprinted upon the Middle Ages their own physiognomy and complexion. One might well say that the longevity of certain views, institutions, and so forth not only finds a ready explanation in the influence which the canonical collections exercised, but also in their function as potent harbingers of a historical continuity which has few parallels in the history of Western Europe. What needs doing is a systematic and careful analysis of the stages by which these numerous conciliar decrees came to be filtered through to Gratian. What we need, if I may be so personal, is another Charles Duggan to master this to my mind urgent task which is ecclesiastically, historically, and, forgive me, sociologically of some considerable interest. The task is no more and no less than to show: (1) the influence of the early medieval councils upon the social complexion of the Middle Ages; and (2) their relevance to later post-Reformation public welfare and social legislation. This cluster of problems may be called the transmission and influence of the councils on later ages.

Of at least equal importance is the question which looks backwards, from the early medieval councils to their sources. What were they? What works of what authors were particularly influential? How were they transmitted to the synodists? What made Cyprian so palatable, and why is only a moderate influence of Tertullian detectable? What part did papal decrees and decretals play in shaping social legislation? How far and in what particular directions did the Bible exercise a noteworthy influence on this segment of conciliar legislation? In what precise respects were secular legislation and secular models—I am mainly thinking of Justinian's legislation—responsible for conciliar enactments? This part of the enquiry to be undertaken I would like to call the genetic problem, in which I naturally would include the influence

37

and assimilation and accommodation of primitive Germanic customs, traditions, and usages, and for this we might want another Brian Tierney.

There is a third category of problems awaiting treatment, and this I would like to call the topographical one. In my sketch I have paid no heed whatsoever to the geographical distribution and diversities of conciliar decrees, which surely is of some importance if one wishes to penetrate into the matrix of society. Why did certain topics receive lengthy and almost monographic treatment in some regions—I am here thinking of the Visigothic councils— whilst the same topic was dealt with in other parts of Christendom within three to four lines? You have certainly noticed that I have not dealt with a fundamental social institution, marriage, the reason being that enactments were so diverse and incorporated so many Germanic customs, that it is extremely difficult to obtain any comprehensive view. The same applies to the dissolution of marriage: why was the divorce by reason of the wife's adultery sanctioned in some councils, for instance in that of Rome in 826, whilst in other parts of Christendom this was not the case? On what grounds could the divorce between a freeman and a slave woman be justified? This topographical treatment of problems would also, I like to think, provide a very welcome yardstick by which the cultural attainments in the different regions could be measured. It would seem that it is at this point that what my old friend Gabriel Le Bras has styled religious sociology comes into its own. Why, to move to a different, though not unrelated, field, were the ordeals kept alive, both by writers and councils, when *prima facie* one would have thought that they could hardly be anything but a denial of some basic Christian tenets? Indeed, no lesser men than Agobard of Lyons or Pope Nicholas I in the ninth century violently attacked the ordeals—and for the right reasons—but without avail. A whole liturgy and a formidable solemn ritual encrusted the performance of the ordeals—all sanctioned and amplified by individuals and councils. We have to wait until the early thirteenth century for the abolition of ordeals—once more by a council.

Lastly, there is a problem to which here and there I have alluded in my sketch, but which needs appropriate *ex professo* treatment, and that is, what role did the ecclesiastical councils, at any rate in the early period, play in regard to secular-royal legislation? Did the councils act as pressure groups? In view of the governmental set-up of the Frankish period, it seems clear that the enforcement of a great many synodal decrees needed the active co-operation of the royal officers, and this again presupposed royal legislation. This particular problem touches on the very nerve-centre of the function of the councils as watch-dogs of the well-being of society. That they saw themselves in this role admits of no doubt. They were the guardians of the spiritual health of early European society. It was a primitive, it was a barbaric, it was a crude age in which the councils acted as an essential leaven that effected or tried to effect a transformation of the character of society from a pagan to a Christian community. It does not need great historical imagination or acumen to realize that within a purely historical context their task as well as their achievements were gigantic. They indicated in a practical manner how the perhaps most pronounced Christian virtue, that of charity, was to be effectively translated into reality, and this in excruciatingly difficult conditions. The synodists did not pursue party politics: the councils were gatherings of men whose corporate efforts and beneficial effects in public life have not been adequately appreciated by posterity. This Ecclesiastical History Society of ours has the scholars in its midst, has the talent and the men and women ready to undertake at least some of the tasks which I have had the privilege of setting forth before you this evening—let us begin to show our own contemporaries what distinguished ancestry modern efforts have in that period which was the *fons et origo* of our own present-day Europe.

NATIONAL SYNODS, KINGSHIP
AS OFFICE, AND ROYAL ANOINTING:
AN EARLY MEDIEVAL SYNDROME

by JANET L. NELSON

ROFESSOR Gabriel Le Bras, a great pioneer in the field of historical sociology, has spoken of the early medieval Church in a bizarre but effective metaphor as 'a dismembered body striving to reunite itself'.[1] The essential task of the hierarchy within each national Church[2] was one of co-ordination—by means of law, doctrine, and the standardization of worship. In the fragmented world of the barbarian kingdoms, the distinctive feature of each episcopate was its ideology of cohesion, the more ardently propounded when social crisis was particularly acute, as in the seventh-century Visigothic kingdom, or the war-torn West Francia of the 830s and 840s. This ideology was, moreover, often intimately associated with movements of monastic reform. Its influence penetrated down into the rural base of society through episcopal visitations, preaching, and provincial councils. To trace all the elements in these complex processes of interaction and change would encompass that much-needed sociology of the early medieval Church which Max Weber did not live to write and no scholar has yet produced.[3] In this paper, as its title

[1] 'Sociologie de l'Église dans le Haut Moyen Âge', in *Settimana Spoleto*, 7, II (1960), 598.
[2] On the early medieval *Landeskirchen*, see H. von Schubert, *Grundzüge der Kirchengeschichte*, 10th edn. rev. E. Dinkler, Tübingen 1937, 130 ff.; H. F. Feine, *Kirchliche Rechtsgeschichte*, 4th edn., Weimar 1964, 147 ff.; and W. Schlesinger, *Beitrage zur deutschen Verfassungsgeschichte des Mittelalters*, Göttingen 1963, 259, pointing out their character as *Gentilkirchen*. For the term 'national church', see the sensible remarks of T. Schieffer and F. L. Ganshof in *Settimana Spoleto*, 7, I (1960), 312 f.
[3] Cf. the Introduction by T. Parsons to Weber's *The Sociology of Religion*, London 1965, xiv; and suggestions scattered throughout Weber's work: e.g. *Max Weber on Law in Economy and Society*, ed. and trans. E. Shils and M. Rheinstein,

implies, my very limited objective is to isolate and examine certain recurrent phenomena and to point to some hitherto unnoticed connections.

Some historians have depicted the bishops of the early Middle Ages as secular magnates wearing different hats, and thus have seen their activities as one among other forms of *Adelsherrschaft*.[1] It is true that bishops were drawn very largely from noble families. But equally significant is the fact that they were royal nominees, and in the periods I shall be considering, kings preferred to seek their bishops in the monasteries.[2] If such promotions can hardly be termed channels of social mobility, they nevertheless created one important precondition for a separation of episcopal from secular interests.

Within each kingdom, the bishops shared in government, usually at the local level, but they also had specialized functions as exponents of ritual and setters of norms in a Christian society. The main limitation on the effectiveness of their performance of these integrative roles was imposed by the incomplete substitution of Christian for pagan beliefs and values:[3] it was this *ignorantia*, the

Cambridge, Mass., 1954, 250 ff., and *From Max Weber: Essays in Sociology*, ed. and trans. H. H. Gerth and C. W. Mills, London 1947, 245 ff., 295 ff. See now also the masterly survey of Le Bras, 'Sociologie de l'Église'; E. Troeltsch, *The Social Teaching of the Christian Churches*, trans. O. Wyon, London 1931, I, 214 ff., and W. Stark, *The Sociology of Religion: A Study of Christendom*, London 1966, are stimulating, but deal only sketchily with the early medieval period.

[1] This approach, first developed by A. Schulte, *Der Adel und die deutsche Kirche*, Stuttgart 1910 (mainly with reference to the later Middle Ages), has, however, corrected a tendency to divorce ecclesiastical history from its social environment. See also H. Mitteis, 'Formen der Adelsherrschaft im Mittelalter', in *Festschrift F. Schulz*, Weimar 1951, 226 ff. esp. 237; K. Bosl, *Frühformen der Gesellschaft*, Munich 1964, 93, 459; K. F. Werner, 'Bedeutende Adelsfamilien...', in *Karl der Grosse*, ed. H. Beumann, Düsseldorf 1965, I, 91 f.

[2] Or among the clergy of the royal chapel: see H. Wieruzowski, 'Die Zusammensetzung des gallischen und fränkischen Episkopats bis zum Vertrag von Verdun (843)', in *Bonner Jahrbücher*, 127 (1922), 1–83. Werner, 'Bedeutende Adelsfamilien', 94, notes the break between Merovingian and Carolingian practice. For further evidence from Spain, Germany, and England, see the works of Thompson, Johnson, and Darlington cited below.

[3] Copious evidence is adduced by E. A. Thompson, *The Goths in Spain*, Oxford 1969, 308 ff.; J. A. Cabaniss, *Agobard of Lyons*, Syracuse 1953, 20 ff.; K. Hauck, 'Geblütsheiligkeit', in *Liber Floridus. Festschrift P. Lehmann*, St Ottilien 1950, 187 ff.; with special reference to kingship, F. Heiler, 'Fortleben und Wand-

cultural barrier to social cohesion, which bishops explicitly set out to combat by means of the *lux conciliorum*.[1] In the national synods of the early Middle Ages, the bishops went into action. These assemblies, in which, despite the presence in some cases of lay participants, the higher clergy formed the overwhelming majority, were convoked by kings to deliberate and act on problems of nation-wide importance. By their very existence, they provided a definite organization for the whole episcopal group: the hierarchy in this respect presents a striking contrast to the lay magnates, who could never be said to have formed anything so precise as an élite.[2] Repeated meetings over time, collective action, and the

lungen des antiken Gottkönigtums im Christentum', in *The Sacral Kingship*, Leiden 1959, 543 ff.; and W. A. Chaney, 'Paganism to Christianity in Anglo-Saxon England', in *Early Medieval Society*, ed. S. Thrupp, New York 1967, 67 ff. See now also J. Le Goff, 'Culture cléricale et traditions folkloriques dans la civilisation mérovingienne', in *Annales ESC*, 22 (1967), 780 ff. On integration and pattern-maintenance in social systems, see T. Parsons, *Societies*, Englewood Cliffs 1966, 11 and 24 ff. It seems to me that the early medieval Church performed both these functions, and that the Parsonian paradigm involves a certain over-schematization which actually diminishes its analytic usefulness for the historian.

[1] Conc. Tol. xi (a provincial synod), prologue, in *PL* 84, 451: 'annosa series temporum subtracta luce conciliorum non tam vitia auxerat quam matrem omnium errorum ignorantiam otiosis mentibus ingerebat'. Cf. Tol. iv, *ibid.* 366: 'de qualitate conciliorum'. See also the Anglo-Saxon *Polity* of *c.* 1000, ed. and trans. B. Thorpe, *Ancient Laws*, i, 428, c. x. '*Incipit de synodo*: It is incumbent on bishops in the synod first of all to consider about unanimity and true concord among themselves, and how they may before all things exalt Christianity and most effectually suppress heathenism.' For synods as 'charismatic assemblies', see N. Baynes, *Byzantine Studies and Other Essays*, London 1955, 111; cf. H. Barion, *Das fränkisch-deutsche Synodalrecht des Frühmittelalters*, Bonn 1931, 110 ff.: 'nur Organe der Kirchenleitung...nicht Versammlungen der Christen, ...sie (i.e. Synods) hierarchischen Charakter trugen und keine Zugeständnisse an demokratische Wünsche ihrer Untergebenen gemacht hätten'. On synods in general, see P. Hinschius, *Das Kirchenrecht der Katholiken und Protestanten in Deutschland*, Berlin 1869 etc., iii, 539 ff.

[2] On the distinction between an élite and a wider (unorganized) ruling class, see R. Sereno, *The Rulers*, Leiden 1962, 99 ff., and the penetrating study of T. B. Bottomore, *Elites and Society*, London 1966, esp. 41 f. The fluidity of the ruling stratum and the various possibilities for achieving social status in early medieval kingdoms have been discussed by R. Boutruche, *Seigneurie et Féodalité*, Paris 1959, 147 ff.; Bosl, *Frühformen der Gesellschaft*, 156 ff.; F. Graus, *Volk, Herrscher und Heiliger im Reich der Merowinger*, Prague 1965, 200 ff. A clearly defined aristocracy with its own characteristic ethos and system of status-stratification

articulation of common concerns fostered a conscious solidarity on the part of the bishops, and a sense of responsibility for the leadership of their whole society within the wider Church of Christendom. We have to thank Professor Ullmann for showing the full significance of this episcopal deployment of the 'hierocratic theme'.[1]

It has rightly been said that no-one in the Middle Ages wanted a weak king;[2] but it might be fair to add that the lay magnates wanted non-interfering kings, who could give a strong lead in time of crisis but would leave local control in noble hands. The bishops, by contrast, needed a strong and continuously active central power to establish Christian norms and habits of worship, and to protect the rural economic basis of the clergy's livelihood. In view of these divergent interests, it seems to me superficial to see the struggles of the bishops against the feudal laity as 'like against like'.[3] Bishops, especially if they had been monks, had interests *qua* bishops which cut them loose from their anchorage in the aristocracy.[4] In two of the four kingdoms which I shall be

came into existence only with the decline of the Carolingian Empire, and matured in the eleventh and twelfth centuries: see G. Tellenbach, 'Zur Erforschung des mittelalterlichen Adels (9–12 Jhdt.)', in *XII Congrès International des Sciences Historiques*, 1965, Rapports 1,318 ff., and G. Duby, 'The Diffusion of Cultural Patterns in Feudal Society', in *Past and Present*, 39 (1968), 3 ff. The distinction between ranking and stratification is stressed by M. Fried, *The Evolution of Political Society*, New York 1967, and by R. Wenskus, *Stammesbildung und Verfassung*, Köln-Graz 1961, 314 and n. 273: the social anthropologist and the historian, from quite different starting-points, reach similar conclusions. The methodological problem of dealing with periods for which no statistics are available has been ably discussed by M. K. Hopkins, 'Elite Mobility in the Roman Empire', in *Past and Present*, 32 (1965), 12 ff. His structural approach seems very useful also for medieval material.

[1] See esp. his *The Growth of Papal Government in the Middle Ages*, 2nd edn., London 1962, 125 ff.
[2] J. M. Wallace-Hadrill, *The Barbarian West, 400–1000*, London 1964, 144. Cf. Schlesinger, *Beitrage zur deutschen Verfassungsgeschichte*, 242, and *idem*, 'Die Auflösung des Karlsreiches', in *Karl der Grosse*, I, 833 ff.
[3] So E. N. Johnson, *The Secular Activities of the German Episcopate*, Chicago 1932, 23.
[4] See Barion, *Das fränkisch-deutsche Synodalrecht*, 332. I would rate very highly the importance of the episcopal ordination rite in aggregating individual to role. The idea of personal regeneration is central to this as to other status-changing rituals: hence the ease of liturgical transpositions from one initiation rite to another. See P. Oppenheim, 'Mönchsweihe und Taufritus', in *Miscellanea Liturgica in honorem L. C. Mohlberg*, Rome 1948, I, esp. 265 ff., and the suggestive remarks of G. H. Williams, *The Norman Anonymous*, Harvard 1951,

considering, the development through national synods of an episcopal group-identity led to the replacement of mixed lay and ecclesiastical councils by two separate assemblies;[1] while in the other two kingdoms, clergy alone deliberated and promoted legislation on doctrinal and ecclesiastical matters (which of course covered a very wide range).[2] If it was the king who, in the first instance, mobilized the episcopate as an instrument of royal government, national synods could nevertheless, like the sorcerer's broom, take on a life and character of their own. The bishops might seek to wield a more direct and extensive control by shifting the balance underlying their alliance with the monarchy: when kings were weak, bishops rallied to their support—but with their own idea of how kings should function. National synods provided the organization and operational means, synodal statements the ideology, which underpinned episcopal attempts to capture the commanding heights of the political structure.

I shall survey briefly the national synods of four areas: Visigothic Spain in the time of Isidore and Julian, West Francia in the time of Jonas and Hincmar, the East Francia of Salomo III and Hatto, and the England of Dunstan and Æthelwold. The crucial role played by leaders both in decision-making and propaganda was hardly a surprising feature of such sustained collective action. This leadership was often formalized as a metropolitan dignity,[3] but it was rooted in the consent and support of the episcopate as a

---

77 ff. and 158 f. Relevant and valuable in this context are M. Fortes, 'Ritual and Office', in *Essays in the Ritual of Social Relations*, ed. M. Gluckman, Manchester 1962, 53 ff., and the fundamental work of A. van Gennep, *The Rites of Passage*, ed. and trans. M. Vizedom and G. L. Caffee, Chicago 1960, esp. 93 ff.

[1] See Barion, *Das fränkisch-deutsche Synodalrecht*, 163 f. and 267 ff.; Hinschius, *Das Kirchenrecht*, III, 554.

[2] Cf. the ninth-century forger, Benedictus Levita, iii, 444: 'Ne laici intersint quando canonica iura ventilantur.' See on the Spanish councils, Thompson, *The Goths in Spain*, 278 ff., and on Anglo-Saxon clerical legislation, R. Darlington, 'Ecclesiastical Reform in the Late Old English Period', in *EHR*, 51 (1936), 385 ff.

[3] Thompson, *The Goths in Spain*, 275; E. Lesne, *La Hiérarchie Épiscopale*, Paris 1905, 95 ff. Metropolitan rivalries could later come to centre on the right to perform royal consecrations: cf. P. E. Schramm, *Der König von Frankreich*, 2nd edn., Weimar 1960, 113 ff., and U. Stutz, 'Die rheinischen Erzbischöfe und die deutsche Königswahl', in *Festschrift H. Brunner*, Weimar 1910, 57 ff.

whole: witness the lists of episcopal subscriptions to synodal decrees, or the collective episcopal conduct of royal consecrations. Professor Darlington has said of the late Old English episcopate: 'It is unlikely that all the members...were equally zealous in the pursuit of reform, but the more active prelates could influence their colleagues in synods.'[1]

Royal control over the seventh-century synods of Toledo was extensive, but not exclusive: the Church has been called 'the main stabilizing element in Visigothic society',[2] and in view of recurrent dynastic crises, the bishops were themselves vitally concerned to establish constitutional norms determining the nature and scope of royal power and the ways in which it might legitimately be acquired. These preoccupations are to be found in the writings of Isidore, and in the deliberations of the synod of 633 over which he presided.[3] The impact of monasticism on the episcopate at this time was strong, and the bishops were much concerned with the maintenance of standards of clerical discipline.[4] They were fully aware of the importance of synods, and criticized King Recceswinth for his failure to summon one during the last seventeen years of his reign[5]—a fact which speaks as tellingly for the extent of royal control as the criticism itself does for the existence of a distinctively hierarchical standpoint. The bishops, even when they could claim a major voice in elections, had reservations about elective kingship.[6] They wanted a stable monarchy which should be the Church's bulwark: hence their support of Wamba, 'offering himself', so the synodists of 675 believed, 'as a new

[1] Darlington, 'Ecclesiastical Reform', 414.
[2] J. N. Hillgarth, A Critical Edition of the *Prognosticum futuri saeculi* of St Julian of Toledo, Ph.D. Thesis, Cambridge 1956 (unpublished), XXVII. See also C. Sanchez Albornoz, 'El Aula Regia', in *Cuadernos de Historia de España*, 5 (1946), esp. 85 ff.
[3] See M. Reydellet, 'La Conception du Souverain chez Isidore de Séville', in *Isidoriana*, ed. M. Diaz y Diaz, Leon 1961, 457 ff.
[4] See E. Perez Pujol, *Historia de las Instituciones Sociales de la España Goda*, Valencia 1896, 106 ff., 143 ff.
[5] Conc. Tol. XI, in *PL* 84, 451: the bishops complain of the ills of society 'quia ecclesiastici conventus non aderat disciplina...et quia non erat adunandorum pontificum ulla praeceptio'.
[6] See J. Orlandis Rovira, 'La iglesia Visigoda y los problemas de la sucesion al trono en el siglo VII', in *Settimana Spoleto*, 7, I (1960), 333–51.

Synods, kingship and royal anointing

restorer of the Church's discipline in these our times'.[1] The many decrees of Visigothic councils aimed at protecting the Church's economic welfare show the bishops in direct and frequent conflict with the ambitions of secular magnates.[2]

As in seventh-century Spain, the West Frankish synods of the reign of Louis the Pious and the early years of Charles the Bald formed a coherent series: repeated meetings of the same bishops gave rise in time to what Hincmar would call *episcopalis unanimitas*.[3] At Paris in 829, the synodists gave lengthy consideration to the respective functions in Christian government of the king, as *minister*, and the bishops, as 'those who make known the will of God' (*divinae voluntatis indices*).[4] They were inspired by the ideals of Charlemagne's 'renovation' of society, and by the monastic reform to which Louis had lent his patronage;[5] his penance at Attigny in 822 was a demonstration of faith in personal renewal.[6] The synodists of the 840s attacked lay magnates who violated canon law in appropriating the Church's property. In face of the consistent development of episcopal policy, both royal reservations and lay reaction became more marked, and with the rebuff at Épernay in 847 when the king rejected much

[1] PL 84, 465: 'ecclesiasticae disciplinae his nostris saeculis novus reparator occurrens'. It was thanks to Wamba that 'lux conciliorum renovata resplenduit', *ibid.* 451.

[2] Cf. Thompson, *The Goths in Spain*, 308: 'On no single subject did the bishops spend more time than on the safeguarding of their churches' property.'

[3] De Divortio, Quaest. 6, in PL 125, 757, apropos the reinstatement by the bishops of Louis the Pious in 834.

[4] MGH, Conc., II, 605 ff. See also J. Reviron, *Les idées politico-religieuses d'un evêque du IXe siècle: Jonas d'Orléans et son 'De institutione regia'*, Paris 1930, esp. 94 ff. and 113 ff. (Jonas' treatise was a restatement of the Paris decrees), and E. Delaruelle, 'En relisant le *De Institutione regia...*', in *Mélanges Halphen*, Paris 1951, 185 ff., esp. 187: 'C'est l'entrée en scène de l'épiscopat... organisé en corps constitué... se prononçant sur les grands interêts de l'État et de la chrétienté.' The conciliar activities of this period are discussed by Ullmann, *Growth*, 125 ff.

[5] See H. Fichtenau, *Das karolingische Imperium*, Zurich 1949, 209 ff.; and the perceptive remarks of J. Winandy, 'L'Oeuvre de S. Benoît d'Aniane', in *Mélanges Bénédictins*, St Wandrille 1947, 235 ff. J. Semmler, 'Die monastische Gesetzgebung Ludwigs des Frommen', in *Deutsches Archiv*, 16 (1960), esp. 384 ff., links the *unitas* of monastic observance with the whole idea of a 'renovatio regni Francorum'.

[6] Cf. Isidore, De Offic. II, xvii, 6, in PL 83, 803: 'Lacrymae enim poenitentium apud deum pro baptismate reputantur.'

of the synodists' programme,[1] the bishops were forced to recognize the inadequacy of synodal action without royal co-operation.

In East Francia half a century later, the synodal development was telescoped. Its beginnings can be seen in the 880s, when the synodists at Mainz promulgated almost verbatim the decrees issued at Paris in 829.[2] Again, a major preoccupation centred on the royal function within the Church: at Tribur in 895, the assembled bishops hailed King Arnulf as 'our pious and gentle comforter and energetic assistant',[3] while a chronicler summed up their work as directed 'against many laymen who were trying to weaken episcopal authority'.[4] During the minority of Arnulf's successor, bishops led by Hatto of Mainz were the real rulers of the kingdom.[5] At the Synod of Hohenaltheim in 916, episcopal interests emerged more clearly than ever opposed to those of the lay aristocracy.[6] In legislating 'for the strength of our kings' (de robore nostrorum regum), these bishops viewed the monarchy as a defence against both encroachments on ecclesiastical property and a more general fragmentation of authority.

Because of the difficulty of distinguishing between royal council and ecclesiastical synod in tenth-century England, it seems justifiable to regard the meetings of that council as analogous to

---

[1] See F. Lot and L. Halphen, Le Règne de Charles le Chauve, Paris 1909, 74 ff.; P. Fournier and G. Le Bras, Histoire des Collections Canoniques en Occident, Paris 1931, i, 130 ff.; Barion, Das fränkish-deutsche Synodalrecht, 297 f.; now also C. De Clercq, 'La législation religieuse franque depuis l'avènement de Louis le Pieux jusqu'aux Fausses Décrétales', in Revue du Droit Canonique, 5 (1955), 280 ff. and 390 ff., and continued ibid. 6 (1966), 340 f.

[2] Mansi, 18, 61 ff.; cf. MGH Conc. II, 649 ff.

[3] MGH Capit. II, 213: 'pius et mitis consolator tamque strenuus adiutor'.

[4] Regino, Chron., ed. Kurze, MGH, SS. rer. Germ., 1, 606: 'contra plerosque seculares qui auctoritatem episcopalem imminuere tentabant'.

[5] See A. Hauck, Kirchengeschichte Deutschlands, 3rd edn. Leipzig 1904, III, 7 ff.; R. Holtzmann, Geschichte der sächsischen Kaiserzeit, Munich 1943, 42 ff.; Schlesinger, Beiträge, 137 f. and 139 ff., and idem, 'Auflösung', 841 f.

[6] The importance of this synod was ably shown by M. Hellmann, 'Die Synode von Hohenaltheim (916)', in Die Entstehung des deutschen Reiches, ed. H. Kampf, Darmstadt 1956, 289 ff. Significantly, the synodists of 916 drew heavily on Visigothic conciliar legislation transmitted by Pseudo-Isidore: see Ullmann, The Carolingian Renaissance and the Idea of Kingship, London 1969, 130.

the earlier Continental synods, which were, after all, in some cases also *concilia mixta*.[1] From the time of Athelstan (924–39),[2] at the core of the king's council was a group of bishops, whom the documents, especially those of Edgar's reign, show to have been constantly together around the king, active in legislation and administration, and most notably of all, in the promotion of monastic reform[3]—which since it involved the expropriation of laymen and the communalization of monks' property, brought them into sharp conflict with what Æthelwold castigated as *secularium prioratus*.[4] These bishops assigned a precise and crucial role to the king in the fulfilment of their aims, rightly seeing in royal *dominium* the one effective safeguard against the magnates' local lordship.

I would now like to draw attention to the fact that the rite of royal anointing made its appearance in each of these four national churches at the same period as the upsurge of synodal activity, and even more precisely, at a fairly advanced stage in the synodal sequence in each case. This is not the place to discuss the evidence in detail, but I have elsewhere tried to establish good grounds for pinpointing the date at which the rite was introduced in Spain to

---

[1] See Darlington, *Ecclesiastical Reform*, 414 ff., and D. Whitelock, *English Historical Documents*, vol. I, London 1955, 68 f., as against C. J. Godfrey, *The Church in Anglo-Saxon England*, Cambridge 1962, 390.

[2] Synod of Gratley, 928, Mansi, 18, 351. Cf. the evidence of conciliar activity (canons and charters) printed in D. Wilkins, *Concilia Magnae Britanniae et Hiberniae*, London 1737, 212 ff.

[3] Surviving monastic charters are especially revealing: see e.g. those printed in W. Birch, *Cartularium Saxonicum*, III, nos. 1047, 1067, 1073, 1283. See also the legislation of Edgar in A. J. Robertson, *The Laws of the Kings of England*, Cambridge 1925, 20 ff., esp. the Code of 962–3 (IV Edgar), probably written by Dunstan: cf. Whitelock, *Documents*, 41.

[4] *Reg. Concordia*, ed. T. Symons, 7. See now the valuable study of E. John, 'The king and the monks in the tenth century reformation', in *Bulletin of the John Rylands Library*, 42 (1959), 61–87. An interesting sidelight on the social issues involved may be found in a Canon of Edgar, ed. Thorpe, *Ancient Laws*, I, 396, c. 13: 'that no high-born priest despise the lower born; because if it be rightly considered, then are all men of one birth'. W. Stubbs, *Memorials of Saint Dunstan*, RS, London 1874, cvii, saw Dunstan's influence here. Cf. also the same idea of natural equality enshrined in the conciliar decrees of Paris (829): *MGH, Conc.*, II, 654.

672, in West Francia to 848, in East Francia to 911, and in England to 973.[1]

In each case, anointing almost immediately came to be regarded, not only by clerics but also by the candidates themselves, as indispensable to king-making. The Visigothic bishops declared in 681 that King Erwig 'regnandi per sacrosanctam unctionem suscepit potestatem'. Charles the Bald asserted in 859 that the archbishop of Sens, together with his episcopal colleagues, 'me...in regni regimine...perunxit'. For the East Frankish clergy, Henry I who had refused to be anointed in 918 was 'a sword without a handle'; in the rubrics of the 'Early German' *Ordo* (produced in East Francia in the first half of the tenth century) the *princeps designatus* only after his anointing is termed *rex*. The Anglo-Saxon Ælfric, writing at the close of the tenth century, used the unequivocal word *smyraö* (instead of the vague *gehalgod*) in reference to royal consecration, and stated that 'the king, after he is consecrated, then has dominion over his people'.[2] After Wamba (672), Charles the Bald (848), Otto I (936), and Edgar (973), no unanointed Christian king ruled in any of the four kingdoms.

Royal anointing has usually been interpreted as purely and simply a Christian substitute for the magical sanctions of pagan kingship:[3] its purpose has been seen as the conferment of a sacred character on the king, and thus the protection of monarchy from the attacks of unruly subjects: 'Thou shalt not touch the Lord's

---

[1] For details, see my unpublished Ph.D. dissertation, Rituals of Royal Inauguration in Early Medieval Europe, Cambridge 1967, esp. 52 ff., 150 ff., 370 ff., and 393 ff.

[2] Conc. Tol. XII, c. 1, in *PL* 84, 471; Charles' *Libellus...contra Wenilonem* (probably written at Hincmar's instigation), in *MGH Capit.* II, 451; the early tenth-century *Vita Udalrici*, in *MGH, SS,* IV, 389; the 'Frühdeutsch' *Ordo*, ed. C. Erdmann, *Forschungen zur politischen Ideenwelt des Frühmittelalters*, Berlin 1951, 83 ff.; Ælfric quoted in Whitelock, *Documents*, 851.

[3] E.g. F. Kern, *Gottesgnadentum und Widerstandsrecht im früheren Mittelalter*, 2nd edn. rev. R. Buchner, Münster 1954, 66 ff.; Schramm, *Herrschaftszeichen und Staatssymbolik*, vol. I, Stuttgart 1954, 127; L. Rougier, 'Le Caractère Sacré de la royauté en France', in *The Sacral Kingship*, 609 ff.; the revealing discussion in *Settimana Spoleto*, 7, 1 (1960), 385 ff. Henry I, refusing the proffered anointing, and satisfied with a more familiar mundane title, saw the debit side of the bargain; cf. Widukind, *Rer. Gest. Saxon.*, I, 26, ed. Lohmann-Hirsch, 39: 'Satis michi est ut...rex dicar et designer.'

Anointed'. This interpretation, though partially accurate, by no means exhausts the meaning of the rite, and indeed overlooks the original essential purpose in the minds of those who designed and performed it. Consideration must be given to the position not only of the consecrated, but also of the consecrators. Kings, even when made rather than born, had hitherto received power through either designation or election; the handing over of insignia by predecessor or electors was the characteristic ritual form of succession. (We saw in the recent Investiture of the Prince of Wales a good example of such an entirely secular transference of power, with clerical blessings tacked on to the royal *fait accompli*.) But anointing meant that the candidate became dependent on the ecclesiastical hierarchy: dependent in what sense?

The idea was certainly not to make a bishop of the king, or to suggest a fusion of kingship with priesthood. It has too often been forgotten that episcopal ordination anointings were unknown at the period when royal anointing was introduced. There is no evidence of ordination anointing in Visigothic Spain and the rite was certainly not practised in Rome before the tenth century. The hands of priests may have been anointed in some parts of Gaul before 751, but the practice seems to have been discontinued, and then revived in West Francia when episcopal head-anointing was introduced in the ninth century.[1] To this day ordination anointing remains foreign to the Eastern Church.

The 'Anointed Ones' of the Old Testament were models for *all* Christians.[2] Although ideas of kingship as such might be strongly influenced by the prototypes of David and Solomon,[3] the

---

[1] See G. Ellard, *Ordination Anointings in the Western Church before 1000 A.D.*, Cambridge, Mass., 1933; M. Andrieu, 'Le sacre épiscopal d'après Hincmar de Reims', in *Revue d'Histoire Ecclésiastique*, 48 (1953), 22–73, esp. 40 ff. Liturgical parallels naturally came to exist between royal and episcopal consecration-rites, but influence worked in both directions, and there is evidence that Hincmar manipulated liturgy very subtly in order to maintain and even to underline the fundamental distinction between the two rites. If the later rite of papal coronation represented an *imitatio imperii* (see Ullmann, *Growth*, 311 ff.), the anointing of the Frankish bishop might be seen as an analogous *imitatio regni*.

[2] So Augustine in *PL* 34, 1355; Isidore in *PL* 83, 823; Bede in *PL* 91, 561, 606. See also P. Dabin, *Le Sacerdoce royal des fidèles*, Brussels 1950.

[3] See E. H. Kantorowicz, *Laudes Regiae*, Berkeley 1946, esp. 56 ff.

association with a physical anointing was clearly not relevant to Merovingian or Byzantine use of these *exempla*: kings themselves, especially the Visigoths, were more attracted by Byzantine models.[1] An explanation of early medieval anointings as a revival of Scriptural practice is neither self-evident nor wholly satisfactory.

It was in the oil rituals of the Church that the memory of that practice was kept most intensely and constantly alive. The *liturgical affinity* of royal anointing was with the rite of Christian initiation,[2] and specifically with the post-baptismal chrismation of the initiate's head performed by the bishop. At least from the fourth century onwards, this post-baptismal unction was characterized as a royal investiture[3] of which the anointings of Scripture represented the mystic type. It is not hard to see how the liturgical transference could suggest itself: the purpose of royal anointing too was to 'make a new man' of the unworthy candidate,[4] and to qualify him for the burdensome tasks inseparable from the dignity conferred. Here were re-echoed those ideals of personal and social regeneration which animated monastic and synodal reformers. The link with the Old Testament was thus indirect, and was transmitted through the baptismal liturgy with its reference to 'the oil wherewith thou hast anointed priests, kings, and prophets'.[5]

Royal anointing, then, was no mere surrogate for long hair, for the aim of the anointers was not simply to exalt the king, but at the

[1] See E. Ewig, 'Zum christlichen Königsgedanken im Frühmittelalter', in *Das Königtum. Vortrage und Forschungen*, III, Konstanz 1956, 36 f.

[2] Cf. the stimulating, but often unreliable, study of J. de Pange, *Le Roi très chrétien*, Paris 1949, esp. 79 ff. and 98 ff., who wrongly postulates a confusion of rites. See also B. Welte, *Die Postbaptismale Salbung*, Freiburg 1939, and J. D. C. Fisher, *Christian Initiation*, London 1965, for discussion of doctrine and liturgy.

[3] See T. Michels, 'Die Akklamation in der Taufliturgie', in *Jahrbuch für Liturgiewissenschaft*, 8 (1928), 76 ff., for the early development of this idea, especially in the Eastern liturgies. Cf. the Merovingian *Missale Gothicum*, ed. L. C. Mohlberg, Rome 1961, 67, where the newly anointed are referred to as 'baptizati et in Christo coronati'; Pope Leo I, *PL* 54, 149: 'omnes enim in Christo regeneratos crucis signum efficit reges'.

[4] Cf. I *Reg.* x, 6.

[5] *Liber Sacramentorum Romanae Ecclesiae Ordinis Anni Circuli. (Sacramentarium Gelasianum)*, ed. Mohlberg, Rome 1958, 73; *The Gregorian Sacramentary*, ed. H. A. Wilson, *Henry Bradshaw Society*, 49, London 1915, 50. Cf. already the third-century *Apostolic Tradition*, ed. B. Botte, Münster 1963, 18 f.

same time to condition and, when necessary, to control his action. At the VIII Council of Toledo in 653, the bishops declared: 'Regem...iura faciunt non persona (It is the laws, not the individual, which make the king).'[1] The synodists at Paris in 829 posed the question: 'Quid sit proprie ministerium regis? (What really is the king's job?)'[2] The achievement of the Synod of Hohenaltheim has been epitomized as 'a re-interpretation of kingship in the sense of a theocratic office'.[3] King Edgar himself, addressing an Anglo-Saxon synod in 967, expressed his readiness to take up 'the sword of Constantine', and to obey episcopal commands.[4] The notion of kingship as office, whether implied or made explicit, was the remarkable common feature of the synodists' statements in all four areas. An office presupposes clearly defined functions, for the officer, as Weber has pointed out, 'is subject to an impersonal order to which his actions are oriented'.[5] As guardians of that higher order in early medieval Christendom, the bishops saw the royal office as an executive post, themselves as the directors of the corporation.

The bishops were also the ritual specialists in a Christian society, and therefore were uniquely qualified to manipulate ritual to express and to implement their own ideas. It is hardly surprising that the rite of royal anointing, both in a creative and a demonstrative sense, made precisely those points which were of prime importance in the view of the hierarchy: first, the auxiliary role of the chosen king, incorporated into his office and actually made capable of assuming it, through the dynamic rite of anointing, and secondly, the episcopal monopoly of king-making —the *sacerdos* being the unique channel of supernatural power

---

[1] *PL* 84, 431. The significance of this statement is stressed by De Pange, *Le roi*, 120 ff., and by H. Beumann, 'Zur Entwicklung transpersonaler Staatsvorstellungen', in *Das Königtum*, ed. Ewig, 215 ff.

[2] *MGH, Conc.*, II, 651–2.   [3] Hellmann, 'Die Synode', 303.

[4] *PL* 138, 515. Cf. IV Edg. 1, 8, ed. Robertson, *Laws*, 32 f.: 'the obedience which we show (the bishops) as representatives of God'.

[5] *The Theory of Social and Economic Organisation*, Oxford 1947, 330. See also Fortes, 'Ritual and Office', 57 ff.; and the penetrating analysis of comparative institutions, and of terminology, by J. Goody, *Succession to High Office*, Cambridge 1966, 1–56, and 170–2, stressing the special characteristics of *royal* office as a 'scarce resource'.

conceived of as *gratia divina*. Here is the central passage of the anointing prayer which appeared in almost all the medieval *ordines* for royal consecration:

Almighty eternal God,...we ask thee to attend to the prayers of our humility and to establish this thy servant in the high rulership of the kingdom, and anoint him with the oil of the grace of thy Holy Spirit wherewith thou hast anointed those priests, kings, prophets, and martyrs who through faith conquered kingdoms, worked justice, and obtained thy promises.

This text, *Omnipotens sempiterne deus*, composed by Hincmar for the consecration of Louis the Stammerer in 877, was used by the author of the 'Seven Forms' *Ordo* (early tenth century), when it passed into the *Ordo* of 'Mainz' in the *Pontificale Romano-Germanicum* (*c.* 960) and from there into the mainstream of the medieval *ordines* tradition.[1]

Moreover, Hincmar would show that anointing, unlike penance, provided a basis for episcopal jurisdiction over the king: Charles the Bald, having been consecrated by the bishops, could be deposed *only* by their decision, and was subject to their 'fatherly correction'. This subordination paralleled that of the bishop to his consecrators, for, as Hincmar succinctly told his erring nephew the bishop of Laon: 'You can be judged by those who had the power to ordain you.' Likewise, in demanding a *professio* or solemn undertaking from the king, Hincmar extended to the royal office the penalty which canon law prescribed for a broken *professio* in the case of a bishop: *privatio honoris* or deposition.[2]

---

[1] The *Ordo* of 877 in *MGH, Capit.*, II, 461–2; the 'Seven Forms', ed. Erdmann, *op. cit.*, 87 ff.; the 'Mainz' Pontifical, ed. C. Vogel and R. Elze, Rome 1963, 246 ff.

Episcopal mediation was most heavily stressed in the 'Seven Forms' texts for the delivery of crown and sword, *ed. cit.*, 88: the kingdom is committed to the royal 'regimen, per officium nostrae benedictionis', the sword is handed over 'per manus episcoporum licet indignas vice tamen et auctoritate sanctorum apostolorum consecratas'.

[2] Cf. the *Libellus* of 859, in *Capit.*, II, 451: 'a qua consecratione (i.e. Charles's anointing in 848)...proici a nullo debueram, saltem sine audientia et iudicio episcoporum, quorum ministerio in regem sum consecratus...quorum paternis

At the last synod over which Hincmar presided, in 881, the Gelasian doctrine of responsibility was given a new and pregnant meaning when the consecration of kings was seen as the concrete application of episcopal *auctoritas*:

so much greater is the responsibility of the priesthood in that they must render account in God's judgement even for the very kings of men, and by so much greater are the rank and prestige of bishops than of kings 'quia reges in culmen regium sacrantur a pontificibus, pontifices autem a regibus consecrari non possunt (because kings are consecrated to their kingship by bishops, but bishops cannot be consecrated by kings)'.[1]

The candidate received from his consecrators not only symbols—crown or spear or sceptre—though these too were soon transferred from secular ritual to ecclesiastical rite, but royal power itself together with the qualities required for its exercise. The king was now the bishops' creature, and in a quite literal sense their right-hand man. This implication of anointing distinguishes it clearly from other ritual forms of king-making which were taken over by the Church. In Byzantium from the fifth century onwards, the imperial accession ritual became increasingly an ecclesiastical affair, but the coronation, whether performed by the senior Basileus or by the Patriarch of Constantinople, was never regarded as dynamic or constitutive.[2]

It is worth noting, in this context, that the bishops of the Western Churches were not initially interested in crowning their kings. There is no evidence for an ecclesiastical rite of coronation in Visigothic Spain, although Byzantine influence may well have brought crown-wearing into royal ceremonial, and perhaps even into a secular accession ritual. Coronation was introduced into the

---

correptionibus et castigatoriis iudiciis...sum subditus'; Hincmar to his nephew, in *PL* 126, 378: 'ab his potes iudicari a quibus potuisti ordinari'; *idem, PL* 125, 1040 f. and Mansi, 16, 601.

[1] *PL* 125, 1071, in the *acta* of the Synod of St Macre-de-Fismes.

[2] See O. Treitinger, *Die Oströmische Kaiser- und Reichsidee nach ihrer Gestaltung im höfischen Zeremoniell*, Jena 1938, 7 ff., 27 ff., and F. Dölger's effective refutation of the contrary opinion of P. Charanis, in *Byzantinische Zeitschrift*, 43 (1950), 146–7.

Frankish royal consecration by the papacy, again probably through a modelling on Byzantine practice. In 848, the deliveries of both crown and sceptre seem to have remained within the framework of a secular ritual of enthronement. Even much later, the actual coronation was of secondary importance in the full rite of inauguration: in the 'Edgar' *Ordo* as performed in 973, three antiphons were prescribed for reasons of emphasis at the entrance of the *electus*, at the anointing, and at the girding-on of the sword.[1]

Of course, ideas of sacral kingship did not die: and in the context of *that* tradition, especially when its pagan origins had been concealed by a Christian theocratic gloss, royal anointing from the later tenth century onwards, when ordination anointings had become widely practised, could be cited as evidence of the king's priestly powers: the 'rex ex nobilitate' engendered 'le roi thaumaturge'.[2] But the ideas of the Norman Anonymous[3] were *not* those of the men who first devised and performed the rite of royal anointing. I suggest that there was in the early medieval period a connection between sustained synodal activity and the introduction of this rite. The link was made by the bishops'

---

[1] Isidore, *Hist. Goth.*, 48, 51, 52, in *MGH, AA*, XI, 286 f.; P. Classen, 'Karl der Grosse, das Papsttum und Byzanz', in *Karl der Grosse*, I, 557 f.; *Ann. Bertin.*, ed. F. Grat, 55 and cf. *ibid.* 71; the 'Edgar' *Ordo*, ed. L. G. Wickham Legg, *English Coronation Records*, Westminster 1901, 15 ff.

[2] See M. Bloch, *Les Rois Thaumaturges*, Strasbourg 1924; H. Beumann, 'Die sakrale Legitimierung des Herrschers im Denken der ottonischen Zeit', in *Zeitschrift für Rechtsgeschichte, Germ. Abt.*, 66 (1948), 1–45; H. Wolfram, *Splendor Imperii*, Graz–Köln 1963, 126 ff. and 137, calling the replacement of the king's *splendor fortunae* by a *splendor fidei* 'ein echt mitteralterlich Kompromiss'.

[3] See Williams, *The Norman Anonymous*, esp. 167 ff. The Anonymous regarded the king's anointing as superior to that of the bishop: *MGH, L de L*, III, tract. IV, 669: 'Nam unctio et sanctificatio sacerdotum ad exemplum Aaron instituta est...et...ad exemplum apostolorum...regis vero unctio instituta est ad exemplum illius quem Deus pater unxit ante saecula.' On these ideas, which drew heavily on expressions contained in the royal *ordines*, see the perceptive remarks of Kantorowicz, *The King's Two Bodies*, Princeton 1957, 42 ff. But both he, and the equally perceptive R. W. Southern, *The Making of the Middle Ages*, London 1953, 97 ff., somewhat misleadingly suggest that the Anonymous was really representative of early medieval attitudes. Stark, *Sociology of Religion*, 58 f., mischievously juxtaposes the Anonymous and the Vicar of Bray, the former's argument being 'a near-perfect reflection of the sentiments which, when the time came, produced the Anglican establishment'.

preoccupation with the function of secular power *intra ecclesiam*,[1] and the problem of controlling its exercise. These series of synods at once manifested and promoted the group-consciousness and ideological maturity of the episcopates, while at the same time, they revealed the dependence of the hierarchy on royal support. The result was a crystallization of the clergy's needs and expectations of kingship. The transmission of rulership by secular and autonomous means now appeared clearly for what it was: an anomaly in the Christian society. Theology and practical need coalesced to suggest a ritual expression for a new social reality.

By way of contrast, one might glance for a moment at Ireland and Byzantium in this period. In both cases, the Church accommodated itself to the wider society in ways quite different from those which evolved in the barbarian kingdoms. No theories emerged of kingship as office, or of the hierarchy as supervisor of the ruler's usefulness. Not the bishop but the charismatic figure of monk or abbot appeared to castigate royal or imperial sin: such interventions were individual, intermittent, and never institutionalized or formalized in law. The absence here of synodal movements comparable to those outlined above may be linked with the fact that the practice of royal or imperial anointing was never introduced by the indigenous episcopates.[2] This is not to postulate a

---

[1] Cf. Isidore, *Sent.* III, 51, 4, in *PL* 83, 723: 'Principes saeculi *nonnumquam* intra ecclesiam potestatis adeptae culmina tenent, *ut* per eandem potestatem disciplinam ecclesiasticam *muniant.*'

[2] On Irish conditions, see P. Fournier, 'Le *Liber ex lege Moysi* et les tendances bibliques du droit canonique irlandais', in *Revue Celtique*, 30 (1909), esp. 228: 'Les conciles n'y tiennent qu'une place secondaire, comme les évêques dont le rôle est singulièrement effacé.' Also valuable are J. Ryan's observations in *Settimana Spoleto*, 7, II (1960), 554 ff. and 584 f., and K. Hughes, *The Church in Early Irish Society*, London 1966. On synods in the Eastern Church, see H. G. Beck, *Kirche und Theologische Literatur im Byzantinischen Reich*, Munich 1959, 38 ff., esp. 55 ff.: only ten local synods are recorded for the whole Empire in four centuries (from 600 to 1000), and nearly all were exclusively concerned with the doctrinal problems of monothelitism or iconoclasm, rather than with administrative or legislative matters, which were in any case looked after by the imperial government. On imperial control, see A. Michel, 'Die Kaisermacht in der Ostkirche', in *Ostkirchliche Studien*, 3 (1954), 1 ff.; for monastic criticisms, see the lively essay of H. Grégoire in N. H. Baynes and H. B. Moss, eds., *Byzantium*, Oxford 1948, 86 ff. On royal inaugurations in Ireland, which

simple causal relationship between institution and rite: rather that these are best seen as interrelated features of specific social and political conditions.

There is time only for a brief mention of the anointings of Pippin in 751 and 754. I have tried to show elsewhere that these were the results of papal initiative,[1] and therefore not cases of the syndrome I have been examining here, though obviously relevant to it. It was no coincidence that the Frankish bishops allowed the practice of royal anointing to fall into abeyance after 751, and did not resume it on their own initiative until the mid-ninth century. Seen in this perspective, the so-called 'delayed anointings' of Charles the Bald and, in the tenth century, of the Anglo-Saxon Edgar, lose their aura of mystery.[2]

I have said that two key ideas lay behind the anointing rite: the executive function of Christian kingship and the mediatory role of the bishops in conferring and legitimizing secular power. These ideas were nowhere more clearly apparent than at a synod; and it is significant that prayers 'pro rege in tempore sinodi' were incorporated into the earliest *ordines* for royal consecration. Two of Alcuin's collects for this purpose were used by Hincmar in the anointing prayer of the *ordo* which he composed for the consecration of Charles the Bald as king of Lotharingia in 869.[3] The reference of one of these texts to the royal *ministerium* was no doubt its chief recommendation; while the whole meaning of the rite was epitomized in its opening prayer, that God's servant 'in

remained entirely secular even in the later Middle Ages, see M. Dillon and N. Chadwick, *The Celtic Realms*, London 1967, 93 ff. G. Ostrogorsky, 'Zur Kaisersalbung und Schilderhebung im Spätbyzantinischen Krönungszeremoniell', in *Historia*, 4 (1955), 246 ff., resumes the evidence, and shows that an imperial anointing was not practised in Byzantium before the thirteenth century, when the rite was imported from the West.

[1] For details, see my unpublished dissertation, ch. III.
[2] Cf. *Settimana Spoleto*, 7, 1 (1960), 397 f. and 403 f.
[3] *MGH, Capit.*, II, 457: 'Et qui te voluit'. Cf. Alcuin's *Benedictio* in the Gregorian Sacramentary, *ed. cit.*, 351. The same collect was employed quite independently by the East Frankish author of the 'Early German' *Ordo*, ed. Erdmann, *op. cit.*, 86. In this form (which differed slightly from Hincmar's text) the prayer passed into 'Mainz', and thus into the later *ordines*. Cf. also the echo in Hincmar's opening benediction, 'Deus qui populis', of two Alcuinian Mass prayers *pro rege in tempore synodi*: Gregorian, *ed. cit.*, 188 and 189.

regni regimine maneat semper idoneus'. Between the two great liturgists Alcuin and Hincmar lies the distance from the monarch acting in synod to the suitable king consecrated by the synodists.*

* I should like to take this opportunity of acknowledging the help and encouragement of Professor W. Ullmann and of my husband, H. G. H. Nelson, both of whom have discussed with me some ideas contained in this paper.

THE CASE OF BERENGAR OF TOURS[1]

by MARGARET GIBSON

'OR he called pope Leo IX not *pontifex* but *pompifex* and *pulpifex*; the Roman Church a council of vanity, the church of the malignant; and the Apostolic See the seat of Satan.' This hostile epitaph, and more in the same vein, was written in 1088, the year that Berengar died.[2] They are perhaps unequal crimes: to call even a scion of the German aristocracy 'not pope but *a maker of pomp*' or (worse still) '*pulp*',[3] and to reject the entire Roman Church as an institution. The charges are based on Lanfranc's indictment of twenty-five years before: that Berengar had ignored the judgements of pope and council and despised the testimony of the faithful throughout the ages, saying that in himself and his followers only was the true Church to be found on earth.[4] It is not for claims like these that Berengar is now remembered: he has his niche in Gratian and the ecclesiastical dictionaries as an exponent of views on the Eucharist rather than as a schismatic from the Roman Church. But in his own day Berengar's eucharistic theology did not strike all men as heretical: Peter Damian, for example, is said to have been undecided.[5] For his contemporaries the issue that Berengar raised was as much one of authority as one of doctrine. When rightly or wrongly Leo IX

[1] I am much indebted to Professor R. W. Southern for his criticism of this paper.

[2] 'Nempe S. Leonem Papam non pontificem, sed *pompificem* et *pulpificem* appellauit; sanctam Romanam ecclesiam, uanitatis concilium et ecclesiam malignantium; Romanam sedem, non apostolicam, sed sedem satanae, dictis et scriptis non timuit appellare': *De multiplici damnatione Berengarii haeresiarchae*, ed. Bouquet, *Rec. Hist. France* (1806), XIV, 35D–36A.

[3] For other, more derogatory, meanings see *pompa*, deceits of the devil (Augustine, *De Symbolo*, IV. 1); and *pulpa*, flesh as distinct from spirit (Isidore, *Etymologiae*, XI. i. 81)—hence 'fleshmaker', referring to the eucharistic words 'Hoc est enim corpus meum'.

[4] Lanfranc, *De corpore et sanguine Domini*, cap. 23 (*PL*, col. 412A).

[5] Martène et Durand, *Thesaurus Novus Anecdotorum* (1717), IV. 103B–C.

and Nicholas II condemned Berengar, he continued to teach and write. For nearly thirty years he provoked papal interest, resolutions in provincial synods, letters and tracts from individual critics: and still there was no final and effective judgement. Because it was so slow to be concluded, Berengar's 'case' illuminates for us how ecclesiastical authority was conceived by the eleventh-century popes and their sympathizers, and how it worked. Three popes in particular were concerned with him: Leo IX, Nicholas II and Gregory VII.

In the spring of 1050 Leo IX condemned Berengar in the annual Easter synod at Rome. Lanfranc, who is our only source for these events, tells an elaborate and not wholly comprehensible tale of a letter from Berengar to Lanfranc that was intercepted and given to 'a certain clerk of Rheims', who in turn brought it to the papal court.[1] Now Leo IX had just returned from the dramatic council of Rheims that had followed the dedication of the church of St Remigius; and the chances are that this letter reached him in the aftermath of the council: here as in other matters Leo's visit had transformed a local issue into one that affected the whole Church. At all events Berengar was called for examination, not to Rome but Vercelli, which the pope expected to visit on his way north in September. Though he was advised that he need not go for trial beyond his own province (Tours), Berengar did set out for Vercelli: but rather than concede such papal interference Henry I of France threw Berengar into prison. So at Vercelli the condemnation stood.[2] Leo's next move however was precisely to try Berengar *within* his own province, at a legatine synod held by the young Hildebrand in Tours in 1054. There Berengar agreed on oath to a formula, which has not survived, but seems to have been innocuous; and I take it that his excommunication, if that had ever

[1] Lanfranc, *De corpore et sanguine Domini*, cap. 4 (*PL*, col. 413A–B). Berengar's letter may be the one printed in the apparatus to the *Vita Lanfranci* (*PL, loc. cit.*, col. 63C–D).

[2] Lanfranc, *De corpore et sanguine Domini* (*PL*, col. 413C); Berengar, *De Sacra Coena*, viii (ed. Beekenkamp, pp. 11–12). Henry I was quick to notice Berengar: he had him examined at a council in Paris (October 1050) and received further advice from bishop Theoduin of Liège (summer 1050). See *PL*, CXLIX, 1422C–1424B (council of Paris); *PL*, CXLVI, 1439B–1442C (Theoduin's letter).

been effective, was lifted. But even then Leo had achieved nothing; for while the synod was in session news came of his death: the legate's authority was therefore void.[1]

For the papal court then by 1055 there were only two ways forward: either Berengar should be judged by his own hierarchy in Touraine; or he should come in person to Rome.

Seen from Touraine, however, there was no reason that he should do either. The details of Berengar's career in the 1040s and '50s often elude us; but broadly it is certain that though he belonged to the hereditary clergy of St Martin at Tours, he made his career in Anjou, as archdeacon and treasurer of the cathedral of St Maurice at Angers. While Geoffrey Martel was count, Berengar was a leading figure in the principal comital church, composing letters for Geoffrey Martel—rather tricky letters—and identifying his interests with the count's. In return he enjoyed complete security: the protection of the count and his bishop, Eusebius Bruno of Angers. Though in principle the archbishop of Tours was his superior, the hard fact was that since 1044 the city of Tours and Touraine had been subject to Geoffrey Martel: the capital of the whole region was Angers.[2] In these circumstances the idea that the archbishop of Tours should try Berengar, still more condemn him, was the merest academic pleasantry. The alternative then was that Berengar should go to Rome. Rome had, however, to consider which of several objects she most desired. Berengar was a contumacious archdeacon, who should be disciplined. At the same time his patron Count Geoffrey had for quite defensible political reasons thrown into prison the bishop of Le Mans, whom the papacy was even more anxious to see released—and as powerless to help.[3] Secondly there was Geoffrey Martel's alliance,

---

[1] Lanfranc, *De corpore et sanguine Domini* (*PL*, col. 413D); Berengar *De Sacra Coena*, XI (*ed. cit.* pp. 16–18). Leo IX died in April 1054; and Victor II was not elected until September.

[2] See L. Halphen, *Le Comté d'Anjou au xie siècle* (Paris 1906), especially pp. 124–6; and for further details A. J. Macdonald, *Berengar and the Reform of Sacramental Doctrine* (London 1930), pp. 24 *app.*, 25 *app.* Berengar's letters are edited by C. Erdmann, *Briefsammlungen der Zeit Heinrichs IV* (Weimar 1950).

[3] The story is told in R. Latouche, *Histoire du comté du Maine pendant le xe et le xie siècle* (Paris 1910) = *Bibl. Ecole Hautes Etudes*, CLXXXIII, 28–9: cf. Erdmann, *Briefsammlungen*, no. 84.

through his wife Agnes, with the emperor, Henry III. Unlike his father, who three times visited Jerusalem, Geoffrey Martel travelled little abroad: his one major foreign excursion was with Agnes to Goslar in 1045. Thence he came with the emperor south to Sutri in 1046 and on to Rome and south Italy. By 1052 Agnes had been repudiated, and the link with Germany was technically broken: but the papacy still had to recognize the close connections over two decades between Anjou and the German court.[1] While Henry III remained the benevolent patron of the papacy, Berengar was safe. He was not worth the diplomatic inconvenience of quelling.

But five years passed, and Nicholas II became pope, in January 1059. By then the diplomatic scene had changed wonderfully: for Henry III was dead (October 1056). The regent in Germany was the Empress Agnes, daughter of the repudiated Countess of Anjou; and in any case after the independent election of Stephen IX in 1057 the papacy felt less beholden to the German court. So when Nicholas II held his first major council at Easter 1059, Berengar was again summoned; and this time he came. During the 1050s he had encountered enough criticism in France—not in the Loire valley but further north in Chartres and parts of Normandy, notably Fécamp—to make a papal exoneration, if he could secure one, very useful.[2] Instead he met an adversary far more dangerous than any pope: the archbishop of Sicily and cardinal bishop of Silva Candida, Humbert of Moyenmoutier. I give him all his titles because they sum up at once his political power as archbishop and cardinal, and his origins and loyalty as monk of Moyenmoutier in the Vosges and secretary to Leo IX while the future pope was still bishop of Toul. Humbert, as is

---

[1] Halphen, *op. cit.* p. 128, 128 *app.* Geoffrey Martel married Agnes of Poitou, widow of William IX of Aquitaine and mother of the Empress Agnes of Germany, in 1032. Lacking a direct heir, he repudiated Agnes to marry successively Grécie and Adela, both of the local aristocracy, and then finally the German Adelaide.

[2] For Berengar's critics in Chartres see the letter cited p. 62 n. 2. above and Erdmann, *Briefsammlungen*, no. 88; in Fécamp, abbot John's *Confessio Fidei*, IV, 5 (*PL*, CI, 1089C–D), written *c.* 1050, and the much more elaborate *De corpore et sanguine Christi* (*PL*, CXLIX, 1375–1424), written a few years later by the abbot's cross-bearer, Durand.

sufficiently proven by his dealings with the Greek Church and with simoniac Latin clergy, was uninhibited by considerations of diplomacy, and sure that he was right. He was also passionately loyal to his old master pope Leo, one of the earliest proponents of his cult as a saint, and the last man to receive equably Berengar's punning remarks on *pompifex, pulpifex,* and the like.[1] Humbert presented to the council in 1059 what is surely the least diplomatic formulation of Eucharistic belief ever to reach a serious assembly:

The bread and wine which are placed on the altar after consecration are not only a sacrament but also the very Body and Blood of our Lord Jesus Christ; and these are physically (*sensualiter*) handled and broken by the priest and torn by the teeth of the faithful. Not—he repeats—just in a sacrament, but in truth.

This formula Berengar swore to—under pressure, he alleged: and we can well believe him. Nicholas II sent it 'to all the cities of France, Germany, and Italy, as many as have been troubled by Berengar's heresy now renounced'.[2] It appears in the book of canon law that Lanfranc gave to Canterbury in the 1070s, in other eleventh-century canonistic collections and—surprisingly—in Gratian's *Decretum*.[3]

At once and vociferously Berengar repudiated his subscription, adding to his list of enemies Humbert's name beside that of Leo IX. 'The inept Burgundian', he wrote, 'cannot tell his right foot from his left in the matter of logic: he so defeats his own arguments that he is actually buttressing the propositions that he seeks to demolish.'[4] In May 1060 Humbert died, and shortly after him Nicholas II; so Berengar continued to all appearances unchecked. But in fact his position was much more precarious. In 1060 Geoffrey Martel had been succeeded by a blundering nephew, who failed to govern Anjou, and was personally hostile to Berengar.

---

[1] See H. Tritz, 'Die hagiographischen Quellen zur Geschichte Papst Leos IX', *Studi Gregoriani*, IV (1952), 194–353, especially 352.

[2] Lanfranc, *De corpore et sanguine Domini*, cap. 2 (*PL*, CL, 409D–412B).

[3] For Lanfranc's book of canon law see Z. N. Brooke, *The English Church and the Papacy* (Cambridge 1931), cap. 5; cf. Ivo, *Decretum*, II. 10 (*PL*, CLXI, 161B) and Gratian, *Decretum*, III. ii. cap. 42 (ed. Friedberg, I, 1328–9).

[4] Lanfranc, *De corpore et sanguine Domini*, cap. 3 (*PL*, CL, 412B–D); cf. Berengar, *De Sacra Coena*, IV (ed. Beekenkamp, pp. 4–5).

M. GIBSON

Early in the 1060s Berengar returned to his native Tours, where he later became *scholasticus* of St Martin's and ultimately chancellor.[1] There he was not without protection; but it was a very different matter from being in the inner citadel of the counts of Anjou.

One of the most illuminating passages in Berengar's story is that just at this point, when politically he was far more vulnerable, the papacy failed to renew or enforce Nicholas II's judgment. Alexander II kept himself informed, but did nothing.[2] Lanfranc, in his *De corpore et sanguine Domini* (*c.* 1063), undertook the defence of Nicholas II's settlement and the good name of Humbert. But Lanfranc, though given full credit by everyone for challenging Berengar, was not in a position to bring him to judgment. Neither was another very able Norman critic, Guitmund of La Croix-St Leofroy, writing ten years later.[3] A Norman provincial council loyally proclaimed its faith, and there are traces of activity in Poitou; but in general there is little concern, and outstandingly there is none in the two places which were competent to execute judgment: the Loire valley and the papal court.[4] Berengar was by now chancellor of one of the greatest

[1] Berengar witnessed several charters in this period for St Julian, Tours and for Marmoutiers. See for example L. J. Denis, *Chartes de S. Julien de Tours 1002–1227* (Le Mans 1912), no. XXXV = *Arch. Hist. Maine*, XII, fasc. 1–2.

[2] A papal legate came to Anjou in 1067: see Erdmann, *Briefsammlungen*, no. 91, pp. 157–9. Alexander II's letters regarding Berengar are mentioned, but not quoted, in the *De multiplici damnatione*, p. 36A: see p. 61 n.2. Four such letters were discovered and published by Edmund Bishop, 'Unedirte Briefe zur Geschichte Berengars von Tours', *Historisches Jahrbuch: Görresgesellschaft*, I (1880), 272–5: but see C. Erdmann, 'Gregor VII und Berengar von Tours', *Qu. und Forsch. aus Ital. Archiv. und Bibliotheken*, XXVIII (1937–8), 48–74 (who thinks that these are forged), and O. Capitani, 'Per la storia dei rapporti tra Gregorio VII e Berengario di Tours', *Studi Gregoriani*, VI (1961), 99–145 (who defends their authenticity).

[3] *De corporis et sanguinis Domini ueritate in Eucharistia* (PL, CXLIX, 1427–1508).

[4] Archbishop Maurilius (1055–67) in a council held at Rouen recognized this formula: 'Credimus...panem in mense Dominica propositum panem tantummodo esse ante consecrationem; sed in ipsa consecratione ineffabili potentia diuinitatis, conuerti naturam et substantiam panis, in naturam et substantiam carnis; carnis uero non ullius alterius, sed illius quae concepta est de Spiritu sancto, nata ex Maria Virgine' (F. Pommeraye, *Sanctae Rotomagensis Ecclesiae Concilia* (Rouen 1677), 74). The date of Maurilius's council is probably 1063. For Poitou (1075) see Th. Schieffer, *Die päpstlichen legaten in Frankreich* (Berlin 1935), 87–8.

religious houses in France; he was actively maintaining his opinions and his right to declare them: and still neither Alexander II nor Gregory VII after him took any action. Even Gregory's exacting interpretation of papal authority did not require him to maintain this old quarrel.

It was at the prompting of Hugh of Cluny that Berengar's case was reopened in Rome. In the spring of 1078 Gregory VII assured Hugh that he would not neglect Berengar;[1] and in November of the same year a Roman council examined Berengar's teaching and declared it not heretical. According to Berengar, this was the formula that both he and the whole council approved:

I believe that the bread on the altar is after consecration the very Body of Christ, born of the Virgin...and the wine his very Blood, that flowed from his side on the Cross.

Berengar stayed on in Rome apparently in peace.[2] Nevertheless we cannot have the whole truth about the 1078 council, for within six months Berengar was being re-examined at a second Roman council in Lent 1079. There, after days of vacillation—the pope advocating prayer for the miraculous revelation of the truth, others favouring the ordeal by hot iron—a new and much more technical formula was imposed on Berengar:

that after consecration the bread was the very Body of Christ and the wine his Blood, not only sacramentally (*per signum et uirtutem sacramenti*) but in its physical being: *in proprietate naturae et ueritate substantiae*.

In addition he was forbidden to expound his Eucharistic opinions, even if orthodox.[3] At that price he returned to Tours, with papal letters of safe-conduct to his count and bishop.[4]

Why had Gregory VII been stricken with so uncharacteristic

---

[1] Gregory VII, *Register*, v. 21: 'De Berengario, unde nobis scripsistis, quid nobis uideatur uel quid disposuerimus, fratres, quos tibi remittimus cum praedicto cardinali nostro, nuntiabunt.'

[2] Martène et Durand, *Thes. Nou. Anec.* (1717), IV, 103.

[3] Martène et Durand, *Thes. Nou. Anec.* (1717), IV, 103E–109E: cf. Gregory VII, *Reg.*, VI, 17a.

[4] For these letters, which are not in Gregory's *Register*, see P. Jaffé, *Monumenta Gregoriana* (Berlin 1865), 550, 564 = nos 24 and 36. No. 36, to Ralph, archbishop of Tours and Eusebius, bishop of Angers, is the more important.

3-2

an interest in Christian doctrine? (He is concerned ceaselessly with good government and liturgical uniformity, but almost never—apart from this one enquiry—with the contents of the Creed.) The probable explanation—it can be no more—is typical of Berengar's career as a whole. Early in 1078 Hugh of Cluny was urging Gregory to examine Berengar; within the year he had been silenced (spring 1079). Now the year after that (June 1080), as the German bishops at Brixen withdrew their allegiance from Gregory, they declared *inter alia* that the pope was tainted with the damnable opinions of Berengar.[1] As heresy is the one charge on which traditionally even a pope may be deposed, this sequence of events is not likely to be fortuitous. Hugh of Cluny, who had a better understanding of the German situation than Gregory, had forewarned him that he could not afford to leave Berengar alone.

Gregory's decision seems to have taken effect: Berengar was thereafter silent. He was growing old, and the loyalties of the time of Leo IX and Humbert were passing. Principally, however, the judgment of 1079 was effective because for the first time to have a decision was politically urgent. Gregory concluded a case that Leo and Nicholas had left unfinished, not because he had a more sophisticated machinery of government than they, nor a better grasp of principle, but because in the situation of 1078-9 to give a clear, orthodox, and effective decision was only common sense.

[1] *MGH, Const.*, I, 119, no. 70.

ECCLESIASTICA AND *REGALIA*: PAPAL INVESTITURE POLICY FROM THE COUNCIL OF GUASTALLA TO THE FIRST LATERAN COUNCIL, 1106–23

by M. J. WILKS

IT IS commonly asserted that in the early years of the twelfth century the medieval papacy was suddenly afflicted with a bad attack of apostolic poverty. The consensus of historical opinion accepts that a pope, Paschal II, who had already distinguished himself by launching crusades against both eastern and western Roman emperors, acted so much out of character that, when forced to deal directly with Henry V over the question of episcopal investiture, he abruptly and to the astonishment of contemporaries 'decreed the poverty of the whole Church'. It was as if St Peter had hiccoughed, and for a brief instant the Roman church was assailed by self-doubt, tacitly admitting that centuries of criticism of ecclesiastical secularity were justified. The attempt by Paschal to renounce the regalian rights of bishops in February 1111 has become regarded by many as the turning point in a process described as weaning the papacy away from strict Gregorian principles, permitting the introduction of a spirit of moderation and compromise which would eventually lead to the Concordat of Worms and 'the end of the Investiture Contest'.[1] Not only are we asked to believe that a pope 'went spiritual' in a moment of papal ascendancy, and yet was able to re-establish ecclesiastical

[1] E.g. P. Zerbi, 'Pasquale II e l'ideale della povertà della chiesa', *Annuario dell'Università Cattolica del Sacro Cuore, 1964–5* (Milan 1965), 207–29; H. V. White, 'Ponthius of Cluny, the Curia Romana and the End of Gregorianism in Rome', *Church History*, XXVII (1958), 195–219 at pp. 198f. Similarly N. F. Cantor, *Church, Kingship and Lay Investiture in England, 1089–1135* (Princeton 1958), 122–4, sees this 'espousal of apostolic poverty' as an example of Paschal's monastic asceticism, although it is not explained how this is appropriate to one described as 'a fanatical high Gregorian'.

power when to all intents and purposes a royal prisoner—which even
the recent ingenious suggestion that Paschal was a concealed pro-
imperial sympathizer can hardly explain[1]—but the whole argument
exhibits a profound misunderstanding of papal attitudes towards the
regalian rights during the Investiture Contest, and fails to discern
the essential continuity of papal policy during the crucial period
of negotiations between the Councils of Guastalla and Lateran I.

The death of the deposed and excommunicate Henry IV on
7 August 1106 provided Paschal II with an opportunity to make
termination of the investiture problem a leading feature of papal
policy, and he opened his campaign for a settlement at Guastalla
on 22 October by renewing the prohibitions of lay investiture of
a bishop with ring and staff already pronounced by Gregory VII
and Urban II.[2] At the same time, however, he began negotiations
with the representatives of Henry V, formally reconciled with the
Roman church earlier in the year, and also to be presumed to have
gained greater freedom of manoeuvre from the death of his
father. But within eight months the negotiations had collapsed.
The German ambassadors declared that the matter could only be
determined 'at Rome, and with swords';[3] and it was to Rome
with swords (we are told that there were thirty thousand German
knights on the expedition)[4] that Henry V came at the beginning
of 1111. Nevertheless, at first the *furor Teutonicus* was muted.
Henry is reported to have been extremely gracious, if somewhat
condescending. He declared his great affection for the Romans;
promised to provide them with peace and righteousness; and
regretted only that he had been so tardy in visiting the city.[5]

[1] P. R. McKeon, 'The Lateran Council of 1112, the "Heresy" of Lay Investiture, and the Excommunication of Henry V', *Medievalia et Humanistica*, XVII (1966), 3–12.
[2] Hefele-Leclercq, *Histoire des Conciles*, v. 1 p. 496: cf. pp. 475–6 for his earlier condemnation of lay investiture at the Council of Rome in April 1102. He had already told Ruthard, Archbishop of Mainz, in November 1105 that the main objective of his pontificate would be to solve the investiture problem: this was no doubt intended for the benefit of Henry V.
[3] Suger, *Vita Ludovici VI*, MGH, SS, XXVI, 50, 'Non hic, inquiunt [legati], sed: Romae gladiis haec terminabitur querela.'
[4] Otto of Freising, *Chronicon*, VII, 14, MGH, SS, XX, 254.
[5] MGH, *Const.*, I no. 82 p. 134.

Henry had in fact reached that moment of truth which dawned on all medieval emperors once in a lifetime, when they realized that they were still only German kings, not Roman emperors, and that only the Roman church could effect the transformation. The price, as Paschal's legates made clear during discussions at Rome and at Sutri between 4 and 9 February, was the Gregorian *libertas ecclesiae*, coupled with the traditional oath of obedience from the emperor-elect and his recognition of the Carolingian donations to the Roman church in central Italy. It was stipulated that there should be no more lay investiture of bishops.[1] At the same time it was agreed by Paschal, through Peter Leonis, that at Henry's imperial coronation the pope would command all imperial bishops and abbots to surrender their regalian rights to the emperor, and would forbid them to be held in future:

domnus papa praecipiet episcopis praesentibus in die coronationis eius ut dimittant regalia regi et regno quae ad regnum pertinebant tempore Karoli, Loduici, Heinrici et aliorum praedecessorum eius...id est, civitates, ducatus, marchias, comitatus, monetas, teloneum, mercatum, advocatias regni, iura centurionum et curtes quae (manifeste) regni erant, cum pertinentiis suis, militiam et castra (regni).[2]

When the terms of the agreement were made known in St Peter's prior to the coronation ceremony on 12 February, there was an uproar which would seem to have been carefully arranged by the imperial forces. The pope and cardinals were hustled away into custody, whilst the German troops in the basilica cut down clergy and congregation.[3] After two months of captivity Paschal agreed

[1] See the royal promise in MGH, *Const.*, I no. 83 p. 137; also Ekkehard's account, *Chronicon ad 1111*, MGH, SS, VI, 244.

[2] MGH, *Const.*, I no. 85 pp. 138–9.

[3] For these events see the *Relatio registri Paschalis* and Henry V's encyclical in MGH, *Const.*, I no. 99 pp. 147f. and no. 101 pp. 151–2 respectively; Ekkehard, MGH, SS, VI, 244–5; and the *Chronica monasterii Casinensis*, IV, 37–9, MGH, SS, VII, 779–80. Henry stated afterwards that all the clergy were opposed to Paschal's scheme, which they regarded as heretical: 'universis in faciem eius resistentibus et decreto suo planam haeresim inclamantibus, scilicet episcopis, abbatibus, tam suis quam nostris, et omnibus Ecclesiae filiis', *Const.*, I no. 100 p. 151; but the papal account clearly says that it was the German bishops (*episcopi transalpini*), the 'familiares regis', who objected: *Const.*, I no. 99 p. 148; and this is supported by Ekkehard's reference to them: 'tumultuantibus in

to recognize lay investiture and abandoned his demand for episcopal surrender of the *regalia*.[1] Two days later, on 13 April, he crowned Henry as emperor.

However familiar this pattern of events, attention still needs to be drawn to two points. In the first place, there is no basis for the suggestion that the February agreement would have reduced the imperial bishops to poverty. Not only were they to retain tithes, oblations, offerings, and the like, but they were also to continue to hold the great episcopal estates with the revenues accruing from them. It was expressly stated that they should have free enjoyment of possessions inherited with the see and not held from the king: 'Et [rex] dimittet ecclesias liberas cum oblationibus et *possessionibus* quae ad regnum *manifeste* non pertinebant.'[2] What were to be given up were the 'manifest *regalia*', the civil positions, rights, and duties granted to a bishop by an act of royal grace.[3] In other

infinitum principibus per ecclesiarum spoliatione, ac per hoc beneficiorum suorum ablatione', VI. 244. It is important not to confuse the objectors of February with the later clerical opposition against Paschal generated by the surrender in April.

[1] *MGH, Const.*, I no. 91 p. 142; *dem*, no. 96 p. 145. Paschal ensured that the grant was declared invalid at the Lateran council of March 1112—'neque vero debet dici privilegium sed pravilegium'—on the grounds of having been extorted by force: Mansi, *Concilia*, XXI, 51.

[2] As defined in the royal promise: *MGH, Const.*, I no. 83 p. 137; and see also Paschal's statement, no. 90 p. 141, 'Porro ecclesias cum oblationibus et *haereditariis possessionibus*, quae ad regnum *manifeste* non pertinebant, liberas manere decernimus, sicut in die coronationis tuae omnipotenti Domino in conspectu totius Ecclesiae promisisti.' It was, significantly, the imperial encyclical which subsequently represented the pope as saying that 'ecclesiae decimis et oblationibus suis contentae sint', no. 100 p. 150.

[3] According to the February Agreement Paschal was to grant: 'Tibi itaque, fili karissime rex Heinrice, et *nunc per officium nostrum* Dei gratia Romanorum imperator, et regno regalia illa dimittenda praecipimus quae ad regnum *manifeste* pertinebant tempore Karoli, Ludevici, Heinrici et caeterorum praedecessorum tuorum. Interdicimus etiam et sub districtione anathematis prohibemus ne quis episcoporum seu abbatum, praesentium vel futurorum, eadem regalia invadant, id est civitates, ducatus, marchias, comitatus, monetas, teloneum, mercatum, advocatias regni, iura centurionum et curtes, quae *manifeste* regni erant, cum pertinentiis suis, militiam et castra regni, nec se deinceps, nisi *per gratiam regis*, de ipsis regalibus intromittant', no. 90 p. 141. 'Manifestly' should be understood in the canonical sense of attested by a written statement or document, literally by a manifest or charter (in the same way that manifest heresy was that in which written proof or evidence was made available). One would need to make a

words, a line is being drawn between two sorts of episcopal wealth: that deriving from endowments and the obligations of Christian subjects under canon law; and those sources of income which a prince might with equal facility have granted to lay magnates if he had been so minded.[1] All episcopal land might have derived from the crown in the first instance, but the lands of the see were given to God and were irrevocable, whereas the regalian lands and offices were revocable grants. There is also, secondly, the apparent paradox that the last thing that Henry V wanted was to recover the grants made *gratia regis*: the *rex* did not, it appears, wish to recover possession of those things which manifestly pertained to the *regnum*, to his kingship. He was absolutely determined to alienate royal rights into the hands of the clergy, the very rights which were acknowledged to be key factors in maintaining good order and security in the realm.[2] We have the curious spectacle of a lay ruler's insistence on clerical control of the administration of his kingdom, matched by a desperate papal attempt to prevent it.

'Domesday survey' of the imperial bishoprics to be able to assess the practical significance of the papal proposal, but there is no reason to suppose that the distinction could not have been made by contemporaries. It is interesting to notice that in thirteenth-century England the crown distinguished between the ordinary revenues of the episcopal estates and other sources of income such as feudalism and patronage when taking the revenue from vacant sees: M. Howell, *Regalian Right in Medieval England* (London 1962), 110f.

[1] The generally current view that Paschal intended to deprive the bishops of the property of the see results from a confusion with lay versions of the meaning of *regalia* in which the distinction was not drawn between episcopal lands and other, secular, rights. Cf. R. L. Benson, *The Bishop-Elect: A Study in Medieval Ecclesiastical Office* (Princeton 1968), 275–6, 281, although for the most part Benson insists on the revolutionary nature of Paschal's proposals, and maintains that the distinction does not develop until later in the twelfth century. For discussion of the *regalia* see I. Ott, 'Der Regalienbegriff im 12. Jahrhundert', *Zeitschrift der Savigny Stiftung für Rechtsgeschichte, Kanonistische Abteilung*,xxxv (1948), 234–304; also A. Scharnagl, *Der Begriff der Investitur in den Quellen und der Literatur des Investiturstreites* (Stuttgart 1908).

[2] Thus Paschal is made to acknowledge in the royally-dictated terms of 11 April that 'Praedecessores enim vestri ecclesias regni sui tantis regalium suorum beneficiis ampliarunt ut regnum ipsum episcoporum maxime vel abbatum praesidiis oporteat communiri', *MGH, Const.*, i no. 96 p. 145; and note Henry's complaint that Paschal was trying to destroy the *status regni* under the plea of exalting and enlarging the royal rights: 'coepit dilatationem et exaltationem regni super omnes antecessores meos promittere; studebat subdole tamen quomodo regnum et ecclesiam a statu suo discinderet tractare', no. 100 p. 150.

Both these features fall logically into place if we look back to the original series of negotiations which followed the Council of Guastalla. Despite an atmosphere of mutual recriminations (Paschal complaining about the failure of the German bishops to attend the Council, and Henry irritated by the pope's refusal to meet him as arranged at Mainz), a German delegation led by Bruno, Archbishop of Triers,[1] was despatched to the papal court at Châlons in May 1107. Since these were to be exploratory talks, little more than preliminary discussions, both sides were more concerned to state their objectives rather than consider possible compromises. Provided that Suger's account can be trusted,[2] the pope, speaking through the Bishop of Piacenza, demanded that bishops should neither be invested by the lay ruler nor obliged to give homage to him:

Super his igitur dominus papa consulte oratoris episcopi Placentini voce respondit,...si [praelatus] virga et anulo investiatur, cum ad altaria eiusmodi pertineant, contra Deum ipsum usurpare; si sacratas dominico corpori et sanguini manus laici manibus gladio sanguinolentis obligando supponant, ordini suo et sacrae unctioni derogare.[3]

In Paschal's eyes these were two quite separate issues. Homage related to the regalian powers of a bishop, and was denounced as derogatory to the sacred office of the bishop acquired by investiture. Four years later Paschal quite consistently took the further step of trying to make homage impossible by abandoning altogether the *regalia* for which it was exacted,[4] thereby preventing,

---

[1] Bruno had been condemned at Guastalla for receiving lay investiture, but after exhibiting due penitence was recognized by Paschal and given the *pallium*.

[2] On the question of Suger's reliability and for further literature, see now Benson, *The Bishop-Elect*, 243–4.

[3] Suger, *Vita Ludovici*, XXVI, 50. Despite Urban II's prohibition at Clermont in 1095 on homage being given to laymen by clergy in canon 17 (Mansi, XX, 817; cf. Hefele-Leclercq, *Histoire de Conciles*, V. I p. 402), note the attempts made in canon 8 of the Council of Rouen in the following year (Mansi, XX, 921; cf. Hefele-Leclercq, V. I p. 445) to distinguish between ecclesiastical fiefs for which homage to a lay lord should not be given, and non-ecclesiastical fiefs for which such homage could be paid.

[4] Note Frederick I's agreement in 1159 that the Italian bishops who renounced their *regalia* should not be required to perform homage, *MGH, Const.*, I no. 179 p. 250.

it was hoped, any possibility of confusion with the endowed lands and intrinsic episcopal powers which investiture conferred. The intention of the German party on the other hand was precisely the opposite. Bruno of Triers at Châlons—like his royal master at Rome—insisted that the distinction must not be made an effective one. An elected bishop must receive *regalia* and do homage and fealty for them in order that (and this is the operative phrase) the king might invest him with the *episcopatus*:

Temporibus antecessorum vestrorum, sanctorum et apostolicorum virorum magni Gregorii et aliorum, hoc ad ius imperii pertinere dinoscitur, ut in omni electione hic ordo servetur: consecratum libere nec simoniace ad dominum imperatorem pro regalibus, *ut* anulo et virga investiatur, redire, fidelitatem et hominium facere. Nec mirum: civitates enim et castella, marchias, thelonea et quaeque imperatoriae dignitatis nullo modo aliter debere occupare [1]

At Châlons Paschal fully appreciated that it was the bishops' tenure of regalian functions which enabled Henry to widen and expand his claim until the king became the source of all episcopal jurisdiction without distinction.[2] The lay theory saw no cause to distinguish between specifically episcopal and specifically regalian powers and possessions, nor therefore between questions of investiture and homage. On the contrary there was every reason not to do so, since the conflation made it possible for the prince to appear as vicar of God, the sole source of all episcopal rights,

[1] Suger, *Vita Ludovici*, XXVI, 50. Similarly in the spring of 1111 Henry V paid lip-service to the distinction but argued that royal investiture was necessary for him to bestow the *regalia*: 'quamvis ille per investituras illas non ecclesias, non officia quaelibet, sed sola regalia se dare assereret', *MGH, Const.*, I no. 99 p. 149. The same point is made by Gerhoh of Reichersberg, *De ordine donorum Sancti Spiritus, MGH, L de L*, III, 280, who refers to the evil by which 'pro regalibus, immo iam non regalibus sed ecclesiasticis dicendis facultatibus ab episcopis hominium fiat vel sacramentum'.

[2] The pope made the same point in February 1111, *MGH, Const.*, I no. 90 p. 141, 'In regni autem vestri partibus episcopi vel abbates adeo curis saecularibus occupantur, ut comitatum assidue frequentare et militiam exercere cogantur... Ministri enim altaris ministri curiae facti sunt, quia civitates, ducatus, marchias, monetas, curtes et caetera ad regni servitium pertinentia a regibus acceperunt. *Unde* etiam mos inolevit ecclesiae intollerabilis, ut episcopi electi nullomodo consecrationem acciperent nisi prius per manum regiam investirentur.'

whilst the bishops were nothing more than imperial officials whose lands and powers were held from the king as the land lord or proprietor of the realm. If all governmental power derived from the king, what was the point of distinguishing a part of it as regalian? Henry's requirement that episcopal rights should be treated as a single royally-bestowed entity led logically to his demand of April 1111 that bishops should retain the *regalia*, just as Paschal's insistence on a distinction of regalian from episcopal capacities led with equal consistency to the abortive renunciation of the former in February of that same year: an attempt to make the bishops completely immune from lay control.

When the implications are borne in mind, it becomes clear why so much of the investiture dispute in the first quarter of the twelfth century centred on the question of whether episcopal jurisdiction could or could not be separated into two distinct categories. Paschal II hoped in the first instance to secure recognition of the distinction, and then to compel imperial acknowledgment that essentially episcopal jurisdiction as such derived from the pope via ecclesiastical investiture, whilst the indisputably royal grants were discarded. In 1111 Paschal took advantage of his superior bargaining position before the imperial coronation and endeavoured to secure both first and second objectives. In the event the gamble failed, and neither was achieved. For Paschal the opportunity was lost and would not be repeated. It was not until after his death, and the brief reign of Gelasius II, that a further attempt could be made. But at his first major council, held at Rheims in October 1119, the next pope, Calixtus II, clearly hoped to be able to announce that he had begun his pontificate with a settlement of this issue. After a series of semi-official discussions held at Strasbourg, the papal negotiators, William of Champeaux and Ponthius, Abbot of Cluny,[1] had arranged that pope and emperor should meet during the course of the council at Mouzon.

[1] For Ponthius, who was Paschal II's godson, see White, *Church History*, xxvii. The account of the Strasbourg meeting is in Hesso, *Relatio de concilio Remensi*, *MGH, L de L*, III, 22 f.; cf. Hefele-Leclercq, *Histoire des Conciles*, v. 1 pp. 569–70, and pp. 576 f. for the Council of Rheims itself. It is of interest to notice that Calixtus II, as Archbishop of Vienne, had taken the lead in the opposition of the French bishops to Paschal II's surrender to Henry V in April 1111.

It was also agreed that the two aspects of episcopal jurisdiction should be distinguished and treated separately. The possessions and rights of the see, here termed *ecclesiastica*, were to be dealt with under canon law: in effect, lay investiture would be prohibited. The regalian capacity, the *saecularia*, were to be subject to the customary laws of the land,[1] by which homage and fealty would automatically be exacted and feudal service required.[2] But when it came to the point, Henry V found the proposed division too much to swallow, and the Council of Rheims had to content itself with yet another condemnation of lay investiture and a further sentence of excommunication on the emperor. It was not until three years later that a firm agreement was established. In the Concordat of Worms, as in Paschal II's compromise with the English monarchy in 1107,[3] Calixtus II gained lay recognition of the separate categories of a bishop's power and possessions: the ecclesiastical lands and rights conferred by the metropolitan's investiture with ring and staff as distinct from the regalian lands

---

[1] Both pope and emperor were to declare 'Quodsi quaestio inde emerserit, quae *ecclesiastica* sunt, canonico; quae autem *saecularia* sunt, saeculari terminentur iudicio'; and Henry should relinquish all claim to the right to invest bishops: Hesso, *Relatio*, p. 24. This compares well with the proposal which Paschal is reported to have made to the German bishops sent to Rome in 1109–10: 'ça tantum quae canonici et ecclesiastici iuris sunt, domnum apostolicum exigere; de his vero quae regii iuris sunt, domno regi se nichil imminuere', *Annales Patherbrunnenses ad 1110* (ed. P. Scheffer-Boichorst: Innsbruck 1870), 122.

[2] According to Hesso's account, William of Champeaux was insistent both at Strasbourg and at Mouzon that bishops would retain the *regalia*: 'scito me, in regno Francorum episcopum electum nec ante consecrationem nec post consecrationem aliquid suscepisse de manu regis. Cui tamen de tributo, de militia, de theloneo, et de omnibus quae ad rempublicam pertinebant antiquitus, sed a regibus christianis Ecclesiae Dei donata sunt, ita fideliter deservio, sicut in regno tuo episcopi tibi deserviunt', p. 22; 'Immo palam omnibus [papa] denuntiat, ut in exhibitione militiae et in caeteris omnibus in quibus tibi et antecessoris tuis servire consueverant, modis omnibus deserviant', p. 25. If he really discussed the *regalia* in these terms, it is hardly surprising that doubts are said to have arisen about the precise meaning of the proposals to be agreed.

[3] 'Annuit rex et statuit ut ab eo tempore in reliquum nunquam per dationem baculi pastoralis vel anuli quisquam episcopatu aut abbatia per regem vel quamlibet laicam manum in Anglia investiretur; concedente quoque Anselmo ut nullus in praelationem electus pro hominio quod regi faceret consecratione suscepti honoris privaretur', Eadmer, *Historia novorum* (ed. M. Rule, *RS*: London 1884), 186; cf. Cantor, *Church, Kingship and Lay Investiture*, 266–9.

and functions for which homage could legally be demanded.¹
But just as in 1107 Paschal II had regarded the continued possession
of *regalia* by the English bishops as a temporary concession which
the papacy would seek to withdraw at a later date,² so after
Worms Calixtus was able to subdue vociferous opposition at the
First Lateran Council by an assurance that the ultimate aim was
the same, a complete denial of the bishop as a proper recipient of
royal acts of grace.³ And for two decades thereafter Gerhoh of

¹ Whilst Henry relinquished 'omnem investituram per anulum et baculum',
Calixtus recognized that the German bishop-elect 'regalia per sceptrum a te
recipiat et quae ex his iure tibi debet faciat'. The same was to apply to the
Italian bishops, except for regalian rights held from the papacy itself: *MGH*,
Const., I nos. 107–8 pp. 159–61. See further A. Hofmeister, 'Das Wormser
Konkordat: Zum Streit und seine Bedeutung', *Festschrift D. Schäfer* (Jena 1915),
64–148. Hofmeister attempts to argue however (pp. 76–81) that Paschal's grant
of February 1111 was of such a revolutionary nature that it had to be a charter
to Henry and his successors in perpetuity, whereas the grant of April 1111 (like
Calixtus's grant in the Concordat of Worms) was only a confirmation of existing
privileges and so was made to Henry alone. The difference is surely between
what represented achievement of a long-term papal policy, and what was
hoped would only be a temporary arrangement.
² See Paschal's letter to Anselm in Eadmer, *Historia novorum*, p. 179: the arrangement should only last 'donec per omnipotentis Dei gratiam ad hoc omittendum
cor regium tuae praedicationis imbribus molliatur'. On the other hand Henry I
bitterly resented the compromise, complained about the imperial retention of
the right of investiture, and threatened to return to the customary position,
according to Anselm's report in 1108: *Opera omnia* (ed. F. S. Schmitt: London
1946–51), V no. 451 p. 399. See further K. Leyser, 'England and the Empire in
the Early Twelfth Century', *TRHS*, Fifth Series, X (1960), pp. 61–83 at pp. 73–4.
³ See the commentary on the Council by Gerhoh of Reichersberg, *De ordine*,
p. 280, recording the doubt and indignation with which the terms of Worms
were received: these were only a partial denial of evil practices for the sake of
peace ('illa propter pacem obtinenda extorta concessio partim est annichilata'),
and he concludes by hoping ('In proximo futurum speramus') that homage and
regalia will eventually be abolished altogether. This view, as also the official
lay view, should therefore be distinguished from the various 'double investiture'
theories which, whilst being attempts to compromise between papal and lay
positions, insisted that royally-conferred *regalia* were rights to be maintained:
e.g. Hugh of Fleury, *De regia potestate et sacerdotali dignitate*, I. 5 (*MGH*, *L de L*,
II, 472), 'Post electionem autem non annulum aut baculum a manu regia, sed
investituram rerum saecularium electus antistes debet suscipere, et in suis ordinibus per annulum aut baculum animarum curam ab archiepiscopo suo, ut nego-
tium huiusmodi sine disceptatione peragatur, et terrenis et spiritualibus potestati-
bus suae auctoritatis privilegium conservetur.' Similarly Geoffrey of Vendome,
Libellus IV (*MGH*, *L de L*, II, 691), suggested that both pope and king should

Reichersberg was to remind the papacy of its unfinished business in this respect.[1]

It can then be shown that throughout the period the Roman church, admittedly with varying degrees of practical success, adhered to a consistent programme in regard to the investiture issue. Against the lay view that a bishop's powers could be simply divided into sacramental *spiritualia* and jurisdictional *temporalia*, received from *sacerdotium* and *regnum* respectively[2]—a view which effectively denied the bishop any governmental power,

invest to demonstrate that episcopal lands and property were held under divine and human law; cf. Ivo of Chartres, *Ep.* 60 (ed. J. Leclercq: Paris 1949), 246–8: but neither writer distinguishes between *ecclesiastica* and *saecularia* in the way that Hugh of Fleury does.

[1] *De aedificio Dei*, 23 (*MGH, L de L*, III, 153), 'sed illud simpliciter affirmo quod sicut laici nullo iustitiae vel falso colore decimarum possessionem sibi poterunt licitam affirmare, quoniam decima *ecclesiastica res* esse non dubitatur, sic illae *regales et militares administrationes* ab episcopis sine certa sui ordinis apostasia gubernari non possunt.' It is difficult to follow Benson's contention, *The Bishop-Elect*, 282, 310, 312, that Gerhoh's viewpoint is a much more radical one than that adopted by Paschal II, and is one which does not obtain support until applied by Conrad of Salzburg in the 1130s. For the dating of Gerhoh's works see D. van den Eynde, *L'oeuvre littéraire de Gerhoch de Reichersberg* (Rome 1957); cf. E. Meuthen, *Kirche und Heilsgeschichte bei Gerhoh von Reichersberg* (Leiden and Cologne 1959) and P. Classen, *Gerhoch von Reichersberg* (Wiesbaden 1960).

[2] E.g. Gregory of Catino, *Orthodoxa defensio imperialis*, 5 (*MGH, L de L*, II, 538), 'De investitura ergo baculi vel anuli quam rex vel imperator quilibet ecclesiae praelatis faciunt,...per quam non sacri honoris gradum, non munus praelationis sanctae, non ministerium spirituale, non ecclesiarum vel clericorum consecrationes, nec aliquod divinum sacramentum; sed potius sui defensionem tribuunt officii, saecularium rerum seu temporalium atque corporalium possessionum omniumque ecclesiae eiusdem bonorum iuris confirmationem.' See also the *Tractatus de investitura episcoporum* (*MGH, L de L*, II, 501). A quarter of a century earlier the same distinction had been used by Guido of Ferrara, *De schismate Hildebrandi*, II (*MGH, L de L*, I, 564), 'Duo siquidem iura conceduntur episcopis omnibus: spirituale vel divinum unum, aliud saeculare; et aliud quidem coeli, aliud vero fori. Nam omnia quae sunt episcopalis officii spiritualia sunt, divina sunt, quia, licet per ministerium episcopi, tamen a sancto Spiritu conceduntur. At vero iudicia saecularia et omnia quae a mundi principibus et saecularibus hominis *ecclesiis conceduntur*, sicut sunt curtes et praedia omniaque regalia, *licet in ius divinum transeant*, dicuntur tamen saecularia quasi a saecularibus concessa.' Guido's awareness and touchiness concerning the papal theory that lands given to a church become subject to divine law and are removed from lay control are apparent in this passage. For numerous other examples see Benson, *The Bishop-Elect*, 206–28.

territorial possession, or income except from the lay prince—
the papacy insisted that a triple distinction must be made. First,
there were the *spiritualia*, the gifts of invisible grace given by the
Holy Spirit through consecration, which conferred sacramental
capacities on the bishop.[1] Half a century later this would be known
as the *potestas ordinis*.[2] Next, there was (again employing later
terminology) his episcopal *potestas iurisdictionis*, comprising the
visible governmental powers and rights of his office, the *episcopatus*,
the care of the faithful within his see.[3] This came to him by investiture: the staff symbolizing his right and power to rule; the ring
his marriage to the bishopric, his juridical capacity to act as head
and embodiment of the see itself:

Episcopus etiam, cum benedicitur, baculum de manu archiepiscopi
accipit, simul et anulum. Baculum quidem ut bene populum regat;
anulum vero ut signum aeterni misterii se percepisse cognoscat...
Unde et nos intellegere decet ideo institutum episcopos vel abbates
baculum de manu episcopi, cum consecrantur, accipere ut noverint se
terrenarum rerum quae ecclesia possidet de manu Domini veraciter tunc
accepisse dominium. In anulo vero misterium sacratissimae coniunc-
tionis, Christi videlicet et eius Ecclesiae, designari certissimum est.[4]

And with this went all the estates and rights vested in the see,
inherited and administered by the bishop *ratione officii* as things

[1] But see G. Olsen, 'The Definition of the Ecclesiastical Benefice in the Twelfth
Century: The Canonists' Discussion of *Spiritualia*', *Studia Gratiana*, XI (1967),
431–46, who illustrates the way in which this basic sense of the term could be
extended to include anything annexed to the sacramental capacity. The *spiritualia* were not an issue in the debate, except in relation to the question of
whether consecration should precede or follow lay investiture and the payment
of homage.

[2] Wilks, *JTS*, n.s., VIII (1957), 71 f.; Benson, *The Bishop-Elect*, 50 f.

[3] Humbert, *Adversus simoniacos*, III, 6 (*MGH, L de L*, I, 205). 'Unde palam est
omne episcopale officium in baculo et anulo eis datum', and these convey the
iura and *cura pastoralis*, to which he applies the term *ecclesiastica*. Cf. Manegold
of Lautenbach, *Ad Gebehardum*, 64 (*MGH, L de L*, I, 416), 'A regibus autem
baculos, pastoralis videlicet sollicitudinis sustentationem indicantes, solent
accipere et anulos.'

[4] Placidus of Nonantula, *De honore ecclesiae*, 55 (*MGH, L de L*, II, 590); cf. Rangerius of Lucca, *De anulo et baculo*, lines 11–14 (*ibid.*, 509); and further examples,
Benson, *The Bishop-Elect*, 121 f., 358. For the concept of the mystical marriage
see Wilks, *Bulletin of the John Rylands Library*, XLIV (1961–2), 489–530.

given to God by the original donors.[1] All these things—powers, rights, buildings, lands, incomes, tithes, offerings and so on—pertained to the episcopal *ecclesia*, and were appropriately summed up by the term *ecclesiastica*. Whoever invested appeared as the source of episcopal jurisdiction, and it was therefore vital for the papacy to prevent imperial bestowal of the *ecclesiastica*. But these had to be carefully distinguished from, thirdly, the *regalia* or *saecularia*, the duties of civil administration which pertained to the *regnum*,[2] and which the king, acting *per sceptrum*, by virtue of his royal function, could equally well grant to a layman: the tenure of dukedoms, counties, cities, castles, marches, royal

[1] The point is repeatedly made by Placidus: 'Quod semel ecclesiae datum est, in perpetuum Christi est. Nec aliquo modo alienari a possessione ecclesiae potest', *De honore ecclesiae*, 7 p. 577; similarly 43 p. 587. These are 'tam parvas quam magnas possessiones quae Deo sanctificatae sunt', *prologus*, p. 568; also 151 p. 635. Cf. Rangerius of Lucca, *De anulo et baculo*, lines 891–2, p. 527. 'Sed dico si rex aliquis castella vel agros contulit ecclesiae, contulit et Domino'; Humbert, *Adversus simoniacos*, III, 2 p. 200. 'Sic episcopalis dignitas potius possessionem, quam possessio episcopalem dignitatem vindicat. Et tamen tale est episcopale officium, ut sine his, quibus debet impendi vel adhiberi, non sit officium, velut si quis dicatur habere licentiam agrum colendi, et ei ager, quem colat, desit... Continet autem episcopalis dignitas res Deo sacratas, continetur quoque ab eis, immo in eis, utputa et ipsa a Deo consecrata.' For the episcopal ring and staff as symbols of investiture with an inheritance see St Bernard, *Sermones de tempore*, *In coena Domini*, 2 (PL, CLXXXIII, 271), 'datur ad investiendum de haereditate aliqua et signa est'.

[2] Anon., *Defensio Paschalis papae*, MGH, L de L, II, 665, 'Sicut enim in ecclesia pastoralis virga est necessaria, qua regitur, et ecclesiastica distinguuntur officia; sic in domibus regum et imperatorum illud insigne sceptrum, quod est imperialis vel regalis virga, qua regitur patria, ducatus, comitatus et caetera regalia distribuntur iura. Si ergo [rex] dixerit quod per virgam pontificalem et anulum sua tantum regalia velit conferre, aut sceptrum regale deserat aut per illud regalia sua conferat'; Gerhoh of Reichersberg, *De aedificio Dei*, 25 p. 154, 'Quae cum ita se habeant, patet ecclesiarum facultates trifariam esse distinctas: in decimarum, videlicet oblationes; et agrorum possessiones; necnon regales ac publicas functiones. Et de decimis quidem nulla est contradictio ¦quin eas laici possideant cum sacrilegis. Agros autem semel in usus pauperum oblatos docuit superior assertio ab ecclesia sub caritatis operimento defendi,...Publicas autem functiones non cura[t] ecclesia multum defendere...quoniam spirituales viri malunt carere talibus, quam ex eorum occasione implicari negotiis saecularibus.' This passage makes it clear that for Gerhoh his technically threefold distinction in episcopal jurisdiction is effectively only a twofold one with regalian functions on one side, and oblations and ecclesiastical lands on the other.

offices, rights of taxation, tolls, and dues, which carried with them all the corresponding obligations of homage, fealty, knight-service, and the like.[1] These had nothing to do with the episcopal office as such: they were grants made, not to God, but to an individual bishop—and should, as Placidus of Nonantula indicated, be renewed to each person who occupied the see if the king wished that particular bishop to hold them:

ducatus, marchias, comitatus, advocatias, monetas publicas, civitates et castra, villas et rura et caetera huiusmodi, ita ad imperatorem pertinent, ut, nisi pastoribus ecclesiae semper cum sibi succedunt iterum dentur, nequaquam ea habere debeant.[2]

It was these personal grants of civil administration which the papacy sought to divide from the episcopal office, and which, far from seeking to accumulate, it was desirable for the bishops to refuse. For the papacy realized that it was the possession of *regalia*, of which the king was unquestionably the immediate provider,[3]

---

[1] Gerhoh of Reichersberg, *De investigatione Antichristi*, 24 p. 333, 'siquidem domnus apostolicus omnia regalia, videlicet ducatus, marchias, comitatus, hominia cum beneficiis, monetas, teloneas, munitiones per universum regnum suum imperio reddere voluisset'; cf. *De aedificio Dei*, 12 p. 142, 'dum episcopi, abbates, abbatissae facta electione ad palatium ire compelluntur, quatenus a rege nescio quae regalia suscipiant, de quibus regi vel hominium vel fidelitatis sacramentum faciant'; cf. Placidus of Nonantula, *De honore ecclesiae*, 56 p. 591, 'sacratissimo autem imperatori quod suum est non negamus, quia et militiam ecclesiae, cum pro tempore opus fuerit, si deservire omnimodis volumus et ordinatum tributum nequaquam negamus'.

[2] *De honore ecclesiae*, 151 p. 634. In this passage Placidus is attacking those who would put all ecclesiastical possessions into the regalian capacity. That he himself did not follow Paschal II in wanting the *regalia* renounced is shown by his adoption of the 'double investiture' theory, the emperor granting 'quod sibimet iure competit' alongside the archiepiscopal investiture with ring and staff: 86 p. 612. This corrects Benson's judgment, *The Bishop-Elect*, 247–8, that Placidus does not distinguish between *ecclesiastica* and *regalia* and represents a 'High Gregorian' position. The way in which the lay theory combined the *ecclesiastica* granted permanently to the episcopal church or office with the personally acquired *regalia* is again well illustrated by Guido of Ferrara, *De schismate*, II, 565, 'Illud etiam innotuit quod saecularia iudicia et placita, semel ecclesiis ab imperatoribus tradita, successorum essent investitionibus confirmanda, si omnia regalia et omnia publica iura perpetim ecclesiis manere non poterant nisi succedentium sibi regum frequenti fuissent iteratione concessa.'

[3] Gerhoh of Reichersberg, *De aedificio Dei*, 23 p. 153, 'theloneum ac caetera sine dubio ad regem pertinentia'.

which gave the lay ruler a lever for the greater claim to be the source of all jurisdiction exercised in the see.[1] The repeated attempts of Henry V to blur or obliterate the distinction between *ecclesiastica* and *regalia*, to apply a twofold rather than a threefold division of a bishop's powers, was a means of retaining episcopal estates within the sphere of the *regnum* and to maintain the see as a proprietary church. This not only created the anomaly in hierocratic eyes that a bishop was superior to the king as a bishop and yet subordinate to him as the holder of *regalia*,[2] but also led to pressing practical problems of obligation when a conflict of duty arose between obedience to papal and imperial commands.[3] Above all, the retention of the *regalia* offended against the proper allocation of functions, forcing the bishop to do work which would be better left to his lay inferiors.[4] It made him into a mere 'fixer of landmarks', concerned with purely feudal things which could only serve to distract him from his preoccupation with his higher governmental function as a bishop.[5] For Paschal and Calixtus, as later for St Bernard, the bishop should not be a

---

[1] Thus the *Tractatus de investitura episcoporum*, p. 502, argues that because from the time of the Donation of Constantine 'per christianos reges et imperatores dotatae et ditatae et exaltatae sunt ecclesiae in fundis et aliis mobilibus, et iura civitatum in theloneis, monetis, villicis et scabinis, comitatibus, advocatiis, synodalibus bannis per reges delegata sunt episcopis, *congruum fuit et consequens* ut rex, qui est unus in populo et caput populi, investiat et intronizet episcopum'.

[2] For some examples of bishops distinguishing between their feudal obedience to the king as *dominus* and their right of office as bishops to instruct and correct him as *filius* see J. E. A. Jolliffe, *Angevin Kingship* (London, 2nd ed., 1963), 17. The father–son relationship of bishop and lay ruler is used in this context by Placidus of Nonantula, *De honore ecclesiae*, 37 p. 585. Cf. Gerhoh of Reichersberg, *De ordine*, p. 277, 'Nonne tale quid agitur quando episcopi regibus hominium facientes et illud sacramento firmantes libertatem ecclesiae compellunt huic mundo servire, cum potius reges debeant ecclesiae servire.'

[3] On this see now R. L. Benson, 'The Obligations of Bishops with *Regalia*: Canonistic Views from Gratian to the Early Thirteenth Century', *Proceedings of the Second International Congress of Medieval Canon Law* (ed. S. Kuttner and J. J. Ryan: Vatican City 1965), 127–37; cf. *The Bishop-Elect*, 325–31.

[4] Paschal II, *MGH, Const.*, I no. 90 p. 141, 'Et divinae legis institutione sanccitum est et sacratis canonibus interdictum ne sacerdotes curis saecularibus occupentur, neve ad comitatum, nisi pro dampnatis cruendis aut pro aliis qui iniuriam patiuntur, accedant. Unde et apostolus Paulus [1 Cor. 6. 4], Saecularia, inquit, iudicia si habueritis, contemptibiles qui sunt in Ecclesia, illos constituite ad iudicandum.'

[5] Cf. my remarks in *JTS*, n.s., XIII (1962), 303–7.

persona mixta, layman as well as cleric, since he already was a prince over Israel, ruling his people and administering the estates of God by right of episcopal office. He did not need, indeed it was positively dangerous and embarrassing for him, to be a royal agent too.

All this was part and parcel of the papal-hierocratic theme as it had emerged during the eleventh century in the principles defined by the Reform Papacy. It is to men like Gregory VII, Humbert, and Damian[1] that we must look for the genesis of this triple division of episcopal power, rather than to the canonists of the later twelfth century—they were simply elaborating a doctrine which had already been authoritatively stipulated by the Roman church itself. We need not speculate, as so many have done, about the precise point in time when Paschal II conceived the idea of renouncing the *regalia*. There was nothing novel or revolutionary involved: and no connection with theories of apostolic poverty or monastic withdrawal from the world. Nor can it be suggested that the early twelfth-century papacy had suddenly succumbed to dualism. The papal distinction between *spiritualia* and ecclesiastical jurisdiction on the one hand, and regalian administration on the other, was certainly seen as a suitable application of the injunction to 'Render unto Caesar...',[2] but in the sense of a functional

[1] See Damian's distinction between the bishop's sacramental *officium* (= *ordo*); the property and rule pertaining to the *ecclesia*; and the property which the bishop administered as *villicus*, not by virtue of his sacerdotal function, and which was conferred by the *baculus* of the secular prince: *Ep.*, I, 13 (*PL*, CXLIV, 220–1); V, 10 (353).

[2] As in the report of Paschal II's argument with the German bishops at the abortive coronation proceedings in IIII: *MGH, Const.*, I no. 99 p. 148. The point is made repeatedly by Gerhoh of Reichersberg, e.g. *De ordine*, p. 274, 'Ego autem quomodo dixi aliquando quae Dei sunt Deo et quae Caesaris Caesari reddenda, ita sum notatus tamquam pontificum et regum adversarius, quia neuter ordo suo iure suisque terminis vult esse contentus dum et reges *pontificalia* et pontifices usurpant sibi *regalia*'; *De aedificio Dei*, 22 p. 153, 'Ducatus, comitatus, thelonea, moneta pertinent ad saeculum. Decima, primitiae caeteraeque oblationes pertinent ad Deum. Illa per mundi principes, ista per pontifices antiquitus tractabantur, ea videlicet cautione ac distinctione, ut neque pontifex in his quae erant ad saeculum, neque princeps in his quae erant ad Deum, praeesset; sed utique suo iure contentus, modum divinitus ordinatum non excederet'; cf. *De investigatione Antichristi*, 27 p. 337; *De novitatibus huius temporis*, 12, 19 pp. 297, 301; Placidus of Nonantula, *De honore ecclesiae*, 56 p. 591.

division between the clerical and lay officers of the Christian society, and not as something to be confused with the lay version of Matthew 22. 21, where there was only a simple separation into spiritualities and temporalities.[1] Moreover, none of this affected the much larger question looming in the background of how Caesar had gained the regalian rights which were to be rendered to him in the first place. Since, as Gregory VII had pointed out, they could only have come from God through the Roman church,[2] there was no reason why another successor of St Peter should not insist that Caesar should keep them to himself when he got them.

---

[1] E.g. Guido of Ferrara, *De schismate*, II, 565.

[2] *Reg.*, VII, 14a (ed. E. Caspar: Berlin 1955), 487: the 'terra imperia, regna, principatus, ducatus, marchias, comitatus, et omnium *hominum* possessiones', granted and revocable by the Roman church, referred to here may be contrasted with the properties of the *ecclesiae*, lands given to God and, like tithes, attached permanently to the *regimen episcopatus* or *episcopale officium*, referred to in I, 80 p. 114 and in the 1078 decree against lay investiture (as given in *MGH, SS*, v, 308–9). This suggests that Gregory accepted without comment the distinction between *ecclesiastica* and *regalia* already employed by Humbert and Damian, and whilst it is true that Gregory seems to have made no attempt to prevent homage being given by clerics to laymen, it is extremely doubtful whether one is justified in classifying Gregory's position as somehow distinct from an alleged 'new policy' developed by Urban II and Paschal II on the basis of Humbertine principles, as argued by Z. N. Brooke, 'Lay Investiture and its Relation to the Conflict of Empire and Papacy', *Proceedings of the British Academy*, XXV (1939), 217–47.

VIRI RELIGIOSI AND THE
YORK ELECTION DISPUTE[1]

by DEREK BAKER

ANY discussion of the conciliar assemblies and decisions of the Church is likely to consider things from the centre—to enumerate those present, to distinguish the issues, arguments, and protagonists, and to emphasize the final decisions. Perhaps, indeed, to over-emphasize them, for there is a tendency to assume that what was decreed at Rome was rapidly implemented in the provinces. Often, of course, this was the case, and the speed with which the decisions of the Third Lateran Council were disseminated is striking testimony to the ability of the twelfth-century Papacy to publicize its policies. The Papacy developed rapidly, however, in the middle years of the twelfth century, and it is dangerous to assume that what was true of the pontificate of Alexander III can also be applied to that of Innocent II. It may therefore be useful to look closely at a major provincial dispute from the first half of the twelfth century, and to attempt to determine how decisively regional practice was affected by papal decrees in one particular instance.

The death of Archbishop Thurstan of York on 6 February 1140 marks an epoch in the history of the northern province. *Homo magnarum rerum et totius religionis amator,* as the historian of Fountains styles him,[2] Thurstan was the last and greatest in the line of able Norman prelates who had rebuilt the Church, under all its aspects, in the North of England. His death coincided with the disintegration of the uneasy peace of Stephen's early years, and contributed to it: 'after his death lawlessness was let loose, disputes were allowed to run on without restraint, open contempt was

---

[1] I am indebted to Professor C. N. L. Brooke and Professor W. Ullmann for help and advice in the preparation of this paper.

[2] *Narratio [de Fundationis Fontanis Monasterii]*, ed. J. R. Walbran, *The Memorials of Fountains Abbey*, Surtees Society, XLII (Durham 1862), I, 8.

shown for the clergy, and lay people behaved with shameless disrespect towards church laws and dignitaries. The unity of the kingdom was broken because everyone did as he pleased';[1] and with the constant threat of Scottish intervention only momentarily checked at the Battle of the Standard, no part of the realm was more vulnerable, more sensitive to controversy, than the North.

Not the least of the issues which exacerbated the passions of these turbulent years was the dispute over the election of Thurstan's successor, a dispute which was to persist throughout Stephen's reign, and to drag on into the early years of his successor. The circumstances of the time ensured a complexity of motive and a wide conflict of interest which previous elections at York had lacked—though Thurstan's own succession had been far from tranquil[2]—and most recent writers have emphasized the political importance of the appointment to Stephen at this particular stage in his career.[3] It was not only, however, the political scene which had changed since Thurstan' appointment in 1114:[4] the ecclesiastical circumstances were radically different too.[5] The revival of regular life in the North had accelerated under Thurstan. The foundations which resulted soon achieved considerable local importance, and came to play a large part in the ecclesiastical developments of the time.[6] In such a matter as the archiepiscopal election of 1140 regular views could not have been ignored, and the traditional right of the religious to be consulted had, in any case,

[1] *John of Hexham*, [ed. J. Raine, *The Priory of Hexham*], Surtees Society, XLIV (1865), 131.
[2] Cf. [Donald] Nicholl, [*Thurstan, Archbishop of York (1114–1140)*] (York 1964), 41–74.
[3] Nicholl, 239–247; [R. H. C.] Davis, [*King Stephen*] (London 1967), 99 ff; [G. V.] Scammell, [*Hugh du Puiset, Bishop of Durham*] (Cambridge 1956), 7–21; B. D. Hill, *English Cistercian Monasteries and their Patrons in the Twelfth Century* (Chicago/London 1968), 15–41, 119–22. This last work, however, needs to be used with caution.   [4] 15 August 1114.
[5] [D.] Knowles, [*The Monastic Order in England*] (Cambridge 1940), 172–190, 227–66; J. C. Dickinson, *The Origins of the Austin Canons and their Introduction into England* (London 1950), 91–162.
[6] The participation of Abbot Richard I of Fountains in the legation of Alberic of Ostia in 1138 as assessor for the northern province exemplifies this: Knowles, 253–4.

recently been reaffirmed in the Lateran decree of 1139, which had gone so far as to declare that the exclusion of *viri religiosi* could render an election null and void.[1]

When these developments are contrasted with the extensive legatine nepotism of Henry of Blois,[2] it is not difficult to see why the York election dispute has been so frequently characterized as a struggle between the commandoes of reform, soon to be led, from headquarters, by St Bernard himself, and the armies of tradition under the direction of the bishop of Winchester:

a new factor had come into play in recent years. The movement that favoured drastic reform measures had suddenly been swept to power in the North of England...the Lateran Council had laid it down that episcopal chapters were not to exclude 'men of religion' from helping them whenever their sees became vacant...the Cistercians on the continent were poised to grasp their opportunity...nor were the English Cistercians less zealous.[3]

In this view the dispute at York was part of a European struggle for freedom of election and for reform. Those who opposed William Fitzherbert did so against the background of St Bernard's successful, but unjustified, intervention at Langres, and acted in accordance with papal policy expressed through the decrees of the Lateran Council of 1139. While they stood for ideals, the Fitzherbert faction simply sought self-interest. It is, in fact, whatever

---

[1] (Cap. XXVIII) 'Obeuntibus sane episcopis, quoniam ultra tres menses vacare ecclesias prohibent patrum sanctiones sub anathema interdicimus, ne canonici de sede episcopali ab electione episcoporum excludant religiosos viros, sed eorum consilio honesta et idonea persona in episcopum eligatur. Quod si exclusis eisdem religiosis electio fuerat celebrata; quod absque eorum assensu et convenientia factum fuerit, irritum habeatur et vacuum.' *Sacrorum Conciliorum Nova et Amplissima Collectio*, ed. J. Mansi (Paris 1757–98), XXI, 523. Cf. *Das Register Gregors VII*, ed. E. Caspar, *Monumenta Germaniae Historica, Epistolae Selectae*, II (Berlin 1955), VII, 14a, cap. 6, 482: *De electione pontificum* (7 March 1080). This laid down that 'clerus et populus remota omni seculari ambitione timore atque gratia apostolice sedis vel metropolitani sui consensu pastorem sibi secundum Deum eligat', and is the preliminary to Lateran II, cap. XXVIII.

These decrees, of course, were no guarantee, as the York election itself shows, that the electors would choose an 'honesta et idonea persona'. See also W. Ullmann, *The Growth of Papal Government* (London 1955), 298–9; *Conventionum Oecumenicorum Decreta* (2nd ed., Vienna 1962), 179, n. 3.

[2] Cf. Scammell, 6.   [3] Nicholl, 240–1.

the actual ramifications of intrigue and negotiation, essentially a clear and simple story. Perhaps, however, too simple, and while it is not my intention to attempt yet another inadequate summary of Professor Knowles's definitive study,[1] it may be worthwhile to focus on the first stages of the York election dispute—before the involvement of St Bernard produced the familiar pyrotechnic polemic and hardened opinion into intransigence—and to reassess these general assumptions in the light of that examination.

The dispute at York began, strictly speaking, with the appeal against the election of William Fitzherbert in January 1141, but before that date three other candidates had been put forward to succeed Thurstan. Thurstan himself had sought to obtain papal permission for the transfer of his see to his brother Audoen, the bishop of Evreux, in 1139.[2] His envoy in this business was Richard, the first abbot of Fountains, and a close friend of the archbishop. Richard had distinguished himself not only in the establishment and direction of his abbey, but also as the assessor for the northern province to Alberic of Ostia on his legatine mission of 1138. In the subsequent year he accompanied the legate back to Rome, high in his favour,[3] to act as Thurstan's envoy and to attend the Lateran Council. Richard, however, died at Rome, and with Audoen's death at the Augustinian priory of Merton shortly afterwards, Thurstan's scheme came to nothing.

Thurstan himself died a few months later, in February 1140, at the Cluniac priory of Pontefract, and for a whole year, as John of Hexham uncharitably remarks,[4] the York chapter prevaricated. Their discussions were not, however, entirely fruitless, and they proceeded to two successive elections. In the first, which John of Hexham does not record, Waldef, prior of the Augustinian house

---

[1] [David] Knowles, ['The Case of St.] William of York', C[ambridge] H[istorical] J[ournal], v, 2 (Cambridge 1936), 162–77, 212–14. See also C. H. Talbot, 'New Documents in the Case of St. William of York', CHJ, x, 1 (1950), 1–15; [A.] Morey, ['Canonist Evidence in the Case of St. William of York'], CHJ, x, 3 (1952), 352–3.

[2] Cf. [A.] Saltman, [Theobald, Archbishop of Canterbury] (London 1956), 90.

[3] Narratio, 70–2.

[4] 'Clerici Eboracenses secundum desideria cordis sui varia et vaga sententia circumacti fuerant toto anno super electione facienda', quoted Knowles, 'William of York', 165, n. 9. Cf. Narratio, 78–9.

of Kirkham, was chosen. Since, however, he was the stepson of King David of Scotland his election was vetoed by Stephen on political grounds.[1] Forced to reconsider,[2] the Chapter, 'at the persuasion of the legate'[3] [Henry of Winchester], then fixed on Henry de Sully, the newly-appointed abbot of Fécamp, and nephew of the king. His reluctance to relinquish his abbacy, however, led Innocent II to refuse to allow the election, and the unfortunate Chapter had to start yet once again. This time their choice, if choice it was, was William Fitzherbert.

It is useful, at this point, to take a closer look at each of these candidates. Audoen was much the same age as Thurstan, and though completely overshadowed by him seems to have possessed the same qualities as his brother. Like Thurstan he had a reputation for piety and continence, and he seems to have been an exemplary bishop of Evreux, if of average ability. In 1139 he was, like his brother, considering retirement from his office.

Waldef[4] came from a completely different stable. The grandson of the Anglo-Saxon Earl Waltheof, he had been brought up at the court of his step-father, King David of Scotland, in the company of his brother Simon, the future earl of Northampton, his step-brother Prince Henry, and of Ailred. He was, apparently, early attracted by things ecclesiastical—building sand-churches while his play-fellows built sand-castles—and in c. 1130 entered the Augustinian priory of Nostell. Four years later, at about the time that Ailred was entering Rievaulx, he was elected prior of Walter Espec's foundation at Kirkham (1122). Six years later he was the first abortive choice of the York electors for Thurstan's vacant see. Jocelin of Furness reports that Waldef rejected *in spiritu vehementi* William of Aumâle's offer to secure Stephen's approval of the election in return for the lease of the archiepiscopal lands in Shirburn,[5] and in the following year Waldef is numbered amongst

[1] Cf. Knowles, 'William of York', 165; [Walter Daniel, *Life of*] *Ailred*, ed. F. M. Powicke (Edinburgh 1950), xliv.
[2] The sequence of events is not absolutely clear here, see Knowles, 'William of York', 165.
[3] 'persuadente legato Henrico Wintoniae', *John of Hexham*, 133.
[4] *Ailred*, lxxi–lxxv.
[5] Cf. *Ailred*, xliv; Knowles, 'William of York', 165.

the opponents of William Fitzherbert, accompanying them to Rome in 1143. Within a few months, however, he had resigned his charge, entered another of Espec's foundations, the Cistercian house at Wardon, and precipitated a crisis at Kirkham. The canons were scandalized, and Waldef's brother, the earl of Northampton, sufficiently angry, for the community at Wardon to consider it in their interests that Waldef should withdraw to Rievaulx. The transition which he had made did not, however, immediately resolve Waldef's spiritual crisis: unlike Ailred he underwent prolonged bouts of doubt and depression,[1] and not until his election as abbot of Melrose in 1148 can his course be said to have been stabilized. In 1159, the year of his death, he was offered the see of St Andrews, and though Ailred, now his superior, urged him to accept, he refused, dying not long afterwards.

The third of these candidates was Henry de Sully, the son of William of Blois,[2] the eldest brother of the king and the legate. Henry of Blois,[3] abbot of Glastonbury, bishop of Winchester, and papal legate, exercised a unique authority over the English church at this time, and used his influence to foster the careers of numerous protégés and relatives.[4] Henry de Sully himself had already been put forward for the see of Salisbury early in 1140, but, passed over by the king, had been given the abbey of Fécamp as consolation. It was his reluctance to part with this office which barred him at York. Later, in 1148, he was again unsuccessfully put forward by his uncle, this time for the see of Lincoln. The priory of Bermondsey did, however, come his way, and towards the end of his life, in 1189, he became a disastrous abbot of Glastonbury, and, finally, bishop of Worcester. He died in 1195.[5]

[1] Cf. *Ailred*, lxxiv–lxxv. [2] Cf. Davis, 4.
[3] Cf. Knowles, 285–93. [4] Cf. Knowles, 285–93.
[5] It is possible that the outline career here given represents two Henry de Sullys rather than one. There is no doubt that the candidate for the see of York had been appointed abbot of Fécamp in 1140, and his abbacy seems to have ended in 1187, possibly on his death—his obit is recorded on 10 January in the obituary of St Benigne, Dijon. If this is so, then it was another Cluniac Henry de Sully who, according to the annals of Bermondsey, became prior in 1186, abbot of Glastonbury in 1189, bishop of Worcester in 1194 (6 January) and died in 1195 (24 October). The annals of Bermondsey are, of course, notoriously confused and inaccurate, but the existence of this deutero-Henry de Sully is sufficiently

I have dwelt at some length on Audoen, Waldef, and Henry de Sully because, unlike William Fitzherbert, their candidature for the see of York seems to have provoked no opposition either within the Chapter or amongst the ranks of the religious of the province—and yet they have remarkably little to commend them for what was at the time probably the most responsible and most demanding office in the English ecclesiastical hierarchy. This is, of course, most obvious with Henry de Sully, but it is true also, I would maintain, of the others. Henry de Sully was a young untried scion of the house of Blois; he had demonstrated no outstanding qualities—indeed, no qualities of any sort—before his election in 1140; he was to achieve nothing thereafter, and the disasters of his later years are a sufficient commentary on the man. Audoen, as his retirement to Merton and speedy death merely serve to emphasize, was a man at the end of his days. He no longer felt either willing or able to manage the minor see of Evreux: he could not have been considered competent to rule the province of York during the Anarchy.

Waldef appears, at first sight, in a rather different light. A man of clear spiritual vocation, he was prior of Kirkham and well known to the electors at York. Brought up at the Scottish court, he was the brother of the earl of Northampton, the step-brother of the earl of Northumberland, and related to William of Aumâle, earl of York.[1] It was, in fact, his birth and these family connections which marked him out: not great spiritual or administrative qualities. Still a young man, though older than Ailred, there was

attested by the records of Glastonbury and Worcester to be above suspicion. It would certainly be a remarkable coincidence if there were two Cluniacs of the same name, both connected to the English royal house, the one making his appearance in England as the other vanished from the scene in Normandy; and if the move from Fécamp to Bermondsey seems remarkable, it is as well to notice that five priors of Bermondsey were appointed to great black monk houses between 1157 and 1189. Without further detailed investigation it seems best to retain a single Henry de Sully until the hypothesis is proved untenable.

Cf. Scammell, 6, n. 4; *Monasticon Anglicanum*, ed. W. Dugdale (ed. J. Caley, H. Ellis, B. Bandinel, 6 vols in 8, London 1817–30), I, 1, p. 5; I, 2, p. 573; V, p. 91; Rose Graham, *English Ecclesiastical Studies* (London 1929), 91–124; [Adrian Morey and C. N. L. Brooke, *The Letters and Charters of Gilbert*] Foliot (Cambridge 1967) 109, n. 2.

[1] Knowles, 'William of York', 165, n. 10.

nothing in his past to suggest that he could cope with the problems of the archbishopric and the North. As his sudden move to Wardon in 1143 was to show, and his continued doubts thereafter to emphasize, he had still not attained personal or spiritual stability. In his later life he was to achieve nothing of any moment. The offer of St Andrews, his preferment to Melrose, like his election at York, and perhaps, even, as prior of Walter Espec's foundation at Kirkham, can more probably be ascribed to his social connections than to qualities of leadership for which there is little or no evidence. The famous story of William of Aumâle's offer to obtain York for him, at a price, helps to emphasize this. Although Waldef refused the offer indignantly, William of Aumâle clearly did not think it altogether out of place to proffer such a bargain; and if Stephen could so easily be brought round, it is plain that neither he nor William of Aumâle could have seen Waldef, whose brother Simon of Northampton supported them, as a real threat to their position in the North. Perhaps the clearest verdict on Waldef, however, is implicit in the failure of William Fitzherbert's opponents ever to put him forward as an alternative candidate for the see of York once battle had been joined. As a man, Waldef must be ranked with the second abbot Richard of Fountains rather than with William of Rievaulx, Ailred, or the first abbot of Fountains.

All three of these prospective archbishops were inadequate, if not undesirable, and the course of each of the three processes ought, if William Fitzherbert's case is considered, to have provoked controversy and strife. Thurstan seems to have taken no account of the wishes of his Chapter, or of the needs of his province, in proposing Audoen. Filial interest alone could have guided him here, and his action is a remarkable illustration of the survival of the dynastic politics of the Anglo-Norman prelates even amongst their most eminent representatives. Even more illuminating, however, is the attitude of the abbot of Fountains towards such manoeuvring. Richard, first abbot of Fountains, as events had shown, was one of the most remarkable churchmen of the time in the North. He was the friend of Thurstan and of Bernard, and highly regarded by Alberic of Ostia. The house which he ruled owed its foundation to a powerful impulse to reform within St Mary's Abbey, York, the wealthiest of northern black monk communities, and he had directed that impulse.[1] If there was a 'party of reform' in the North he was one of its outstanding leaders, and yet he was prepared to co-operate in, to effect, a change of archbishop based solely on dynastic interest.

Nor does the matter end there. If Waldef's family and social connections are overlooked, and it is accepted, on very inadequate grounds, that he was fit to be archbishop, then it is very surprising that there was no objection to Stephen's arbitrary veto of his election. The York Chapter was not apt to be slow, or afraid to be outspoken, in defence of its rights, as events were to show. With Henry de Sully, too, it is remarkable that there was no reaction to the pressure and nepotism of king and legate. Had Henry de Sully resigned from Fécamp he would have been accepted, apparently without question, as archbishop.

In these circumstances it is difficult to accept the general verdict of recent writers, of whom Scammell may perhaps be taken as representative, that 'for Stephen to secure York, or later Durham, meant an automatic affront to the views, aspirations and power of the reformers, who objected to the unsatisfactory methods and candidates of the royal party'.[2] There is, as we have seen, more to the York election dispute than this, and if it is difficult to see why the Chapter and the religious of the province should accept such unsatisfactory candidates, and concur in conduct on the part of king and legate in the earlier elections which, when related to William Fitzherbert, they would reject, some explanation may be suggested by considering William Fitzherbert himself and those who opposed him.

Whatever criticism may be levelled against him, when set beside Waldef and Henry de Sully, William Fitzherbert is a man amongst boys. His social background compared with that of Waldef, and for nearly thirty years[3] he had been treasurer of

[1] *Narratio*, 6–29; L. G. D. Baker, 'The Foundation of Fountains Abbey', *Northern History*, IV (Leeds 1969).   [2] Scammell, 9.

[3] [C. T.] Clay, [*York Minster*] *Fasti*, I, Yorkshire Archaeological Society, Record Series, CXXIII (Wakefield 1958), 22.

York and archdeacon of the East Riding. He was easily the senior member of the York Chapter. The dean, William de Sainte Barbe, did not take office until *c.* 1135/6.[1] The precentor, William d'Eu, was not appointed until between July 1139 and Thurstan's death in February 1140.[2] Only the archdeacons Walter of London and Osbert of Bayeux, who appear in office as witnesses to a charter between 1121 and 1128,[3] can in any way compare with the treasurer in length of service, and it is perhaps significant that it was Walter of London and his fellow archdeacons who, John of Hexham records, led the opposition to William.

William was elected archbishop, most sources agree, by the majority of those present, but under pressure from William of Aumâle, acting, apparently, on the king's behalf, 'most of them agreed on the person of William the Treasurer, William, earl of York, who was anxious for his promotion, being present... opposed to this election was master Walter of London, archdeacon of York with his brother archdeacons.'[4] As the dispute developed charges of unchastity and simony were levelled at the archbishop-elect, but the principal accusation from the very start was one of intrusion.[5] This is how John of Hexham saw it.[6] Gervase of Canterbury recorded that Stephen gave the see to 'a certain clerk' called William, but added that the electors were divided, and that in those circumstances Archbishop Theobald refused his assent.[7] The historian of Fountains while mentioning royal intervention and legatine patronage simply remarks that William 'was a man of high birth, worthy enough for the bishopric, if his election had been canonical'.[8] This general impression is reinforced by the list of those who appear against him in the appeal to Rome. John of Hexham ranges the archdeacons against him; William d'Eu, the precentor, appears amongst his opponents before Innocent II in 1143, while the priors of Hexham and Nostell, prebendaries of York, showed themselves opposed to

---

[1] Clay, *Fasti*, I, 1.   [2] Clay, *Fasti*, I, 12.

[3] E[arly] Y[orkshire] C[harters], ed. W. Farrer and C. T. Clay (12 vols., Edinburgh/Wakefield 1914–65), II, no. 936, p. 275.

[4] *John of Hexham*, 133.

[5] Knowles, *William of York*, 166, 168.   [6] *John of Hexham*, 133.

[7] Cf. Saltman, 91.   [8] *Narratio*, 80.

him.[1] The Chapter was not large at this date,[2] and when the antagonism of Robert, the custodian of the hospital at York, of Waldef of Kirkham and Cuthbert of Guisborough, of William of Rievaulx and Richard II of Fountains, is added to that of William Fitzherbert's adversaries within the Chapter, his free election seems inconceivable.[3]

Intrusion in this sense, however, was not uncommon, nor can it be taken to imply major personal failings in William Fitzherbert. A recent historian has termed him 'wealthy, indolent and immoral',[4] but while he was certainly a man of wealth, position, and influence within both the Church of York and northern society in general, there is much to be said in his favour. It may be that the policies and standards he represented were not those of the new orders, but there seemed to be no objection to his re-appointment to York after the death of Henry Murdac, St Bernard, and Eugenius III in 1153; he had no difficulty in coming to terms with the monks of Fountains on his return to England in 1154;[5] he achieved a reputation for sanctity, and in 1226, after due inquiry into his merits by the Cistercian abbots of Rievaulx and Fountains, and the Cistercian bishop of Ely, he was canonized by Pope Honorius III.[6]

It is significant in this context that William de Sainte Barbe, the dean of York, and future bishop of Durham, who has been characterized as a moderate reformer,[7] did not appear amongst William Fitzherbert's opponents, and it should be stressed that not all those who did oppose him possessed uniformly laudable characters. In particular is this true of the archdeacon of Richmond, Osbert of Bayeux. Thurstan himself had not been above a little gentle nepotism, and Osbert had owed his advancement to his uncle. Osbert had been one of the leaders of the anti-Fitzherbert faction in 1141, and his animosity was sustained. In the summer of

---

[1] For Robert Biseth see Knowles, "William of York' 166; Nicholl, 241–2. For Athelwold see Knowles, *loc. cit.*, 173; Nicholl, 245.

[2] Clay, *Fasti*, II (1959), v–ix.

[3] 'Fuerunt autem qui reclamaverunt personae graves et religiosi, abbates, priores, archidiaconi, et decani...' *Narratio*, 79.

[4] Scammell, 10.   [5] *Narratio*, 109–10.

[6] The present writer has a paper in preparation on the canonization of St William of York.   [7] Scammell, 8.

1154, as archdeacon of York, he led others in a fresh appeal to Archbishop Theobald against William Fitzherbert, newly-appointed to his see, and on the archbishop's sudden death[1] proceeded, in conjunction with the dean, to the hasty and questionable election of Roger of Pont l'Evêque to the archbishopric. Osbert then found himself accused of poisoning the late archbishop, and when the case finally came to trial before Archbishop Theobald, failed to clear himself on oath and by compurgation of his fellow canons. He appealed to Rome, and though he subsequently claimed to have been acquitted by Adrian IV, there is no doubt that he was relieved of his archdeaconry. Even before this he had fathered a child, and on his return to secular life he married, fathered further children, took over land in the honour of Skipton, and acted as steward to Hugh de Tilly.[2]

None of the other members of the York Chapter had as chequered a career as Osbert, but it is as well to notice that the Chapter, litigious and controversial by tradition, was, as Archbishop Gerard had complained long before,[3] riddled with nepotism and long-established self-interest, and it is, perhaps, against this background that the early stages in the York election dispute become most intelligible.

The details of William Fitzherbert's early career are few, and it is impossible to do more than guess at the tensions and rivalries which may have existed within the York Chapter and grown up around the long-established figure of the treasurer. That such tensions did exist is evident from the venom with which Osbert of Bayeux pursued his former colleague, and it is clear that the Chapter regarded William as anything but the nonentity which he appears in so much contemporary writing. The local politics and interests of the York Chapter, in fact, and of the families directly associated with it by membership or benefaction—or, as with Espec, by both—seem to me to underlie the early stages of

---

[1] 8 June 1154.

[2] Cf. Knowles, *William of York*, 166 ff. 175–7, 213–14; Nicholl, 244–5; Clay, *Fasti*, I, 46; Morey, 352–3; *Foliot*, Ep. 127, pp. 164–5; *The Letters of John of Salisbury, I: The Early Letters*, ed. and trans. W. J. Millor and H. E. Butler, revised C. N. L. Brooke (Edinburgh 1955), no. 16, pp. 261–2.

[3] Cf. Nicholl, 43–4 and references there given.

the dispute at York. It is difficult to explain the York Chapter's acceptance of any of the first three candidates for the archbishopric: they had so little to commend them. It may have been this very nonentity, however, which recommended them to a Chapter very conscious of its own interests—such age or youth, incapacity or inexperience, might seem relatively easy to control and direct. With the established and experienced William Fitzherbert, however, things were likely to be very different, and with his election the representatives of the new orders could be mobilized, possibly through the relatives of their patrons and founders within the Chapter,[1] as they had not been for that of Henry de Sully.

All this is, of course, hypothesis; but it is, I would submit, a more credible hypothesis than one which seeks to submerge the complexity of motive, action, and reaction at York within the wave of reform which was, apparently, sweeping Europe in the wake of that great leviathan St Bernard,[2] and does so on very inadequate grounds. There is, as far as I know, no clear indication that the Cistercians and Augustinians who opposed William Fitzherbert were influenced to oppose him by St Bernard's conduct of the election dispute at Langres.[3] There is, indeed, no evidence that they became involved at all until after the archdeacons had moved against the treasurer. In the wider view, there is nothing to show that the reaffirmation of the right of *viri religiosi* to participate in episcopal elections at the Lateran Council of 1139 exercised any influence on the outbreak or course of the York election dispute. Whatever it may have later become, or seemed to become, in the hands of St Bernard, the dispute at York sprang from the rich soil

[1] For example, Nicholas de Trailli, canon of York and holder of the prebend of Strensall, who was one of the four sons of Aubreye, the second sister of Walter Espec. In *c.* 1180 he described to Ranulf de Glanville the method of electing the last prior of Kirkham, whom, on behalf of his uncle Walter Espec, together with the canons, he had presented to the archbishop and had instituted at the archbishop's request. It is interesting to notice his association with Hugh Murdac, canon of York and possibly nephew of Archbishop Henry Murdac, as a witness to two grants in the period 1150–3. Cf. Clay, *Fasti*, II, 20–1, 70–1.

[2] See, for example, Scammell, 6–12; Nicholl, 240–2; Knowles, 254; Knowles, 'William of York', 165.

[3] Though it should be noted that St Bernard had corresponded with Thurstan about his wish to resign his see: Nicholl, 233–4.

4-2

of capitular rivalry and local family relationship, and this St Bernard himself may have come to realize. Henry Murdac, the representative he sent to England in 1144, may have come as the archetypal Cistercian reformer—'a reformer *in manu forti*, a consuming fire'[1]—but it is surely not without significance that he was a native of York, a former protégé of Thurstan, and a member of a widely-influential local family.[2]

[1] Knowles, 255.

[2] See above, p. 98 n. 3 and the referencest here given. Geoffrey Murdac witnessed Archbishop Thurstan's charter to Beverley (1115–28) at the head of a distinguished list of witnesses, and appeared as a benefactor of St Mary's, York, in Henry II's confirmation of 1156–7: see *EYC*, I, 91, 272; II, 358. Henry Murdac appears as itinerant justice in 1189, Ralph Murdac as constable of Nottingham castle at about the same time. Nicholas Murdac appears in a grant to Fountains *c.* 1170–80, in other grants and as canon of Ripon *c.* 1200: see *Narratio*, 101, 199, 255. See other references to the family in *EYC*, and in particular *EYC*, II, 406. For Archbishop Henry see the outline career in *Foliot*, 541.

COUNCILS AND SYNODS
IN THIRTEENTH-CENTURY CASTILE
AND ARAGON[1]

by PETER LINEHAN

IN 1228 Gregory IX dispatched as his legate to the Spanish Peninsula the Paris theologian and Cardinal-Bishop of Sabina, John of Abbeville, the first legate sent there since before the Fourth Lateran Council and the last to come during the entire thirteenth century in the cause of ecclesiastical reform. During his stay, which lasted for some fifteen months, he held at least three councils, but of only one of these—the Lérida Council of March 1229—have the statutes come down to us intact.[2] Though he visited Portugal as well as Castile and Aragon, this brief communication is concerned only with John's impact on the Castilian and Aragonese Churches during the central years of the century, and with a summary consideration of the quite different reception which John's reform programme received in each place.

As the legate observed, both kingdoms were virgin territory untouched by the spirit of the Fourth Lateran Council;[3] and virgin territory they both remained for almost a decade thereafter,

---

[1] The text of this communication has been left almost exactly as it was delivered at the Conference. A fuller account of the subject will be found in ch. 2–5 of my doctoral dissertation published as *The Spanish Church and the Papacy in the Thirteenth Century* (Cambridge 1971). For the text of the *Summa*, see P. A. Linehan, 'Pedro de Albalat, arzobispo de Tarragona y su Summa Septem Sacramentorum' in *Hispania Sacra*, XXII (1969), 9–30.

[2] For John's career and writings, see *Histoire littéraire de la France*, XVIII (Paris 1835), 162–77; F. Stegmüller, *Repertorium Biblicum Medii Aevi*, III (Madrid 1951), 340–4. The Lérida statutes are published in *España Sagrada*, ed. H. Flórez *et al.* (Madrid 1747–1879), XLVIII, 308 ff. A vernacular translation of those of the Valladolid Council (autumn 1228), discovered in a León MS by Risco, is in *ibid*. XXXVI, 216 ff. The third council was held at Salamanca in February 1229: cf. J. González, *Alfonso IX*, II (Madrid 1944), 619–20 (where the Council is wrongly dated 1228).

[3] *España Sagrada*, XXXVI, 216; XLVIII, 308.

until 1238 when the Aragonese Church was given as its leader Pedro de Albalat, an Archbishop of Tarragona who was, in every respect, John of Abbeville's spiritual heir.[1] For the greater part of that decade—from 1229 when Pedro was sacrist of Lérida where the legate held his council, until 1237, when John died—the two men were in touch with one another. Indeed, on the strength of some correspondence between them which has survived in the Cathedral Archive of the Pyrenean see of Urgel, it may be said that Pedro was John's agent in Aragon and kept the flag of reform, if not flying, then at least unfurled at a time when the incumbent Archbishop of Tarragona, Sparago de la Barca, was making little or no effort to obey the legatine regulations about holding provincial councils 'at least once a year'.[2] Pedro's formal episcopal apprenticeship began in 1236 with his promotion to Lérida.[3] There he prepared the ground for what may be regarded as one of the outstanding archiepiscopal careers not only of thirteenth-century Spain but also of thirteenth-century Europe.

Pedro was, indeed, the very model of a thirteenth-century archbishop. His run of annual councils was broken only twice in twelve years—when he was abroad for the abortive Roman Council of 1241 and the First Lyons Council of 1245.[4] His initial act at his first provincial council in 1239 was to make John of Abbeville's reform programme his own;[5] and from then until his death in July 1251 he gave particular attention to the two items upon which the legate had concentrated: clerical education and

[1] *Reg. Greg. IX*, 4072. R. Beer recognized in Pedro 'eine der bedeutendsten Gestalten des Katalanischen Klerus jener Zeit': 'Die Handschriften des Klosters Santa Maria de Ripoll', *Sitzungsberichte der phil.-hist. Kl. der kaiserlichen Ak. der Wissenschaften*, CLVIII (1908), 69. But he is still awaiting his biographer. Cf. E. Morera Llauradó, *Tarragona Cristiana*, II (Tarragona 1899), 274–89.

[2] P. A. Linehan, 'La carrera del obispo Abril de Urgel: la Iglesia española en el siglo XIII', *Anuario de Estudios Medievales*, V (forthcoming).

[3] J. Villanueva, *Viage literario a las iglesias de España*, XVI (Madrid 1851), 134–8.

[4] Conciliar statutes published in J. Tejada y Ramiro, *Colección de cánones y de todos los concilios de la Iglesia de España y de América*, III (Madrid 1849), 349 ff.; VI (1862), 29 ff. Cf. F. Fita, 'Concilios tarraconenses en 1248, 1249 y 1250', *BRAH*, XL (1902), 444–58. For a brief account of these councils, see F. Valls Taberner, 'Notas sobra la legislació eclesiàstica provincial que integra la compilació canònica Tarraconense del Patriarca d'Alexandria', *AST*, XI (1935), 251–72.

[5] Tejada y Ramiro, VI, 30.

clerical concubinage. He threatened his suffragans with durance vile at Tarragona if they should miss the annual council, and the same penalty was specified for clergy who failed to appear at diocesan synods.[1] He proved tireless as a visitor of his province, having warned the luckless bishops at that same first council that he meant to descend upon them without prior warning.[2] In this he was as good as his word, and they at first were as bad as might have been expected. But they improved. For whenever vacancies occurred Pedro secured the appointment of bishops of his own persuasion. And this meant Dominicans, by and large. John of Abbeville had assisted the friars during his legation, and had been accompanied on his rounds by Raymond of Peñafort himself.[3] Pedro too was closely associated with the Order of Preachers. By 1248 there were five Dominican bishops in his province, one of them—Andrés of Valencia—being his own brother, and four of them being products of St Raymond's Barcelona convent.[4] Together Pedro and Raymond issued a code of conduct for dealing with heretics—probably at a *sede vacante* synod held at Barcelona in October 1241—which Henry Charles Lea and many others before and after have discussed at great length.[5]

What they have not, however, discussed at any length is the *liber sinodalis* issued on the same occasion—though not, perhaps, for the first time—by Pedro himself, which, despite Raymond's proximity, seems to have been all the Archbishop's own work.[6]

[1] Tejada y Ramiro, VI, 36.   [2] Tejada y Ramiro, VI, 32.
[3] AHN, 1724/15; *Vita Sancti Raymundi*, ed. F. Balme and C. Paban, *Raymundiana*, VI: i, 22.   [4] Linehan, Ph.D. diss., 129–32.
[5] Printed C. Douais, 'St Raymond de Peñafort et les hérétiques', *Moyen Age*, III (1899), 315–25. For a review of the literature on the subject, see H. Maisonneuve, *Études sur les origines de l'Inquisition* (Paris 1960), 287. Maisonneuve dates it 1242. A. Dondaine calls it 'le premier document digne du nom de manuel de procédure inquisitoriale': 'Le manuel de l'Inquisiteur (1230–1330)', *Archivum Fratrum Praedicatorum*, XVI (1946), 96.
[6] Villanueva, XVII, 212, mentioned 'las escelentes constituciones sobre sacramentos, vida clerical, etc' promulgated by Pedro on this occasion. But that is all. Part of the eucharistic section is published, from AC Barcelona, *Constituciones Synodales et Provinciales*, fo. 180v–181v, in *Scrinium*, IV–VI (1952), 73–5. Comparison of this fragment with the text of the other Barcelona MS of the Summa, *Libro de la Cadena*, fo. 128va–9ra, offers almost forty variants. The anonymous

Pedro de Albalat's *Summa Septem Sacramentorum*, as the work came to be known, was disseminated throughout the province. Pedro promulgated it himself in his own archdiocese at a synod of uncertain date. In 1258 his brother, Andrés of Valencia, reissued the Barcelona version at a diocesan synod, and three years later ordered all his clergy to furnish themselves with copies of it.[1] It has not, however, yet been published as such or studied—though when it is, the main point about it to be noted will surely be its almost total lack of originality. Apart from the purely didactic material on the Sacraments, the *Summa* contains sections on synodal procedure, the religious instruction of the faithful, and clerical morality; and it draws throughout on that common source of so much of the literature of this type and period: the Paris statutes attributed to Bishop Odo de Sully (1196–1208).[2]

editor has not noted these variants which he describes as 'simples e insignificantes errores de transcripción', though some represent substantial differences. Pedro had previously, in the winter of 1238–9, held a *sede vacante* synod at Pamplona: AC Toledo, X.2.K.1.12.

[1] J. Sáenz de Aguirre, *Collectio Maxima Conciliorum Omnium Hispaniae et Novi Orbis*, v (Rome 1755), 197–202, 206. According to Aguirre (p. 197), Andrés described the *Summa* as having been edited 'per venerabilem archiepiscopum predecessorem domini P. Tarraconensis ecclesiae'. But the MS—AC Valencia, MS 163—reads *dominum*: information kindly supplied by Don Ramón Robles, canon-archivist of Valencia. Cf. E. Olmos Canalda, *Códices de la Catedral de Valencia* (Valencia 1943), 122. Andrés also referred to its having been edited by Pedro 'in synodo Ilerdensi' (*loc. cit.*): a Lérida synod which must have occurred either while Pedro was bishop of Lérida or *sede vacante* while he was archbishop, namely in 1238 or 1247–8. And the synodal statutes of Pedro's successor at Lérida, Raimundo de Sischar, point to the earlier of these dates, for while, in common with the *Summa*, they draw heavily on Odo de Sully, they also contain a number of features and phrases found in the *Summa* but not in Odo. They are printed by Villanueva, XVI, 297–308, without indication of date. Sáinz de Baranda, *España Sagrada*, XLVII (Madrid 1850), 175, ascribes them to the year 1240.

[2] For the influence of these statutes, see C. R. Cheney, *English Synodalia of the Thirteenth Century* (Oxford 1941), 55–6, 82–4; *idem*, 'The Earliest English Diocesan Statutes', *EHR*, LXXV (1960), 1–29. As early as 1230 they had reached the South of France: L. de Lacger, 'Statuts synodaux inédits du diocèse d'Albi au XIII siècle', *Rev. hist. de droit français et étranger*, VI (1927), 434 ff. Not long after, they were known in Portugal: I. da Rosa Pereira, 'Manuscritos do direito canónico existentes em Portugal', *Arquivo histórico da Madeira*, XIII (1962–3), 36 ff.

As Artonne has remarked, the production of a *liber sinodalis* was regarded by contemporaries as *l'oeuvre capitale d'un évêque*.[1] And Archbishop Pedro was, in almost every respect, a paragon. But it cannot be claimed that he was universally successful. For the Spanish clergy were less amenable to discipline than they were attached to their girl-friends;[2] and the stern penalties which John of Abbeville had prescribed for *clerici concubinarii*—to wit, excommunication and suspension—evidently held no terrors for them. In a bull addressed to the province of Tarragona in 1245 Innocent IV lamented the ineffectiveness of ecclesiastical sanctions.[3] The clergy of Aragon seem to have been quite as indifferent to such threats as those of Bavaria at the same period: 'Non timebant tonitras et fulmina Romanorum, quia non darent pro ipsorum suspensionis et excommunicationis sententiis fabam.'[4] And if they ran any risk at all it was a calculated risk, for the automatic imposition of penalties of such gravity was bound to bring the public ministry of the Church to a grinding halt. Within three years of John of Abbeville's legation Gregory IX admitted as much when he empowered the Archbishop of Braga to absolve more than seventeen hundred illegitimate Portuguese clerics whom John's hard line had caused to be suspended,[5] and thereafter the popes vied with the Spanish clergy in whittling down the adamantine programme of the sometime papal legate.[6] Eventually, in June 1251, Innocent IV surrendered the Ark of the Covenant by conniving at clerical concubinage, for a consideration. In future the Spanish bishops were to fine the culprits, not suspend them. After all, there was no accounting for taste. It was left for them to

---

[1] A. Artonne, 'Le livre synodal de Lodève', *Bibliothèque de l'Ecole des Chartes*, CVIII (1949–50), 71.

[2] The strength of their determination may be inferred from the gloss in AC Barcelona, *Constituciones Synodales et Provinciales*, fo. 183r to the *Summa*'s explicit prohibition of the sharing of quarters with women 'nisi esset persona de qua nulla suspitio possit haberi': Nota quae mulieres permittuntur habitare cum sacerdotibus.

[3] AHN, 161/2: *Non absque dolore* (2 October 1245).

[4] Cited C. C. Bayley, *The Formation of the German College of Electors in the Mid-Thirteenth Century* (Toronto 1949), 10.

[5] In July 1232: *Reg. Greg. IX*, 829.

[6] Linehan, Ph.D. diss., 77–9.

decide, and, quite incidentally, the papal surgeon of twenty years before was written off as a heavy-handed butcher.[1]

Doubtless this was realistic. But it was not reform. Indeed it undermined the whole programme of reform which Innocent III's slavish interpreter, John of Abbeville, had preached. And the death, one month later, of John's faithful follower, Pedro de Albalat, dealt a further, fatal, blow. Still, while he had lived, Pedro had created something of an impresson. And he cast a long shadow, even after his death. As Argaiz noted in the seventeenth century, his tally of councils beat the previous, Visigothic, record.[2] Even Matthew Paris had a word to say about him, on account of his hawkish intervention at the Lyons Council.[3]

Matthew may also have heard of Pedro's opposite number in Castile, for the Archbishop of Toledo, Rodrigo Ximénez de Rada, had been present at the great Christian victory at Las Navas de Tolosa in 1212. But there the similarity ended. Rodrigo (1208–47) was the very antithesis of Pedro. At the time of his translation to Toledo from the see of Osma Innocent III had expressed the hope that he would prove himself a stout champion of *libertas ecclesiastica*.[4] But Innocent and his successors were to be disappointed. When, for example, Rodrigo's own suffragan and successor at Osma, Bishop Melendo, called on him for assistance against King Fernando III in 1218, after the monarch had deprived the prelate of certain property, the Archbishop unerringly chose the line of least resistance and sent a pathetically lame letter to the executors of the papal mandate in Melendo's favour, asking them to release him from the awkward task of reading the King a lecture, 'quia sicut nobis ita aliis poteritis demandare'.[5]

---

[1] 'Cum per varietatem personarum et etiam regionum poenae sint proinde variandae, ne ad instar imperiti medici omnium curare occulos uno colyrio videremur, uti vobis qui conditionem personarum et locorum vestrae provintiae melius scire potestis...committimus...quatenus...clericis poenas et concubinis predictis per sententias memoratas impositas in poenas alias...commutetis, eiusdem legati sententias auctoritate apostolica postmodum relaxantes'; Tejada y Ramiro, VI, 49.   [2] G. de Argaiz, *Soledad Laureada*, II (Madrid 1675), fol. 53v.

[3] *Chronica Majora*, ed. H. R. Luard, *RS*, IV, 540.

[4] D. Mansilla, *La documentación pontificia hasta Inocencio III (965–1216)* (Rome 1955), no. 398.

[5] J. Loperráez, *Descripción histórica del Obispado de Osma*, III (Madrid 1788), 57.

If ever Rodrigo faced the acid test, this was it. And his abject failure was typical of his entire archiepiscopal career. His tendency to kowtow to the King goes part of the way towards explaining why it was that we find no Castilian parallel either for the Alcañiz Council of 1250 at which Pedro de Albalat excommunicated Teobaldo I of Navarre for having harassed the Bishop of Pamplona,[1] or indeed for any of Pedro's councils. With a single possible exception,[2] there is no sign of any council in the province of Toledo during Rodrigo's thirty-nine years as its leader. Not that he lacked for reminders: apart from John of Abbeville, both Honorius III (in no uncertain terms) and Gregory IX prompted him to do his duty.[3] Far, however, from shining as a defender of *libertas ecclesiastica*, Rodrigo it was who permitted the foundations of royal control of the Castilian Church, the notorious *Patronato Real*, to be laid by failing to oppose Fernando III's appropriation of the Church's tithe-income.[4] The reforming reputation upon which his various biographers and hagiographers have insisted is quite spurious.[5] He was the last person to hold councils if his king disapproved of assemblies which, as Pedro de Albalat was demonstrating over the border, might be turned against the King himself. And that the King did indeed disapprove of and prohibit the holding of councils was explicitly stated by the Castilian bishops in a memorandum on the conduct of Fernando's son and heir, Alfonso the

---

[1] Tejada y Ramiro, VI, 47–8; J. Goñi Gaztambide, 'Los obispos de Pamplona del siglo XIII', *Príncipe de Viana*, XVIII (1957), 97 ff.

[2] In 1221 Rodrigo referred to certain disciplinary instructions 'secundum quod in concilio apud Guadalfaxaram a nobis olim fuerat constitutum': D. de Colmenares, *Historia de la insigne Ciudad de Segovia* (Segovia 1637), 188. Though the statutes of this Guadalajara Council have never been unearthed, Rodrigo's biographers have made much of them. M. Ballesteros Gaibrois, for example, regards them as 'la mejor prueba del celo desplegado por el prelado español': *Don Rodrigo Jiménez de Rada* (Barcelona 1936), 107.

[3] AC Toledo, I.5 A.1.1: publ. D. Mansilla, *La documentación pontificia de Honorio III* (Rome 1965), no. 246; I.6.C.1.21: bull *Parum est* (13 February 1229).

[4] D. Mansilla, *Iglesia Castellano-leonesa y Curia Romana en los tiempos del rey San Fernando* (Madrid 1945), 57.

[5] See, in addition to Ballesteros Gaibrois, E. Estella Zalaya, *El fundador de la Catedral de Toledo* (Toledo 1926), V, 93; J. Gorosterratzu, *Don Rodrigo Jiménez de Rada* (Pamplona 1925), 220–2.

Wise, which they dared to submit to Pope Nicholas III in 1279.[1]

Partly in the expectation of rich rewards of reconquered territory—an expectation in which they seem to have been largely disappointed[2]—the Castilian bishops allowed themselves to become totally identified with the royal court, with the result that when that court collapsed they were, literally, crushed. In 1258 the palace of Segovia caved in. Several prelates were injured; the King escaped unscathed.[3] And, as they dusted themselves down, they cannot have been indifferent to the much happier condition of their episcopal brethren next-door, in Aragon, who in the previous year had been granted by their king very generous exemptions from the terms of the strict sumptuary legislation then in force.[4] Indeed it is certain that they were not indifferent. For in that year, 1257, ten years after the death of Archbishop Rodrigo, they had declared jointly that thereafter they would hold two provincial councils annually. But this was no more than a declaration, and it came to nothing. It is, manifestly, not proof (as it has been alleged to be) of an already established flourishing conciliar tradition akin to that of the Aragonese Church.[5] Moreover, when Alfonso the Wise regained the political initiative which, momentarily in 1257, he had lost, their hands were tied again. Twenty-two years later they informed Nicholas III of their difficulties. But yet again their efforts were abortive.

The relationship of Church and (if one dare use the word here) State which obtained in Castile may not have been of Archbishop Rodrigo's making. Still, without reducing the issue to one of personalities, it may be said that he made no effort to change it. And his failure to hold councils was one very important aspect of his neglect. We find no *Summa Septem Sacramentorum* in Castile, and no Dominican bishops, as we do in Aragon. What we do find

---

[1] *Reg. Nich. III*, 743.

[2] I hope to substantiate this on another occasion.

[3] *Chronicón de Cardeña*, in *España Sagrada*, XXIII, 374; Gil de Zamora, 'Biografías de San Fernando y de Alfonso el Sabio', ed. F. Fita, *BRAH*, v (1884), 322–3.

[4] Tejada y Ramiro, III, 386.

[5] Such was the interpretation of F. Fita who published the episcopal declaration 'Concilio de Alcalá de Henares (15 enero 1257)', *BRAH*, x (1887), 151–9.

is a captive Church, and a poor Church which rejected the Dominicans and treated them as carpet-baggers on account of that poverty. St Dominic's fate during the decades after his death was that of a prophet in his own country.[1]

This general conclusion may not be readily acceptable to historians of medieval Spain. For it is a commonplace of the subject that churchmen were synonymous with prosperity and influence, and that—in the words of one historian—in the thirteenth century the clergy 'reached the zenith of its social power and prestige'.[2] If, however, a rather longer view be taken it may be possible to dovetail this account with what has been discovered, by study and experience, of the subject from Visigothic to modern times. The view has quite recently been expressed that from the sixth century to the twentieth Spain's rulers have been so many dummies manipulated by the priests. In this interpretation Franco is seen as only the latest in a succession of Dalai Lamas.[3]

It is difficult to reconcile this view with what we read in the newspapers about the Spanish Church now. It rather looks as if the dummy has developed a mind of its own, or—to change the metaphor—as if, for the first time, the tail is wagging the dog.

But, in fact, there is nothing new about this. Scholars have been hard at work for years demolishing the view that the Church held the whip-hand in Visigothic and Counter-Reformation Spain. It is becoming increasingly clear that neither the Roman pope nor the Spanish bishops have ever deflected the Catholic monarchs far from the course of their political ambitions. Dr Lynch has substantiated George Borrow's observation that 'love of Rome had ever slight influence over her—that is, Spain's—policy' and concluded that 'the domination of the Church by the Crown was probably more complete in Spain in the sixteenth century than in

---

[1] See P. A. Linehan, '*Ecclesie non Mittentes*: the thirteenth-century background', *Studia Albornotiana*, II (1969), forthcoming.

[2] S. Sobrequés Vidal, *La época del patriciado urbano* (*Historia social y económica de España y América*, ed. J. Vicens Vives, II, Barcelona 1957), 164. Similarly, C. Sánchez-Albornoz, *España: un enigma histórico*, I (Buenos Aires 1956), 356, 358, 687; J. H. Elliott, *Imperial Spain 1469–1716* (London 1963), 20; R. S. Smith in *Cambridge Economic History of Europe*, I, ed. M. M. Postan (2nd ed. Cambridge 1966), 433.

[3] Eduardo Romero, *Tiranía y teocracia en el siglo XX* (Mexico 1958), esp. 18, 23, 42.

any other part of Europe, including Protestant countries with an Erastian system'.[1] And strikingly similar conclusions have been reached by students of sixth-century Spain, in the light of a reassessment of the balance of power within the Visigothic Councils. 'The Church by this time had virtually become a department of the State.'[2] 'Of the two parties to the councils, the Crown and the Church, the Crown was dominant and the Church was subordinate...It was the kings, not the bishops, who governed Spain and with it the Spanish Church.'[3] When, therefore, Américo Castro maintains that the Visigothic theocracy 'is regarded by many as the logical antecedent of the Spain of Philip II' he is perfectly right, but right for quite the wrong reasons.[4] Spain's rulers were far from helpless. No mute, inglorious Dalai Lamas they!

A reinterpretation of the ecclesiastical history of medieval Castile along the lines suggested would, therefore, simply show that San Fernando and Alfonso the Wise followed the example set by Reccared after the Third Toledo Council of 589 and foreshadowed that of Philip II three hundred years later. Dogmatism would be out of place here, and the question is perhaps best left wide open. Still, it may be appropriate to finish on a positive note, by drawing attention to one element within this continuous theme.

The phenomenon of the tail wagging the dog is certainly no novelty. Honorius III complained about a similar—and in his view, unnatural—practice in the course of the letter which he sent to Archbishop Rodrigo and his suffragans in 1219. They were, he said, dumb dogs;[5] and though there are contemporary parallels which suggest that the epithet was commonly employed in denunciations of episcopal waywardness,[6] it is nevertheless interest-

[1] *The Bible in Spain* (Everyman's ed.), 3; J. Lynch, 'Philip II and the Papacy', *TRHS*, 5th ser., II (1961), 24.
[2] J. N. Hillgarth, 'Coins and Chronicles: propaganda in sixth-century Spain and the Byzantine background', *Historia*, xv (1966), 500.
[3] E. A. Thompson, *The Goths in Spain* (Oxford 1969), 281–2.
[4] *The Structure of Spanish History*, trans. E. L. King (Princeton 1954), 68.
[5] Mansilla, *Documentación pontificia de Honorio III*, no. 246.
[6] In particular, James of Vitry, *Historia Occidentalis* (Duaci 1597), 270–5: *De negligentia et peccatis prelatorum*; and the anti-episcopal tirade of the Spaniard,

ing to note that this was neither the first nor the last time that the biblical tag was applied to the Spanish bishops. Honorius I had said exactly the same about them in the 630s,[1] and in July 1937, in a very different context, it was cited again. In their collective letter to the bishops of the rest of the world, the Spanish bishops justified their choice of sides in the Civil War by insisting that they could not have remained silent without incurring 'the terrible title of *canes muti* with which the Prophet censured those who, though in duty bound to speak out, nevertheless remained silent in the face of injustice'.[2]

It was an epithet which the rather less conscientious bishops of Castile seven hundred years before did not mind having applied to them. But Honorius III, on their behalf, did mind; and it was not the least of his complaints that by having failed to hold councils in the four years that had elapsed since the Lateran Council they had laid themselves open both to the charge and its consequences.

Diego García, written the year before Honorius's letter: *Planeta*, ed. M. Alonso (Madrid 1943), 405. Both mention *canes muti* and many more of the biblical phrases used by the Pope.

[1] *PL*, LXXX, col. 668. Cf. Thompson, 185.

[2] Cardenal Isidro Gomá y Tomás, *Pastorales de la Guerra de España* (Madrid 1955), 154.

THE BYZANTINE REACTION TO THE
SECOND COUNCIL OF LYONS, 1274

by DONALD M. NICOL

O N Friday 6 July 1274 the reunion of the Greek and Roman Churches was solemnly proclaimed at the Second Council of Lyons. It was a great occasion, and an occasion of great rejoicing for Pope Gregory X who had convened the assembly. In some ways the Greeks, or the Byzantines, had responded to his invitation rather more satisfactorily than his own people. For of the thirteen crowned heads of western Europe who had been invited to attend only one had found it possible to accept. But the Byzantine Emperor from distant Constantinople had sent his own representative in the person of his Grand Logothete George Akropolites; and with him had come a former Patriarch of Constantinople, Germanos, and the Metropolitan of Nicaea, Theophanes. The Council had opened at Lyons in May 1274. But the Byzantine legates had been delayed by shipwreck on their long journey, and it was not until 24 June that they reached their destination. They were welcomed with the kiss of peace by the Pope and all his cardinals and presented the sealed documents that they had brought with them from the Emperor Michael Palaiologos and from the Byzantine clergy. Five days later, on the Feast of Saints Peter and Paul, the Pope celebrated Mass in the cathedral at Lyons. The Epistle and the Gospel were read in Greek as well as in Latin. Thomas Aquinas had been commissioned, perhaps rather tactlessly, to deliver a speech on the errors of the Greeks. But he died on his way to the Council; and so the Byzantine legates were spared the shame of having to listen to the catalogue of heresies and faults that they were supposed to be abjuring. But Cardinal Bonaventura preached a sermon on the unity of Christendom. The Roman form of the Creed was then recited, first in Latin and then in Greek. The Greek clergy were

D. M. NICOL

required to repeat the offensive doctrine on the Procession of the Holy Spirit three times.[1]

The formal declaration of Union came a week later at the fourth session of the Council. After a sermon delivered by Peter, Cardinal Bishop of Ostia, the Pope recalled the three objects of the Council. He then read out Latin translations of the letters from the Byzantine Emperor and the Orthodox bishops which were the tangible evidence of the fact that the second of those objects, the submission of the Greek Church to Rome, had now happily been accomplished. The Grand Logothete Akropolites swore an oath in the name of his Emperor to remain obedient to the Church of Rome, to respect the primacy of the Holy See, and to abide by the Roman version of the Creed. The Pope then recited the *Te Deum* and preached another short sermon; and the ceremony concluded with a further recitation of the Creed led by the Pope in Latin and by the ex-Patriarch in Greek. Again the Byzantine legates were asked to repeat the words *Qui ex Patre Filioque procedit* twice. The pleasing story that the Bishop of Nicaea kept his mouth shut at this point in the proceedings has now, alas, to be rejected as a myth. The recent edition of the full text of the *Ordinatio Concilii Generalis Lugdunensis* reveals that this tale depends, like so many of the *divertimenti* in the history books, on a faulty manuscript reading. Nevertheless, it would not be untrue to say that the only moments when the dragon of theology reared its head at the Council of Lyons were during the repetition by the Greeks, five times in all, of the word *Filioque* in the Creed. Nothing shows more clearly that this was the biggest item on the agenda. But there was no agenda, and the item was never discussed.[2]

[1] The standard work on the Second Council of Lyons is now that by B. Roberg, *Die Union zwischen der griechischen und der lateinischen Kirche auf dem II. Konzil von Lyon (1274)* (Bonner Historische Forschungen, 24), Bonn 1964 [Cited hereafter as Roberg, *Union*]. Other recent accounts may be found in S. Runciman, *The Sicilian Vespers*, Cambridge 1958, and D. J. Geanakoplos, *Emperor Michael Palaeologus and the West*, Cambridge, Mass., 1959.

[2] See now A. Franchi, *Il Concilio II di Lione (1274) secondo la Ordinatio Concilii Generalis Lugdunensis, Edizione del testo e note* (Studi e Testi Francescani, 33), Rome 1965. The tale about Theophanes keeping his mouth shut during the recitation of the *Filioque* was accepted by A. Fliche, 'Le problème oriental au

In the course of his sermon at the fourth session of the Council, Pope Gregory told of his joy and gratitude that the Greeks had returned to the obedience of the Roman Church of their own free-will and without seeking any material advantage or reward. This last statement, if it did not come from the mouth of a Pope, might be classed as a misrepresentation of the truth. Even the recorder of the Acts of the Council, in a rare burst of critical commentary, qualifies the Pope's remark about the disinterested motives of the Greeks with the words 'de quo multum dubitabatur'—about which there was much doubt.[1] For Pope Gregory, even in his hour of joy, can hardly have forgotten the political considerations that prompted the Byzantine Emperor to his action. It is not my intention to describe the political context in which the Union of Lyons was effected. The facts are well known. The Byzantine Empire, restored in 1261 after the disastrous episode of the Fourth Crusade and the so-called Latin Empire of Constantinople, lived under a mounting threat of invasion by the western powers interested in retrieving their losses in the eastern Mediterranean. The Emperor Michael VIII Palaiologos did what he could to avert the danger by diplomatic and military measures. But he had the wit to see that the ultimate deterrent to his Latin enemies lay in the moral authority and the restraining influence of the Pope.

The Popes were inclined to feel that the Byzantines, so long as they clung to their heresies and remained in schism from Rome, were among those in need of a crusade, if only for the salvation of their own souls. The fear that a western imperialist venture

---

second concile oecuménique de Lyon (1274)', *Orientalia Christiana Periodica*, XIII (*Miscellanea G. de Jerphanion*, 1947), 483. It has been repeated by, e.g., S. Runciman, *Sicilian Vespers*, 165, and by D. M. Nicol, 'The Greeks and the Union of the Churches: The preliminaries to the Second Council of Lyons, 1261–1274', *Medieval Studies presented to A. Gwynn, S.J.*, ed. by J. A. Watt and others, Dublin 1961, p. 477 and note 69. Cf. Roberg, *Union*, p. 145 n. 51. But see Franchi, *op. cit.*, p. 91 lines 296 f., where the corrupt text of previous editions of the *Ordinatio* is restored to read: 'Quo completo, patriarcha Grecorum incepit similiter: *Credo in unum Deum*, in greco; quod per cum, et archiepiscopum Nic[enum]...' instead of 'Archiepiscopum Nicosiensem'. Cf. *ibid.* p. 39.

[1] Franchi, *Il Concilio II di Lione*, p. 86 lines 246–9: 'et dicens (dominus papa) qualiter, contra opinionem quasi omnium, Greci libere veniebant ad obedientiam Romane Ecclesie, profitendo fidem; et recognoscendo primatum ipsius; nichilque temporale petendo, de quo multum dubitabatur'.

directed against Constantinople might be glorified with the name of a holy war became very real when Charles of Anjou took over the Kingdom of Naples and Sicily in 1266. For Charles was the Pope's champion, and he was well placed and eager to mount an attack on the Byzantine Empire across the Adriatic Sea. The Emperor Michael VIII had seen the danger coming. He had tried to forestall it by suggesting to the Pope that talks might be resumed on the re-union of the Greek and Roman Churches. It was in fact the Byzantine Emperor and not the Pope who first proposed that the matter might be discussed at a council of the Church. For he knew that by removing the schism he would remove the only moral pretext for a crusade against his Empire. No Pope would give his blessing to an attack on a Christian ruler who had shown himself willing to repent of his errors and return to the fold.[1]

But in the course of the years before 1274 the matter went much further than the Emperor Michael had ever envisaged or intended. He discovered that the Union of the Churches could not be achieved in a day. His own people, and especially the Orthodox bishops and monks, warned him that they would follow him only so far in the way of making concessions to the Latins. But as long as Charles of Anjou was at hand and ready to repeat the experiment of the Fourth Crusade, the Byzantine Emperor saw no alternative to accepting the conditions of Union laid down by the Papacy. Such were the political and military pressures under which the Union of Lyons was achieved in 1274. They give the lie to Pope Gregory's claim that the Greeks had come back to the fold of Rome voluntarily and without hope of any material compensation. But the claim itself is instructive. For it illustrates the fact that, while the Union of Lyons was a spiritual triumph for Pope Gregory, it was a diplomatic triumph for the Emperor Michael. Charles of Anjou was so cross about it that he bit the top off his sceptre.[2]

[1] For Michael VIII's dealings with Pope Urban IV see Roberg, *Union*, 36–52; Geanakoplos, *Emperor Michael*, 139 f., 175 f.
[2] This curious anecdote about the behaviour of Charles of Anjou is related independently by the Byzantine historian George Pachymeres and by the Italian chronicler Bartolomaeo of Neocastro, although they refer to different

The Byzantine clergy and people reacted no less violently. The Emperor Michael Palaiologos had enemies nearer home than Charles of Anjou. There were those, notably in Asia Minor where the Empire had survived in exile after the Fourth Crusade, who looked on him as a usurper who had deliberately excluded the rightful heir to the throne. It was a fact that Michael had ignored the hereditary claims of the house of Laskaris. It was a scandal that he had secured his own position as Emperor by blinding the young John Laskaris. The Patriarch Arsenios had refused to countenance the crime and excommunicated the Emperor. It had taken Michael three years to get rid of Arsenios and appoint another Patriarch of Constantinople in the person of Germanos III, the same who was later to be sent to the Council of Lyons. But Germanos too had refused to absolve him of his crime; and he too had had to be levered out of office. Not until the very end of 1266 did Michael find a Patriarch who was prepared to admit him back into the Orthodox Church. He was a monk called Joseph.[1] Thus for the

occasions. Pachymeres, *De Michaele Palaeologo*, ed. I. Bekker, Bonn 1835, v, 26: 1, p. 410 lines 4–8: ἑώρων οὖν ἐκεῖνον (τὸν κάρουλον) ὁσημέραι τῶν ποδῶν τοῦ πάπα προκυλινδούμενον, καὶ ἐς τοσοῦτον ταῖς μανίαις συνισχήμενον ὥστε καὶ τὸ ἀνὰ χεῖρας σκῆπτρον...ὀδοῦσιν ἐκ μανίας καταφαγεῖν...Bartolomaeo of Neocastro, *Historia Sicula*, ed. G. Paladino, in L. A. Muratori, *Rerum Italicarum Scriptores*, XIII, 3 (1921), 22: 'iracundia fervidus, dentibus frendet, rodens robur, quod in manu tenebat'.

[1] The affair of the deposition of Arsenios is told in some detail by Pachymeres, *De Michaele Palaeologo*, IV, 3: 1, pp. 257–71. The final proceedings against him were instituted on the Akathistos Feast, 7 April 1264; and he was deposed at the end of May 1264. There was then a vacancy of one year in the Patriarchate of Constantinople, until the election of Germanos III on 25 May 1265. Germanos was deposed on 14 September 1266, to be succeeded by Joseph I on 28 December 1266. The chronology of the patriarchates of Arsenios and Germanos was established by I. Sykoutres, Συνοδικὸς Τόμος τῆς ἐκλογῆς τοῦ πατριάρχου Γερμανοῦ τοῦ Γ΄, Ἐπετηρὶς Ἑταιρείας Βυζαντινῶν Σπουδῶν, IX (1932), 178–212. His conclusions seem to have passed unnoticed by some subsequent authorities, e.g., G. Ostrogorsky, *History of the Byzantine State*, 2nd English ed., Oxford 1968, 461. But see now V. Laurent, 'La chronologie des patriarches de Constantinople au XIIIᵉ S. (1208–1309)', *Revue des études byzantines*, XXVII (1969), 142–4. On the career of the Patriarch Joseph, who is commemorated as a confessor in the Orthodox Calendar on 30 October, see the article by L. Petit in *Dictionnaire de Théologie Catholique*, VIII, 1541–2; H.-G. Beck, *Kirche und theologische Literatur im byzantinischen Reich*, Munich 1959, 676. Like some other notable anti-unionists Joseph came from the monastery of Mount Galesios near Ephesos.

first five years of his reign Michael VIII was denied the sacraments of his own Church and even forbidden to set foot in St Sophia. Any other Emperor in this situation would have been highly unpopular in Constantinople. But the people of the capital, recently liberated from foreign rule, had never known any other Emperor; and for the most part they were willing to overlook the methods by which he had reached his throne.

In the provinces, however, people were not so forgiving. The brave Patriarch Arsenios, who had defied his Emperor on a matter of moral principle, had a great following; and for long after his death Byzantine society was troubled by a deviationist party, a church within the Church, calling themselves the Arsenites. Many of them were monks, who generally represented the most conservative and extreme element in the Byzantine Church. Michael VIII was therefore unpopular enough with a large and influential section of his subjects, without having to persuade them to sink their prejudices against the Roman Church. The ways in which he tried to do so are narrated in some detail by the Byzantine historian George Pachymeres. The unity of the Church was, of course, an axiom and an ideal for the Orthodox no less than for the Catholics. But they saw no reason why they should be required to change or mend their ways to suit conditions laid down by the Popes. For in the Byzantine view it was the Popes who had led the Roman Church into innovations for which there was no warrant in the canons of the Councils or the Fathers. It was unfortunate for the harassed Emperor Michael that it was the Popes who held the whip hand with regard to Charles of Anjou. Pachymeres describes the Emperor's dilemma and the lengths to which he went to present to his people the idea of Union with Rome on Rome's terms. He explained to the Patriarch and his synod that the Empire's very existence was at stake and that there was no other way of averting disaster. The Popes made many demands, but ultimately they could be reduced to three mere formalities: commemoration of the Pope's name in the diptychs of Constantinople; acknowledgement of his right of appellate jurisdiction; and recognition of the Primacy of the Holy See. No harm could possibly come to the Orthodox faith from paying lip-service to these conditions. Rome, after all, was separated from Constantinople by a vast expanse of sea which no Pope was likely to traverse in order to exert his authority.[1]

The Emperor therefore proposed that his bishops should practise that principle or talent for compromise which the Byzantines were wont to call *oikonomia*, or 'economy'; in other words they should make a slight concession to circumstances, using their heads rather than their hearts, lest worse evil befall.[2] Above all, the Emperor tried to steer their thoughts away from the deep waters of the theological and doctrinal issues, which were so dear to the Byzantine mind. But in this he failed. For the bishops knew well enough that the terms and conditions of Union stipulated by the Popes were by no means confined to mere formalities and questions of protocol. Pope Gregory X, who had initiated the Council in 1272 and invited the Emperor to attend it, was certainly more understanding of the Orthodox position than some of his predecessors. He was almost as anxious to secure peace in the world as peace in the Church; and he was even prepared to make some small concessions on his own account. In the end, however, the Orthodox would have to be brought to accept not only the Roman form of the Creed, but also many alien and distasteful forms of doctrine and ritual. For they would have to adopt Rome's ruling on such old and fundamental points of controversy as the *Filioque* and the use of unleavened bread in the sacrament; they would have to accept a definition of the Pope's Primacy 'cum potestatis plenitudine', which was far beyond their comprehension;

---

[1] Pachymeres, *De Michaele Palaeologo*, v, 12, 18: 1 pp. 374–6, 386–7. Nikephoros Gregoras, *Historia Byzantina*, ed. L. Schopen, Bonn 1829–30, v, 2: 1, pp. 125–7.

[2] The Emperor defined the matter as *oikonomia* not *kainotomia*, 'compromise' and not 'innovation'. Gregoras, *Historia Byzantina*, v, 2: 1, p. 126 lines 17–18, p. 127 lines 9–11: οἰκονομίας δ' ἐστιν ἔμφρονος, ἀνάγκης κατεπειγούσης ζημιωθῆναι μικρὸν κέρδους εἵνεκα μείζονος ('*Oikonomia* is the policy of a prudent man, to suffer a small loss for the sake of a greater advantage when under pressure of necessity'). Cf. Pachymeres, *De Michaele Palaeologo*, v, 18: 1, p. 387 lines 8–14, where the Emperor recalls the many 'economies' which the Fathers of the Church had made for its benefit, and even cites the Incarnation as an instance of such *oikonomia*. On the principle of *oikonomia* in general see D. J. Geanakoplos, 'Church and State in the Byzantine Empire: A Reconsideration of the Problem of Caesaropapism', in *Byzantine East and Latin West: Two Worlds of Christendom in Middle Ages and Renaissance*, Oxford 1966, p. 74 and note 58.

and they would have to subscribe to a novel doctrine of the after-life called Purgatory, which they had hardly even heard of.[1]

It is remarkable that any Byzantine delegation ever went to the Council of Lyons at all. For those in favour of conceding any points to the Latins were always outnumbered. The opposition centred at first on a respected theologian called John Bekkos, who was archivist of St Sophia. Bekkos expressed the most moderate and polite form of the Orthodox objection to Union with Rome. In his view the Latins were technically in heresy, even though they had never been condemned or anathematized by any Council of the Church. Such statements took the matter into the realm of theology, which the Emperor was at pains to avoid. He had Bekkos arrested and put in prison.[2] The opposition then rallied round the Patriarch Joseph whose opinions, though equally moderate, commanded a wider audience. In June 1273 Joseph felt bound to point out to the faithful that pressure was being put upon them to connive at the innovations that the Latins had made in the Creed; and he reminded the Emperor that, in the Christian tradition, such questions could only be decided by an oecumenical council. The Patriarch of Constantinople, even to please his Emperor, could not act on his own in so important a matter; he must consult the opinion of his colleagues in the other patriarchates of Alexandria, Antioch, and Jerusalem.[3]

[1] On the policy of Pope Gregory X towards Byzantium see Roberg, *Union*, 95–102. But the basic requirements for the 'return' of the Greeks to the Church of Rome remained those spelt out in detail for Michael VIII by Pope Clement IV in his letter of 4 March 1267. A. L. Tautu, *Acta Urbani IV, Clementis IV, Gregorii X (1261–1276)*, Pontificia commissio ad redigendum CIC orientalis, Fontes, ser. III, vol. V, 1, Vatican City 1953, no. 23, pp. 61–9. Cf. Geanakoplos, *Emperor Michael*, 201–3; Roberg, *Union*, 58–64.

[2] Pachymeres, *De Michaele Palaeologo*, v, 12:1, pp. 376–8. Gregoras, *Historia*, v, 2: 1, pp. 127–8.

[3] The Patriarch Joseph issued two anti-unionist documents in 1273. One took the form of an *Apologia* setting out the Orthodox objections to negotiations with the Roman Church. It was drawn up by a commission headed by the monk Job Iasites and including the historian Pachymeres. The other, published in June 1273, was an encyclical containing a testament of loyalty to the Orthodox faith signed by most of the members of the Patriarch's synod. This too was composed with the help of Job Iasites and with the active encouragement of the Emperor's sister Eulogia. The Greek text of the *Apologia* is in J. Dräseke, 'Der Kircheneinigungsversuch des Kaisers Michael VIII. Paläologos', *Zeitschrift für*

The Emperor began to foresee that he might have to silence Joseph and appoint yet another Patriarch. It is a measure of his determination to push through the Union of Lyons that he was prepared even to contemplate such a step. For he had already run through two Patriarchs in the space of a few years. But Charles of Anjou was straining at the leash in Italy; and the Pope had yet to be convinced that the Byzantines were willing to fulfil the only conditions that would remove them from the crusading list. What the Emperor needed was a spokesman for the cause of Union who would lend it an air of respectability and counterbalance the statements of the Patriarch Joseph. He picked on John Bekkos, who was still under arrest. Bekkos was supplied with select passages from the Fathers to while away his hours in prison. He knew little or no Latin; but the passages were, where necessary, translated; and they were carefully chosen to illustrate the basic identity of belief between Orthodox and Catholics, particularly with regard to the Procession of the Holy Spirit. Bekkos had a scholarly turn of mind, and he enjoyed theology. He soon came to the conclusion that he had been over-hasty in condemning the Latins as heretics outright. Misguided they might be; and their approach to theology was deplorably materialistic. But in the prevailing political circumstances he came to feel that the Union of the Churches was permissible and desirable, so long as the rites and customs of the Orthodox Church remained unaffected. The Emperor then released Bekkos from prison and encouraged him to impart his findings to others.[1]

In this way an official unionist party was formed in opposition to the Patriarch Joseph and his supporters; and it became at last possible for the Emperor to send a hopeful reply to the Pope's invitation to a council to be held at Lyons. In January 1274 Joseph was confined to a monastery pending the outcome of that Council. It was agreed that, if Union were achieved, he would

---

wissenschaftliche Theologie, XXXIV (1891), 332–5. The encyclical is in V. Laurent, 'Le serment anti-latin du Patriarche Joseph Ier (Juin 1273)', *Echos d'Orient*, XXVI (1927), 396–407 (text and translation, 405–7). See Nicol, 'The Greeks and the Union of the Churches', 467–70.

[1] Pachymeres, *De Michaele Palaeologo*, V, 14: 1, pp. 380–4. Gregoras, *Historia*, V, 2: 1, pp. 128–30. Cf. Nicol, 'The Greeks and the Union of the Churches', 471–2.

either accept it or resign.[1] Two months later the Byzantine delegation left for France. They took with them the detailed profession of faith signed and sealed by the Emperor Michael and by his young son and heir Andronikos, and also a document of submission from some of the Orthodox bishops. So far as the Emperor was concerned no one could doubt that he was, or purported to be, a whole-hearted convert. But the submission of the Byzantine clergy was phrased in much more general terms, and it was hardly representative of the feeling of their Church. The document referred to the ceaseless striving of the Emperor to overcome the prejudices of his people; and the forty-odd bishops who signed it confined their remarks to somewhat ambiguous platitudes about the special position of the apostolic See of Rome. The crucial points of theology were deliberately and simply omitted. But, such was the spiritual optimism of Pope Gregory X and the diplomatic talent of Michael VIII, that the document had the desired effect. The Union was accomplished. The Patriarch Joseph resigned, and John Bekkos was appointed Patriarch in his place.[2]

The bishops had done well to warn the Pope that the Byzantine hostility to the Union was obstinate and to imply that the Emperor was unable to stifle it completely. For Pope Gregory's successors were gradually to discover that the Emperor's efforts to implement the terms of that Union after the event were never likely to succeed. Yet the Popes, who in other circumstances were so quick to condemn the practice of Caesaropapism, confidently expected the Emperor Michael to bully his people into adopting a course of action that was repugnant to their conscience. The more he bullied them the more they closed their ranks against him and denounced what they called his 'latinizing' policy. For the more

---

[1] Pachymeres, *De Michaele Palaeologo*, v, 17: 1, pp. 384–6.
[2] The Latin versions of Michael VIII's two letters of submission have been re-edited by Roberg, *Union*, Anhang 1, nos. 6 and 7, pp. 239–43, 243–7; cf. pp. 261–3 for a discussion of the transmission of the texts. For earlier editions of these documents and of the submission of Andronikos II, see F. Dölger, *Regesten der Kaiserurkunden des oströmischen Reiches*, III, Munich–Berlin 1932, nos. 2006, 2007, 2072. Cf. Nicol, 'The Greeks and the Union of the Churches', p. 477 and note 70. The Latin text of the submission of the Byzantine clergy has also been re-edited by Roberg, *Union*, Anhang 1, no. 5, pp. 235–9.

conservative among them felt every bit as strongly as the Popes about the practice of Caesaropapism.[1]

The most conservative element in Byzantine society was the Church. But it was conservative in a dynamic and not a static manner. Its members considered their inherited faith and doctrine to be worth conserving and worth protecting from the deviations and innovations that had gained currency in other branches of the Christian Church. An Emperor who suggested tampering with the Orthodox faith forfeited his title to be the elect of God, and therefore put his subjects in danger of losing God's special protection. Michael VIII had given his assurance that, whatever other concessions he might make to the Roman Church, he would never allow so much as one jot or one tittle of the Orthodox Creed to be changed.[2] But everyone knew that he himself had included the *Filioque* in his own profession of faith to the Pope; and everyone found out that the Byzantine bishops at Lyons had been obliged to recite the Creed in Roman style. The extremists in the Byzantine Church, or the zealots as they were called, thought that the Emperor had fallen into heresy. Even the moderates felt that he had pushed his people too far. For the methods that he employed to make the Union work raised the basic question of the nature and extent of imperial authority over the Church.

Byzantine lawyers and canonists had, in times past, made various pronouncements about the ideal relationship between Church and State. The Patriarch Photios in the ninth century had declared that the peace of the Emperor's subjects in things spiritual and things temporal depended upon the complete and harmonious co-operation of Empire and Church. The canonist Theodore Balsamon in the twelfth century had affirmed that the Emperor should serve his people both in soul and in body, but the Patriarch was concerned only with the welfare of their souls.[3] The emphasis

---

[1] This point is well made by Halina Evert-Kappesowa, 'Une page de l'histoire des relations byzantino-latines II: La fin de l'union de Lyon', *Byzantinoslavica*, XVI (1955), 301–2, 311–12.

[2] Pachymeres, *De Michaele Palaeologo*, v, 20: 1, p. 395 lines 7–16.

[3] The views of Photios, as expressed in the *Epanagoge* of Basil I and Leo VI, are translated in E. Barker, *Social and Political Thought in Byzantium*, Oxford 1957, p. 92, §8; those of Balsamon, *ibid.* p. 106. For other opinions see D. J.

varied; but there was a general understanding that Emperor and Patriarch, State and Church, somehow complemented each other and that neither could exist without the other. Canonists might concede that, since the Emperor had the last word in the election of a Patriarch, then he could also exercise the right to depose a Patriarch. But he must have valid reasons for doing so, and he ought not to make a habit of it. Michael VIII deposed three Patriarchs in the course of his reign, two because they refused to admit him back into the Church, the third, Joseph, because he refused to subscribe to the Union of Lyons. It is no wonder that the zealots in the Church regarded Michael as the enemy of all they stood for. The Arsenites, who upheld the principles for which the Patriarch Arsenios had suffered, refused to recognize either of his appointed successors. But in the circumstances of the Union of Lyons they joined forces with their enemies the Josephites, who remained loyal to the anti-unionist Patriarch Joseph. For both parties were agreed that the State could not dictate to the Church in matters of faith and doctrine; and they found a common enemy in the Emperor Michael VIII.[1]

In later years, when the Union was no more, John Bekkos, who had by then been sent into exile, recalled a time not of peace and concord but of bitterness and scandal. 'What can one say', he writes, 'when women and children still in the nursery, when men whose knowledge is limited to agriculture or manual labour cry criminal to anyone who so much as whispers about the Union of the Churches?' The situation reminded him of a celebrated passage in the writings of Gregory of Nyssa. Gregory had complained that it was impossible to go to the bakers or the barbers without getting involved in arguments about the relationship of the Son to the Father. Bekkos complains that 'children at school, women chatting over their distaffs and spindles, farmers and labourers, all of them now have only one subject in the forefront of their minds

Geanakoplos, 'Church and State', in *Byzantine East and Latin West, passim*; and for a late fourteenth-century interpretation see V. Laurent, 'Les droits de l'empereur en matière ecclésiastique. L'accord de 1380/82', *Revue des études byzantines*, XIII (1955), 5–20.

[1] Pachymeres, *De Michaele Palaeologo*, v, 23: 1, pp. 399–401.

and conversations—the Procession of the Holy Spirit from the Son'.[1]

No doubt the uneducated could not fully understand the theology of the Trinity. No doubt also that their interest in the matter was whipped up by mobs of fanatical monks and professional demonstrators, as the Byzantine historians admit.[2] But the principle at stake was, as they saw it, the nature of their Orthodox Creed. And all, zealots and moderates, literate and illiterate alike, were agreed that that Creed was unchangeable. For its form had been determined under the guidance of the Holy Spirit at the seven oecumenical councils of the Church; and, as the Patriarch Joseph had reminded his Emperor, nothing in it could be modified except by the consent of *all* the bishops of the Church in another oecumenical council. At its highest and most informed level the Byzantine objection to the Roman form of the Creed with the addition of the word *Filioque* was based not only on theological grounds. It was based on the fact that the addition had been sanctioned by the fiat of the Pope alone without reference to his colleagues in the Pentarchy of Patriarchs. No council of the whole Church had ever discussed or approved it.[3]

Any such innovation in the Creed was technically heresy. But almost all Byzantine theologians condemned the *Filioque* out of hand in any case. They thought that it upset the delicate balance between the three persons of the Trinity; and they felt that it was another instance of the distressing materialism of the Latin mentality, which was for ever trying to define the undefinable and to

---

[1] John Bekkos (Beccus), περὶ ἀδικίας..., *De Injustitia qua affectus est, a proprio throno ejectus* (or *De Depositione Sua Orationes*), I, in *PG*, CXLIII, col. 984.

[2] Gregoras, *Historia*, V, 2: I, pp. 127–8, goes so far as to say that, though there were those who gladly and bravely courted martyrdom for their principles, they were outnumbered by the rabble of sensation-mongers in the towns and villages, some of whom dressed themselves up in hair shirts and travelled around stirring up trouble and prophesying doom in parts of the world where they were safe from the Emperor's agents.

[3] This was one of the points that worried Demetrios Kydones during the process of his conversion from Orthodoxy to Catholicism. See his letter to Barlaam of Calabria, in *PG*, CLI, cols. 1291–2; and cf. D. M. Nicol, 'Byzantine requests for an oecumenical council in the fourteenth century', *Annuarium Historiae Conciliorum*, I (1969), 81.

pry into the mysteries of God.[1] The ordinary people of Byzantium were ready enough to believe the worst of the Latins after 1204. Many believed, and their Emperor had at first encouraged them to believe, that God had restored their Empire to them as a reward for their steadfast adherence to Orthodoxy during the years of Latin rule. Their Emperor seemed now to have forgotten his debt to God. But most of his people stubbornly declined to take his realistic point of view. No military or political threat to their material existence would frighten them into endangering their immortal souls by accepting a heretical doctrine. And so, as John Bekkos later lamented, 'men, women, old and young, all sorts and conditions of men thought this peace [in the Church] to be a division and not a union'.[2]

There were, of course, those who supported the Emperor. A few did so from conviction. Some did so because they agreed that the Union of the Churches was a necessary piece of 'economy' in the circumstances. And some saw their careers best served by swearing with their tongues and not their hearts. George Akropolites, the Grand Logothete, had in former days composed tracts against the errors of the Latins. But he was a conscientious civil servant. He changed his mind and was prepared to go to Lyons as his Emperor's deputy.[3] Nikephoros Choumnos, a younger man with a longer career to look forward to, discreetly accepted the Union

---

[1] The Byzantines were very fond of supporting their 'apophatic' view of theology with a famous passage from Gregory of Nazianzus about the futility of 'prying into the mysteries of God'. Gregory Nazianzenus, *Theologica quinta: De spiritu sancto*, in *PG*, XXXVI, col. 141. Cf. S. Runciman, *The Great Church in Captivity. A study of the Patriarchate of Constantinople from the eve of the Turkish conquest to the Greek war of independence*, Cambridge 1968, 93 f. The passage was quoted by the Greek-born Franciscan John Parastron who was sent to Constantinople by Pope Gregory X and acted as one of the interpreters at Lyons: Pachymeres, *De Michaele Palaeologo*, V, 11: 1, p. 372. It was quoted also by Nikephoros Gregoras in 1334, when he advised the Emperor Andronikos III against holding theological discussions with two papal legates in Constantinople: Gregoras, *Historia*, X, 8: 1, p. 513; and again by Nikephoros Choumnos in his *Epitaphios* on Theoleptos of Philadelphia, ed. J. F. Boissonade, *Anecdota Graeca*, V, Paris 1832, 191.

[2] Bekkos, περὶ ἀδικίας, in *PG*, CXLIII, cols. 952–3.

[3] The two treatises of George Akropolites against the Latins are printed in *Georgii Acropolitae Opera*, ed. A. Heisenberg, II, Leipzig 1913, 30–45, 45–66.

which he was later to denounce with such pious horror. So also did the historian George Pachymeres.[1] The learned George of Cyprus, who was later to become the Patriarch Gregory, was at first a unionist; though there was thought to be some excuse for one who had been brought up in the French Kingdom of Cyprus; and subsequently he made elaborate apologies for his lapse.[2] Men like Isaac, the Bishop of Ephesos, declared the Union to be acceptable as the kind of economy or compromise which the Church had often had to make as the lesser of two evils. Meletios, Bishop of Athens, said that he would support it only provided that he would not have to subscribe to the dogma or doctrine of the Latins.[3] Maximos Planoudes, one of the ablest scholars of Byzantium in the thirteenth century, shifted his ground with the prevailing theological wind. Planoudes had mastered the Latin language, a rare accomplishment in the Greek world of his day. He translated some of the works of Boethius and St Augustine into Greek; and his services as a Latinist were naturally of great value to the unionist cause. But he was not a theologian by choice. In the 1270s he turned out a little piece defending the addition of the *Filioque* to the Creed; ten years later, when the Union was no more, he turned out two more pieces denouncing it, by way of apology for his temporary aberration.[4]

The most interesting of the unionists, however, were the very few among the Byzantine clergy who supported the Emperor as a

[1] See J. Verpeaux, *Nicéphore Choumnos, homme d'état et humaniste byzantin (ca. 1250/1255–1327)*, Paris 1959. George Pachymeres, who died about 1310, wrote a short treatise on the Procession of the Holy Spirit (in *PG*, cxlii, cols. 924–9), in which he came down in favour of the formula derived from the writings of St John of Damascus, that the Spirit proceeded 'through' the Son, a formula which was anathema to many of the Orthodox. Pachymeres also subscribed for a time to the Union of Lyons, though he remained at heart an anti-unionist. Cf. Beck, *Kirche und theologische Literatur*, 679.

[2] On Gregory (George) of Cyprus see Verpeaux, *Nicéphore Choumnos*, 29–36; Beck, *Kirche und theologische Literatur*, 685–6.

[3] Pachymeres, *De Michaele Palaeologo*, VI, 23 : I, pp. 480–3.

[4] On the theological works of Planoudes see Beck, *Kirche und theologische Literatur*, 686–7, and V. Laurent, in *Dictionnaire de Théologie Catholique*, XII, 2247–52. Laurent believes that Planoudes was conscientiously inclined towards Catholicism, and that his anti-Latin tracts were composed under intimidation after the Union of Lyons had been denounced in 1283.

matter of conscience. They were more honest men than most of their contemporaries, and more honest than the Emperor himself. Prominent among them were Constantine Meliteniotes, who succeeded Bekkos as archivist of St Sophia, and the archdeacon George Metochites, the father of the more celebrated philosopher and statesman Theodore Metochites. Both took part in embassies to the West, and both clung to their convictions even after the Union had been repudiated. But both had succeeded in satisfying themselves that the Latin doctrine on the Procession of the Holy Spirit had some warrant in the Greek Fathers. It was therefore not an innovation or a technical heresy.[1] Another convinced unionist was Theoktistos, Metropolitan of Adrianople, a friend of Maximos Planoudes. He too remained faithful to his conversion, and when the Union was formally renounced in 1283 he was deposed from his see. He left Byzantium for Rome, and in 1310 he was to be found in Paris.[2]

The most notable and the most voluble convert, however, was John Bekkos. But Bekkos caused the Emperor much embarrassment by insisting that the Union could never be more than a pretence unless the Orthodox were brought to admit that it was permissible on theological grounds. Bekkos set himself to bring the whole matter into the open, and by so doing he stirred up the hornets' nest of theology, which is the last thing that the Emperor wanted. Things got so bad that he had to be forcibly restrained, and he retired to a monastery for a while.[3] But Bekkos also fell foul of the Emperor by urging him to be a little more merciful to the anti-unionists. For what people in after years remembered most vividly about the time when the Union was enforced were the persecutions and punishments meted out to its opponents by the Emperor. As Pachymeres writes, 'apart from the Emperor and

[1] On Constantine Meliteniotes (of Melitene) and George Metochites see Beck, *Kirche und theologische Literatur*, 683-4.

[2] V. Laurent, 'Un théologien unioniste de la fin du XIII⁰ siècle: Le Métropolite d'Andrinople Théoctiste', *Revue des études byzantines*, XI (*Mélanges Martin Jugie*, 1953), 187-96; Beck, *Kirche und theologische Literatur*, 684-5.

[3] There is much literature on the career of John Bekkos. See, e.g., the references in Beck, *Kirche und theologische Literatur*, 681-3; Nicol, *op. cit.*, *Medieval Studies presented to A. Gwynn*, 471-2; Roberg, *Union, passim*.

the Patriarch [Bekkos] and some of their close associates, everyone
loathed the peace, the more so as the Emperor tried to impose it
by force and with outrageous penalties'.[1]

The persecution of the anti-unionists in Byzantium increased in
proportion to the ever more exacting demands of the Popes after
the death of Gregory X in 1276. For Gregory's successors became
more and more sceptical about the nature of the Union which was
said to have been achieved at Lyons. The fact of its achievement
had been proclaimed at Constantinople in a ceremony in the
imperial chapel on 16 January 1275. But it was not until the winter
of 1276 that the Patriarch Bekkos was able to get together a synod
of bishops and laymen to ratify it. At the same time he excommunicated all who refused to accept it. In April and again in
July 1277 he presided over meetings of his synod at which these
declarations were confirmed. But Pope Nicholas III, who was
appointed in November 1277, was still not satisfied that everything possible was being done. Nicholas instructed his legates to
Constantinople to secure professions of the Roman faith from
every member of the Orthodox clergy individually and by word
of mouth. Worse still, the Emperor was to receive a Cardinal-
legate as papal plenipotentiary in Constantinople, and the clergy
were to beg the favour of absolution from Rome for their errors
and confirmation from Rome of their orders. These demands
went far beyond anything that the Emperor had expected; and to
the Byzantine Church they were intolerable. But he could not
now see his way to turn back. And when his people declined to be
persuaded he took to terrorizing them into acquiescence.[2]

The anti-unionists were declared to be traitors. Their property
was confiscated by the state. The prisons were crowded with
monks, priests and laymen arrested on evidence or suspicion of

[1] Pachymeres, *De Michaele Palaeologo*, VI, 30: 1, p. 505.
[2] Halina Evert-Kappesowa, 'Une page de l'histoire des relations byzantino-
latines. Le clergé byzantin et l'Union de Lyon (1274–1282)', *Byzantinoslavica*,
XIII (1952), 83 f., 89 f.; Geanakoplos, *Emperor Michael*, 305–17; Roberg, *Union*,
170 f., 196 f. For the chronology of these events, however, see now R.-J.
Loenertz, 'Mémoire d'Ogier, protonotaire, pour Marco et Marchetto nonces de
Michel VIII Paléologue auprès du Pape Nicholas III. 1278 printemps-été',
Orientalis Christiana Periodica, XXXI (1965), 374–408, especially 385–6, 400–2.

treason; many of the opposition leaders were blinded, mutilated, or banished; and the barren islands of the Aegean were peopled with political exiles. Refugees from the reign of terror in Constantinople found their way to the separatist Byzantine states in Trebizond or in northern Greece, whose rulers had never recognized Michael VIII as Emperor. They welcomed the victims with open arms. It suited their political purposes to be able to pose as the champions of true Orthodoxy against the heretical usurper in the capital. The ruler of Thessaly broadcast his reputation for Orthodoxy by convening an anti-unionist synod in the winter of 1276–7. It was attended by about a hundred monks and abbots with eight bishops, who almost unanimously anathematized the Pope, the Emperor and the Patriarch. The Emperor found it especially discouraging that so many of his own relatives were out of sympathy with his policy and even engaged in plotting against him. Among them was his favourite sister Eulogia, whose daughters were married to the rulers of Bulgaria and Epiros. The rulers of Epiros and Thessaly were excommunicated by the Patriarch John Bekkos. But their political manoeuvres were rather more worrying to the Emperor than the state of their souls. For both were known to be on the best of terms with Charles of Anjou.[1]

George Pachymeres has some horrifying tales to tell of the reign of terror in Constantinople. Manuel Holobolos, the public orator of the Great Church and a Professor at the University, had been one of the first to make an open protest against the Union of Lyons. He was submitted to a public flogging with ten others who had defied the Emperor and was then sent into exile.[2] Theodore Mouzalon, who was later to be made Grand Logothete, dis-

[1] Halina Evert-Kappesowa, 'La société byzantine et l'Union de Lyon' *Byzantino-slavica*, x (1949), 28–41. The anti-unionist council held in Thessaly is described in the report of the imperial protonotary Ogerius. Cf. V. Grumel, 'En Orient après le IIe Concile de Lyon', *Echos d'Orient*, xxiv (1925), 321–4, who dated the council to December 1277. See also D. M. Nicol, 'The Greeks and the Union of the Churches. The Report of Ogerius, Protonotarius of Michael VIII Palaiologos, in 1280', *Proceedings of the Royal Irish Academy*, 63, Sect. C, 1 (1962), 8; Geanakoplos, *Emperor Michael*, 309; Roberg, *Union*, 195. But see now Loenertz, 'Mémoire d'Ogier', 385–6, 400–1.
[2] Pachymeres, *De Michaele Palaeologo*, v, 20: 1, p. 394. Cf. Evert-Kappesowa, 'La société', 31–2.

obeyed an order to go to Rome on the Emperor's business; he was ordered to be flogged by his own brother until he submitted. Understandably, he was one of the prime movers in denouncing the Union as soon as the Emperor was dead.[1] George Moschabar, the Professor of New Testament exegesis at the patriarchal school, escaped the worst; for he published his numerous anti-Latin polemics anonymously and revealed their authorship only when the coast was clear. They included a Dialogue with a Dominican friar which, like almost all his works, deals with the Procession of the Holy Spirit.[2]

The Emperor went out of his way to make sure that the Pope and his legates would be aware of what was going on in Constantinople. The report that he sent back with the legates of Pope Nicholas III in 1278 itemizes many case-histories of persecution, for which the Emperor clearly expected to get credit as proof of his heroic efforts and his good intent. It is a most revealing document, for it names not simple monks or ignorant fanatics but several blue-blooded members of the Byzantine aristocracy.[3] The brothers Manuel and Isaac Raoul, who were closely related both to the Emperor Michael and to the Empress Theodora, were imprisoned and later blinded. Two of the Emperor's nephews suffered the same treatment for refusing to deny their faith. Andronikos Palaiologos, a cousin of the Emperor, who had held high military rank, died in prison. Such was the Emperor's anxiety to impress the Pope's legates that in 1279 he sent them on a conducted tour of the prison in which some of these noble offenders were being held. The legates were shown round by Isaac, Bishop of Ephesos, who was none too keen on the Union

---

[1] Pachymeres, *De Michaele Palaeologo*, VI, 26:1, p. 496. Theodore Mouzalon later wrote a treatise 'against the blasphemies of John Bekkos', under the name of Gregory of Cyprus, whose pupil he had been. Part of it is printed in *PG*, CXLII, cols. 290–300. Cf. Beck, *Kirche und theologische Literatur*, 680.

[2] On George Moschabar see V. Laurent, 'Un polémiste grec de la fin du XIIIe siècle. La vie et les oeuvres de Georges Moschabar', *Echos d'Orient*, XXVIII (1929), 129–58; *idem*, in *Dictionnaire de Théologie Catholique*, X, 2508–9; Beck, *Kirche und theologische Literatur*, 677–8.

[3] The definitive edition of and commentary upon the Report of Ogerius is now that of R.-J. Loenertz, in *Orientalia Christiana Periodica*, XXXI (1965), 374–408. See above, p. 129, n. 2.

himself. Manuel Raoul, who was chained in a dungeon, found the sight of the Bishop of Ephesos more than he could stomach; for he justly felt that it was all wrong that a bishop should be at liberty while so many laymen were languishing in gaol for fighting the bishop's cause. Manuel is said to have gathered up the chain that bound him and, edging forward as near as he could, to have launched it at the bishop with foul intent. He missed, for the weight of the chain dragged on his neck and pulled him back.[1]

The monks were the victims of particularly vicious treatment. Many of them were devoted Arsenites and so had prior cause to be hostile to the Emperor. But when it came to the defence of Orthodoxy against the Latins, their example and their appeal had more influence with the ordinary people than the reasoned arguments of intellectuals and theologians. Some of them were undoubtedly hypocrites or fanatics. Job Iasites, who was the chief adviser and right-hand man of the Patriarch Joseph, was the author of several of the anti-unionist encyclicals that emanated from the patriarchate, before he and his master were rounded up and sent into exile.[2] Some of them were saints and martyrs, or were to be accounted so by the Orthodox Church. Theoleptos, later to be made Bishop of Philadelphia and to become one of the father figures of Orthodox mystical speculation in the fourteenth century, was a young monk of twenty-five years old when the Union of Lyons took place. He left his monastery to go to Constantinople with the sole purpose of accusing the Emperor to his face of propagating heresy. He was arrested, beaten and thrown into prison.[3] Meletios of the monastery of Mount Galesios near

---

[1] Pachymeres, *De Michaele Palaeologo*, VI, 16: 1, pp. 459–60.

[2] On Job Iasites see Pachymeres, *De Michaele Palaeologo*, V, 14: 1, p. 380. Cf. L. Petit, in *Dictionnaire de Théologie Catholique*, VIII, 1487–9; Beck, *Kirche und theologische Literatur*, 677. M. Petta, 'Inni inediti di Iob monaco', *Bolletino della Badia greca di Grottaferrata*, N.S., XIX (1965), 81–139, is inclined to doubt the identification of Job Iasites, the polemicist, with Job the monk called Meles or Melias, the hymn-writer and hagiographer.

[3] One of the principal sources for the career of Theoleptos of Philadelphia is the *Epitaphios* on him composed by Nikephoros Choumnos, ed. Boissonade, *Anecdota Graeca*, V, Paris 1832, 183–245. This contains 'a brief refutation of the Latin dogma concerning the Procession of the Holy Spirit, against which he (Theoleptos) held out firmly and struggled most manfully'. See also J. Gouil-

Ephesos and his fellow-monk Galaktion also travelled to Constantinople to denounce and publicize the Emperor's blasphemies. They were both exiled to the island of Skyros. But in 1279 the Emperor ordered Meletios to be sent to Rome with another anti-unionist monk called Ignatios, so that the Pope could see the kind of people he had to deal with. When they were returned to Constantinople, Meletios was put in prison and had his tongue cut out for comparing the Emperor to Julian the Apostate. His companion in exile Galaktion was blinded. Both survived, however, and were to be acclaimed among the principal heroes of the hour when Orthodoxy was restored in 1283.[1]

Like the Patriarch Joseph, Meletios was honoured as a confessor in the Orthodox Calendar. His *magnum opus*, still unpublished, was composed during his exile in Skyros. It must be one of the very few theological tracts written in pentedecasyllabic verse, and bad verse at that. One of its seven books is entitled 'Against the Italians or Latins'. The reader is cautioned against taking communion with such heretics for fear of doing irreparable damage to his immortal soul. Meletios lists some forty divergences between Catholics and Orthodox, quite apart from the well-known errors which put the Latins in heresy. They range from such enormities as baptism by single immersion and the use of saliva in the collation of the sacrament for baptism, to making the sign of the cross with all five fingers, and the wrong way round, and the celibacy and beardlessness of the Latin clergy.[2]

Accusations of this nature brought the waywardness of the Catholics home to ordinary people in the Byzantine world. They were easier to understand than the *Filioque* business, dreadful

---

lard, in *Dictionnaire de Théologie Catholique*, xv, 339–41; Beck, *Kirche und theologische Literatur*, 693–4; J. Meyendorff, *Introduction à l'étude de Grégoire Palamas* (Patristica Sorbonensia, 3), Paris 1959, 30–3 and *passim*.

[1] Pachymeres, *De Michaele Palaeologo*, VI, 18, 24: I, pp. 462, 489. On Meletios Homologetes or the Confessor, see L. Petit, in *Dictionnaire de Théologie Catholique*, x, 535–8; Beck, *Kirche und theologische Literatur*, 678–9. Cf. Dölger, *Regesten der Kaiserurkunden*, III, no. 2048 and references. The Patriarch Joseph also came from the monastery on Mount Galesios; see above, p. 117, n. 1.

[2] Only a part of this work has been published. See references in Petit, in *Dictionnaire de Théologie Catholique*, x, 538; Beck, *Kirche und theologische Literatur*, 679.

though that was. Why, the Latins even sat down to Mass and allowed dogs and cats into their churches; and their Pope claimed to be able to forgive sins not only in the past but also in the future.[1] Some of the western misapprehensions about the errors of the Greeks were, of course, no less curious. Jerome of Ascoli, for example, a Franciscan who wrote a report on the matter for Pope Gregory X, had it that the Greeks considered fornication to be a smaller sin than contracting a third marriage. He had also got it into his head that the Greeks had condemned and excommunicated the Pope and all the Latins at the Council of Nicaea in 325. The simple difficulty of communication accounted for some of these misunderstandings. The Dominican Humbert of Romans complained that, at the time of the Council of Lyons, there was not a single man at the Curia who was fully competent to translate the correspondence coming in from Byzantium.[2]

But the poetical polemics of Meletios the Confessor were sober stuff when compared with some of the propaganda put about by less worthy monks. For when they were forbidden to hold meetings and address the people, the monks secretly circulated pamphlets condemning the Emperor and the Patriarch and ridiculing the beliefs and practices of the Roman Church. A decree went out that those caught with such documents were to be put to death if they refused to burn them. One form of such literature was an imaginary Dialogue between a pious Orthodox called Panagiotes and a Catholic called simply Azymites, or the Unleavened-Breader; or a Debate between a most holy martyr for the faith called Constantine and a Roman Cardinal. The argu-

[1] Cf. Evert-Kappesowa, 'La société', 33–4.
[2] Jerome of Ascoli's report to Pope Gregory X has been re-edited by Roberg, *Union*, Anhang I, no. 2, pp. 229–31. The *Opus Tripartitum* of Humbert of Romans (Humbertus de Romanis) is printed in part in J. D. Mansi, *Sacrorum Conciliorum nova et amplissima collectio*, XXIV, Venice 1780, 109–32 (for older and fuller versions see Roberg, *Union*, 270). His views on the difficulties of communication between Greeks and Latins are contained in Cap. XVII, ed. Mansi, 128: 'Sed vix in curia Romana invenitur, qui sciat legere litteras ab eis missas, et legatos ad eos missos oportet habere interpretes, de quibus nescitur utrum intelligant, aut decipiantur.' The language problem as it affected unionist negotiations in the thirteenth century is discussed by Roberg, *Union*, Anhang II, pp. 248 f.

ments were trivial or absurd, but the Cardinal inevitably lost the battle of wits.[1]

There are monks on Mount Athos today who will still hark back to the terrible things that the heretical Emperor Michael Palaiologos did to their brethren in the thirteenth century. As late as 1872 a sort of war memorial was erected in the courtyard of the Bulgarian monastery of Zographou to commemorate the heroic end of twenty-six martyrs for true Orthodoxy. The inscription on the monument relates how they were burnt to death on that spot by the Pope of Rome six hundred years before. Written and oral tradition has it that the Emperor Michael and the Patriarch John Bekkos visited the Holy Mountain of Athos in person, and that three of the monasteries which refused to submit to the Emperor's will were plundered and their inmates massacred. The story goes no further back than the fifteenth century and is surely apocryphal.[2] But it reflects a memory of the special persecution that was inflicted on the monasteries after the Union of Lyons. For, in the words of Pachymeres, the monks counted the days until they should be rid, not of their Emperor (for they could no more live without an Emperor than a body can live without a head), but of the sufferings that they were being forced to endure.[3]

[1] Pachymeres, *De Michaele Palaeologo*, VI, 24. 1, pp. 490–2. For editions of the Dialogue with the Roman Cardinal see Beck, *Kirche und theologische Literatur*, 680; cf. Evert-Kappesowa, 'La société', 34. The 'Dispute between Panagiotes and the Azymites' has been more recently discussed by M.-L. Concasty, 'La fin d'un dialogue contre les Latins azymites d'après le Paris. Suppl. gr. 1191', *Akten des XI. internationalen Byzantinistenkongresses München 1958*, Munich 1960, 86–9. Other more or less informed anti-Latin tracts of this nature were written by, e.g., Lazaros, a monk from Thessaly, some of whose correspondence also survives. Cf. L. Petit, in *Dictionnaire de Théologie Catholique*, IX, 87–8; Beck, *op. cit.*, 680. The letter of Lazaros to the Bishop of Larissa is on the topic of 'not taking communion with the heterodox Italians', and exhorts the bishop to stand fast by the Orthodox faith, to anathematize the Latins and to drive them out utterly as corrupt and rotten members of the body: text in C. Simonides, 'Ορθο-δόξων 'Ελλήνων θεολογικαì γραφαì τέσσαρες, 2nd ed., London 1865, 215–18.
[2] See especially S. Binon, *Les origines légendaires et l'histoire de Xéropotamou et de Saint-Paul de l'Athos* (Bibliothèque du Muséon, 13), Louvain 1942, 110–13. Cf. F. W. Hasluck, *Athos and its Monasteries*, London 1924, 29; J. Anastasiou 'Ο θρυχούμενος διωγμòς τῶν 'Αγιορειτῶν ὑπο Μιχαὴλ Η τοῦ Παλαιολόγου καὶ τοῦ 'Ιωάννου Βέκκου, Thessalonike 1963.
[3] Pachymeres, *De Michaele Palaeologo*, VI, 24: 1, p. 490.

In 1281 Pope Martin IV excommunicated the Byzantine Emperor and thus declared the Union of Lyons to be at an end. Michael Palaiologos was no longer to be considered in any sense a Catholic prince. Pope Martin was the creature of Charles of Anjou. It was he who gave his blessing, at long last, to what he described as a just war for the restoration of the Latin Empire of Constantinople. In July 1281 plans were drawn up in the papal palace at Orvieto for the great crusade which was to be led by Charles of Anjou. Charles had succeeded in uniting to his cause not only Venice, who was to supply the ships, and the Pope, who was to supply the moral cover, but also nearly all of the Balkan powers. It is no wonder that contemporaries should have thought that the King of Sicily was about to make himself monarch of the world.[1] But in March 1282, when his preparations were already far advanced, the citizens of Palermo broke out in rebellion and massacred their French oppressors. The rising, which came to be called the Sicilian Vespers, spread like wild-fire all over the island of Sicily. The armada that Charles had assembled was utterly destroyed; and his empire and his dream of mastering the world were shattered.

This is not the place to assess the part played by the Byzantine Emperor Michael in underwriting the Sicilian Vespers and so promoting the downfall of his most persistent enemy.[2] What seemed ironical to his own people was that, after all, the Union of Lyons had proved to be a quite unnecessary imposition; for divine providence had, in the end, seen to the salvation of their city and their Empire. The Pope himself had renounced the Union. The Emperor would surely now do the same and ask the forgiveness of his Orthodox subjects for all the misery he had caused them. The strange thing is that the Emperor Michael never

[1] Gregoras, *Historia*, v, 1: 1, p. 123 lines 10–12, writes of Charles's dream of mastering the whole empire of Julius Caesar and Augustus by the conquest of Constantinople. Cf. Marino Sanudo Torsello, *Istoria del Regno di Romania*, ed. C. Hopf, *Chroniques gréco-romanes inédites ou peu connues*, Berlin 1873, p. 138: '...si chè in somma detto Rè Carlo era quasi in quella grandezza e potentia, che'l poteva essere, e nondimeno ebbe a dire, che quel, che aveva, era poca cosa ad uno, che aspirava alla Monarchia del Mondo'. Cf. Geanakoplos, *Emperor Michael*, 335 f.; Roberg, *Union*, 214 f.

[2] See Geanakoplos, *Emperor Michael*, 344 f.; Runciman, *Sicilian Vespers*, 201 f.

did so. He died in December 1282, only eight months after the Sicilian Vespers. Perhaps he hardly had time enough to change his mind and reverse his policy. His only reaction to the news that the Pope had excommunicated him was to remark bitterly that this was a poor reward for all his sacrifices on behalf of the Roman Church. He forbade the Pope's name to be commemorated in the Liturgy. But when it came to renouncing the Union of Lyons he hesitated. He delayed making a decision on the matter until it was too late. But one can hardly pretend that he died as a Roman Catholic. A priest, presumably a unionist Orthodox, gave him communion at the end. But otherwise he died, as the monk Meletios had forewarned, somewhat in the manner of Julian the Apostate.[1]

The moment of Michael VIII's passing was the moment of truth for the Orthodox Church. Nothing is more eloquent of the Byzantine reaction to the Council of Lyons than the scene that is said to have been enacted at the little village in Thrace where the Emperor died on the night of 11 December 1282. His son Andronikos, who was at his deathbed, had the body hurriedly carried away from the spot where they were encamped. No grave was dug. The corpse was to be left where it was laid down, though Andronikos ordered it to be covered over with a mound of earth to protect it from wild animals. Such was the form of burial prescribed for heretics and apostates. And these things, says the historian Gregoras, Andronikos did not from hatred of his father, for no son was ever more dutiful, but from hatred of the things that his father had done in the perversion of the true faith. It was never suggested that the mortal remains of Michael VIII should be brought to Constantinople; though some years later they were placed in a coffin and moved to a safer resting place in a monastery in Thrace.[2] But the Orthodox Church never forgave him. In later

---

[1] Pachymeres, *De Michaele Palaeologo*, VI, 30: I, pp. 505–6. Only Pachymeres, VI, 36: I, p. 531, relates that the Emperor received the sacrament *in articulo mortis*.

[2] This is the account of Nikephoros Gregoras, *Historia*, V, 7: I, pp. 150–5. The removal of the Emperor's body to the monastery of Christ Soter at Selymbria in Thrace in 1285 is attested by Pachymeres, *De Andronico Palaeologo*, I, 37: II, pp. 107–8; and by the compiler of the Short Chronicle of 1352, ed. R.-J. Loenertz, 'La chronique brève de 1352. Texte, traduction et commentaire', *Orientalia Christiana Periodica*, XXIX (1963), 345.

times it was popularly believed that the flesh of the Emperor's corpse had refused to rot away. This was a sure sign that a man had died in heresy. It had happened to Nestorios, and you could hardly do better than that. The Cretan scholar Arsenios Apostolis in the fifteenth century suffered a like fate for the same reasons as Michael VIII. He too had fallen into the Roman heresy; and it was reported that his corpse had turned black and bloated, with the skin stretched tight like a drum. Such was the end of the Emperor Michael Palaiologos who, it was said, had tried to save the city of Byzantium by trading its soul to the Latins.[1]

His son Andronikos, though only twenty-four years of age, lost no time in taking the step that his father had hesitated to take. Within a fortnight of his accession to the throne Andronikos

[1] Popular belief in the incorruptibility of Michael VIII's flesh is attested by the fourteenth-century unionist Manuel Kalekas in his tract *Adversus Graecos*, lib. IV, in *PG*, CLII, col. 211A: '...asserunt, Lugdunense concilium tyrannicum fuisse, ipsius quoque, qui illud conflavit, regis cadaver, integrum, ut aiunt, perdurans, illius animae iniquitatem annuntiare, quia hujusmodi concilium coegit, autumant'. Kalekas declares this belief to be ridiculous, since in other cases the incorruptibility of the mortal remains is taken to be a sign of the sanctity and not of the wickedness of the deceased. But in this he shows himself to be curiously ignorant of the folk-lore of his own people. For it was widely held that the corpses of those who died in heresy or under sentence of excommunication remained black and swollen until such time as they were posthumously absolved, or at least for a period of a thousand years. Du Cange, *Glossarium ad Scriptores mediae et infimae Graecitatis*, Lugduni 1688, 1621, s.v. Τυμπανίται, describes this as the term applied in later Greek to those 'qui in excommunicatione mortem obierunt, & quorum cadavera post obitum *ad tympani morem turgentia*, nigra, deformia apparent, eaque incorrupta...'. The case of Arsenios Apostolis is graphically described in the *Historia Patriarchica Constantinopoleos*, ed. B. G. Niebuhr, Bonn 1849, 149; see also D. J. Geanakoplos, *Greek Scholars in Venice. Studies in the Dissemination of Greek Learning from Byzantium to Western Europe*, Cambridge, Mass. 1962, 200. The Sultan Mehmed II the Conqueror was so intrigued to learn of this belief among Christians that he commissioned the Patriarch of Constantinople Maximos III (1476–1481/2) to find him a specimen of the corpse of one who had died in this fashion. Maximos not only produced the black and uncorrupted body of an excommunicated woman, but actually caused the flesh to dissolve by pronouncing absolution over it. See the full account in the *Ecthesis Chronica*, ed. Sp. P. Lambros (Byzantine Texts, ed. J. B. Bury), London 1902, 36–8. For a case of such a happening in Thessaly in the fifteenth century see D. M. Nicol, *Meteora. The Rock Monasteries of Thessaly*, London 1963, 114 and note 1.

made it clear that the Union of Lyons was to be formally renounced and condemned. He was aware that his own future as Emperor probably depended on his forswearing the oaths of submission to Rome that his father had made him take when he was of tender age; and he was under very strong pressure to do so, not least from his aunt Eulogia who had been living in exile. Eulogia even convinced the widowed Empress Theodora that she might as well abandon any hope of the salvation of her late husband's soul. Another of Michael's victims, Theodore Mouzalon, who had now been raised to the office of Grand Logothete, also strongly advised the young Emperor to make an immediate and public confession of his sins. Andronikos needed little persuasion, for he was devoutly Orthodox and something of a theologian. He was distressed to think that he would have to remove John Bekkos from the patriarchate, for he was very attached to him. But he could not override the feelings of the majority of his subjects. On 26 December 1282 Bekkos was arrested and taken to a monastery in Constantinople. He went quietly and no violence was done to him. A few days later the former Patriarch Joseph, now an elderly invalid, was carried back to the patriarchate on a stretcher. The streets were thronged with cheering crowds and the church bells were ringing.[1]

The prisoners and survivors of Michael VIII's reign of terror were now set free and became the heroes of the hour. The monks Meletios and Galaktion, the one rendered dumb, the other blind, for the sake of Orthodoxy, were paraded as martyrs. The zealots and the monks made the most of the occasion. The cathedral of St Sophia was purified with holy water and re-dedicated, as it had been when the Latins left the city in 1261. The monks took it upon themselves to impose various penances on those who had favoured Union with Rome or, worse still, taken communion with the Latins. A monk called Gennadios announced in a fearsome voice that their sins were exceeding great and that the Gospel had been violated. The Patriarch Joseph was too ill to be able to take much part in these cathartic proceedings. But he was prevailed upon to

[1] Pachymeres, *De Andronico Palaeologo*, I, 2–4: II, pp. 14–15, 17–19. Gregoras, *Historia*, VI, I: p. 160.

139

decree that all unionist bishops and priests must be excommunicated for three months, and the laity according to their guilt.
Priests like Constantine Meliteniotes and George Metochites, who
had served as envoys to the Pope and even attended Mass with
him, were defrocked.[1] The Emperor allowed these things to
happen even against his better judgment so that, as Pachymeres
puts it, 'the storms of yesterday might be stilled and peace be
restored, and that his own conscience, which had been sorely
troubled by having to support his father's actions, might be set
at rest'.[2]

But the excitement mounted and the storms were not stilled.
The cry went up that prominent unionists should be brought to
trial as traitors, and that John Bekkos should be prosecuted as a
heretic and as a usurper of the patriarchal throne. A council of
bishops was convened in Constantinople in January 1283. The
Patriarch Joseph was too weak to preside, but the presence of the
Patriarch of Alexandria lent it some authority. The Grand Logothete Theodore Mouzalon proposed that all documents attesting
the Union of Lyons should be burnt. The bishops then formally
charged John Bekkos with heresy. He was condemned and sent
into exile. He was not, as yet, otherwise victimized, for the
Emperor saw to it that he was made as comfortable as possible.
But the zealots had won the first round. All the decisions made by
the council were confirmed in writing by the Emperor. One of
them related to his deceased father. Michael VIII was never to be
honoured by any memorial or requiem, nor was he to be given
a Christian burial.[3]

But the more fanatical of the anti-unionists continued to call for
a public confession of their guilt from all those who had betrayed
Orthodoxy. The aged Patriarch Joseph died in March 1283. The
scholar Gregory of Cyprus was appointed in his place. His own
past was not above suspicion. But he tried to placate the extremists
by calling another council in Constantinople. The dowager
Empress Theodora, the widow of Michael VIII, was there required

[1] Pachymeres, *De Andronico Palaeologo*, I, 4–7: II, pp. 19–25.
[2] Pachymeres, *ibid.* II, pp. 22–3.
[3] Pachymeres, *ibid.* I, 8–12: II, pp. 25–38.

to make a profession of her Orthodox faith, to repudiate her past, and to swear that she would never ask that her late husband should be decently buried.[1] But the zealots would not rest until John Bekkos had been made to repent; and the Patriarch was forced into convening yet another council in Constantinople in 1285. It was this council that did most to salve the wounded conscience of the Orthodox Church. Bekkos was brought back from his exile to stand trial. Also in court were his associates, or accomplices in crime, Constantine Meliteniotes and George Metochites. Bekkos had rather wanted to be given a chance to state his case and clear his name at a public hearing, and he was foolish enough to defend his theological position by producing a string of citations from the Fathers. Nothing could have been more ill-advised in the circumstances, for he showed himself to be aggressively unrepentant. He and his colleagues were again convicted of heresy. The Emperor intervened personally to give them a last opportunity to recant, but they remained adamant. And in the end they were removed to prison.[2]

The council of 1285 also produced a *Tomos* or declaration of the Orthodox ruling on the Procession of the Holy Spirit. It was drawn up by the Patriarch Gregory of Cyprus, and it became the starting-point of another round of passionate theological debate and dissension in Constantinople. But the dispute was a Byzantine one, in the sense that both sides assumed the *Filioque* clause at least to be unacceptable. There was no argument about the fact that Latin theology and its principal supporters among the Greeks

---

[1] Pachymeres, *ibid.* I, 13–19: II, pp. 38–55. Gregoras, *Historia*, VI, 1:1, pp. 162–7. The first council in the church of the Blachernai in Constantinople was held early in May 1283. The text of the Empress Theodora's recantation and profession of faith is printed in C. Simonides, Ὀρθοδόξων, 85–8, and in J. Dräseke, *op. cit.*, *Zeitschrift für wissenschaftliche Theologie*, XXXIV (1891), 353–4. See also S. Petrides, 'Chrysobulle de l'impératrice Théodora', and 'Sentence synodique contre le clergé unioniste', *Echos d'Orient*, XIV (1911), 25–8, 133–6.

[2] Pachymeres, *De Andronico Palaeologo*, I, 34–6: II, pp. 88–102. The second council of Blachernai lasted for six months, in four sessions, from February to August 1285. V. Laurent, 'Les signataires du second synode des Blakhernes (été 1285)', *Echos d'Orient*, XXVI (1927), 129–49; *idem*, 'Notes de chronologie et d'histoire byzantine de la fin du XIIIᵉ siècle. 3: La date du second synode des Blachernes sous Grégoire de Chypre', *Revue des études byzantines*, XXVII (1969), 217–19.

D. M. NICOL

had been well and truly outlawed.¹ By 1285 therefore many old scores had been settled. But by general consensus of Orthodox opinion the villain of the piece had been named and condemned in the person of John Bekkos. The Emperor Michael had been led into heresy from political motives. But the false Patriarch Bekkos had added insult to injury by trying to explain and defend that heresy. Indeed he went on doing so even in his prison cell, scribbling away about the Procession of the Holy Spirit as long as he could hold a pen. He died in 1297, and his corpse is perhaps still somewhere to be found, incorruptible, black and blown up like a drum.²

The accession of Andronikos Palaiologos was hailed in many quarters as the beginning of a new era. But those whose duty or conceit it was to deliver eulogies of the new Emperor had to be as tactful as possible about his father; for part of the form of a Byzantine encomium was studied praise of the recipient's ancestors. The art of rhetoric was almost expressly invented for circumventing difficulties of this nature. The blame for what Andronikos's father had done could be laid at the door of his Patriarch John Bekkos. And so it was. Nikephoros Choumnos, in his Eulogy of Andronikos, excuses the young Emperor for the act of 'economy' which he had been obliged to perform by subscribing to the Union of Lyons. But he praises him to the skies for renouncing that Union as soon as he came to the throne. 'At once', he says, 'all the corruptions that had been wickedly insinuated into [our faith] flowed away, and the arch expounder of foolish doctrine [Bekkos] fell and was expelled from the sanctuary and from the altar...while his associates in madness, who had condemned God and the Holy Spirit...were humiliated and forced to bow their heads in shame.'³ Again in the Epitaph that

¹ On the significance of the *Tomos* of 1285 see Meyendorff, *Introduction à l'étude de Grégoire Palamas*, 26–8; Runciman, *The Great Church in Captivity*, 99.
² V. Laurent, 'La date de la mort de Jean Beccos', *Echos d'Orient*, xxv (1926), 316–19. The polemical writings of John Bekkos, including his treatise against the *Tomos* of Gregory of Cyprus, are for the most part contained in *PG*, cxli. Cf. Beck, *Kirche und theologische Literatur*, 683.
³ Nikephoros Choumnos, *Enkomion of the Emperor Andronikos Palaiologos*, ed. J. F. Boissonade, *Anecdota Graeca*, ii, Paris 1830, 1–56, especially 53.

142

he wrote on Theoleptos of Philadelphia, Choumnos recalled the underhand way in which John Bekkos and his friends had gone about their business. 'To begin with', he says, 'they described the affair as *oikonomia* and as an exercise in peace.'

And those who engineered it said, 'What is so terrible if, while preserving our own Orthodox beliefs and traditions safe and sound and unaltered, we keep our enemies at bay by making one small concession, namely to commemorate the name of their chief bishop at our altars?' But this was trickery, this was the ambush that they laid for our Church. And the Patriarch Bekkos advised and persuaded the Emperor that it was better to go all the way with the Romans than just to pretend that we were in communion with them. Such was the craft and evil cunning of Bekkos...But things did not turn out as he wished. For he failed to reckon with the fact that he had turned the champions of true Orthodoxy yet more violently against him. Such a one was our soldier for Christ [Theoleptos].[1]

The Patriarch Gregory of Cyprus likewise lays the blame on John Bekkos and eulogizes Andronikos as the restorer of Orthodoxy and the faith. 'For it was you', he writes, 'who brought low [Bekkos] the arrogant one, he who had besieged and almost broken down the stronghold of our confession. It was you who dismissed him and committed his works to the flames.' For Gregory, Andronikos II was to be acclaimed as the New Constantine, the emulator of the first Christian Emperor, the father of all Orthodox Emperors, who had combined the imperial authority with the piety of a saint.[2] At an earlier date Gregory had said much the same things about the father of Andronikos. His Eulogy of Michael VIII is addressed to the Emperor Michael Palaiologos, the New Constantine.[3] But the rules of the game of rhetoric applied more to form than to content. On the other hand, the court poet Manuel Philes certainly voiced the true feelings of most

[1] Nikephoros Choumnos, *Epitaphios for the blessed and most holy Metropolitan of Philadelphia Theoleptos*, ed. Boissonade, *Anecdota Graeca*, v, Paris 1832, 183–245, especially 197–9.
[2] Gregory of Cyprus (Gregorios Kyprios), *Enkomion of Andronikos Palaiologos*, ed. Boissonade, *Anecdota Graeca*, i, Paris 1829, 359–93, especially 381–4.
[3] Gregory of Cyprus, *Enkomion of the Emperor Michael Palaiologos and New Constantine*, ibid. 313–58.

of the Byzantines when he described Andronikos II as 'the light of the Church, the guardian of true dogma, who calmed the tempests that had disturbed the faith of our fathers...the corner-stone of religion'.[1]

It would be hard to maintain that the cause of Christendom as a whole benefited much from the Union of Lyons. But the Ortho-dox Church gained immensely. It gained in its hold on the hearts of the Byzantine people, for the persecutions had bred a rich crop of martyrs and confessors for their faith. It gained also in authority and prestige. For the Emperor Andronikos II, unlike his father, was pious to a fault. He saw it as his Christian duty to compensate for the harm that his father had inflicted on the Church and to heal the wounds in society. He was only partially successful, for the Byzantine Church emerged from its sufferings not only triumphant but also divided among its own members. But its quarrels advertised its restored freedom and vigour, and above all they were of its own making. No Cardinal-legate from Rome acted as arbiter of its disputes. During the reign of Andronikos II, in the generation after the Union of Lyons, the Byzantine Church behaved as if the Church of Rome simply did not exist. For over forty years after 1282 there was no direct communication of any kind between Byzantium and the Papacy. The first sign of a thaw came in 1327, with an exchange of letters between Andronikos II, the King of France and Pope John XXII.[2] His grandson Andro-nikos III, who came to the throne in 1328, found it politically expedient to negotiate with the Papacy. But all his dealings were done in secret; and all his emissaries to the Curia were foreigners and not Byzantines. The most famous of them was Barlaam of Calabria, who went to Avignon in 1339; but Barlaam took care to warn the Pope against supposing that any Byzantine Emperor could again impose Union on his subjects by force. The matter was still so inflammatory in Constantinople that, in Barlaam's own words, 'the Emperor does not dare to let it be known that

[1] *Manuelis Philae Carmina*, ed. E. Miller, II, Paris 1857, pp. 376 lines 26 f., 377 lines 19 f.

[2] H. Omont, 'Projet de réunion des églises grecques et latines sous Charles le Bel en 1327', *Bibliothèque de l'Ecole des Chartes*, LIII (1892), 254–7; *idem*, 'Lettre d'Andronic II Paléologue au Pape Jean XXII', *ibid*. LXVII (1906), 587.

he is interested in the Union of the Churches; for if he did then many of his nobles and of his people would seek an occasion to murder him for fear that he was proposing to do to them what Michael Palaiologos had done [to their ancestors]'.[1]

Barlaam was also at pains to dispel the illusion which the Popes found so comforting, that their predecessor Gregory had made a noble and generous gesture to the Greeks at the Second Council of Lyons and that the Orthodox Church had since gone back on its word. For, as he pointed out to Pope Benedict XII, 'no one will ever be able to make the Greek people accept [the rulings of] that Council unless another one be held; because the Greeks who took part in it were sent there neither by the four Patriarchs who govern the Eastern Church nor by the people. They were sent there only by the Emperor, who tried to bring about the Union of the Churches by force and not by free will.'[2]

In the Byzantine view, therefore, the Second Council of Lyons was a local synod of the Roman Church. It was very far from being an oecumenical council. And yet a form of words affecting the fundamentals of Christian theology had there been imposed upon a small delegation from the Byzantine Empire without debate or discussion of any kind. This had been the work of the misguided Emperor and more particularly of his ill-gotten Patriarch John Bekkos. These are the two names that figure most prominently in later Byzantine references to the subject. The name of Pope Gregory X is seldom mentioned; and his gathering at Lyons in 1274 was remembered, if at all, as an episode which had prompted the great persecution of the Orthodox in the reign of Michael VIII.[3] In the long history of the Orthodox Church the

---

[1] *Barlaami abbatis legati Graecorum de unione Ecclesiarum sermo ad Pontificem et cardinales*, ed. O. Raynaldus, *Annales ecclesiastici*, ed. A. Theiner, Barri-Ducis 1870, xxv, *ann.* 1339, §§20–31 (= *PG*, CLI, cols. 1331–42), especially §31.

[2] *Ibid.* §21.

[3] In 1367 the ex-Emperor John Cantacuzene, in his Dialogue with the papal legate to Constantinople, Paul of Smyrna, looked back on the so-called Union of the Churches in the time of Michael VIII as the cause of more harm than good. 'For out of it had come tyranny and a great persecution, but no benefit; and therefore it had not endured for long, and things had reverted to their former condition.' J. Meyendorff, 'Projet de concile oecuménique en 1367: Un Dialogue inédit entre Jean Cantacuzène et le légat Paul', *Dumbarton Oaks Papers*,

council held in Constantinople in 1285 was of far greater significance. For that council had finally condemned the unrepentant heretic who had perverted the faith. Some felt that its decisions were of oecumenical authority, since the Patriarchs of Constantinople and Alexandria had been there, and the two other eastern Patriarchs had approved of what was done. It was therefore at least rather more representative of Orthodox opinion than the Council of Lyons; and in the minds of some people, such as the fifteenth-century Patriarch Gennadios Scholarios, it remained more representative than the Council of Florence. For it had held to and confirmed the received truth of the oecumenical councils of past ages, adding nothing to the faith and taking nothing away. And this, after all, does not signify that the faith has stopped, or has not grown up with those who continue to believe in their own form of it as a way of life and death.[1]

xiv (1960), pp. 147–77, especially § 13, pp. 173–4. The Second Council of Lyons was later regarded as a 'Robber Council'. Cf. Geanakoplos, *Emperor Michael*, 236 f.

[1] For the opinion of Gennadios Scholarios on the Council of 1285 see Meyendorff, *Introduction à l'étude de Grégoire Palamas*, 26; J. Gill, *Personalities of the Council of Florence and other essays*, Oxford 1964, 215–18; Runciman, *The Great Church in Captivity*, 99.

THE COUNCIL OF LONDON OF 1342

by BRENDA BOLTON

Now that the statutes formerly ascribed to Winchelsey and Reynolds have been shown to derive from other sources, those of John Stratford, issued after the Second Council of London (1342), are seen to stand out as the most significant body of provincial legislation in the later Middle Ages.[1] Their relative importance is enhanced by the paucity of such legislation in this period in comparison with the considerable volume produced in the course of the thirteenth century.

On investigation, Stratford's constitutions appear significant in the corpus of medieval 'administrative' canon law.[2] Not only do they show signs of the friction existing between the lay and ecclesiastical jurisdictions and experienced both by Pecham and Winchelsey, but also of the recurring clerical concerns, frailties of conduct, and malpractices of church courts and officials alike. Provincial legislation springs partly from local imperfections, and partly from more general circumstances. Political considerations may have been critical in the decision to issue constitutions. There is justification, therefore, for first examining the political context in which these constitutions arose.

By 1340, Stratford's position was ambiguous and unenviable.[3]

---

[1] C. R. Cheney, 'The So-Called Statutes of John Pecham and Robert Winchelsey', *JEH*, XII (1961), 21–5; C. R. Cheney, 'The Legislation of the Medieval English Church', *EHR*, CXCIX (1935), 193–224, 385–417; *Councils and Synods 1205–1313*, ed. F. M. Powicke and C. R. Cheney, 2 vols. Oxford 1964, 1382–93. This is the basic printed collection of national and provincial legislation up to the fourteenth century and is henceforth quoted as *C & S*.

[2] Wilkins (1737) II, 675 et seq., 696–702, 702–9; Wm Lyndwood, *Provinciale*, Oxford 1679, 43–54.

[3] Stratford held the chancellorship of England three times between 1330 and 1340, and in 1339 was *dux regis* in the king's absence although he failed to convince parliament of the need to grant adequate supplies for the war with France. See A. B. Emden, *A Biographical Register of the University of Oxford to A.D. 1500*, Oxford 1957–9, 1796–8; M. McKisack, *The Fourteenth Century*,

Bound by his chancellorship to ensure the observance of recent royal statutes, he could see that these very statutes placed his clergy under an intolerable and exceptional burden of taxation, in direct contravention of the bull *Clericis Laicos*. Tenths which produced growing resentment were taken in 1338 and in 1340, and a ninth imposed at the same time caused an impassioned outburst from Adam Orleton, Stratford's old political rival.[1] Further attempts to raise money resulted in the demand for a moiety of the wool crop from the clergy and for procurations to be diverted as a forced loan. Stratford, in the *littera privata* directed to his suffragans, suggested that, to compensate for this last diversion, they should retain a corresponding part of the tenth.[2]

The commissions of *trailbaston*, which, among other things, were empowered to inquire into the conduct of royal officers, had amerced or imprisoned clerics and laity alike and were interpreted as instruments, not only of extortion, but of a direct and concerted attack on ecclesiastical liberties. The issue, in fact, still centred on the writ of prohibition and the difficulty of separating purely temporal from purely spiritual pleas. One method by which the clergy relieved their feelings, and indeed brought pressure to bear, was by compiling lists of *gravamina* defining specific areas of conflict.[3] Once Stratford had resigned the chancellorship, he was able to present the seven *gravamina* of 1341.[4] Following the precedent supplied by Pecham at Lambeth in 1281, these dealt

Oxford 1959, chapter VI, 'Edward III and Archbishop Stratford 1330–43', 152–181; G. T. Lapsley, 'Archbishop Stratford and the Parliamentary Crisis of 1341', *EHR*, xxx (1915), 6–18, 193–215; B. Wilkinson, 'The Protest of the Earls of Arundel and Surrey in the Crisis of 1341', *EHR*, xlvi (1931), 177–193.

[1] *Winchester Cathedral Chartulary*, ed. A. W. Goodman (1927), 221. On clerical subsidies see D. B. Weske, *The Convocation of the Clergy* (1937), 67. An indication of the tremendous financial pressure placed by Edward III on the country may be obtained from E. B. Fryde, 'Edward III's Wool Monopoly of 1337', *History*, New Series, 37 (1952), 8–24. For the effects of the war on the diocese of Worcester see R. M. Haines, *A Calendar of the Register of Wolstan de Bransford* (1966), l–li. Subsequently referred to as *Cal. Reg. Brans.*

[2] *Cal. Reg. Brans.*, 511–12.

[3] The most recent study of clerical grievances appears in W. R. Jones, 'Bishops, Politics and the Two Laws: the *Gravamina* of the English Clergy 1237–1399', *Speculum*, 41 (1966), 209–45.

[4] *Rotuli Parliamentorum*, II, 129a–130b.

with benefit of clergy, seizure of ecclesiastical property, indictment of ecclesiastical judges, and sentences of excommunication against those violating the Charter.

Edward, dismayed by the cost and futility of his Flemish campaign and determined to lay the blame elsewhere, issued writs preventing the publication of ecclesiastical censures against collectors of royal taxes. At the same time, there was published an indictment of Stratford for his 'incapacity', attributed, but without proof, to Adam Orleton, the old and half-blind Bishop of Winchester.[1] In his dignified reply to what he entitled the *libellus famosus*, Stratford challenged the king on the grounds that the arrest of clerks ran counter to the *privilegium fori*, and claimed that their judgment without proper trial was an infringement, not only of ecclesiastical rights, but of those of all peers of the realm.[2] The archbishop sent a copy of a Charter of the Church's liberties to the bishops and secured certain temporary concessions. These included guarantees against arbitrary arrest and encroachments by the laity on ecclesiastical jurisdictions and allowed the remission of the ninth by those clergy who were not summoned to Parliament and had not, therefore, given consent.

By 1341, Stratford had disassociated himself to a considerable degree from affairs of the realm and was able to devote more time to his metropolitan duties.[3] The Fourth Lateran Council (1215) had ordered the regular holding of provincial assemblies to maintain ecclesiastical discipline by 'correcting excesses and by moral reformation'.[4] The onus of reiterating and reaffirming the decrees

---

[1] *Foedera*, II, ii, 1147–8; *Anglia Sacra: Sive Collectio Historiarum, Partim Antiquitus, Partim Recenter Scriptarum, de Archiepiscopis et Episcopis Angliae, A Prima Fidei Christianae Susceptione ad Annum MDXL*, ed. H. Wharton (1691), I, 23–7.

[2] For clarification on this point see W. Ullmann, 'A decision of the Rota Romana on the benefit of clergy in England', *Studia Gratiana*, XIII (1967), Collectanea Stephan Kuttner III, 458–62; L. C. Gabel, *Benefit of Clergy in England in the Later Middle Ages* (Smith College Studies in History), (Northampton, Mass. 1929); R. Génestal, *Le privilegium fori en France du Décret de Gratien à la fin du XIVe siècle*, 2 vols (Paris 1921–4). For the excuse to the *Libellus Famosus* see *Anglia Sacra*, ed. Wharton, I, 28, 32.

[3] Stratford was Archbishop of Canterbury (1333–48) but his archiepiscopal register has not survived, and this is a major void in the study of fourteenth-century ecclesiastical history.

[4] Lateran IV cap. 6. *Conciliorum Oecumenicorum Decreta*, Herder (1962), 212–13.

of the Lateran and of subsequent councils, particularly Lyons II (1274) and Vienne (1311), lay with the archbishop. By the 1340s a procedural pattern seems to have emerged in these assemblies. Each suffragan received a personal summons to attend or to send his proctor unless he wished to be punished as an absentee, while a general summons was sent to abbots, priors, and members of the lower clergy. When new legislation was to be formulated, it could be derived from material gathered by officers specially appointed in each diocese to investigate matters needing reform. These officers then reported back to their bishops, and the ensuing legislation was promulgated by formal reading at the Council. The injunctions were later published in diocesan synods, often with the proviso that they should be regularly recited.[1]

Although the principle was well-established that provincial councils *ought* to be held annually, the political crisis of the early 1340s and the consequently embittered relations between the king and his archbishop had made this difficult to effect.[2] We find Stratford complaining to Simon Montacute of Ely that the tribulations and adversities of office had, thus far, prevented him from fulfilling his obligation in this respect.[3]

The summons to the Council of 1341 to be held at St Paul's on the day after St Luke, 19 October, was sent out in the normal way

[1] I am indebted to Dr Roy M. Haines for abstracting material from the unpublished register of Bishop Adam Orleton of Winchester. This indicates the national importance of the reforms under discussion among the clergy of the Winchester diocese before the Council of 1341. Three points emerge. First, the liberties granted to churches and ecclesiastical persons should not be diminished. Secondly, since the king had alienated so many of his goods, he could not support those burdens incumbent upon him without imposing 'tallias et alia . . . onera importabilia' on the clergy and people of the realm. It should, therefore, be laid down by the Council that such alienated goods be recovered and no more distributed 'et quod omnes huiusmodi bona decetero recipientes excommunicentur nisi sit cum consensu tocius parliamenti'. Lastly, the king was to be asked not to burden with royal commissions, abbots, priors and other religious who held their temporalities in free alms, or other ecclesiastical persons whose benefices consisted in spiritualities. Such persons should not be forced by commissions of this kind to become involved in secular business contrary to church teaching, *Reg. Orleton*, I, fol. 107 recto.

[2] Weske, *Convocation*, 250–2. In practice only three provincial councils were held in the 1340s: 1341, 1342 and 1347.

[3] Wilkins, II, 680.

by the Bishop of London, Ralph Stratford, in his capacity as Dean of the province of Canterbury. It was issued on 10 August and we have evidence of its transmission to the suffragans by 18 September.[1] On the archbishop's authority the bishops were cited *praecise et peremptorie* and the abbots, priors, clergy, and heads of chapters, *non praecise sed causative*, should it appear to their interest or advantage to come. On 1 October, the king warned Stratford against challenging and derogating from royal authority in the coming Council, and there exists a similarly dated letter sent to Ralph, Bishop of Bath and Wells, warning him to do nothing contrary to the royal dignity.[2] The political crisis appears virtually to have sabotaged the 1341 assembly, for Murimuth records that the publication of canons 'to preserve the liberties of the Church and ensure a moral reformation' was postponed. Eight bishops were present at the Council and it is possible that others had simply not attended, owing to the king's threats.[3]

On 23 October, immediately after the Council assembled, the king and Stratford met and resolved their differences *ad honorem ecclesiae Anglicanae*.[4] There is evidence that by November, in a more relaxed political climate, bishops and clergy of the province were deliberating on matters of reform and were drawing up written proposals for submission and consideration at the next Council.

The summons to the Council of 1342 was issued on 28 August, when the dean of the province cited the diocesans to appear personally in St Paul's on 14 October, and shows that part of its business was to resume discussions which had begun earlier but

---

[1] *Winchester Cathedral Chartulary*, p. 222. Wilkins, II, 675, 680. For the usual procedure of summons see Weske, *Convocation*, 119–24. Bishop Orleton's mandate for the execution of the archbishop's summons was addressed to the prior and chapter of Winchester and dated Waltham 13 September 1341, *Reg. Orleton*, I, fol. 107 recto.

[2] CCR, 1341–43, p. 335. Wilkins, II, 680.

[3] The Bishops of London, Chichester, Salisbury, Ely, Bath, Coventry, St David's and Bangor. *Continuatio Chronicarum*, ed. E. M. Thompson, RS (1889). Adam Orleton being *corporali molestia prepediti* appointed Master John de Usk, his official, and Master John de Trilleck to act as his proctors, *Reg. Orleton*, I, fol. 107 v. For a general study of the bishops see J. R. L. Highfield, 'The English Hierarchy in the reign of Edward III', *TRHS*, 5th Series, VI (1956), 115–38.

[4] *Winchester Cathedral Chartulary*, p. 219.

which had been deferred. In the words of the summons 'other arduous matters which have recently arisen to the detriment of the state of the Church and clergy' were also to be investigated.[1] On this occasion no one was to be excused on pain of canonical punishment for contumacy, unless for some essential reason which nevertheless had to be declared and proved at the Council. Summonses to Ralph of Shrewsbury,[2] Thomas Bek of Lincoln,[3] John Grandisson of Exeter,[4] and Adam Orleton of Winchester have survived.[5] Representatives of the diocesan clergy were cited to appear together with the heads of exempt houses other than mendicants and proctors of absent bishops.[6] Of those recorded as present, seven bishops had attended the previous Council of 1341, while four were newcomers.[7] We know, too, that Bishop Bransford did not remain long in London as he was about to make a visitation of his diocese,[8] and that John Grandisson stayed at least until 21 October when he personally acted in London as a judge in the case of John de Sodbury.[9]

A study of the provenance of Stratford's canons has been made.[10] Three sets were printed by Wilkins, of which the first version appears to have been drawn up after the Council of 1341 but not published. The second series, a revision of the first, has been dated 10 October 1342 and concentrates on clerical reform. It has been argued that, from the material under discussion at the Council of 1342, those chapters of *gravamina*, dealing mainly with the limits

---

[1] *Cal. Reg. Brans.*, pp. 205–6. In 1341 and 1342, Stratford observed the prescriptions of canon law far more carefully than in previous councils, E. W. Kemp, *Counsel and Consent* (1961), 104–5.

[2] *Register of Ralph of Shrewsbury*, ed. T. S. Holmes, 2 vols, Somerset Record Society (1896), II, 454. [3] Wilkins, II, 710.

[4] *Register of John Grandisson*, ed. F. C. Hingeston-Randolph (1899), 968–9.

[5] *Reg. Orleton*, I, fol. 114r.

[6] *Cal. Reg. Brans.*, p. 206. Bishop Orleton sent the names of the religious houses which had been duly summoned 'Nomina premunitorum', *Reg. Orleton*, I, fol. 107r.

[7] Ralph of London and the Bishops of Coventry and Lichfield, Salisbury, Chichester, Bath and Wells, Ely, and Bangor. The Bishops of Exeter, Worcester, Lincoln, and Hereford were newcomers.

[8] *Cal. Reg. Brans.*, p. 94. His visitation of the Worcester diocese lasted from 5 to 11 November 1342.

[9] *Reg. Grandisson*, II, 968–9. [10] C. R. Cheney, *JEH*, XII, 415–17.

of lay jurisdiction, were set aside to be re-examined subsequently and reissued in a third series: Ralph of Shrewsbury received a copy in June 1343.[1] It also seems likely that Stratford was the last archbishop to issue his constitutions directly in council, since his successor, Islip, ordered canons to be transmitted to his suffragans by letter from the Bishop of London.

The significance of Stratford's constitutions was not lost on Lyndwood, the fifteenth-century canonist, and he obtained material for some of his longest and most instructive glosses from them.[2] Between the 1281 constitutions of Pecham and 1430, sixty chapters are glossed, including all twenty-nine of Stratford's. Although it is not within the scope of this paper to deal with the individual points raised in these glosses, it is perhaps worth noting their extent and interest.

Before attempting an assessment of the constitutions, two points should be made. Such provincial canons rarely formed systematic codes of law. Although they sometimes contained familiar chapters and repeated well-known and accepted legislation, they generally sprang into being in response to particular demands and needs. In 1341, for instance, Stratford had written in considerable distress to the Bishop of Ely about the excesses which were occurring daily in his province.[3] Moreover, Stratford was a Doctor of Civil Law and had been Dean of the Court of Arches in 1321.[4] This may explain, in part, his preoccupation with the regulation of fees and procedure in the church courts.[5] After all, what better experience could he have had? Furthermore, he had acted as university proctor in the dispute with the Dominicans over the requisite qualifications for degrees in theology, and seems

[1] *Reg. Ralph of Shrewsbury*, II, 454.
[2] William Lyndwood (c. 1375–1446), the principal authority on English canon law, was chancellor to the Archbishop of Canterbury (1414–17) and an official of the court of Canterbury (1417–31). He was created Bishop of St David's in 1422 and by 1430 had collected the synodal constitutions of fourteen archbishops of Canterbury from Langton to Chichele which he glossed elaborately. See Emden, *Register*, 1191–2.   [3] Wilkins, II, 680.
[4] Stratford produced a long series of statutes for the Court of Arches, Wilkins, II, 681–95.
[5] On church courts see I. J. Churchill, *Canterbury Administration*, 2 vols (1933), 380–499.

B. BOLTON

to betray, in his frequent reiteration of their offences, the antagonism of the secular clerk to the religious.

The set of constitutions dated 10 October 1342 concerns itself with various aspects of clerical reform in which neither bishops nor archdeacons escape criticism. There was an apparent threat to parochial structure, as parish churches were suffering considerable financial loss at the hands of the religious orders and laity alike. By the fourteenth century many people sought to have their own chapels and thus, to some extent, withdrew from ordinary parochial worship to the detriment of the system. The canon *quam sit inhonestum* forbade the unlicensed celebration of mass in unsuitable places or in private oratories.[1] Bishops were not to grant such licences except to 'magnates or nobles' living at a distance from parish churches or to those who were feeble or ill. The appropriators of parish churches who had neglected almsgiving were to pay annually under pain of sequestration. When the religious orders were the appropriators, they were often guilty of such extensive encroachments in the parishes that the remaining parishioners had insufficient funds with which to fulfil their responsibility to repair the nave and everything pertaining to it.

Several chapters deal with the regulation of fees and church courts. Excessive charges were not to be made for essential administrative documents or certificates, and specific fees were prescribed for these and for inductions. A scale of charges was also appended to the injunction *adeo quorundam* to prevent 'immoderate' sums being charged for probate of wills, a repetition of Mepham's constitution of 1328.[2] Bishops were ordered to pay adequate stipends to their ministers so that the lesser clergy were not forced to accept *douceurs* or to overcharge. Visitation procurations were, by the regulation *quamvis lex naturae*, to be limited to one a day, and no money was to be taken at all from places where defects in the church fabric were discovered.[3] Such visitations were to be made triennially by bishops and regularly, probably each year, by archdeacons.

1 Wilkins, II, 696 c. 1; Lyndwood, *Provinciale*, 233.
2 Wilkins, II, 698 c. 6; Lyndwood, *Provinciale*, 170. This injunction gives rise to a well-known gloss on the English *consuetudo*. See p. 181.
3 Wilkins, II, 698 c. 7; Lyndwood, *Provinciale*, 223.

Stratford was concerned that the expense of holding episcopal consistory courts and archidiaconal chapters tended to fall upon particular rectors or monasteries. They were held at the same places and therefore constituted a continuous charge. He also attempted to reduce the additional expense caused by citations outside the deaneries. The canon *quoniam reus* forbade archdeacons to commute corporal penance in cases where the offender had lapsed more than once, and when they handled fines, the money was not to be diverted to their own use but was to be used to maintain church fabric.[1] Apparitors were the officers responsible for serving citations and the preamble to the canon concerning them mentions the excessive increase in their number. Fifty years later Chaucer's summoner would demonstrate that they had earned a well-deserved reputation for extortion. Bishops of the province were allowed a single mounted apparitor, while each archdeacon had to content himself with only one on foot.[2]

Purgation was to be made in the deanery of accusation and the injunction *licet quis purgari* ordered that in cases of fornication and adultery there should be a maximum of six and twelve compurgators respectively.[3]

The chapter *esurientis avaritiae* is of considerable importance.[4] It was concerned with lay interference in ordinary presentation, particularly on the pretext of past episcopal voidances, and followed the lines laid down by Benedict XII in a long letter to his nuncio in England in 1337. The king was increasing his nominal patronage and was bringing pressure to bear upon the bishops by writs of *quare impedit* and *quare non admisit*. Any cleric who attempted to make use of such writs was to be excommunicate and thus incapacitated from accepting the benefice in question, while

---

[1] Wilkins, II, 700 c. 10; Lyndwood, *Provinciale*, 323. For a note on the injunction *excussis*, by which the costs of courts and chapters were to be defrayed by the principals, see R. M. Haines, *The Administration of the diocese of Worcester* (1965), 108. Also Lyndwood, *Provinciale*, 99.

[2] Wilkins, II, 700 c. 9. Lyndwood, *Provinciale*, 225. On apparitors see B. L. Woodcock, *Medieval Ecclesiastical Courts in the diocese of Canterbury* (1952), 45–9.

[3] Wilkins, II, 700 c. 11; Lyndwood, *Provinciale*, 313.

[4] Wilkins, II, 701–2 c. 12; Lyndwood, *Provinciale*, 143. Ottobon's constitution *de intrusis*, C & S, 759.

any bishop who concurred was to be suspended for three months.[1]

The third series of constitutions deals mainly with friction caused by the lay infringement of ecclesiastical liberties, and generally attempts to denigrate the laity. In a scornful preamble, the injunction *exterior habitus* mentions those clerics who despised the tonsure and who wore their hair, often powdered and curled, hanging down to their shoulders in an effeminate fashion. Contrary to canonical sanctions, they bedecked themselves in fur-edged cloaks with long hanging sleeves, caps, tippets, costly belts and rings, red and green shoes with long toes, and knives which looked like swords. These fourteenth-century fops were given six months to have their hair cut, subject to suspension at the end of that period.[2]

The whole vexed question of the avoidance of tithes by the laity remained prominent, and an apparently original injunction enforced the ceduous wood tithe *sylva caedua*, considered by the clergy to include all mature trees when felled and any subsequent growth. Laity and clergy alike appeared to have been taking advantage of the lack of definition, and in spite of Stratford's attempt to resolve this ambiguity, *sylva caedua* seems to have remained a subject of dispute.[3] The question is raised again in the

[1] For a detailed study of the writs of *quare impedit* and *quare non admisit* see F. Cheyette, 'Kings, Courts, Cures and Sinecures: The Statute of Provisors and the Common Law', *Traditio*, XIX (1963), 295–349. Royal 'recoveries' of benefices continued despite the severe measures promulgated by Stratford in 1342, *Hemingby's Register*, ed. H. M. Chew, Wiltshire Archaeological and Natural History Society, XVIII (1962), 31, 173–4, 185–6.

[2] Wilkins, II, 703; Lyndwood, *Provinciale*, 16. This injunction repeated those of Ottobon, Council of London (1268), c. 5, *C & S*, 752 and Pecham, Council of Lambeth (1281), c. 22, *C & S*, 914.

[3] Wilkins, II, 704 c. 5; Lyndwood, *Provinciale*, 189–90. This nomenclature, always used by the tithe owner claiming for payment of tithe, became subsequently linked with the *legal* definition of what wood could be tithed. The tithe from wood provided a valuable source of income for parish churches and this was not neglected by the clergy. In 1343, the Commons complained that unprecedented tithes of *hautboys* and *suboys* were being taken, *Rot. Parl.* II,142. A distinction was finally drawn between great wood which yielded no annual increase and underbrush or non-timber trees, and after 1371 no wood of 20 years or more was titheable, *Rot. Parl.* II, 319a. The struggle over the tithing of wood led not only to ill-feeling between clerics and laity but brought the whole vexed

gravamina of 1376 when laymen were resorting to royal writs of prohibition to prevent action against them by the church courts, and in 1377 Simon Sudbury warned the Vicar of Cranbrook that his parishioners were infringing the injunction laid down by Stratford.[1]

Lay abuses were also apparent when benefices were farmed, and the injunction *licet bonae memoriae* recalled the earlier constitutions of Otto and Ottobon and threatened the religious orders should they act contrary to the spirit of the canon.[2] Further regulations, recalling Mepham's statute of 1328, dealt with clandestine matrimony contracted illegally *ad loca remota*, and attempted to prevent the frequent misconduct at funerals and *vigilia mortuorum* by forbidding popular resort to the houses concerned.[3] To judge by the canon *quia divinis*, which forbade parishioners to fell trees or mow grass in churchyards, the medieval public seems to have been drawn to use these places for unsuitable and irreverent behaviour.[4] There is also the economic aspect, for grazing and timber rights could be important to a local vicar. In addition, laymen were guilty of taking offerings from churches. There is a most interesting example of the injunction *immoderate temeritatis* in operation in the diocese of Worcester very soon after the publication of the constitutions.[5] Forty-nine wax candles burning in Ipsley church at Candlemas 1344 were stolen, and Stratford's canon was immediately invoked against the offenders.

question of jurisdiction over tithes into the king's court. The plaintiff would describe *all* wood indiscriminately as *sylva caedua* on the grounds that this was a generic term covering all young, and therefore titheable, trees. The defendant in turn would claim that it was not coppice wood at all, but wood of mature growth, and thus exempt by the act of Edward III. *Sylva caedua* is dealt with by N. Adams, 'The Judicial Conflict over Tithes', *EHR*, LII (1937), 1–22; J. Selden, *A Historie of Tithes* (1618), 236–40; S. Degge, *The Parson's Counsellor with the law of tithes or tithing* (1681), 237–45. I am most grateful to David Gransby for allowing me to see the relevant chapter in his unpublished M.Phil. thesis on Tithe Disputes in the Diocese of York 1540–1640 (1968).

[1] Wilkins, III, 113. [2] Wilkins, II, 703 c. 3; Lyndwood, *Provinciale*, 154.

[3] Wilkins, II, 707 c. 11. See also R. M. Haines 'Bishop Carpenter's Injunctions to the Diocese of Worcester in 1451', *BIHR*, 40 (1967), 203–7; Lyndwood, *Provinciale*, 275.

[4] Wilkins, II, 709 c. 14; Lyndwood, *Provinciale*, 267. This also appears as one of the so-called statutes of Pecham, *C & S*, c. 8, 1123; Cheney, *JEH*, XII, 19.

[5] Wilkins, II, 705 c. 6; Lyndwood, *Provinciale*, 191; *Cal. Reg. Brans.*, p. 104.

The statute *bonae memoriae*, a repetition of the canons of Boniface (1261) and reiterated by Pecham (1281), attempted to safeguard the rights of the testator by forbidding the appropriation of the goods of any cleric dying intestate.[1] Another chapter, *ita quorundam*, was directed against the 'improbitas' of certain ecclesiastical judges.[2] It referred to interference with the actions of executors, both of beneficed clerks and other persons, who were prevented from making a distribution of goods in accordance with the testator's wishes. A problem was raised by the disposal of such goods, which since Ottobon's decree *cum mortis incerta* was not within the jurisdiction of the bishop.[3] Stratford ordered a division of the goods into three parts for the settlement of debts, for pious uses and the salvation of the deceased's soul, and for the next of kin. Bishops were to retain *nothing* for themselves except a reasonable amount *pro labore*. A clever practice which Stratford attempted to halt was that by which laymen, prelates, and beneficed clerks granted away their goods *inter vivos* so that their creditors were defrauded and dilapidations could not be secured.[4]

Other potential sources of friction came from the sequestration of ecclesiastical benefices, a regular method of coercion, and from the initiation of fraudulent processes in distant counties, thereby obtaining sentences unbeknown to the defendants.[5] The chapter *accidit novitate* provides a complicated list of lay infringements of clerical jurisdiction.[6] Lay lords were generally guilty of hindering the exercise of jurisdiction. Not only did they prevent their villeins and their lay tenants from responding to ecclesiastical judges outside their lordships, they also indicted and brought into

[1] Wilkins, II, 705 c. 7; Lyndwood, *Provinciale*, 171; Boniface, Council of Lambeth (1261), *C & S*, 681; Pecham, Council of Lambeth (1281), *C & S*, 913.

[2] Wilkins, II, 706 c. 8; Lyndwood, *Provinciale*, 179.

[3] Ottobon, Council of London (1268), *C & S*, 771. In practice, bishops regularly claimed this right.

[4] Wilkins, II, 706 c. 9; Lyndwood, *Provinciale*, 161. The statutes of George Neville, Archbishop of York, refer to this injunction of Stratford in 1466, Wilkins, III, 601.

[5] Wilkins, II, 709 c. 16; Lyndwood, *Provinciale*, 97.

[6] Wilkins, II, 707–8 c. 12; Lyndwood, *Provinciale*, 261. This gloss deals with canonical opinion on the use of pecuniary penance and its limitation to *ex officio* cases.

the secular courts ecclesiastical persons and matters which should properly have been dealt with in the ecclesiastical forum. They allegedly disrupted ecclesiastical court proceedings and prevented the punishment of transgressors. All such offences were to incur the sentence of greater excommunication.

The injunction *saeculi principes* attempted to deal with the infringement of the *consuetudo* whereby, at the request of the bishop, excommunicates arrested by the secular arm were then released. Excommunicates who were released without reference to the parties at whose instigation the sentence was brought, or who had been imprisoned for a cause not belonging to the ecclesiastical sphere and were subsequently released, were to incur solemn excommunication.[1]

In comparison with other fourteenth- and fifteenth-century provincial legislation, Stratford's constitutions appear to be of considerable importance. All twenty-nine of the *capitula* are extensively glossed by Lyndwood, and further light may sometimes be shed on them by a comparison with the contemporary manuals of instruction for parish priests which indicate many of the same interests and preoccupations.[2]

An examination of grievances against ecclesiastical courts down to the seventeenth century will reveal precisely those points raised by Stratford. One wonders whether the constitutions had a noticeable effect on diocesan administration or on the operation of consistory courts or visitation. The comparative study of episcopal registers may eventually help us to reach a solution to these problems.

The injunctions provide an explicit statement of the particular needs of the Church at this period, but it is also interesting to observe to what degree they are coloured by Stratford's own legal training. The preoccupation with court procedure, probate, fees, and fines certainly is not that of the theologian. Behind much of

[1] Wilkins, II, 708 c. 13. The most recent study of excommunication is F. D. Logan, *Excommunication and the Secular Arm in Medieval England*, Pontifical Institute of Medieval Studies, Studies and Texts, 15 (1968), 75-6.

[2] On pastoral manuals see W. A. Pantin, *The English Church in the Fourteenth Century* (1955), 207-8; L. E. Boyle, 'The *Oculus Sacerdotis* and some other works of William of Pagula', *TRHS*, 5th Series, v (1955), 81-110.

his legislation lies a defence of church property at the parochial level, where indeed it was most vulnerable. One tends to forget that the lesser clergy were not very far removed from their parishioners in social status and influence, and therefore needed more protection than corporate religious bodies. Finally, like all recent archbishops, particularly Pecham and Winchelsey, Stratford is constantly trying to oppose secular encroachment. The *gravamina* are not new, and it was the constant repetition of the same complaints which indicates how insecure was the position of the Church and how vulnerable it was to the impact of purely secular politics.

EDUCATION IN ENGLISH
ECCLESIASTICAL LEGISLATION OF
THE LATER MIDDLE AGES

by ROY M. HAINES

ROVINCIAL and diocesan legislation provided a coherent system of religious education at a time when opportunities for study were few.[1] It is true that in content little was new, but there was much in the way of reiteration, development and expansion, with particular attention to the practical details of implementation.

Mediaeval education is often discussed in terms of clerical education on the one hand, and of lay education on the other. In this context they are one. The priest had first to learn before he could teach, and what was taught can roughly be summed up as faith, morals, and knowledge of the Church's law. It remains true that some things were more appropriate for the clerical than the lay ear. Thus Peter des Roches, Bishop of Winchester (1205–38), required priests to expound the Trinity, the Passion and the Incarnation, but only 'secundum quod convenit laicis',[2] while Archbishop Pecham ordered that Ottobon's constitution on clerical concubinage[3] should be published quarterly in rural chapters

[1] The education of the clergy is discussed by J. R. H. Moorman, *Church Life in England in the Thirteenth Century*, Cambridge 1946, chap. 8. For the following century much can be learned from parts 2 and 3 of W. A. Pantin, *The English Church in the Fourteenth Century*, Cambridge 1955. See also chap. 1, 'The Fifteenth-century background', in Joan Simon, *Education and Society in Tudor England*, Cambridge 1967; Peter Heath, *The English Parish Clergy on the Eve of the Reformation*, London/Toronto 1969, chaps. 5, 6; H. G. Richardson, 'The parish clergy of the thirteenth and fourteenth centuries', *TRHS*, 3rd ser., VI (1912), 118–19, 124–5.

[2] Statutes of Winchester I (1224), c. 51: *Councils and Synods*, ed. F. M. Powicke and C. R. Cheney, 2 vols. Oxford 1964, 134. Hereafter this work is quoted as *C & S* with page reference (the pagination being continuous through both volumes).

[3] Legatine Council of London (1268), c. 8: *C & S*, 756–7.

'exclusis tamen laicis'.[1] As Lyndwood explains, the same information could be treated on two levels. Everyone should know the
articles of faith, but he who had the cure of souls, with the
responsibility of instructing others, must know them 'explicite et
distincte', that is, in such a manner as to be able to explain and
support them. It sufficed for others, 'simplices vel laici', that they
should believe such articles 'implicite'.[2] In any case there is con-
venience in the separate treatment of clerical and lay education in
so far as the manner of instruction is concerned.

A major premise of legislators was that if clerical and more particularly sacerdotal ignorance or unsuitability could be remedied,
the effect on the laity would be correspondingly salutary. Some
went out of their way to elaborate upon the theme. Bishop
Richard Poore (1217–28), for instance, in a preamble to the first
series of Salisbury statutes, suggests that if the Lord's seed is to
germinate and produce fruit the ground must first be cleared, the
weeds rooted out. Starting with a chapter on the irregularity of
priests and clerks, he proceeds to the matter of ordination and the
quality of ordinands, and thence to the basic elements of the faith
and of moral behaviour.[3]

What were the essentials of priestly knowledge? Bishop Grosseteste (1235–53) in the initial chapter of his Lincoln statutes provides an exemplar for future legislators.[4] Every shepherd of souls
and parish priest should know the ten commandments, the seven
'deadly' sins (criminalia)[5]—to the intent that they be avoided, the

[1] Council of Reading (1279), c. 13: C&S, 851.
[2] W. Lyndwood, Provinciale, Oxford 1679, p. 1 ad ver. sciat.
[3] Statutes of Salisbury I (1217 × 1219): C&S, 59 et seq. D. W. Robertson jr.,
'Frequency of Preaching in Thirteenth-Century England', Speculum XXIV
(1949), 378–9, argues the novelty, with respect to both formulation and
content, of those of Poore's constitutions which deal with matters of faith.
[4] Or so it appears. At one time Professor Cheney considered that Grosseteste's
statutes leaned heavily on those of Cantilupe. Compare English Synodalia of the
Thirteenth Century, Oxford 1941, 119–24, with C&S, 265–6. They are now dated
'1239?': Statutes of Lincoln, c. 1: C&S, 268. Cf. Worcester III (1240), c. 34;
Norwich (1240 × 1243), c. 1; Winchester II (1247?), c. 1; Durham II (1241 ×
1249), cc. 1, 2; Ely (1239 × 1256), c. 1; Wells (1258?), c. 43; Exeter II (1287),
c. 20: C&S, 304, 345, 403, 423–4, 516–17, 609–10, 1017.
[5] M. W. Bloomfield, The Seven Deadly Sins, Michigan 1952, 43–4, warns against
confusing the 'cardinal', 'chief', or 'capital' sins with the 'deadly' or 'mortal'

seven sacraments—with special emphasis on penance, and have a simple understanding of the faith as contained in the greater and lesser creeds and in the *Quicunque vult*.[1]

Naturally the statutes contain many expository chapters on the sacraments, but none so terse as that of Richard of (Droit)wich, Bishop of Chichester (1245–53). For the preacher it provides a neat, though not original, framework, on the subject of life's journey: baptism was for *ingredientes*, confirmation for *proeliantes*, eucharist for *itinerantes*, penance for *redeuntes*, extreme unction for *exeuntes*, orders for *ministrantes*, and marriage for *laborantes*.[2]

But most legislators favoured expansion rather than contraction, and some referred their readers to additional material. Associated with the Coventry statutes of Bishop Stavensby (1224–38) are tracts on the seven 'deadly' sins (*criminalia*)[3] and on confession.[4] Roger de Wesebam, a slightly later occupant of the see (1245–56), compiled *Instituta* for the pastoral guidance of his clergy.[5] At Lincoln Grosseteste was responsible for a *summa*, the *Templum Domini*.[6] A masterpiece of compressed, tabular presentation, it

sins, the latter being those which inevitably lead to damnation. In the statutes '*criminalia*' and '*capitalia*' are regularly used of *superbia, invidia, ira, accidia, avaritia, luxuria*, and *gula*, but these are also termed '*mortalia*' by those who commented upon or implemented Pecham's legislation: e.g. Lambeth MS. 460 (15th cent.), fol. 31; *Wykeham's Register*, ed. T. F. Kirby, Hants. Rec. Soc. XIII (1899), II, 371; *The Register of John Stafford, Bishop of Bath & Wells 1425–1443*, ed. T. S. Holmes, Som. Rec. Soc. XXXII (1916), II, 173.

[1] The Apostles', Nicene, and Athanasian creeds. Cf. BM Add. MS 6158, fol. 134v ('Incipit tractatus domini Roberti Grosteth' de confessione'), which contains the same syllabus.

[2] Statutes of Chichester I (1245 × 1252), c. 1: *C & S*, 452. An earlier expanded version is to be found in Bishop Poore's Salisbury statutes (1217 × 1219), c. 15: *C & S*, 65; cf. Exeter I (1225 × 1237), c. 14: *C & S*, 232. A later one is in Exeter II (1287), c. 1: *C & S*, 986. See also *Provinciale*, p. 43 ad ver. *Baptisma, Confirmatio, Poenitentia, Eucharistia, Extrema Unctio*.

[3] The subject had many exponents. See M. W. Bloomfield, *The Seven Deadly Sins*, and the same author's 'A preliminary list of Incipits of Latin works on the virtues and vices, mainly of the Thirteenth, Fourteenth, and Fifteenth Centuries', *Traditio* XI (1955), 259–379.

[4] Statutes of Coventry (1224 × 1237), c. 27: *C & S*, 214; and for the tracts, *C & S*, 214–20, 220–6.

[5] This short piece is printed by Professor Cheney, *English Synodalia*, 149–52, from Bodley MS 57, fols. 96r–97v.

[6] Bodleian Lib., Bodley MS 631, Rawlinson MS. A. 384.

was deservedly popular.[1] Within Worcester diocese Walter Cantilupe's penitential tract, which has not survived, was required reading.[2] For Exeter Bishop Quivil (or Quinel) provided a penitential *summula*, a draught of spiritual medicine, his *Altissimus de terra*.[3] Perhaps the best known of all such tracts, though in origin not a separate piece, merely the ninth chapter of Archbishop Pecham's Lambeth constitutions of 1281, is that known by the memorable incipit *Ignorantia sacerdotum*.[4] To this we will have to return.

Apart from the works written or inspired by bishops and often specifically associated with their legislative activity, there was a growing body of thirteenth-century *summae* or manuals of pastoral theology.[5] Here for the lettered priest was material related to the constitutions but more expansive than they could hope to be.

Didactic matter, then, was readily available, but how could this be used effectively, and how, once appropriate standards were reached, could they be maintained?

The quality of ordinands remained a problem throughout the Middle Ages—and beyond. Certainly many of them left much to be desired in the thirteenth century, and the *Sermo exhortatorius* of William of Melton suggests that at the beginning of the sixteenth they were far from satisfactory.[6]

---

[1] There are some 70 extant manuscripts (L. E. Boyle, 'The *Oculus Sacerdotis* and some other works of William of Pagula', *TRHS*, 5th ser., v (1955), 82 n. 3) of which 65 are listed by S. H. Thomson, *The Writings of Robert Grosseteste*, Cambridge 1940, 138–40. Cf. Bloomfield, 'A preliminary list of Incipits'.

[2] Statutes of Worcester III (1240), cc. 35, 97: *C&S*, 305, 320. It could have been at Syon in the early sixteenth century: *C&S*, 305 n. 1, quoting M. Bateson, *Catalogue of the Library of Syon Monastery, Isleworth*, Cambridge 1898, 191. The index to the catalogue has 'William' rather than 'Walter' (*ibid.* 244), so William de Blois remains a possibility.

[3] Statutes of Exeter II (1287), c. 20: *C&S*, 1018. For the text of the *summula*: *ibid.* 1061–77.   [4] Council of Lambeth (1281), c. 9: *C&S*, 900–5.

[5] Dr Pantin (in this following Professor Leonard Boyle) lists eight, including the *Templum Domini*: *The English Church*, 219. See also, H. G. Pfander, 'Some Medieval Manuals of Religious Instruction in England and Observations on Chaucer's Parson's Tale', *Journal of English and Germanic Philology* XXXV (1936), 243–58; E. J. Arnould, *Le Manuel des Péchés dans la Littérature Religieuse de l'Angleterre*, Paris 1940, 1–59.

[6] *Sermo Exhortatorius cancellarii Eboracensis his qui ad sacros ordines petunt promoveri*, Argentorati 1514 (Bodl. Fasc. e. 186). The BM copy is by Wynkyn de Worde (London 1510?). Heath, *English Parish Clergy*, 70 et seq., discusses this sermon.

The Fourth Lateran Council laid the onus of instructing priests on the bishops who ordained them. It was better to have a few good ministers than many bad ones, for if the blind were to lead the blind both would fall into the ditch.[1] As the legate Otto pointed out, there was much about the sacraments in the canons, but it was no easy task to go through those volumes. So men who were undertaking the cure of souls or the priesthood were to be examined on such matters.[2] Bishop William de Blois of Worcester (1218–36) ordered that the Wednesday to Friday prior to ordinations should be set aside for the examination of candidates, and the business at Worcester and elsewhere was still being taken seriously in the fourteenth century.[3] Another danger was that some who aspired to orders did so for temporal advantage, perhaps the extortion of benefices from those who ordained them—a practice specifically condemned by Bishop Robert Bingham of Salisbury (1229–46).[4]

The archdeacon of course had special responsibility for the clergy within his jurisdiction. By no means the least of his duties was to ensure minimal clerical education, not only by publishing the texts of the constitutions, but also by giving practical tuition. At Salisbury, for instance, the archdeacons were directed to expound in simple words the summary of the faith contained in the first canon of the Fourth Lateran Council.[5] Likewise Cardinal Otto's constitutions directed archdeacons to instruct priests in particular, teaching them what they ought to know about the sacraments of baptism, penance, the eucharist, and matrimony.[6]

Should the clergy's superiors fail in their duty of instruction, the defect could be remedied by having the constitutions made

[1] IV Lateran, c. 27: *Extra* I, 14, c. 14.
[2] Legatine Council of London (1237), c. 2: *C&S*, 246–7: '...set quia non est leve canonum girare volumina et ignorare medico medicinale officium nimis grave...'
[3] Statutes of Worcester II (1229), c. 61: *C&S*, 180. R. M. Haines, *The Administration of the Diocese of Worcester*, London 1965, 172.
[4] Statutes of Salisbury II (1238 × 1244), c. 19: *C&S*, 373–4.
[5] Statutes of Salisbury I (1217 × 1219), c. 3: *C&S*, 61. Cf. Durham II (1241 × 1249), c. 4: *C&S*, 424. *Extra* I, 1, c. 1.
[6] Legatine Council of London (1237), c. 2: *C&S*, 246–7: reiterated by Cardinal Ottobon (1268), c. 19: *C&S*, 768. Cf. Chichester I (1245 × 1252), c. 40: *C&S*, 459.

available in every church.[1] At Exeter, to take one of many instances, vicars and rectors were to have a copy of Bishop Quivil's statutes in their churches so that both they and other parish priests might frequently look them over, revolving the text in their minds until they had it by heart. In this way they would be better prepared to expound the contents to the laity in the vernacular.[2]

In Worcester diocese that careful legislator William de Blois went further. Every chaplain with cure was to come to the diocesan synod bearing with him a copy of the constitutions, and prepared, under penalty of suspension, to answer questions about them or to read them out.[3] A schoolmasterly touch is added by his successor, Cantilupe. Both his constitutions and his tract on penance were to be read out in every (archidiaconal?) chapter. If any difficulty arose, it was to be explained. When one reader left off, another was to continue. There was to be no prior warning, the president of the chapter was merely to hand over the constitutions to any chaplain he chose for him to read them. The same practice was to be observed with respect to the penitential tract. Lack of a copy or ignorance of the contents was to bring a fine of half a mark.[4] In the early fourteenth century we find Bishop Stapledon of Exeter (1308–26) ordering a newly instituted rector, whom he found to be 'in literatura minus sufficiens', to learn his predecessor's *summula*, *Altissimus de terra*, by heart. But when the time-limit expired the rector neither knew the tract nor did he fully understand it. The patron of the living, Sir John de Carminow, is said to have interceded to save him from deprivation.[5]

[1] Statutes of London II (1245 × 1259), c. 1: *C &S*, 634. Cf. Statutes of Salisbury I (1217 × 1219), c. 114: *C &S*, 96; Statutes of Norwich (1240 × 1243), c. 55: *C &S*, 354; etc.

[2] Statutes of Exeter II (1287), c. 56: *C &S*, 1059: '...totiens illam respiciant et revolvant donec quasi cordetenus eam intelligant et sciant pandendam laicis facilius exponere in vulgari'.

[3] Statutes of Worcester II (1229), c. 51: *C &S*, 179.

[4] Statutes of Worcester III (1240), c. 102: *C & S*, 321.

[5] *The Register of Walter de Stapeldon*, ed. H. C. Hingeston Randolph, London/Exeter 1892, 242. The incident is quoted by K. Edwards, 'Bishops and Learning in the Reign of Edward II', *CQR* cxxxviii (1944), 80, and by H. H. Walker 'Notes for a study of Bishop Walter de Stapeldon and the Church in the West Country in the early 14th century', *Devonshire Assoc. Trans.* xciii (1961), 319.

Cardinal Ottobon directed all archbishops and bishops, abbots and priors, whether exempt or not, and also chapters of cathedral churches, to have a copy of his canons.[1] The bishops were to see that they were read yearly in their synods, word for word.[2] By Pecham's time the amount of material to be recited in this way was embarrassingly large, so he reviewed the practice. Stephen Langton's Council of Oxford (1222) had provided the fount, from which clear source had flowed as a stream the legislation of Otto, from which in turn had come that of Ottobon. Thus with respect to those three councils' regulations for the clergy's reformation it was enough that Ottobon's constitutions be recited, but with certain additions, of which the most important came from the Second Council of Lyons (1274). In the second place there was the legislation of Boniface concerning ecclesiastical liberties, then Magna Carta with its supporting sentences of excommunication against violators, and lastly the various sentences of excommunication abstracted from all three sets of canons.[3]

Clerical education, then, was envisaged as a continuous process from the examination prior to the assumption of orders, by way of the teaching of fundamentals and reiteration of legislation in diocesan synods and archidiaconal chapters, and the dissemination of individual copies of statutes so that in any case there could be no excuse for ignorance, which were it to be brought to light in synod would incur appropriate penalty.

Arrangements in individual dioceses varied, and some had more notable legislators than others. At best the system seems a sound one, dependent for its effectiveness, however, on the attention which clerical superiors gave to their educational responsibilities.

Why then was it that at the very end of the great period of thirteenth-century legislation, at the Council of Lambeth (1281), Archbishop Pecham found it necessary to issue the canon *Ignorantia sacerdotum*?[4] Is this to be taken at its face value as an indictment

---

[1] Legatine Council of London (1268), c. 36: *C&S*, 782–3.
[2] For the synod and its functions, see *English Synodalia*, chap. 1.
[3] Council of Reading (1279), c. 1: *C&S*, 834–6, 851, and cf. 474–5.
[4] *C&S*, 900–5.

of clerical ignorance; admission that former legislation and all that accompanied it had failed dismally?

The opening words recalled those of canon 24 of the Fourth Council of Toledo, which is incorporated in the Decretum.[1] There the priest is urged to know the scriptures and the canons. His whole work is said to consist in preaching and *doctrina* (theology); the instruction of men in knowledge of the faith and the discipline of works. Ignorance, adds the Pecham preamble, brought error rather than *doctrina*.

There has been much discussion of Pecham's constitution. Dr Douie in her study of the archbishop is not impressed by his decree, which she described as resembling Bishop Weseham's 'manual'[2] and as being in large part derived from a work of Gautier de Bruges, Pecham's former teacher, who became Bishop of Poitiers.[3] By contrast, Professor Cheney did not regard the dependence of Pecham on Gautier de Bruges to be certain. He considered the archbishop's chapter to be 'of a didactic sort more common in diocesan [than provincial] statutes', and that 'it provided parish priests with the rudiments of religious instruction which they needed for themselves and for the teaching of their flock'.[4] On this point Professor Boyle remarked that 'some, beguiled perhaps by the famous opening sentence about the ignorance of priests, seem to represent Pecham's enactment as a manual of practical theology designed to combat ignorance'. In his view it is 'simply a syllabus which lists or defines what responsible parish priests should preach to their parishioners'.[5] On the other hand, D. W. Robertson maintained that Pecham was trying to dissipate 'theological ignorance' by providing some insight into the systematic theology of the Schools.[6]

There are two distinct points here, that of derivation, and that of purpose. It seems to me on comparing the *Instructiones* of Gautier de Bruges with Pecham's work that they are very close

[1] D. 38, c. 1.
[2] D. L. Douie, *Archbishop Pecham*, Oxford 1952, 134 et seq.; *English Synodalia*, 149–52 (Weseham's *Instituta*).
[3] *Un Traité de Théologie inédit de Gautier de Bruges*, ed. A. de Poorter, Société d'Emulation de Bruges, Mélanges V, Bruges 1911, 1–44.   [4] *C&S*, 887–8.
[5] 'The *Oculus Sacerdotis*', 82.   [6] *Art. cit.*, *Speculum* XXIV, pp. 385–6.

only in the treatment of the fourteen articles of faith, where indeed they are sometimes verbally identical. Otherwise, not only is the order of subject matter quite different, but also, by and large, the treatment. It is true that from time to time the same phrases occur, sometimes to an extent that cannot be explained by the common material. Undoubtedly the outline of instruction in Weseham's *Instituta* is similar to that of Pecham's canon, but such coincidence is hardly surprising. In other respects the two tracts seem to be very different.

In any case, here we are more concerned with the second point, that of the purpose of Pecham's canon. The argument put forward in this paper is that in the legislators' view the basic content of clerical and lay education was the same. Here we are speaking only of minima, of course. The difference lay in depth: the clergy had to preach and expound their knowledge, the laity had merely to receive and accept it. That is why the basic syllabus of Grosseteste was so often repeated.

The Winchester statutes of Bishop Gervais in the 1260s speak of 'multi inscii et illiterati' who usurp the pastoral office. The bishop's official and the archdeacons' officials were to make enquiry as to whether rectors or vicars were greatly deficient in learning and whether they knew *inter alia* the commandments, the seven sacraments, the seven deadly sins, and had some simple knowledge of the faith.[1] These constitutions were written into the later register of Pontissara, to whom they are attributed by its editor.[2] Pontissara, it may be noted, ruled the see of Winchester between 1282 and 1304, that is immediately after the issue of Pecham's canon. As late as 1287 the Grosseteste syllabus was incorporated in one of Bishop Quivil's Exeter statutes, of which the incipit, 'Omnium mater errorum ignorantia precipue in sacerdotibus est vitanda', comes straight out of that canon of the Decretum which could have inspired Pecham.[3]

---

[1] Statutes of Winchester III (1262 × 1265), c. 95: *C&S*, 721. Cf. Statutes of Worcester III (1240), c. 67: *C&S*, 313.

[2] *Registrum Johannis de Pontissara*, ed. C. Deedes, C & Y Soc. XIX (1915), 207. Cf. *English Synodalia*, 103–8.

[3] Statutes of Exeter II, c. 20: *C&S*, 1017; D. 38 c. 1. The seven sins are here termed '*mortalia*'. On the continent a version of the statutes of Daniel Vigier,

Pecham's syllabus was wider in scope—and more explicit—than that of Grosseteste, for it included fourteen articles of faith (twelve was the usual number), the ten commandments, the two additional precepts of the Evangelist, the seven works of mercy, the seven 'capital' sins, the seven principal virtues, and the seven sacraments. All ministers of the Church ought to know them, he declared, and so that none should have the excuse of ignorance, he would set them down in summary form.[1]

In short, Pecham's intention seems to be the provision of a basic syllabus, designed as a *terminus a quo* rather than a *terminus ad quem*. Many who came after were to elaborate upon it,[2] including Archbishop Thoresby in the so-called *Lay Folk's Catechism* for the more simple,[3] and Lyndwood in his *Provinciale* for the *iuris periti*.[4] Long treatises in Latin and English respectively follow recensions of Pecham's canon in manuscripts now at Lambeth[5] and the Bodleian.[6] The author of the latter, who tells us that he is a priest and a graduate in law, while acknowledging his indebtedness to Lyndwood's 'golden' gloss (though in fact it is hard to establish),

Bishop of Nantes, which have been dated 1320, commences: 'Cum propter ignorantiam sacerdotum, maxime curatorum, multa pericula immineant animabus.' *Répertoire des Statuts Synodaux des Diocèses de l'Ancienne France du XIIIe à la fin du XVIIIe siècle*, ed. André Artonne et al., Paris 1963, 317.

[1] *C&S*, 901.

[2] See J. L. Peckham, *Archbishop Peckham as a Religious Educator*, Yale Studies in Religion no. 7, Scottdale, Pennsylvania 1934. The author goes into much greater detail than is possible here, tracing (pp. 83–97) Pecham's influence upon ecclesiastical legislation and (pp. 98–113) on clerical manuals and other works in Latin and English. But the statement that 'As far as the writer knows, no other important ecclesiastical legislation existed in England which prescribed a definite outline of religious instruction for the laity except that which flows in the general channel marked out by the Lambeth decrees' (pp. 93–4), is to ignore Grosseteste and all that went before Pecham.

[3] Ed. T. F. Simmons and H. E. Nolloth, *EETS*, orig. ser., CXVIII (1891); Pantin, *English Church*, 211–12. Archbishop Islip's lost *brevis libellus* (Pantin, 212 n. 3: a reference to Lambeth Reg. Islip fol. 182 provided by Dr Highfield) could also have looked back to Pecham.

[4] *Provinciale*, 1, 42, 54. *Ignorantia sacerdotum* provides Lyndwood's initial gloss.

[5] Lambeth MS 460.

[6] Bodleian Lib. MS Eng. th. c. 57. There is an introduction to this manuscript by P. Hodgson, '*Ignorantia sacerdotum*: a fifteenth century discourse on the Lambeth constitutions', *Review of English Studies* XXIV (1948), 1–11.

prefers something less 'diffuse, intricate with law, and hard of intellect'.[1]

The canon was taken up by subsequent legislators. Thomas Arundel in his 'preaching constitutions' ordered parish priests and stipendiary vicars to confine their preaching to those matters set out in Pecham's *Ignorantia sacerdotum*, which was to be available in every church of the province within three months of the publication of Arundel's own constitutions.[2] Somewhat later, John Stafford, Bishop of Bath and Wells (1425–43), had the canon translated into English and likewise directed that his version be placed in every church in the diocese. The archdeacons were to provide copies for a cost of not more than sixpence.[3] In the northern province *Ignorantia sacerdotum* was reissued by Archbishop George Neville (1465–76) and, some half-century later, in 1518 by Cardinal Wolsey.[4]

To sum up: doubtless many priests in Pecham's day did not measure up to his minimum standards, but the incipit of his ninth canon has a rhetorical flavour and may owe more to the fervour of the reformer than to the qualified assessment of the administrator. Arguments from its re-publication must also be treated with caution. None the less, there were priests, even long after Pecham's time, who failed to reach his minimum requirements. A Winchester rector during William of Wykeham's episcopate (1366–1404) had to swear to learn those basic elements of faith and sacerdotal duty contained in the Lambeth constitution, under penalty of forty shillings.[5] Bishop John Stafford's translation was made with the express intention of easing the task of that 'simplex sacerdos' for whom Pecham had shown concern.[6] At the beginning of the sixteenth century the 'curate' could look to the printed book for treatment of these familiar themes.[7]

---

[1] Bodleian Lib., MS Eng. th. c. 57, fols. 3r, 6r.
[2] Lyndwood, *Provinciale, Const. Prov.*, 65.
[3] *The Register of John Stafford*, II, 173. Stafford was archbishop of Canterbury 1443–52.
[4] Wilkins, III, 599–601, 662, 664–5.   [5] *Wykeham's Register*, II, 371.
[6] Pecham's canon is entitled in many MSS 'De informatione simplicium sacerdotum'.
[7] The *Exoneratorium Curatorum*, London 1520? (Richard Pynson), or *Exornatorium Curatorum*, London 1520? (Wynkyn de Worde), is based on Pecham's canon.

To turn to the instruction of the laity, to which end clerical education was primarily directed. Those with cure of souls should guide the people by their example and exhortation, instructing them in right doctrine and clean living.[1] Pecham's injunctions for the parish clergy of Canterbury diocese stress the threefold nature of the cure of souls: preaching, dispensing of the sacraments, and the hearing of confessions.[2] Provincial and diocesan legislation envisaged lay education as being effected in four principal ways: by the direct instruction of children and adults in the faith, by regular preaching, by means of the confessional, and by making known sentences of excommunication—a negative guide to behaviour.

Bishop Poore's statutes direct parish priests to call children together often for instruction in the creed, the Lord's Prayer, and the Hail Mary, and to admonish parents to do likewise.[3] In the *Templum Domini* the same threefold formula is declared a necessity for the laity: the Creed—*ad fidem*; the Lord's Prayer—*ad caritatem*; the Hail Mary—*ad spem*.[4] With the proper way to make the sign of the Cross such instruction was frequently repeated.[5] Norwich statutes laid down that on every Sunday at Prime and Compline the priest was to say the Lord's Prayer and Creed with deliberation, his parishioners listening carefully so as to comprehend what was said.[6] In later statutes the confessional is named as the means of examining laymen in their understanding of the faith, so that in case of defect remedial instruction could be given.[7]

As with children, so with parents, the purpose of instruction was the salvation of souls, for it was a fundamental tenet that anyone who did not firmly believe the catholic faith could not be saved.[8]

[1] Statutes of York I (1241 × 1255), c. 1: *C&S*, 485–6; Chichester II (1289), c. 1: *C&S*, 1082–3.　　[2] *C&S*, 1079.
[3] Statutes of Salisbury I (1217 × 1219), c. 5: *C&S*, 61. Later, Exeter statutes add 'vel saltem instrui faciant ab expertis': Exeter I (1225 × 1237), c. 2: *C&S*, 228.
[4] Bodley MS 631, fol. 190v.　　[5] E.g. *C&S*, 269, 346, etc.
[6] Statutes of Norwich (1240 × 1243), c. 7: *C&S*, 346.
[7] E.g. Statutes of Winchester II (1247?), c. 10: *C&S*, 405.
[8] Statutes of Exeter II (1287), c. 20: *C&S*, 1017–18: '...tanto tenentur studiosius informare quanto quilibet qui fidem catholicam firmiter non crediderit salvus esse non poterit'.

Although the laity were to be taught about the sacraments, their administration was a priestly affair, except in the case of baptism, which was to be performed by the laity in emergency when no priest was to be had. For this reason careful instruction was needed with respect to the precise words which had to be used.[1]

Appropriate moral behaviour was to be taught by priestly example, but also by preaching on that important topic, the seven deadly sins, for which purpose it was necessary that the priest's study 'be set to know vices from virtues'.[2] Other matters were more within the sphere of social mores, such as the repeated instruction not to lie on the baby during sleep, the purpose of marriage, and the upbringing of children in the fear of the Lord.[3]

Although in much provincial and diocesan legislation there is frequent mention of 'monition' and 'exhortation', it is clear that preaching was considered the fundamental didactic tool for reaching a wide audience. Stephen Langton at the Council of Oxford (1222) urged parish priests not to be 'dumb dogs' (*canes muti*), but to minister to their people the food of the word of God.[4] But some undoubtedly were dumb, so Bishop Stavensby of Coventry diocese directed that a sermon or tract on the seven deadly sins was to be read out on Sundays or other feasts.[5] The more resourceful doubtless used it merely as a model. Pecham laid priests with cure under obligation to expound his syllabus four times a year. This was to be done simply 'absque cuiuslibet textura fantastica'.[6] And as we have seen, in dangerous times Arundel did not want the inexperienced preacher to venture beyond the Pecham outline.

Thus legislation gave much direction as to the matter of the

---

[1] Statutes of Canterbury I (1213 × 1214), cc. 31, 32: *C &S*, 31; Salisbury I (1217 × 1219), c. 22: *C &S*, 68–9; Council of Oxford (1222), c. 29—it being one of the archdeacon's duties to see that proper instruction was given: *C &S*, 115; etc.

[2] Bodleian Lib., MS Eng. th. c. 57, fol. 9r.

[3] Statutes of Worcester III (1240), cc. 25, 27: *C &S*, 302.

[4] *Ibid.* c. 15: *C &S*, 110.   [5] *C &S*, 214–20.

[6] Council of Lambeth (1281), c. 9: *C &S*, 901. For Pecham's own use of the sermon see D. L. Douie, 'Archbishop Pecham's Sermons and Collations', *Studies in Medieval History presented to F. M. Powicke*, ed. R. W. Hunt *et al.*, Oxford repr. 1969, 269–82. On the general problem of the frequency of preaching in the thirteenth century, see Robinson, *art. cit.*, *Speculum* XXIV.

sermon, and occasionally a hint as to the manner. But this is comparatively little when one bears in mind the space given to penance and the confessional. Various chapters devoted to the subject are tracts in themselves, not to mention those lengthier works associated with the statutes.

The Fourth Lateran decree *Omnis utriusque sexus* laid down the minimal requirement of annual confession to one's parish priest.[1] Here was a great pastoral opportunity. The confessional provided a more personal means of instructing parishioners in the faith than did the sermon *ad omnes*. Peter des Roches in his Winchester statutes (1224) required priests to use the confessional for giving simple instruction in the Trinity, the Passion, and the Incarnation. They were also to make sure that penitents knew the Lord's Prayer and the Apostles' Creed, at any rate in English.[2] Regular legislation demanded only such basic essentials, but occasionally the priest had to deal with more unusual items, such as enjoining the reservation of harvest gleanings for the needy and aged.[3]

The great period of English ecclesiastical legislation was over well before the close of the thirteenth century. By comparison the output of the fourteenth and fifteenth centuries is meagre. Only Archbishop Stratford's constitutions with their twenty-nine chapters[4] stand out as a substantial contribution, and much of their material is not new. There was no need for further wide-ranging legislation, as the old remained in force and, if need be, particular canons could be re-published, as was *Ignorantia sacerdotum*. Additional matters not covered by earlier legislation might be dealt

[1] *Extra* 5, 38, c. 12. Cantilupe advised the faithful to make confession before Christmas, Easter and Pentecost, so that 'confessione purgati digne possint suum recipere salvatorem'. Statutes of Worcester III (1240), c. 31: *C&S*, 304. Cf. Salisbury I (1217×1219), c. 38: *C&S*, 72-3.
[2] C. 51: *C&S*, 134.
[3] Statutes of Worcester II (1229), c. 24: *C&S*, 174.
[4] These are the constitutions of the second and third series glossed by Lyndwood. There was also a first (draft?) series. Wilkins, II, 675-8, 696-702, 702-9; Cheney, 'Legislation of the Medieval English Church' (part 2), *EHR*, CXCIX (1935), 415-17. Discussed by Brenda Bolton, 'The Council of London of 1342', in this volume. BM Add. MS 6716 contains (fol. 811) a form which the 'curatus' of one church could use to notify the 'curatus' of another that (marriage) banns had been called three times. This was to implement [Stratford's] constitution 'Humana concupiscentia'.

with by the publication of individual constitutions, by *ad hoc* mandates, or indeed by the visitation process.[1]

The needs of the later centuries were perhaps more sophisticated. The number of literate laymen was increasing, while incumbents of the fourteenth century went to the university in appreciable numbers, thanks to Boniface VIII's constitution *Cum ex eo*.[2] There was a growing literature in Latin and English concerned with pastoral theology, confession, preaching,[3] and mysticism, with legal glosses for those so minded. All of this served to enlarge the horizons of men of those days, even if there was persistent elaboration of well-worn themes. The foundation had been firmly laid by the legislation of the thirteenth century.

[1] For a set of 'minor constitutions', see R. M. Haines, 'Bishop Carpenter's Injunctions to the Diocese of Worcester in 1451', *BIHR* XI (1967), 203–7.

[2] L. E. Boyle, 'The Constitution *Cum ex eo* of Boniface VIII: Education of Parochial Clergy', *Mediaeval Studies* XXIV (1962), 263–302; R. M. Haines, 'The Education of the English Clergy during the later Middle Ages: some observations on the operation of Boniface VIII's constitution *Cum ex eo* (1298)', *Canadian Journal of History* IV (1969), 1–22.

[3] See H. Caplan, *Mediaeval 'Artes Praedicandi', a Hand-List*, New York 1934.

THE REPRESENTATION
OF THE *UNIVERSITAS FIDELIUM*
IN THE COUNCILS OF THE
CONCILIAR PERIOD

by JOSEPH GILL

THE Council of Pisa was the fruit of a long period of gestation. Intermittently over centuries canonists had discussed where in various contingencies the supreme authority in the Church lay—with the pope, the cardinals, the *universitas fidelium* in a general council. Twice in the fourteenth century theory was nearly tested by practice, when Philip the Fair opposed Boniface VIII and when Louis of Bavaria faced John XXII. The final challenge was given by the Great Schism. Begun in 1378 it dragged on for decades, causing irreparable damage to Christian Europe. Neither of the rival 'popes' showed any genuine goodwill to end it. So others, particularly in France, lent a hand. When Benedict XIII in Avignon refused the *via cessionis* (abdication) and paid only lip-service to the *via discussionis*, the court of Paris withdrew its obedience and the theologians of the French universities justified the royal action. Canonists like Conrad of Gelnhausen and Henry of Langenstein wrote treatises to uphold the superiority of the *universitas fidelium*, i.e. a general council, over pope and cardinals. But who could summon a council? And who could best represent the *universitas fidelium*?

It had been the cardinals who had started the schism when, confident that they were the chief power in the Church, they declared Urban VI's election invalid. They were the prime movers in the summoning of the Council of Pisa and in its running. In Constance, four years later, those same cardinals were fighting to retain a semblance of their previous importance, and bishops in the four or five 'Nations' were the chief authority representing the *universitas fidelium*. In Basle neither cardinals nor bishops counted for much; it was the mass of doctors and masters who claimed to represent the Church universal and who dominated the conciliar scene. The Council of Florence found still another solution, but within the same general pattern.

The rest of this paper is devoted to examining this suggestion of a shift of power within the four councils of the conciliar period.

THE COUNCIL OF PISA 1409

In 1378 Cardinal Amiel, one of those who at Anagni elected Clement VI, wrote: 'Pope and cardinals are in the Church of Rome in such a way that they are the Church of Rome, which received the keys and the power of binding and loosing...It is the Roman Church, which consists of the cardinals, that is said to preside over all chapters and churches of the world.'[1] The cardinals who took action at Pisa expressed themselves in much the same way. In a letter inviting Manuel II, Emperor of Constantinople, to send representatives to their council they wrote: 'We Cardinals of both Colleges whose daily burden should be and is, according to the Apostle, "anxiety for all the churches", who, too, by Levitical law are the helpers of the High Priest,...are united in a single proposal of unity,...namely by convoking a general council...[to which] by our letters and envoys we require patriarchs, archbishops, bishops...everywhere' to come.[2]

Patriarchs, archbishops, bishops, etc., did go in large numbers to join the twenty-two cardinals in Pisa, and in the church of St Michael, where the sessions were held, they were arranged 'in such a way, though, that my lords the cardinals were seated on a bench, as it were presidents, with their backs to the altar and their faces towards the bishops and the others arrayed before them'.[3] Actually, only in the first few sessions did a cardinal act as president. When Simon de Cramaud, Patriarch of Alexandria, arrived on 26 April as head of the French delegation, he was made president and in the sessions sat after the senior cardinal, though at

---

[1] Quoted by O. Přerovský, *L'elezione di Urbano VI e l'insorgere dello Scisma d'Occidente*, Rome 1960, 81.

[2] Mansi, 27, 171B.   [3] Mansi, 27, 361B. Cf. also 116A.

the conciliar Masses his place was with the prelates after the Camerarius, the Archbishop of Narbonne.[1] But he was president more in name than in fact.

It was the cardinals who were the real directors of the council, and nothing of moment was done without consulting them. When on 15 April the envoys of Bavaria challenged the council's right to exist, they 'as presidents...sent notaries to each of the seats of the other prelates to seek their opinions'.[2] 'On 24 April...because my lords the cardinals had put into writing the whole history of the division in the Church...for the space of three hours the advocate of the council read it out in a loud and audible voice.'[3] Possibly there was some criticism of their methods. At any rate, on 8 May, 'the Cardinal of Preneste said that his brethren had no desire to do anything in the pursuit of union without the council and, because not everybody could be present at these deliberations, it would be good that they should appoint some to be present always when there was discussion and to report the result to the others'.[4] The opinion of the cardinals was awaited before the question of proceeding against the absent cardinals was decided.[5] Five days after the deposition of the two 'popes' on 5 June, 'the advocate of the council asked whether it was the council's will that my lords the cardinals should depute some to draw up an account of the legal process and should announce the sentence and execute it over the whole world'.[6] Then, with both 'popes' deposed, a new one was to be elected. A suggestion that, since there was present only one cardinal whose elevation dated from before the Schism, the council itself might elect was given scant attention. The cardinals for their part promised that the new pope could continue the council to effect reform of the Church, and then it was agreed that there should be no prejudice to their rights as electors, the council supplying any possible defect in the present instance. Alexander V was generous in granting graces, but he gave none to the detriment of the cardinals.

Of the four chief sources for the Council of Pisa, from which

[1] Mansi, 27, 125 D.
[2] Mansi, 27, 362 A.
[3] Mansi, 27, 5 E–6 A.
[4] Mansi, 27, 7 E–8 A.
[5] 17 May: Mansi, 27, 9 B.
[6] Mansi, 27, 404 E.

the above account is drawn, none records the numbers of voters pro and con any motion, still less their status. There are extant, however, two lists of names which are instructive. The one is attached to the decree deposing the two 'popes'. It is signed by 24 cardinals, 80 bishops and 4 bishops elect, 62 abbots, 12 priors, various generals of orders, and procurators of princes, bishops, abbots, or others. Of the signatories only one, Nicholas Rishton, 'utriusque iuris doctor ac causarum palacii apostolici auditor', did not sign as a 'mitre' or as a procurator of another. In actual fact he was a member of the embassy representing Henry V of England (Mansi, 27, 336D), and that may be the reason why he signed, even though it is not noted with his signature. Another non-'mitre', William Bruni, 'decretorum doctor canonicus Magalon-ensis', signed both *proprio nomine* and also as procurator of the Archbishop of Arles: one wonders why he, a non-'mitre', wrote *proprio nomine*, for in this he is unique. This list bears witness to some 235 people participating in the council.[1]

The other list of names is found in Mansi, 27, 331-56: 'Nomina patrum qui Pisano concilio interfuerunt.' It is a register of the names and qualifications of members under the dates on which they were incorporated, and lists 24 cardinals, 95 bishops with 2 bishops elect, 84 abbots and many generals or provincials of orders, procurators of princes, universities, bishops, abbots, chapters, etc. The embassies of princes are, with only five or six exceptions, made up exclusively of clerics. No non-bishop or non-abbot is there *pro se*. A few of the signatories of the deposition are not found on this list and, on the other hand, some on this list are not among the signatories. That is to be expected, of course, of those who were incorporated after 5 June, when the deposition of the two 'popes' was decreed. Surprisingly, however, Antony, Cardinal of S. Maria in Via Lata, who was registered on 7 June, signed the decree of deposition though without asserting that he was present at its promulgation, whereas Francis, Bishop of

---

[1] J. Vincke, *Schriftstücke zum Pisaner Konzil. Beiträge zur Kirchen- und Rechts-geschichte*, III, Bonn 1942, 177–205. Dr M. Harvey very kindly sent me photographs of these pages, for which I am very grateful. (For further discussion of Rishton's part in the council, see Dr Harvey's paper which follows.—Ed.)

Melos, who registered on 13 June, wrote *presens fui, consensi et subscripsi.*

At each session, after the solemn Mass and the litany, it was only 'familiaribus dominorum cardinalium et aliis omnibus vocem in concilio non habentibus extra ecclesiam devectis' that conciliar business began.[1] But who had a 'voice' in the council? The Religious of St Denis mentions in his account for the second session (devoted almost entirely to formalities): 'his peractis, publice indictum fuit auctoritate concilii ut omnes, nunciis et doctoribus exceptis, ab ecclesia recederent'.[2] But the only other relevant notice suggests that doctors had no general right to be present: 'Quo facto, dixit unus notarius ex parte totius concilii quod omnes, qui non haberent vocem in concilio, irent extra ecclesiam, exceptis doctoribus, magistris in theologia et servitoribus de mitra dominorum cardinalium. Tunc omnes vocem non habentes exiverunt.'[3]

The general procedure seems to have been that each province (i.e. not merely Nation; most Nations had several ecclesiastical provinces) elected one representative who was present at the non-public deliberations with the cardinals, who then reported back to a meeting of his electors where the topic was discussed and agreed upon. Presumably he thereupon delivered to the cardinals the decision arrived at. Later in public session the conclusion was proclaimed and a vote taken in writing. The impulse for this arrangement came, it seems, from the cardinals when the Cardinal of Preneste suggested the appointing of deputies.[4] The French immediately agreed that if possible an archbishop, otherwise a bishop or a doctor, should represent each province and 'it was decided that the same should be done by the other nations, and that only such delegates should remain during the deliberations'.[5] In the sessions, 'posthaec fuerunt vota sedentium in synodo per notarios super praemissis petitionibus scrutata. Et placuit omnibus.'[6] The phrase 'vota sedentium' is frequent in this

---

[1] 15 April; Mansi, 27, 123A. [2] Mansi, 27, 3D.
[3] 10 May, VIII session; Mansi, 27, 126E.
[4] Mansi, 27, 7E–8A; cf. above.
[5] Mansi, 27, 8A. [6] Mansi, 27, 127C.

version of the Acts (e.g. 122 C, 126 C: or *vota singulorum* in another version, e.g. 365 E, 395 D). It is probably the equivalent of *vocem habentium*, which would certainly include all prelates but probably not doctors as such.[1]

It is true that Cardinal d'Ailly wrote in a memorandum at the Council of Constance that at Pisa doctors 'signed their names to the final decrees' and Cardinal Fillastre that: 'You will find in it [Pisa] almost a hundred persons of this sort, especially doctors and licentiates, officially admitted and subscribers to the verdict against Pedro de Luna and Angelo'.[2] Fillastre's remark may be no more than a gloss on d'Ailly's, and both probably refer to the list of signatories described above. It should, however, be noted that, Rishton and Bruni apart (and they are doubtful exceptions), all the 'doctors and licentiates' functioned as procurators of more official principals. Or the two cardinals might have been thinking of a special meeting of all doctors, 105 in number (except for 6 or 8 licentiates), held under the chairmanship of the Archbishop of Milan to ascertain their views on the deposition of the 'popes': they all concurred and signed the statement, which was read out in the following session on 29 May.[3]

THE COUNCIL OF CONSTANCE 1414

For the convoking of the Council of Pisa the cardinals had been fully responsible. For the Council of Constance they shared responsibility with Sigismund, King of Hungary. When he proposed to John XXIII the summoning of a council, it was they who made the pope reply and accept; and later, when the time came to open the council, in spite of his reluctance they prevailed on him to go. The first session was held on 16 November; the second not till 2 March. Meantime the council was organizing itself. It followed the style of the Council of Pisa (of which it considered itself to be the continuation) by dividing into Nations, but with this difference, that these were no longer sub-divided into ecclesi-

[1] *Domini cardinales, quasi presidentes, ibidem...miserunt notarios ad singulas sedes aliorum prelatorum...*, 15 April, IV session, Mansi, 27, 362 A.
[2] *The Council of Constance*, trans. L. R. Loomis, New York & London 1961, 214, 215.　　　　　　　[3] Mansi, 27, 400 AB.

astical provinces, each with a single vote, but the Nation itself was the sole unit, whose decision was settled by votes of the members. In Constance the division into Nations was not altogether guileless. It was meant to counteract a manoeuvre of the pope who, it was said, to provide himself with support, on the eve of the council had appointed some fifty new Italian prelates.

If John was distressed by being thus checkmated, he was even more disconcerted by the turn that the council was taking. The general demand was for unity in the Church to be achieved not by insisting on the solution of Pisa (as the Italian Nation proposed), but (as the other Nations urged) to be obtained anew by treating the two deposed popes as if they were not deposed and by forcing John himself to abdicate, though for the council then at Constance he was the only legitimate pope. In the vanguard of this latter movement were the cardinals, and at least two of them (d'Ailly and Fillastre) were even advocating widening the suffrage in the council to allow a deliberative vote to others besides prelates.[1]

The flight of John XXIII on 21 March from Constance to Schaffhausen changed the situation radically. It threatened the Council with dissolution. Nine cardinals followed the pope, but only on the first stage of his flight. In Constance, with the aid of the other seven cardinals Sigismund managed to allay the panic and to keep the council in existence. Thereafter John had lost all authority, and the King of the Romans was the real head of the council. The abdication of John became more than ever the immediate purpose to be attained and with that there was allied a determination to reform the Church in head and members.

---

[1] It should, however, be noted that d'Ailly stipulated: 'To begin with, a distinction should be drawn between the subjects to be treated in the Council. They may be either such as relate solely to the Catholic faith, the sacraments, and purely spiritual aspects of the Church, with which the holy fathers of old dealt in their general councils. In such a case the canon law has much to say and what I am now writing nothing at all. Or else they may relate to the ending of the present Schism and the establishment of unbroken unity and peace. In which case the following remarks are pertinent.'

Fillastre seemingly went further. Having spoken of anyone with a cure of souls or learning as suitable for the council, he proceeds: 'As for ambassadors of kings and princes, clearly they should be given a voice in matters that concern the Universal Church, such as church union and faith' (Loomis, *The Council of Constance*, 213, 216).

The position of the cardinals was rendered equivocal and difficult. They were all nominees of a pope. They were all *fratres nostri* of the pope. The majority of them had in fact joined John in his flight even though temporarily, and the rest were suspected of being too favourable to him. They were the 'members' destined for reform with the head, and not considered likely to be enthusiastic co-operators in the process of their own reformation. Add that the Sacred College contained no German and no Englishman, who might have been a liaison between it and the two most radical of the Nations.

The most complete, single account of the Council of Constance is the narrative history written by Guillaume Fillastre, Cardinal of St Mark.[1] Obviously it is sympathetic to the College, but the events it narrates are amply confirmed by other documents. Fillastre's story in brief is of the war waged against the College by Sigismund with the backing of the German and English Nations (and till 1417 also of the French), of the resistance offered and of the final justification. The tension began as soon as John XXIII left Constance in flight. At the third session (26 March) the cardinals were not informed beforehand of the agenda and only two of them attended, one (d'Ailly) to preside, the other (Zabarella) to read out the decrees; and these two functioned only to prevent others taking over what were traditionally offices of the cardinals. Then the three Nations of France, Germany and England, without informing the cardinals, prepared a number of decrees declaring the council validly constituted for the ending of schism and for the reform of the Church of God in head and members, subordinating pope and everyone else to its God-given authority, and enjoining presence and co-operation of all suitable persons. This time only the able diplomacy of Sigismund, anxious to avoid an open rift at this juncture, persuaded the cardinals to attend (30 March). But Zabarella omitted in his reading of the decrees phrases that he judged incorrect—the phrases, in fact, that were the most radical imposing reform and conciliar superiority. Then came news of John's further flight. There was, therefore, still another solemn

[1] H. Finke, *Acta Concilii Constanciensis*, II, Münster im W. 1923, 13–170. Eng. trans., Loomis, *The Council of Constance*, 200–465.

184

session, the fifth, held on 6 April, to promulgate the fuller version of the decrees of the week before. Four cardinals refused to attend. Cardinal Orsini, however, presided, and seven others were present, but of these Zabarella refused to read the decrees, and the rest had previously declared that they were participating only to avoid scandal.

The Nations, so Fillastre narrates, continued to treat the cardinals with complete contempt, showing them the texts of the decrees that they had elaborated and agreed on only shortly before they were approved in session. After repeated complaints the College proposed that it should be considered as a Nation since 16 cardinals were nearly as numerous as, and much more eminent than, the 20 Englishmen of the English Nation, of whom only three were bishops. Their request was refused: they were told to join their respective Nations. However, they were allowed to appoint deputies to sit and act with the deputies of the Nations. In point of fact for the rest of the Council the cardinals did not join their Nations but in practice seem to have functioned as a Nation. At every session the cardinal of Ostia, the president, for the cardinals gave his *placet* before the four functionaries 'deputed for the four Nations to read, check, etc., what the synod had decided upon' uttered in turn their *placets*.[1]

On 18 July 1415, with no cardinal, 16 prelates and doctors, and 4000 horse, Sigismund set off to treat in the council's name with Peter de Luna, Benedict XIII, about abdication. In his absence nothing of importance was to be done. He was away a year and a half and ended his journey in England when he allied himself with Henry V against France. While he was away the friction between the cardinals with the Italian Nation and the other three Nations continued. After Sigismund's return in January 1417 the College found new supporters. The French Nation, bitter at Sigismund's English alliance, broke off from the German and English Nations. At the same time the Spanish Nation was coming into being and its sympathies lay rather with the French and Italians. The rift had been building up for some time, because the French had sided with the Aragonese in a squabble about precedence and even

[1] Cf. Mansi, 27, 606 D, 623 D, 682, etc.

publicly protested at the minute English delegation being considered a Nation at all, on a par with the much bigger Nations of Germany, Italy and France.

With Sigismund's return a new question came to the fore, which after the deposition of Benedict XIII (26 July) became an open quarrel. He with the German and English Nations wanted first to reform the Church in head and members and then to elect a new pope. The cardinals with the Italians, French and Spaniards placed the unity of the Church first, i.e. a new pope, and then reform. Tension mounted rapidly. Sigismund tried to intimidate his opponents and even thought of arresting at least some of the cardinals on trumped up charges. He exercised great influence through his loyal henchmen—the Bishop of Salisbury, president of the English Nation, the Patriarch of Antioch, president of the French Nation, and the Bishop of Milan, president of the Italian Nation. His opponents resisted with growing confidence. Mauroux was not only deprived of the presidency of the French Nation in May 1417 but even excluded from the Nation altogether, though he was a Frenchman. In June the Archbishop of Milan lost his presidency. The Bishop of Salisbury died on 4 September and Henry V of England changed his orders to the English delegation, freeing them from the obligation he had imposed to support all Sigismund's motions. In the end both the cardinals and Sigismund had to accept a compromise, but it was one that included all the cardinals as voters in the conclave for the election of a pope and the need of a two-thirds majority of their vote, along with others. It was a cardinal who was elected. At the end of it all the College emerged unsubdued but not triumphant. It had been challenged as never before and did not again recover its old prestige and power in the Church.

Though the cardinals retained at least externally their traditional functions in the Council of Constance, the real power in it lay with Sigismund and the Nations. Within the Nations there seems no doubt that the members voted as equals. But it is not clear precisely who were the members and how many there were in each Nation. Obviously all bishops and abbots were members. For the rest there does not seem to have been any central bureau where all members of the council, irrespective of Nation, had to register. Instead, each Nation apparently registered its own. An attempt was made to establish qualifications to be observed by all. The French and Italians, some little time after February 1416,[1] in a project, 'De forma et ordine concilii et de personis ac rebus ad Concilium pertinentibus',[2] proposed 'Nullus inscribatur nisi qui pro se vel ab alio missus venerit ad concilium et pro concilio' and each should be 'in dignitate constitutus vel doctor vel licentiatus in theologia vel iure'. The German Nation to which the project was referred expanded the qualifications to include any authorized proxy, anyone in administrative office, canons of cathedrals *Rector vel plebanus*; and at the end added: 'Let this article be omitted for the time being and let us come together in peace and work for the common good as we have been doing.' No version of these regulations seems to have been officially adopted by the council, but in practice what they proposed about presidents and the various functionaries seems to have been observed.

But possibly not all the members of a Nation had a right to vote. On one occasion in mid-May 1415 the German Nation, either because of its own bad conscience or as a result of complaints from others, proposed self-amendment by imitating the French Nation, which (they said) distinguished between those having a vote and those with no vote, locating them separately in the meetings and having notaries to control who voted and how.[3]

As voting was done in the Nations, in the sessions there was registered only the assent of the cardinals as a body and of each of the Nations as a body. Hence there are no definitions with lists of names to allow the inquirer to analyse the composition of the council. There is, however, a useful list of signatories to the agreement of Narbonne, that was accepted by the council on 4 February 1416. It contains the names of 20 cardinals, 2 patriarchs, 46 archbishops or bishops, 30 abbots, and 120 others, i.e. 98 'mitres' and 120 others. Several of the bishops and many of the

---

[1] Finke, *Acta Concilii Constanciensis* II, 577.   [2] *Ibid.* 742–58.
[3] *De modo suffragia aptius colligendi*: H. von der Hardt, *Magnum oecumenicum Constantiense concilium*, Helmstadt 1697–9, IV, 190 seq.

abbots were also delegates of princes or proxies for other bishops or abbots. Of the rest—canons, priors and graduates of various sorts, and 72 without any degree noted—all except 14 are registered as proxies of some individual or institution (9 of them *pro se et pro*...).[1]

Another interesting account is that given of a prolonged debate spread over many meetings of the French Nation on the subject of papal annates. Everyone was supposed to voice his opinion, but it is not certain that they did so before the Nation became thoroughly tired of the subject and (though not without opposition) applied the guillotine. 102 votes are recorded of 1 patriarch, 9 bishops, 13 abbots (these spoke first), then in any order apparently of 10 doctors, 32 masters, 12 priors, 21 proxies, and 4 others.[2] Fillastre asserts that by 21 March 1415 the French was 'the greatest of all the Nations both in numbers and in the quality of its members, for it included four hundred men of distinction'.[3] In that case the votes of some three hundred members, including such outstanding personalities as Gerson, are not recorded in this debate on the annates.

THE COUNCIL OF BASLE 1431

The Council of Basle was convoked by Martin V just before his death to meet in 1431. His successor Eugenius IV for various reasons tried to prorogue it before ever it had really got going. Of the few who were present in the council in the last months of

[1] Mansi, 27, 817–24. The figures given by von der Hardt, *op. cit.*, IV, 592–602, are slightly different and in general lower.

[2] Mansi, 28, 166 seq. Priors might also be doctors, and proxies usually had some rank or degree. Some of the bishops, abbots, and graduates not noted in the voting as proxies were also proxies; they claimed to register their proxy vote (apparently in vain) only after the threat of closure. So probably the 21 proxies noted above were only proxies with no vote *pro se*.

Some inquirer compiled statistics of all those present in Constance for the council. He records 3 patriarchs, 22 cardinals, 5 more patriarchs of other obediences, 17 archbishops, 33 titular bishops, 99 diocesan bishops, 110 abbots, and among the many other items noted in the 38 columns of categories and names, one finds *curtesani quos reperi in domibus* MD; *simplices presbyteri quos reperi in domibus* MDCC; and near the very end, *mulieres communes ad minus* DCC, without saying where he found them (von der Hardt, *Magnum oecumenicum Constantiense*, V, 12–50).

[3] Finke, *Acta Concilii Constanciencis*, II, 23: Loomis, *Council of Constance*, 221.

1431, several had taken part in the Council of Pavia-Siena, which Martin had contrived to bring to a speedy end. They were not going to be tricked again and were determined on reforming the Church before they separated. So they set their faces against prorogation and resolved to remain and function where they were. From the start, then, there was friction between pope and council. It was soon open war. Appealing to and widening the principle of conciliar superiority decreed in Constance the council attracted large numbers of adherents, summoned the pope to present himself before it, and threatened cardinals and curia if they did not attend.

Of the twenty-one cardinals in 1431 most wilted before the unyielding determination of the council. By the end of 1432 only five remained faithful to the pope. The rest were either on missions or had openly made their submissions to the council. The maximum number that voted at any time seems to have been seven, in late 1433 and early 1434, after which they began to return to their allegiance to the pope, even though he was then in exile from Rome, first in Florence and later in Bologna. In the council they were treated with great respect. Though too few to wield any great influence as a body (and perhaps because of that) they played a full part in the deliberations, were as critical of Eugenius as most others, had the council insist that they should receive their emoluments, and began to drift back where they belonged, the papal Curia, even before it was certain that Eugenius's star was in the ascendant. Their value to the council probably was not so much the personal merits that they undoubtedly possessed or because their adherence to the council was also a denuding of the pope of his most intimate support, as that their presence gave a kind of completeness to the council, making it seem to represent every section of the Church, even the highest. Assuredly the council was enormously indebted to two members of the Sacred College in particular—Cesarini who for the years of its legally conciliar activity was its director and the warranty of its respectability, and after him Aleman without whom the attenuated remnant of the *conciliabulum* would have distintegrated.

Bishops at Basle were relatively few, whereas there was always a multitude of functionaries of dioceses and cathedrals and of graduates of various sorts, some as procurators of bishops or abbots or chapters, etc. The numbers and qualities of those voting are rarely recorded but there are enough data extant to indicate general proportions.[1]

	Total number of members	Quality of members	Approximate proportion
9 April 1432 (*MC* II, 151)	81	9 bishops 16 abbots (= 25 'mitres')	1 in 3
27 April 1433 (*MC* II, 355)	265	6 cardinals 44 'mitres'	1 in 5
5 Feb. 1434 (H. v, 79)[2]	422	7 cardinals 3 patriarchs 50 bishops 30 abbots (= 7 cardinals + 83 'mitres')	1 in 5
5 Dec. 1436 (H. iv, 348)	355	3 cardinals 2 patriarchs 17 bishops 28 abbots (= 3 cardinals + 47 'mitres')	1 in 7

These figures denote the numbers actually present and active on the days indicated. They take no account of the number and rank of the members absent sent on various missions by the council, a number which sometimes was fairly considerable. A rough cross-check can be made from the lists of *incorporati*, i.e. newly registered, as recorded by John of Segovia (in this more complete than the lists in Haller) for approximately the same dates.

[1] These data are taken from *Monumenta conciliorum generalium saec. XV*, 3 vols. and index (Vienna 1857–86), a full and accurate account written by an ardent conciliarist and participant in the council, John of Segovia, referred to hereafter as *MC*; and J. Haller and others, *Concilium Basiliense, Studien und Documente*, 8 vols., Basle 1896–1936, a collection of documents, with introductions.

[2] At the 17th session of 26 April 1434 there were 105 'mitres', 'quo numero in aliqua sessionum sanctae Basiliensis synodi ante vel post nunquam interfuit major' (*MC*, II, 649).

	Total number of new members	Quality of members	Approximate proportion
May 1432 (*MC* II, 184)	33	1 cardinal 6 bishops 6 abbots (= 1 cardinal + 12 'mitres')	1 in 3
May 1433 (*MC* II, 355)	78	1 patriarch 23 bishops 1 abbot (= 25 'mitres')	1 in 3
April 1434 (*MC* II, 650)	82	10 bishops 9 abbots (= 19 'mitres') 3 non-'mitres'	1 in 4
May 1435			
May 1436	15	3 'mitres'	1 in 5
May 1437		6 non 'mitres'	

The proportions, then, for the two sets of figures are roughly the same. The only significant difference is for 1433, but John of Segovia notes that the influx in May of that year was particularly high because in the previous February the pope had approved of Basle as the seat of the council and had urged prelates to attend.

All those who registered as members—and their number rose to about 500—were divided into four Deputations dealing respectively with faith, reform, peace, and general purposes. The Deputations, with in each an equal number of the four Nations—French, German, Italian, and Spanish—and of the 'mitres', prepared the matter for the general congregations, in which, as in the Deputations, all the members had an equal vote.

It was not to be expected that so many members would all be worthy of their office. The council itself passed legislation limiting membership (in addition, of course, to 'mitres' and their superiors) to certain graduates, and those only if they had a mandate.[1] It excluded religious of the Mendicant Orders, unless with a licence from their superiors.[2] In February 1434 it determined the qualifications for members 'that, besides prelates, abbots, bishops, and their superiors, there could be admitted masters, licentiates or

[1] 25 May 1433, Haller, *Concilium Basiliense*, II, 414.   [2] 3 July 1433, *ibid.* 441.

bachelors in theology, doctors or licentiates in one of the two laws, important dignitaries, archdeacons, deans, provosts or canons of cathedral churches possessed of a mandate from their chapters'.[1] Two months later, Cesarini warned those responsible to be attentive 'that a multitude be not indiscriminately admitted, because it is no small burden and honour to be admitted in so sublime a gathering to judicate for the whole world'.[2]

Wide though the qualifications were, they were apparently being exceeded, for the need to repeat the regulations was frequent.[3] So there is probably a deal of truth in the caustic criticisms of Agostino Patrizio, of John Palomar,[4] of Aeneas Sylvius,[5] of Ambrosio Traversari,[6] and of Pope Eugenius,[7] who were all agreed (in the words of N. Valois) that 'Many a time, among the Fathers who legislated for the whole world, there were to be seen cooks and grooms...or again clerks, vagabond religious, servants ...who in the evening doffed their long [clerical] habits to serve at table or perform other domestic duties for their masters'.[8] John of Segovia in his history of the council wrote of 'bishops and their superiors whose presence is said to be substantial to the celebration of general councils' (MC, II, 130) and noted that the cardinals 'because they are considered to be part of the body of the pope' were not distributed among the Deputations, but 'the others were deputed to act together with them' (ibid. 272); none the less he defended in lyrical terms the 'one man, one vote' principle of Basle (ibid.). Elsewhere he claimed to be a defender of the rights of bishops, deprecated the behaviour of members who interrupted proceedings by making an uproar and by banging of feet, and recorded with disapproval even an occasion, when a crowd of 'inferiors' with no prelate at all present passed a resolution on an important matter and demanded that it be accepted as con-

[1] MC, II, 580. [2] Ibid. 651.
[3] 23 Jan. 1434, Haller, Concilium Basiliense, III, 11; 10 Apr. 1434, ibid. 66; 2 Aug. 1434, ibid. 461; 9 Nov. 1434, ibid. 563, etc.
[4] Quoted by E. Cecconi, Studi storici sul Concilio di Firenze, I, Florence 1869, 151.
[5] C. Fea, Pius II, pontif. max., a calumniis vindicatus, Rome 1823, 117.
[6] A. Traversari, Ambrosii Traversari...latinae epistolae, ed. L. Mehus, Florence 1759, no. 176.
[7] Raynaldus, Annales ecclesiastici, an. 1436, VIII.
[8] N. Valois, Le Pape et le Concile, Paris 1909, I, 313.

ciliar.[1] It was not quite as bad as that, but it was getting on that way when the *conciliabulum* deposed Eugenius IV on 25 June 1439. Among some 300 present (*MC*, III, 528) there were 1 cardinal, 1 patriarch, 11 bishops, and 13 abbots (Haller, V, 524)—and Nicholas of Cusa asserted that not more than four of the bishops had received consecration (*MC*, III, 1132).

THE COUNCIL OF FLORENCE 1438

The Council of Ferrara–Florence was unique among councils held in the West, indeed in the whole series of general councils, for it was an encounter of two Churches to reach agreement on a fundamental point of doctrine, and so to unite. As the council was held in the West the Latin Church was numerically the stronger, though the Eastern Church was well represented with the Patriarch of Constantinople there in person, the other three eastern patriarchs acting through procurators, sixteen metropolitans from the patriarchate of Constantinople, and eight delegates from four other oriental Churches. Agreement was reached, not by a count of heads (when the Latins would always have overwhelmed the Greeks), but when after discussion and some amendments the Greeks accepted several written doctrinal statements presented to them. These were then put together to form the decree of union promulgated on 6 July 1439.

So, in the Council of Florence there was no organization regulating discussion and voting that applied to both the Churches, analogous to those of Constance and Basle. But within only the Latin section of the council there was. Obviously certain qualifications for membership were established, and on 10 February 1438 a bureau for registering members was set up, but what those qualifications were and how many members were registered there is no record extant. Whatever the number, they were divided not into Nations (as in Constance) or into Deputations (as in Basle) but by hierarchical rank into three Estates—cardinals, archbishops, and bishops; abbots and other regulars; doctors, dignitaries of churches, graduates. The votes of two-thirds of any Estate were requisite for the assent of that Estate to any measure,

---

[1] Haller, *Concilium Basiliense*, I, 40, n. 4.

and the assent of all the Estates was necessary for a conciliar decision.[1]

Since the Latin acts and protocol of the Council of Florence are lost, there are no minutes extant of any meeting of an Estate (the main discussions were obviously in the general congregations between Greeks and Latins), but there is a fugitive reference to them apropos of the final stages of negotiation with the Greeks— fortunately for us, because without it there would be no knowledge of this arrangement at all. After Cesarini, at the pope's bidding, had informed a gathering of all the Latin members of the successful progress of the meetings with the Greeks, the pope bade them meet in their Estates to elect four persons from each to form a committee to act with the Greeks in drawing up the final decree. Andrew da Santacroce, the author of the narrative, thereupon explains what the Estates were. This is the first time the Estates are mentioned in his account, apropos of the events of 27 June 1439. It cannot have been the first time they functioned.

CONCLUSION

This closer examination of the composition of the conciliar councils and the rights of their members confirms the hasty judgement proposed in the introduction to this paper, that cardinals were the leaders at Pisa, bishops at Constance, and graduates at Basle. In Florence theologians did the talking, and little is known for lack of documents of the influence of cardinals and bishops among the Latins.

There is a further question, perhaps worth hinting at: in what way did these councils of the conciliar period represent the Universal Church? The Council of Pisa included in the preamble to its decree deposing the 'popes' the phrase, 'representing the Universal Church'; but the cardinals throughout had acted as 'the Roman Church which is said to preside over all chapters and churches of the world',[2] i.e. as head of the Church they had acted for the Church, as it were from above. On the other hand, the

---

[1] *Andreas de Santacroce, advocatus consistorialis: Acta latina Concilii Florentini*, ed. G. Hofmann (= *Concilium Florentinum Documenta et Scriptores*, VI), Rome 1955, 256–7. [2] Cf. above, p. 178.

Council representation in the conciliar period

Councils of Constance and Basle justified all their actions precisely on the principle enunciated at the 5th session of 6 April: 'this council, legitimately assembled in the Holy Spirit, forming a general council and representing the Universal Church, holds its power directly from God.' They purported to be acting, as it were, from below, as the embodiment of the Universal Church. By canon law, only cardinals, bishops, and mitred abbots, with perhaps the Generals of Religious Orders, had, I believe, a right of voting. On what grounds did the rest claim to vote? As representatives? But probably not a single member of these councils had been elected to represent anyone. The bishops were present *ex officio* as bishops, as successors of the Apostles who, according to age-long tradition, formed the councils. The rest came as procurators appointed by princes, bishops, abbots, universities, chapters (these last might have been chosen by election)— a minute even if élite proportion of the Universal Church—or even, particularly in Basle, they were only minor functionaries of churches who wanted a holiday, or were seeking preferment, and whose office was their open sesame to the council. That they should vote as representing the Universal Church was an innovation based apparently on a fiction.

NICHOLAS RYSSHETON AND THE
COUNCIL OF PISA, 1409 [1]

by MARGARET HARVEY

I N November 1408 Henry IV finally decided that England
would support the Council of Pisa, called by the cardinals in
defiance of the rival popes in the Great Schism. The decision
seems to have met little opposition, but it must have involved at
least some readjustment of ideas for Englishmen. There were of
course good traditional arguments in favour of the Council, and
we know now that the Government had not always taken a
rigidly pro-Roman stand in moves to end the Schism, but Henry's
English ecclesiastical contemporaries at least had been used to a
policy which supported the Roman pope and which insisted that
if a Council were called, only their pope (Gregory XII) could call
it. In accepting Pisa they were accepting a Council which would
proceed whether or not he supported it, and a policy knowingly
designed to secure his removal, with or without his consent.[2]
How did they justify their action?

We know how the King justified himself (or rather we know
what he said officially). He referred to information contained in
the speech on behalf of the dissident cardinals delivered before
him on 28 and 29 October 1408 by Cardinal Uguccione. In
particular Henry insisted that Gregory had broken the oath he had

---

[1] I would like to thank my former supervisor, Professor E. F. Jacob, for the help
he gave me when I first became interested in the manuscript discussed below, and
Professor H. S. Offler for a great deal of kindness in reading a draft of this paper.

[2] English background in E. Perroy, *L'Angleterre et le grand Schisme sous Richard II,
1378–1399*, Paris 1933, with recent modifications by J. J. N. Palmer, 'England
and the Great Western Schism' in *EHR*, LXXXIII (1968), 516–22; H. Junghanns,
Zur Geschichte der Englischen Kirchenpolitik von 1399–1413, Freiburg i. Br. 1915.
The best discussions of the powers of councils are in B. Tierney, *Foundations of
the Conciliar Theory*, Cambridge 1955; and J. Moynihan, *Papal Immunity and
Liability in the Writings of the Medieval Canonists, Analecta Gregoriana*, 120,
Series Fac. Iuris Canonici, Sect. B, no. 9, Rome 1961.

made in the conclave and renewed at his coronation in 1406.[1] Evidence and argument about this had formed a large part of Uguccione's case. Officially, therefore, the English thought Gregory at least suspect if not guilty of perjury, and of deliberately prolonging the Schism.

The official view is of course much easier to discover than the attitudes of individuals to that view. The aim of this paper is to draw attention to the writings of an Englishman who did discuss the legitimacy of supporting Pisa and also considered some questions which arose as the Council progressed. These make a welcome addition to the very scanty evidence about the attitudes of Englishmen to the Council and to their role in it.

The writings are the work of Master Nicholas Ryssheton.[2] He was a Lancastrian lawyer, and a doctor of both laws, trained partly in Bologna, who had practised as Auditor of Causes in the Curia between 1385[3] and about 1400. By 1400 he had returned to England and become Auditor of Causes in the Court of Arches. There probably he met and befriended Robert Hallum, who later as Bishop of Salisbury was to lead the English delegation to Pisa. Ryssheton became a successful diplomat and from 1403 was frequently abroad on royal missions. It is not surprising, therefore, that when Henry IV decided that as well as supporting Pisa he would send to Gregory XII one last appeal to attend it, Ryssheton was one of the ambassadors sent to make the appeal. In February 1409, therefore, Ryssheton was at Rimini, but the appeal was a failure. Ryssheton and his colleagues came on to Pisa, arriving about 25 March 1409. On 4 May the newly arrived English delegation chose him to be its auditor of witnesses against the popes.

[1] The oath printed in M. Souchon, *Die Paptswahlen in der Zeit des Grossen Schismas*, Braunschweig 1898, I, 285–95, chapters IV, V. Uguccione's speech is printed in full in *St Alban's Chronicle 1406-1420*, ed. V. Galbraith, Oxford 1937, 136–52. I hope soon to publish a full account of Henry IV's letters of 1408, many of which are contained in MS BM Harley 431, especially ff. 14–14 v, 15 v–16, 47 v.

[2] For Ryssheton's career the major sources are in A. B. Emden, *Biographical Register of Oxford Graduates to 1500*, Oxford 1959, III. The MS discussed here was not known to Emden. All references to Ryssheton's career are from Emden unless otherwise stated.

[3] Lambeth Palace Library, Register of Courtenay (Canterbury), f. 61 v.

Ryssheton therefore was clearly one of the leading members of the English Nation at the Council of Pisa.

His writings are four *quaestiones* in MS Theol. Lat. fol. 251 from the Deutschstaatsbibliothek in Berlin.[1] The major part of the manuscript contains one of the main notary's diaries used by Professor Vincke for his 'Acta'.[2] Ryssheton's work is on extra paper sheets bound in at the end, clearly not part of the main manuscript. They are in many ways very different in production from the diary.[3] In the early sixteenth century John Leland saw a *Determinatio de Schismate* by Ryssheton in a manuscript in Westminster Abbey,[4] but this has long since vanished. It is possible that the Berlin manuscript is a copy of the same thing, though Ryssheton had written other works on aspects of the problem.[5]

It would not be possible here to give a full account of all the complicated arguments of the *quaestiones*, so I will confine myself to what I consider their most interesting features. Of the four short pieces, at least the first seems to have been delivered before

---

[1] I thank the Stiftung Preussischer Kulturbesitz, Depot der Staatsbibliothek in Tübingen, for permission to use this manuscript and for help in reading it by ultra-violet lamp. The manuscript has now been transferred to Berlin.

[2] J. Vincke, 'Acta Concilii Pisani' in *Römischer Quartalschrift*, XLVI (1938), 82. Professor Vincke cites there MS Berlin 420, but this is a misprint for the manuscript cited in the text.

[3] V. Rose, *Verzeichniss der Lateinischen Handschriften der Königlichen Bibliothek zu Berlin*, Berlin 1903, II, 2, 575 (no. 631). The MS came into the Library in 1821. Its origin is unknown. Ryssheton's work is at the end, ff. 108–11v. It is in a smaller hand, in darker ink with many more lines to the page. Marginalia have sometimes been cut off to reduce the sheets to the right size. There is no water mark on these last sheets, in contrast to the earlier section. The hand is early fifteenth century and, contrary to what Rose suggests, Mr N. Ker considers that it is probably not English.

[4] *J. Lelandi antiquarii de rebus Brittanicis Collectanea*, ed. T. Hearne, Oxford 1715, III, 49.

[5] In the Berlin MS he refers to writings of his own which show that Gregory XII had been properly cited to Pisa, f. 109v: 'legitime requisitus iuxta formam scripturarum mearum in convocacione facta in ecclesia sancti Pauli London nuper exhibitarum'. This probably refers to the Convocation of January 1409 when the delegation to Pisa was chosen, cf. Junghanns, *Kirchenpolitik*, 35, 51; Wilkins, III, 312–13. Ryssheton delivered a major speech to Gregory at Rimini, but nothing remains of this except the report used in evidence at Pisa, cf. Vincke, 'Acta', 281; *idem, Briefe zum Pisaner Konzil*, Beiträge zur Kirchen- und Rechtsgeschichte, I, Bonn 1940, no. 95. This is probably the *requisicio* referred to above.

the cardinals in the Council[1] and all four seem to have been presented to Alexander V when the Council was over.[2] The first piece at least is semi-official. The preface indeed says 'Anything I shall say I say as a private person and not as an ambassador or nuncius'[3] but the protest seems merely prudential, since the first *quaestio* undoubtedly represents the 'party line' which Henry IV had adopted from Uguccione. One proof of this is that in it Ryssheton is often quoting thought for thought and sometimes even word for word (though of course without acknowledgment) from Uguccione's speech.[4]

The first and longest *quaestio*[5] was intended to prove that Gregory had perjured himself and fallen into schism and heresy. The theory behind it was that in order to fulfil the oath which all the cardinals had taken in 1406[6] (promising to resign if the other pope resigned or died and to use all other reasonable means to end the schism) the Pope was obliged both to resign and to agree to the cardinals' Council. A great deal of information about the

[1] There is a heading now only partly visible by ultra-violet light which reads: f. 108: 'Presentetur pape ex parte N. Auditoris de Anglia super facto scismatis. Materia tradita Reverendissimis in Christo patribus et dominis utriusque collegii sancte Romane ecclesie Cardinalibus super facto scismatis... [illegible] scandi ex parte Nicolai de Ryssheton utriusque iuris doctoris minimi ac causarum palacii apostolici Auditoris eciam defensione processus facti in generali concilio contra g. et b. nuper contendentes.' The first piece begins 'Reverendissimi Patres et domini mei singularissimi'.

[2] f. 111v: 'Ideo, pater sancte, sanctitas vestra, auctoritate generalis concilii, declaravit ex duabus obedientiis seu duobus collegiis Cardinalium unicum fuisse et esse collegium, et ita fuit obtenta in elecione quod due partes dominorum Cardinalium cuiuslibet obedientie concurrerent in elecione eadem sanctitatis vestre iuxta c. *licet de vitanda* ad tollendum omne dubium prout supra consului, quamvis alii contra et male. Cetera suppleat sanctitas vestra.'

[3] f. 108: 'quicquid dixero illud dicam tanquam privata persona non tanquam ambassiator seu nuncius'.

[4] E.g. The passage in *St Alban's Chronicle*, p. 149, from 'Nam si lex' to 'c. consuetudo' is word for word (though the order is altered) at f. 108v. See below, p. 202, n. 2. Ryssheton was almost certainly borrowing from Uguccione and not vice-versa, because whereas Uguccione quoted in support the doctors of Bologna in their withdrawal of obedience (which happened 20 December 1407, Fliche et Martin, *Histoire de l'Eglise*, vol. xiv (1962), 137), Ryssheton quoted both the Bolognese and the Florentines who had provisionally withdrawn on 26 January 1409 and finally on 25 March (Fliche, p. 145). Cf. Berlin 251, f. 109; *St Alban's Chronicle*, 147–8.   [5] ff. 108–9v.   [6] See p. 198, n. 1 above.

frantic diplomacy of the years 1407 and 1408 was assumed, and its implications discussed, to show that Gregory had not taken the *via cessionis* seriously. Ryssheton argued that the Pope could not be dispensed from his oath because it concerned a matter of divine law—the union of the Church.[1] Gregory's Council of Cividale was too partial and one-sided to fulfil his obligation.[2] He could not declare the cardinals deprived for going to Pisa because they were needed for a new election.[3] Furthermore the cardinals were equally bound to keep the oath, and were obliged to desert Gregory if there was no other way of fulfilling it. In arguing this Ryssheton was relying on Uguccione,[4] and he was equally dependent on him for the next bit of the argument, which was that Gregory was obliged to accept the Council. This was because of the final clause of his oath (the public good of the Church), and because of the oath's collegiate form, which obliged the individual to follow the wishes of the majority (just as was the case in cathedral or monastic chapters).[5]

---

[1] f. 108: 'illud descendit a iure divino attestante sacra scriptura ibi dum dicitur: 'vovete et reddite etc.' (Ps 75. 12), item alibi: 'reddite domino iuramenta vestra' (Mt. 5.33), et sic reddenda sunt deo cui magis obediendum quam hominibus (Acts 5. 29). Cum eciam papa in hoc casu non habet potestatem contra legem divinam nec contra ipsum deum, c. *sunt quidam* xxvi. q. i (sic c. xxv, q. 1,c.6) quia respicit statum universalis ecclesie propter unionem et probatur per dictum pauli ii ad. cor. ultimo (II Cor. 13. 10) ubi dicitur quod potestas pape est ad edificationem non ad destructionem quia par in parem etc.' *St Alban's Chronicle,* 147.

[2] Vincke, 'Acta', 283; L. Schmitz, 'Die Quellen zur Geschichte des Konzils von Cividale', *Römischer Quartalschrift,* VIII (1894), 217–58; f. 108v: 'quia hic agitur de titulo papatus inter duos contendentes et sic in causa propria non potest esse iudex et pars…dominus G. asseruit quod noluit habere scismaticos in concilio suo…et ipse vocat quoscumque scismaticos sibi non obedientes', cf. *St Alban's Chronicle,* 150.

[3] f. 108v: 'quantumcumque Cardinales utriusque collegii fuerint reputati excommunicati, privati seu alias inhabiles apud dominum G., tamen quoad mixturam et unionem predictam et futuram elecionem pape eosdem Cardinales voluit dominus G. pro Cardinalibus habere et reputari ac super nihilitate eorum ex certa scientia sua et consensu a principio accomodato intelligi.' Authorities are *Digest* 5, 1, 1 and 42, 1, 57; *Codex,* 3, 13.

[4] *St Alban's Chronicle,* 147.

[5] f. 109: 'Nam causa finalis huiusmodi instrumenti est publica utilitas ecclesie universalis et omnium Christianorum que insurgit ex unione ecclesie. Forma eciam fuit communis et collegialis. Unde licet Collegium ut Collegium, cum sit

The law seemed to confine the right to call a council to the pope alone,[1] but Ryssheton, again borrowing from Uguccione, argued that this law need not always be obeyed:

One may reply that convocation pertains to a certain and undoubted Pope and not to a doubtful Pope. [Ryssheton at the outset had made it clear that he accepted Gregory as Pope 'as to his initial entrance', so 'doubtful' refers to his present status.] And supposing that it pertains only to the Pope, according to the canons, however we must judge according to the mind and reason of the canons, and not according to the words or the superficial meaning of the words as the Jews did, because if a canon or a law lacks reason it is to be abolished [DI.c.5. *consuetudo*]. And if a relevant case is not to be found written in the law, reason itself has the force of law.[2]

The mind or reason of the law confining convocation to popes was to prevent disturbance and maintain obedience, but the cardinals were precisely trying to unify the Church. There were no legal precedents, and therefore one was left with use of reason. The most reasonable solution was a General Council called by the obvious authority: the cardinals, whose status in the Church was next after the Pope. Uguccione had supplied the authority here—Hostiensis, where he discussed where power resided when the Pope died and concluded that it rested with the cardinals.[3]

res inanimata, non potest ligari pena periurii. l. *proponebatur* ff. *de iudiciis* (*Digest* 5, 1, 76), singulares tamen persone ipsius Collegii possunt ligari periurium (*sic*). Unde cum hoc iuramentum...sit actus collegialis sed in actibus collegialibus et capitularibus minor pars, et presertim unus prout dominus G., habet sequi majorem partem ex illa obligacione renovata, per titulum *de hiis qui fiunt a majore parte capituli* (*Decretals*, III, tit. 11) et c. *cum omnes, de constitutionibus* (*Decretals*, I, tit. 2, c. 6) sed maior pars collegii Cardinalium conclusit de loco civitatis Pisarum, igitur dominus G. tenetur sequi conclusionem illorum quo ad locum Pisarum per eos electum.'   [1] D. XVII.

[2] f. 108v: 'Respondetur quod convocacio concilii pertinet ad papam certum et indubitatum et non ad papam dubitatum etc. Et presupponendum quod pertinet ad papam tantum secundum illos canones, tamen debemus iudicare secundum mentem et racionem ipsorum canonum et non secundum verba et corticem verborum prout faciunt Iudei, quia si canon vel lex caret racione extirpanda est. 1. di. *consuetudo* (D.I.c. 5). Et si casus occurens non repperiatur in lege scriptus, racio ipsa habet vim legis.' *St Alban's Chronicle*, 149–50.

[3] *St Alban's Chronicle*, 150–1. Hostiensis on *Decretals*, V, tit. 38 c. 14, quoted Tierney, *Conciliar Theory*. See Moynihan, *Papal Immunity*, 115–16. Hostiensis was an authority especially in favour of the Council to judge a case of papal heresy.

Ryssheton proved from Joannes Andreas that a General Council was the competent judge whether a pope had fallen into heresy and could condemn him for it.[1] He also argued that to persist in schism, thus leaving Christians in doubt who was pope and denying the doctrine 'one holy Church', was itself heresy.[2] In fact the present case rested really on notoriety, and the law, referring to Achasius and Anastatius with their *Glossa Ordinaria*, showed that the cardinals were right to withdraw even before a formal condemnation.[3]

This is a conservative statement, basically justifying the Council and its aims with the argument that a pope who is a notorious and persistent schismatic and therefore a heretic can be condemned and saying that Gregory could be treated as if he had resigned and the papacy were vacant. Provided that one accepts Ryssheton's equation of schism and heresy (and he had good authority for it),[4] this argument is traditional. The other *quaestiones* show the same attitudes.

Judging by its contents the second piece[5] was written very shortly after the main body of the English arrived at Pisa on 30 April 1409. It proved that the cardinals had the right to summon a Council and to cite the rival popes to attend it, even though they did not have jurisdiction over the popes. The occasion for writing must have been the discussion about the status of the cardinals and whether the popes had been properly cited, upon which the English insisted after the 6th session (30 April). We know that in the course of these discussions Hallum drew attention to the dubious status of those cardinals who had not yet withdrawn obedience, and that this problem was eventually settled by a decree (10 May). Furthermore we know that after lengthy discussion the English changed their minds about the validity of the

---

[1] On Sext, v, tit. 2, c. 5. Quoted in Moynihan, *Papal Immunity*, 120, n. 29, and see 119–22.

[2] f. 109: 'Item propter pertinaciam et tolleranciam scismatis antiquati xxx annis et ultra, corrumpit illum articulum principale fidei nostre videlicet "unam sanctam ecclesiam".'

[3] D. XIX, c. 9; C. XXIV, q. 1; and see Tierney, *Conciliar Theory*, 38, 62.

[4] f. 109v, quoting C. XXIV, q. 3, c. 26 and q. 1, c. 21 and gloss; C. XXV, q. 1, c. 5. See *St Alban's Chronicle*, 148, for the same argument.

[5] f. 110–110v.

initial citation by the cardinals and by 28 May had accepted it.[1] Though Ryssheton was prepared, out of caution, to allow that the popes might be summoned again, he was convinced of the validity of the initial summons. He compared the status of the cardinals in the Council with that of an archbishop in his provincial synod, where he convoked the synod and could summon wrongdoers although he was not their judge.[2] To those who argued that cardinals were not ordinaries like archbishops he quoted *si duo forte contra fas*, with Huguccio's gloss which argued that in a disputed election the cardinals had the right to call a Council.[3] Essentially Ryssheton regarded the Council as a legal *processus* on a par with a provincial synod dealing with a contumacious priest.

He was certainly not prepared to give the Council any rôle beyond what tradition assigned to it. This comes out also in the third *quaestio*[4] which denies to the Council any right to make a grant from papal revenues of lands, offices, or benefices to Gregory or his relatives if the Pope will resign. This *quaestio* was probably written between about 10 and 18 April 1409, while a group of cardinals were discussing such an offer with Carlo

[1] For all this see *Register of Chichele* (Canterbury), ed. E. F. Jacob, *Canterbury and York Society*, 1937 seq., I, xxx; C. J. Hefele, *Histoire des Conciles*, trans H. Leclercq, Paris 1916, VII, pt. 1, 38–9; J. Lenfant, *Histoire du Concile de Pise*, Utrecht 1731, vol. I, bk. III, p. 74; P. Uilbein (ed.), *Acta Fac. Artium Universitatis Vindobonensis, 1385–1416*, Publikation des Instituts fur Österreichische Geschichtsforschung, VI, pt. 2 (1968), 318, for a letter from the Ambassador of the University at the Council, 7 May; L. Schmitz, *art. cit.*, *Römischer Quartalschrift* VIII, 372, gives the outcome.

[2] f. 110: ' Unde dicit textus eiusdem capituli (?) *si primates* (C. V, q. 2, c. 4) si bene videatur, quod si primas, qui non est iudex, vocavit concilium et huiusmodi concilium actu tenetur, si sunt aliqui vocandi vel citandi ad concilium, citabit primas non concilium, sed si tales vocati fuerint contumaces, concilium excommunicabit non primas. Ergo sub pari forma Cardinales qui non sunt iudices, possunt ad concilium sic citare et convocare citandos et convocandos et presertim dictos contendentes, et non possunt excommunicare non venientes contumaces.'

[3] f. 110v: 'sicut primates habent iurisdictionem ordinariam ad convocandum concilium provinciale, sic Cardinales habent potestatem et iurisdictionem ad convocandum concilum generale inter duos contendentes super papatu, lxxix di. *si duo forte* (D. LXXIX, c. 8) per Hug(uccionem)'. For the gloss of Huguccio, see Tierney, *Conciliar Theory*, 76–7. For Huguccio's views see also Moynihan, *Papal Immunity*, 75–82.

[4] f. 110v.

Malatesta, Gregory's representative.[1] Ryssheton argued that the offer would not do.[2] The papacy at that time was like a vacant benefice, vacant because of the heresy and schism of its occupants, and there could be no question of compensation for these crimes. The vacant benefice must not be burdened, especially with a grant like this one, which smacked of simony.[3] There was in any case a conciliar decree which forbade unreasonable alienation of ecclesiastical property and it was unsuitable that the decrees of one council should be over-ruled by another.[4]

The final piece[5] underlines Ryssheton's desire that this most unusual of councils should as far as possible stick to tradition. The question was whether, when the papacy was vacant by deprivation or rejection, the right to elect rested with the cardinals or with the cardinals and the Council. The French were discussing this bitterly from 10 June 1409, and had also arranged talks with the other nations.[6] A major difficulty was whether, in these circumstances, the newly united college of Cardinals, the status of most of whom could be questioned, had authority to elect, or whether the extra authority of the Council was needed to strengthen them. In the end (13 June) the Council agreed that the election rested with the cardinals, 'but if, and in so far as there is need, this is to be done by the authority of the Council'.[7] Ryssheton wrote probably just before or during the Conclave (which began 15 June) and supported the Council's conclusion.[8] He recognized that some might have their doubts about the status of the College (though he denied that the doubts were justified), and

---

[1] Hefele, *Histoire des Conciles*, 12 and 18 seq.; E. Martène and U. Durand, *Veterum Scriptorum et Monumentorum Amplissima Collectio*, Paris 1733, VII, col. 1049 seq.

[2] 'Crederem quod non, absque argumentis.'

[3] *Decretals*, III, tit. 5, c. 21; and III, tit. 14, c. 2 and the *Glossa Ordinaria* to it were among the authorities cited to prove this.

[4] *Decretals*, III, tit. 5, c. 8, which is a ruling of the Council of Tours, 1163.

[5] f. 111–111v.

[6] Martène, *Veterum Scriptorum*, col. 1098 and 1103.

[7] Hefele, *Histoire des Conciles*, 49–51; Souchon, *Die Papstwahlen*, II, 41 seq. and esp. 52 seq.

[8] He quotes the definitive sentence of 13 June: (f. 111v) 'illa pretensa privacio dominorum Cardinalium facta post tercium diem mensem maii anni ultimi elapsi est declarata nulla per sententiam diffinitivam latam a generali concilio'. For this sentence see Vincke, 'Acta', 304.

he agreed that if the two parts of the cardinals disagreed, the result might be another disputed election. He thought, however, that these problems were not sufficient to justify altering the traditional method of election laid down in *Licet de vitanda*[1] and other legislation. It is interesting to notice that here he rejects the apparent authority of *si duo forte contra fas*, which said that in a dispute over the election of the Pope the new election pertained to the clergy.[2] Ryssheton pointed out that here Gratian was quoting a civil law, and cited Guido de Baysio to show that Gratian was to be approved for the authorities he cited, but not necessarily for the solutions that he drew from them.[3] Ryssheton's compromise solution to ensure that the election was beyond dispute was that the Council commission the cardinals, and that no important men (noncardinals understood) from the Nations at the Council should be included.[4] In a note at the end, written after 1 July 1409, Ryssheton reminded Alexander V that this was the solution adopted, though others counselled otherwise (and badly).[5]

If these pieces are typical of English opinion, and if the first at least is semi-official, the English were not radicals. In the unprecedented crisis Ryssheton was prepared to observe the spirit rather than the letter of the law; he regarded the Council like a provincial synod, and the papacy as a benefice whose incumbent might have to stand his trial in some cases like any erring clerk.

---

[1] *Licet de Vitanda* is *Decretals*, I, tit. 6, c. 6, from Lateran Council 1179 ordering a two-thirds majority of cardinals for the election of the Pope. Also quoted were Sext., I, tit. 6, c. 3; Clementines, I, tit. 3, c. 2.

[2] See p. 204, n. 3 above.

[3] f. 111: 'cum sit lex civilis prout patet ex eiusdem subscriptione quamvis canonizata, quia canonizacio non probat eam servandam in foro ecclesiastico, cum in canonibus repperiatur contrarium...Ideo Gracianus canonizando legem non poterat nobis inponere neccesitatem observandi eam in foro ecclesiastico, sed servabitur in foro suo, quamvis conpilacio Gratiani est approbata. Idem est in libro sententiarum, quod notat Archidiaconus ix di. *si quis nesciat.*' *Si duo forte* was a letter of the Emperor Honorius. For Guido's theory, see G. de Baysio, *Rosarium seu in Decretorum Volumen Commentaria*, Venice 1601, at D. IX, c. 8, f. 11v.

[4] f. 111v: 'eligatur (papa) a duabus partibus Cardinalium utriusque obedientie cum auctoritate generalis concilii per viam comissionis seu concessionis vel compromissi, in dominos Cardinales universaliter vel particulariter, ad cautelam et ex superhabundanti prout melius et honestius et facilius poterit obtineri a concilio.'

[5] See p. 200, n. 2 above.

But Ryssheton was not prepared to give the Council new untraditional powers nor to charge the Pope with any crime other than that for which he could traditionally be tried and deposed. This is all a long way from conciliarism or from the Council of Constance, and if Ryssheton really was to some extent a royal spokesman, we can see one reason why royal policy seems to have met with such widespread support from churchmen.

THE CONDEMNATION OF JOHN WYCLIF
AT THE COUNCIL OF CONSTANCE

by EDITH C. TATNALL

T HE Council of Constance was perhaps the most dramatic of all the ecumenical councils of the Church. Called under stress by an anti-pope whom it proceeded to depose, it was the scene of the fire that burned John Hus and the arena for the debate of the most potent political theories of the time. It was fitting that it should be an occasion for the condemnation of the works of John Wyclif, the firebrand heretic of the preceding century.

Consideration of Wyclif's condemnation at Constance is usually overshadowed by the condemnation of John Hus, of which process the action concerning Wyclif was a part. However, for the purposes of this paper, the focus will be placed on the total condemnation process of the two men specifically insofar as it concerns Wyclif. When this is done, an interesting succession of events at the Council emerges from the general mass of its records.

Wyclif, of course, had died as the result of a stroke in 1384. He had at that time already been condemned as heretical by Pope Gregory XI, who in 1377 had extracted nineteen erroneous conclusions from Wyclif's treatise *De Civili Dominio*, I.[1] There would seem to have been little point in raising him for new condemnation at Constance if there had not been some contemporary representation of his ideas. This was seen in John Hus.

Thus the story of Wyclif at Constance begins with the early arrival of Hus at the Council. Hus was convinced of his own innocence of heresy, but realized that he might be in some danger.[2]

---

[1] Mansi, XXVI, 565 f. Cf. R. L. Poole's notes to the text in Johannis Wyclif, *Tractatus De Civili Dominio, Liber Primus*, ed. Reginald Lane Poole, London 1885.

[2] Jaques Lenfant, *Histoire du Concile de Constance*, Amsterdam 1714, I, 25–6.

Hus arrived at the Council on 3 November 1414 in the company of three Bohemian lords to whose care he had been entrusted by the Emperor Sigismund and his brother, Wenceslas.[1] The day after his arrival he was received with two of the lords by Pope John XXIII. The lords informed the pope that Hus had the safe conduct of Sigismund, and the pope pledged himself to use all his power to see that no injustice would be visited upon Hus while he was at the Council.[2]

The first suggestion of Wyclifian doctrine at Constance came from the mouth of Hus in a sermon he preached before clergy soon after his arrival.[3] He referred to the Church as the whole body of the predestinate ('Omnium praedestinatorum universitas'),[4] and thus he uttered the first doctrine for which he was later to be condemned.[5]

As Wyclif's works had already been condemned by John XXIII as a part of an action against Hus in a council at Rome in the winter of 1412–13,[6] it is not clear why Hus was permitted to preach such a sermon at Constance. Hus was evidently relying upon the assurances of safety he was thought to have received from the pope and the Emperor Sigismund.

Hus's case was not mentioned in the first session of the Council, but he was in trouble immediately upon the arrival on the scene of Michael de Causis, an enemy from Prague.[7] Despite all the assurances of safety, Hus was in fact taken prisoner at the instigation of de Causis, Stephen Paletz, a professor of theology from Prague, and others. When this was protested by John de Chlum, one of the Bohemian nobles who had accompanied Hus, on the grounds of the assurances by emperor and pope, John XXIII

---

[1] Lenfant, *Histoire*, 19.
[2] Lenfant, *Histoire*, 28.
[3] *Ibid.*   [4] Lenfant, *Histoire*, 29.
[5] 'Unica est sancta Universalis ecclesia, quae est praedestinatorum universitas.' Mansi, xxvii, 754. Cf. 'Ecclesia autem sancta katholica, id est universalis, est omnium predestinatorum universitas'. Magistri Johannis Hus, *Tractatus De Ecclesia*, ed. S. Harrison Thomson, University of Colorado Press 1956, 2. Cf. 'Ecclesia catholica sive apostolica sit universitas predestinatorum'. Johannis Wycliffe, *Tractatus De Civili Dominio, Liber Primus*, ed. Reginald Lane Poole, London 1885, 358.
[6] Mansi, xxvii, 505 f.   [7] Lenfant, *Histoire*, 36.

placed the blame upon the cardinals and bishops in whose hands indeed he himself was finding his fate.[1]

Hus's troubles at this point were two-fold. First of all, he became gravely ill in his prison at the Dominican monastery, so much so that the pope is said to have sent doctors to restore his health in order that it might not appear that he had died a natural death.[2] Secondly, the eight articles which were being held against him by his enemy, Michael de Causis, were indeed close to the ideas of the recognized heretic, Wyclif.[3]

The first official mention of Wyclif himself at Constance came in the first session in the reading of the agenda to be discussed at the Council.[4] Clearly John XXIII wished to have the full Council confirm the condemnation he had made himself in 1412. This confirmation was accomplished in the fifth session of the Council of Constance. It included approval of the burning of Wyclif's books, and it is clear that by this time the condemnation of Wyclif was to be considered as a part of the prospective condemnation of Hus.[5] Hus was being detained for holding the views of Wyclif, and the procedure was set up whereby the Council would condemn forty-five articles attributed to Wyclif which had already been condemned at the Universities of Paris and Prague.[6] At this session also we find the prospect that even the memory of Wyclif is to be condemned and that his bones are to be exhumed from their burial place in consecrated ground.[7] A committee was formed to pursue the matter against both Wyclif and Hus.[8] At this point it seems that some opposition may have begun to develop in the persons of Cardinal Deacon Francisco Florentina and the Cardinal William of Saint Mark from Paris. Neither of these men was on the appointed committee, and as the chronicler observes, many words passed between them.[9] The

[1] Lenfant, *Histoire*, 38.   [2] Lenfant, *Histoire*, 39.
[3] Lenfant, *Histoire*, 40.   [4] Mansi, XXVII, 539. Lenfant, *Histoire*, 35.
[5] 'Item, quod in eadem sessione committatur materia fidei per hoc sacrum Concilium cum plena auctoritate, quoad doctrinam ipsius Joannis Wicleff, nec non Joannis Hus, & suorum sequacium, reverendissimis patribus...videant super materia Joannis Huss, hic propter errorem ipsius Joannis Wicleff, detenti.' Mansi, XXVII, 592.
[6] *Ibid*. Cf. c. 594.   [7] Mansi, XXVII, 595.
[8] Mansi, XXVII, 597.   [9] *Ibid*. Re the names and orders, cf. c. 606.

committee received a report from these cardinals at the sixth session of the Council concerning the confirmation of the condemnation of Wyclif's memory, of the forty-five articles of Wyclif's that had been condemned at Paris and Prague, and in addition, two hundred and sixty articles which had been condemned at Oxford.[1]

In the seventh session the Council was busy with the condemnation of Pope John XXIII. William of Saint Mark and Francisco Florentino were present also at this session.[2] In addition to the matter of the pope, this session heard a citation read against Jerome of Prague in his capacity as a follower of John Hus.[3] It was decided that the eighth session was to be devoted to matters of faith, and in particular to the condemnation of the memory of Wyclif.[4] Thus, Wyclif's condemnation took place in the context not only of the condemnation of Hus, but of the deposition of the pope who had called the Council.

The eighth session opened 4 May 1415. William of Saint Mark was one of those present, and the citation against John Wyclif, to be the principal order of business at this session, was presented by Henry of Piro, one of the promoters and proctors of the council and synod.[5] At issue were the two sets of Wyclifian theses. What may be an important difference between them was that the original forty-five theses had also been studied and condemned at the *studia* of Paris, while the list of two hundred and sixty theses had evidently been brought to the Council by the English delegation following their condemnation at Oxford.[6]

The Archbishop of Genoa read in general session the forty-five theses specifically mentioned as having been condemned in the *studia* at Paris. However, he was interrupted before he could read the two hundred and sixty further theses by William Cardinal of Saint Mark. Apparently the ground for this was that this set had not been sufficiently studied at Paris, and the cardinal asked that the reading and condemnation of the two hundred and sixty theses be

---

[1] Mansi, xxvii, 611.   [2] Mansi, xxvii, 623 f.   [3] Mansi, xxvii, 628.
[4] Mansi, xxvii, 629. Cf. also Lenfant, *Histoire*, 144 f. and Heinrich Finke & Johannes Hollnsteiner, *Acta Concilii Constanciensis*, ii, Munster 1923, 34 f.
[5] Mansi, xxvii, 630.
[6] Hefele–LeClercq, *Histoire des Conciles*, vii, pt. 1, 226. Mansi, xxvii, 635.

reserved to the next general session.[1] According to the account recorded by Mansi, this was approved in a vote by nations.[2] However, Lenfant suggests that the German nation might have preferred to condemn the two hundred and sixty unread articles along with the other articles and works of Wyclif over the opposition of the Cardinal of Saint Mark.[3]

In any event, the forty-five theses were read and condemned at the eighth session. Also condemned were Wyclif's books, the *Dialogus*[4] and *Trialogus*,[5] which had already been condemned at the council at Rome in 1412.[6] His books were definitely condemned to be burned and the reading of them was prohibited,[7] and in addition his bones were actually to be exhumed and ejected from consecrated ground.[8]

All this left the two hundred and sixty theses which had been condemned at Oxford still unread at the Council of Constance. These theses were not mentioned again in the eighth session. Lenfant notes that all the decrees against Wyclif had been pronounced in the name of the Council without any mention of the pope.[9] The reason for this may be discerned in the fact that in the ninth session, to which they had been held over, despite the fact that William of Saint Mark, Francisco Florentino, and Henry of Piro were all present, Wyclif's two hundred and sixty theses were not taken up because the session was devoted to the much more serious business of condemning Pope John XXIII.[10]

The foregoing leads one to ask whether there might not be some theses among Wyclif's two hundred and sixty which the Paris delegation might have been concerned not to have publicly condemned in the eighth session just before taking up the

---

[1] Mansi, xxvii, 630. Lenfant, *Histoire*, 156 f. Finke & Hollnsteiner, *Acta*, ii, 34. Cf. Hefele–Leclercq, *Histoire des Concils* vii, pt. i, 226, where Cardinal Filastre is named as the interrupter.   [2] Mansi, xxvii, 631.   [3] Lenfant, *Histoire*, 172.

[4] Johannis Wyclif, *Dialogus Sive Speculum Ecclesie Militantis*. ed. Alfred W. Pollard, London 1886.

[5] Joannis Wyclif, *Trialogus cum Supplemento Trialogi*, ed. Gotthard Lechler, Oxford 1869. And see Wilkins, iii, 229–30. Margaret Aston, *Thomas Arundel: a Study of Church Life in the Reign of Richard II*, Oxford 1967, 332.

[6] Mansi, xxvii, 505 f., 632–4.

[7] *Ibid.* 634.   [8] *Ibid*, 635 f.

[9] Lenfant, *Histoire*, 157.   [10] Mansi, xxvii, 640 f.

condemnation of John XXIII in the ninth. In connection with the consideration of the detention of John Hus, which was taken up in the tenth session,[1] the observation was made that the German and Gallican nations had agreed to vote each as a unit on the floor of the Council, having resolved any differences in meetings of their respective groups beforehand. In this context the chronicler comments that the whole Gallican nation asserted that they knew nothing of the two hundred and sixty articles by Wyclif. The chronicler adds that thus sinister suspicions were avoided and dissensions truly appeared.[2] Lenfant suggests that there was some contention between the German and Gallican nations in the matter.[3] In any event, later in the session Cardinal William of Saint Mark was permitted to leave the session due to illness,[4] and with this the matter of Wyclif's two hundred and sixty theses seems to have been lost in the more pressing business of healing the schism in the Church and deposing Pope John XXIII.[5]

Wyclif's case was finally laid to rest in session fifteen in connection with the final condemnation of Hus. Here a list of articles was read as having been formed and taught by both John Wyclif and John Hus.[6] Hus responded to these in his own defence.[7] One of the chief accusations against Hus was that he had taught the errors of Wyclif in Bohemia. He replied that he had not taught the errors of Wyclif or anyone else, and if Wyclif had propagated such errors in England, it was a problem for the English.[8] At another point in the examination, Hus said that he hoped Wyclif was saved, although he realized that he might have been damned, and that whichever it was Hus hoped his own soul might go where Wyclif's was. At this the whole assembly broke into laughter.[9] Clearly Hus was more humorous on this occasion than Wyclif ever would have been.

Finally in the formal condemnation of Hus, they read a list of articles specifically attributed to him.[10] It is in this list that we

---

[1] Mansi, XXVII, 655 f.
[2] Mansi, XXVII, 658.
[3] Lenfant, *Histoire*, 172 f.
[4] Mansi, XXVII, 660.
[5] Mansi, XXVII, 661 f.
[6] Mansi, XXVII, 748 f.
[7] Lenfant, *Histoire*, 200 f.
[8] Lenfant, *Histoire*, 203.
[9] Lenfant, *Histoire*, 205.
[10] Mansi, XXVII, 754 f., where thirty articles are given. Cf. Lenfant, *Histoire*, 210–24.

finally see the condemnation of the most important article for Wyclif's ecclesiological theory, that the true Church is the whole body of the predestined.[1] When Hus was confronted with this he gave precisely the answer that would have been given by Wyclif himself. He said that he recognized that the proposition was his and that it was clear in the writings of St Augustine on St John.[2] Thus we see that the Wyclif story at Constance must be followed all the way through the condemnation of Hus to see it as a whole.

It is interesting to see which specific teachings of Wyclif were condemned and in what order. The first doctrine to be taken up in the forty-five original articles[3] was that of the eucharist, where they condemned Wyclif's denial of transubstantiation. This can certainly be inferred from Wyclif's writings,[4] as can most of the other theses in this list, even if Wyclif was not always directly quoted. Another in this category is that a bishop or priest in mortal sin cannot perform valid sacraments.[5] Wyclif's thesis that clerics should not possess temporal property[6] is covered in the list. Also implied is his whole theory of dominion in article 15, which says that no one is a civil lord, prelate, or bishop if he is in mortal sin.[7] The position taken from *De Civili Dominio*, I, and already condemned by Pope Gregory XI in 1377,[8] is given to the effect that temporal lords are able forcibly to remove temporal goods from clerics who habitually abuse them.[9] Article 24

[1] 'Unica est sancta Universalis ecclesia, quae est praedestinatorum universitas.' Art. I, Mansi, XXVII, 754.

[2] Lenfant, *Histoire*, 210.

[3] Mansi, XXVII, 632 f.

[4] On this point especially Johannis Wyclif, *De Eucharistia Tractatus Maior*, ed. Johann Loserth, London 1892.

[5] Wyclif says that the mass is more efficacious insofar as the priest is more good than bad. Then he goes further: 'Dicunt enim quod denarius est melior in manu prudentis quam fatui, et tamen negant sacramentum esse melius in ministerio iusti qui facit cum illo fructum centuplum quam in ministerio reprobi qui cum illo dampnificat se ipsum et populum.' *De Eucharistia*, 113–14. Cf. *De Civili Dominio*, I, 284 f., in passages condemned by Pope Gregory XI. On the pope, *op. cit.*, 415 f.   [6] Wyclif, *Dialogus*, p. 3.

[7] Wyclif, *De Civili Dominio*, I, 12, 21 f., 102. On the pope, *De Ecclesia*, 17–19.

[8] Mansi, XXVI, 565 f.

[9] Wyclif, *De Civili Dominio*, I, 267, 345, 351.

reiterates Wyclif's clear preference that religious brothers live by the labour of their hands rather than by begging.[1]

Article 27, that everything comes to pass by absolute necessity, is a thesis that is all too easy to derive from Wyclif if one does not search diligently for his very careful qualifications.[2] Similar are article 26, that the prayers of the foreknown (to damnation) are not valid;[3] article 30, that excommunication by the pope is not to be feared[4] because he is the Antichrist;[5] 32, that to enrich the clergy is against the rule of Christ;[6] and 36, that the pope and other clerics who have possessions are heretics.[7]

The accusers recognized the difficulty in article 41, which says that it is not necessary to salvation to believe the Roman Church to be supreme over other churches. They add that this is an error if the Roman Church is understood as the Universal Church. However, this is precisely Wyclif's point in the passages from which this is derived. He maintained that the Roman Church was *not* to be equated with the Universal Church, which for Wyclif of course was the whole body of the predestined.[8]

An interesting point that they chose as an error is the position which is certainly implied in Wyclif, article 33 in the list, that Pope Sylvester and the Emperor Constantine erred in the 'donation' to the Church.[9] Thus we see that the Council of Constance still accepted the validity of the Donation of Constantine.

Others of the articles are complete misinterpretations of Wyclif. An example is article 6, that God must obey the Devil. This is

---

[1] Johannis Wyclif, *Tractatus De Officio Regis*, ed. Alfred W. Pollard & Charles Sayle, London 1887, 159 f.
[2] Wyclif, *Trialogus*, 40, 121-2.
[3] Wyclif, *De Eucharistia*, 114. Cf. Johannis Wyclif, *De Civili Dominio*, II, ed. Johann Loserth, London 1900, 49 f., where Wyclif questions whether prayers *on behalf* of the foreknown are valid.
[4] Wyclif, *De Civili Dominio*, I, 255, 274 f.; *Dialogus*, 25; *De Ecclesia*, 19; Johannis Wyclif, *Tractatus De Potestate Pape*, ed. Johann Loserth, London 1907, 31.
[5] Wyclif, *De Potestate Pape*, 118 f.
[6] Wyclif, *De Potestate Pape*, 82 f.; *De Officio Regis*, 160 f.
[7] Wyclif, *Dialogus*, 6-7. Cf. *De Ecclesia*, 88.
[8] Wyclif, *De Ecclesia*, 14-18, 85-8; *De Civili Dominio*, I, 381 f., 415 f.; *De Potestate Pape*, 32 f., 95 f.
[9] Johannis Wyclif, *De Civili Dominio*, III, ed. Johann Loserth, London 1903, 215 f.; *De Officio Regis*, 36 f.; *De Potestate Pape*, 226-31.

derived again from Wyclif s very complicated doctrine of necessity. Another that would have shocked Wyclif himself is article 44, which suggests that Saints Augustine, Benedict, and Bernard might be among the damned if they unrepentantly held material possessions. Taken out of its probable context of an example of his irony (the closest Wyclif comes to humour), this is a really low blow at Wyclif, for especially Augustine and Bernard are quoted frequently in Wyclif's writings.

With all this, what seems especially interesting is that in this basic list of articles to be condemned the brethren did not include Wyclif's basic doctrine of the Church, that the true Church is the whole body of the predestined, when this doctrine is basic to everything else that Wyclif has to say about the Church.

What then of the two hundred and sixty theses which were brought down from Oxford, but were not read at Constance? First of all, it should be noted that they are not in any way derived from the forty-five theses which were first condemned at Paris and Prague and then officially condemned at Constance. Thus it cannot be maintained that the ground for their suppression was that they were merely subsidiary to the original forty-five.

The two hundred and sixty, however, also purport to be excerpts from Wyclif's writings. The actual list as given in Wilkins's *Comilia* consists of two hundred and sixty-seven theses. This list deserves close study by Wyclif scholars. Some of the articles are evidently taken from Wyclif's later period of writing during which he was actually equating the pope with the Anti-Christ.[1] A number of them deal with the doctrine of the eucharist, and therefore may indeed be said to have been condemned in principle with the forty-five theses.[2] However, the document as a whole amounts to a ringing manifesto against the established order in the Church. Wyclif is quoted against religious orders, temporal property in ecclesiastical hands, even elaborate tombs. Especially significant is article 61, where it is suggested that it would be good for the Church to depose the pope with his cardinals

[1] E.g., Art. 4, in list as given in Wilkins, III, 339–49. Cf. Wyclif, *De Potestate Pape*, 118 f.

[2] E.g., Art. 65–71, 121 f., 160–70, 259–63.

and Caesarian prelates, by which Wyclif means bishops who hold secular as well as ecclesiastical offices.[1]

There is no doubt that the reading of any list of two hundred and sixty theses would have been soporific at the Council of Constance. However, the actual content of these theses strongly suggests that the Gallican nation at Constance, which was deeply involved in the process of deposition of Pope John XXIII, would have very good reason to suppress the condemnation of these particular theses as heretical in the eighth session of the Council just before an actual act of papal deposition, which as we have seen was begun in the ninth session.[2]

Even at Oxford they did not condemn Wyclif's basic concept of the true Church as the whole body of the predestined in this set of two hundred and sixty theses. Thus, as far as Wyclif's condemnation at Constance was concerned, this doctrine was not condemned specifically. Such a condemnation waited for the condemnation of John Hus. The first doctrine condemned in the list specifically attributed to Hus was the following: 'Unica est sancta Universalis ecclesia, quae est predestinatorum universitas.'[3] As we have seen, Hus's rejoinder was that this may be found in the writings of St Augustine, and thus he implied that the Council was putting itself in the ironic position of condemning as heretical one of the Fathers of the Church.

---

[1] '61. Experimento cognoscimus, quod mortuo papa vel deposito, cum suis cardinalibus et praelatis Caesareis, non minus, sed amplius prosperatur ecclesia. Nam quantum ad sacramentum confirmationis, cum sacramento ordinis, et benedictione chrismatis, cum ecclesiis dedicandis, quae appropriantur episcopis, videtur quod Christus perpendiculariter residens in caelis super justos presbyteros daret illis potestatem talia faciendi.' Wilkins, III, 342. Cf. Wyclif: 'Ergo per idem summus sacerdos Romane ecclesie deponi poterit et dampnari.' *De Civili Dominio*, I, 414.

[2] On Jean Gerson in this connection, see John B. Morrall, *Gerson and the Great Schism*, Manchester 1960, 92, 98, 109. Cf. on Pierre d'Ailly, Francis Oakley, *The Political Thought of Pierre d'Ailly*, New Haven 1964, 73, n. 17; 112; 157 f. These authors show clearly that Gerson and d'Ailly both took great care to disassociate themselves from Wyclif, but that this should have been so necessary seems significant.

[3] Mansi, XXVII, 754.

SOME ASPECTS OF
ENGLISH REPRESENTATION AT THE
COUNCIL OF BASLE

by A. N. E. D. SCHOFIELD

IN several papers already published I have attempted to provide an account of English relations with the Council of Basle and of the English role within the Council; in the course of these studies I have also tried to identify as many as possible of the Englishmen who can be traced at Basle during this period.[1] There is room, however, for a few further observations, and I trust that these will prove a useful supplement to my earlier work.

Of the two delegations that went to the Council from England, the first arrived early in 1433 and stayed only a few months, the second went in 1434 and was present for about a year until mid-1435. Both were despatched from England as the result of missions from the Council to this country led by Gerardo Landriani, the Bishop of Lodi. On each occasion the king's council resolved to send representatives to Basle and the Convocation of Canterbury then decided likewise. The members of the first delegation were active in Basle, but they did not formally join the Council since they declined to take the oath of incorporation by which entrants to the Council submitted to its authority and discipline. They were admitted to the discussions about the four Hussite articles of faith, perhaps because the Hussites had also

---

[1] 'The First English Delegation to the Council of Basel', *JEH*, XII, no. 2 (Oct. 1961), 167–96; 'The Second English Delegation to the Council of Basel', *ibid.* XVII, no. 1 (Apr. 1966), 29–64; 'England, the Pope, and the Council of Basel, 1435–1449', *Church History*, XXXIII, no. 3 (Sept. 1964), 248–78; and *Reunion*, VI, no. 62 (June 1965), 3–28. Many of the matters touched upon in the present paper are treated at greater length, with citation of sources and relevant authorities, in the above articles. This paper is devoted to the English at Basle, to the exclusion of the Normans, Gascons, and Irish; on the last mentioned, see 'Ireland and the Council of Basel', *Irish Ecclesiastical Record*, CVII, no. 6, 5th ser. (June 1967), 374–87.

refused to be incorporated. A further instalment of the delegation was planned but never sent. The members of the second delegation were allowed to take a modified form of the oath and some of them participated in the Council's work.

Let us look first at these English delegations. The terms 'delegation', 'national delegation' or 'official delegation', which do not occur in any equivalent form in contemporary sources, are nevertheless suitable descriptions for the two groups of representatives sent by the English government with the co-operation of the Church in response to appeals from the Council. The earlier one comprised royal ambassadors and representatives or delegates of the province of Canterbury. (York appears to have been overshadowed in this respect by the southern province.) The royal ambassadors were named in a procuration dated 1 December 1432.[1] Their colleagues, the representatives of Canterbury, were named in a procuration issued by the archbishop on 16 September that year.[2] Convocation, which was then in session, voted a subsidy for their maintenance.[3] A series of official documents can be traced relating to the payment of the members of the delegation and other matters such as the issue to them of licences to take gold and silver abroad.[4] A distinction was usually made therein between ambassadors and those whom we may call clerical representatives or delegates, between those described as going to the Council 'in praesenti Ambassiata Regis'[5] and those going there 'in Obsequium Regis de Licencia Regis... pro Clero Regni Regis Angliae'.[6]

[1] Foedera, Conventiones, literae et cuiuscumque generis acta publica, ed. T. Rymer, The Hague 1740, IV. 4. 187.
[2] Emmanuel College, Cambridge, MS 142, ff. 165–6b.
[3] The Register of Henry Chichele, Archbishop of Canterbury (1414–1443), ed. E. F. Jacob, 1943–7, III, 233, 236.
[4] Proceedings and Ordinances of the Privy Council of England, ed. Sir H. Nicolas, 1835, IV, 123–6; Foedera, IV. 4. 183–94; Calendar of French Rolls, 48th Report of the Deputy Keeper of the Public Records, 1887, 289–93; Calendar of Patent Rolls, Henry VI, 1907, II, 248–67.
[5] For example, when Brouns, the Dean of Salisbury, was granted letters of protection, Dec. 1432; Foedera, IV. 4. 188–9.
[6] Cf. when Pertrich (Partriche), the Chancellor of Lincoln, was granted letters of protection, Dec. 1432; ibid.

Some of those described in this way as ambassadors also appear in the archbishop's procuration just mentioned, and one is led to the conclusion that a nucleus of this first delegation had a double status, thus making it a closely integrated body; of its members who are known definitely to have reached Basle, about half may have been both royal ambassadors and clerical representatives.[1]

This twofold structure of the first delegation is again apparent in the two English protestations that were made at Basle during 1433 against the Council's procedure by 'deputations', the international commissions that had been established instead of the 'nations', the national or regional groupings, that had been set up at the Council of Constance. The first protestation was made in the name of Henry, King of France and of England, by three ambassadors who seem also to have had the status of clerical representatives. The second protestation was made on behalf of the Archbishop of Canterbury, the prelates and clergy of his province, and the English church and nation by four members of the delegation, three of whom were clerical representatives; the fourth, the Prior of Holy Trinity, Norwich, had participated in the other protestation and, appropriately, seems to have had a double status.[2]

The second delegation was appointed in a similar manner. The ambassadors' names can be found in royal procurations and a letter of credence issued in May and June 1434.[3] Convocation had decided that a maximum of eight doctors of theology or of canon or civil law might be sent on behalf of the province; however, no subsidy was granted, and this delegation lacked a non-ambassadorial contingent such as the first one had.[4] There was a small band of members of the first delegation still at Basle during the winter of 1433–4 and probably still there when the second delegation arrived. They cannot have been more than a handful; presumably they were not incorporated and were waiting for further instructions

[1] See Appendix A. Those who seem to have had double status were: Polton, Fitzhugh, Worstede, Brouns, Symondesburgh.
[2] 'The First English Delegation to the Council of Basel', *JEH*, xii, no. 2, 181–2.
[3] *The Official Correspondence of Thomas Bekynton*, ed. G. Williams (*RS*, 1872), ii, 259; *Foedera*, v. 1. 9; *Calendar of Patent Rolls, Henry VI*, ii, 342.
[4] *The Register of Henry Chichele*, iii, 249.

and reinforcements. (This does not contradict the existence of two distinct delegations.) But the presence in Basle of this small group could explain why Convocation thought it unnecessary to nominate more delegates in 1434.

The names of the members of the two delegations who are known to have gone to Basle are listed in two appendices attached to this paper. There are ten names from each delegation. Since three persons were in both of the delegations, the total of individuals amounts to seventeen. These men were well qualified by training and experience for the missions entrusted to them, but each delegation was small and was reduced in size still further by deaths and departures. The total figure includes three bishops (two of whom died in Basle), two abbots, one prior, one count, and two knights. By contrast, the delegation originally planned for 1433 would have amounted to as many as twenty-eight people. A few would have been in the retinues of more important personages and would themselves not have been of great weight, but there would have been eight bishops, including the Archbishop of York and Cardinal Beaufort. This grand design was never implemented.

So far we have considered royal ambassadors and other representatives who were under some measure of royal control. This preoccupation needs no justification. The delegations have an obvious importance as the expression of the kingdom's official, formal presence and support, and the Council was very dependent on the good-will of secular rulers, especially at the more critical moments in its life. The Council, of course, claimed to be a general council, representing the Universal Church, and guided by the Holy Spirit. By adopting 'deputations' instead of 'nations' the Fathers of Basle no doubt wished to eliminate, as far as possible, the national influences and rivalries that had been so much in evidence at Constance. They did not expect only prelates to come, although these, like the ambassadors of secular rulers, were important for the prestige and continued existence of the Council; it was an accepted feature of the Council that prelates often sent proctors of lesser status who acted for them; moreover, regulations concerning admissibility, drawn up in 1434, admitted to the

Council certain cathedral dignitaries, canons representing their chapters, and graduates down to bachelors of theology and licentiates in either law.[1] Was there, then, another side to English representation? Did bishops, chapters, and religious orders send representatives to Basle readily and independently of the delegations? Did some individuals perhaps go there impelled by enthusiasm for the conciliar cause? Any answers to these questions must be somewhat tentative, but they can be attempted.

To go back almost to the beginning of the Council, during the autumn of 1431 Cardinal Cesarini, the president, began to summon prelates and on 20 September he sent a summons to Archbishop Chichele.[2] The archbishop was ordered, under threat of excommunication, to come to the Council or to send proctors, who should be men of suitable education and character, well experienced in ecclesiastical affairs, with full powers. The summons was to be transmitted, subject to the same penalties for non-compliance, to all prelates, exempt and non-exempt, in his province, as well as to all chapters of cathedral churches therein which were customarily required to send representatives to general councils. One result was that John Stafford, the Bishop of Bath and Wells, appointed six proctors in December 1431.[3] Most of them were already proctors at the papal curia; one, the Bishop of London, was later an ambassador at Basle; but only one of these six was at the Council before the first delegation. This was John Gele, who was incorporated in March 1432 on behalf not only of the Bishop of Bath and Wells but also of the Bishops of Lincoln and Worcester.[4] Although a Canon of Lübeck and originally from Saxony, Gele was also Vicar of Harberton in Devon and a graduate of Oxford; he must therefore be allowed the distinction of being the first English churchman to have been incorporated in the Council.

---

[1] *Monumenta Conciliorum Generalium Saeculi XV. Concilium Basiliense Scriptores,* ed. F. Palacky, etc., Vienna 1857–86, II, 34–5, 579–80.

[2] *Ibid.* 32–4; Wilkins, III, 518–19.

[3] *The Register of John Stafford, Bishop of Bath and Wells (1425–1443),* ed. T. S. Holmes (Somerset Record Soc., 31, 32, 1916), 115–16.

[4] *Concilium Basiliense. Studien und Quellen zur Geschichte des Concils von Basel,* ed. J. Haller, etc. Basel 1896–1936, II, 52–3, 55–6.

William Swan, who had had long experience as a proctor at the papal curia, might also have been at the Council, perhaps before Gele, as proctor for the same bishops. John Keninghale, the English provincial of the Carmelites, was there by the autumn of 1432. In neither case, however, is there a record of incorporation.[1]

Otherwise, the tardy response of the English hierarchy to Cesarini's summons seems to have been overtaken by the organization of the first national delegation in 1432–3. From that time, a number of procurations can be traced which indicate what the general practice must have been.[2] Members of the delegations already at the Council are sometimes named; however, it is clear that an obligation was recognized to send others to supplement the delegations. But some names tend to recur, and we can see that multiple procurations were common, so that a small number of men might ultimately represent the hierarchy and chapters of an entire province.

During the first five or six years of the Council there were probably at least as many Englishmen there outside the delegations as within them; that would give us a total of about forty English at Basle; they were not all present together, of course, but at various times during that period. Probably most of those who were outside the delegations were proctors rather than sympathizers with the Council who had gone there independently. But what we see demonstrated here are rather perfunctory attempts to satisfy the obligation to take part in the Council.

The religious orders in England sent few of their members; it

---

[1] *Concilium Basiliense*, II, 245, 272; 'The First English Delegation to the Council of Basel', *JEH*, XII, no. 2, 179 and n. 7; 'The Second English Delegation to the Council of Basel', *ibid*. XVII, no. 1, 46–7.

[2] *Literae Cantuarienses*, ed. J. B. Sheppard (*RS*, 1887–9), III, 163–4; *The Register of Thomas Langley, Bishop of Durham (1406–1437)*, ed. R. L. Storey, 1956–61, IV, 91–4; *The Register of Edmund Lacy, Bishop of Exeter (1420–1455)*, ed. F. C. Hingeston-Randolph, 1909, 1915, II, 621; *The Register of John Stafford*, II, 184; cartulary of Reading Abbey, Salisbury Diocesan Record Office, f. 10ab; for names of proctors nominated by Chichele to watch over his interests, see A. Zellfelder, *England und das Basler Konzil (Historische Studien*, ed. E. Ebering, Band 113, Berlin 1913), 120–9, 297–311.

is mostly the Benedictines who are in evidence.[1] The English universities did not formally participate in the Council, although Oxford had been ready at one stage to send delegates if the money could be found.[2]

At this point we may briefly consider an unpublished royal letter, a copy of which is contained in the cartulary from Llanthony Priory now at the Public Record Office.[3] The king explains that he is writing in similar vein to all his prelates and notable abbots. From his ambassadors at the Council he has heard that the English there have been too few in number to achieve the standing they had enjoyed at Constance and other councils or to succeed in forming a 'nation'. The French, meanwhile, have arrived in force. He therefore exhorts the addressee to go to Basle or to send a proctor, who should be a notable or worthy clerk, to arrive by Easter, if possible. He disapproves of the tendency towards multiple procurations and says that he has given instructions that henceforth no one shall be proctor for more than one prelate and abbot. This letter bears the date, 10 February, but no year is given. It might have been written in 1434, when the second delegation was being organized, or, more probably, in 1435, when that delegation was already at the Council but depleted, and on that same date, 10 February, a new procuration for royal ambassadors was issued.[4] This letter is evidence both of

---

[1] In Dec. 1432 the Abbots of St Albans, Glastonbury, and St Mary's, York, were appointed to represent the English provincial chapter. *Documents Illustrating the Activities of the General and Provincial Chapters of the English Black Monks, 1215–1540*, ed. W. A. Pantin, Camden Soc., 3rd series, LIV (1937), III, 105; the last two were in the second delegation. See also *Memorials of St Edmund's Abbey*, ed. T. Arnold (*RS*, 1896), III, 252–7.

[2] *The Official Correspondence of Thomas Bekynton*, II, 104, 354; *Epistolae Academicae Oxoniensis*, ed. H. Anstey, 1898, I, 72–4.

[3] PRO C115/A3, f. ccxlviii. There is a copy or draft of a similar, although shorter and perhaps incomplete, royal letter, also like the above mentioned in English, in British Museum Cotton Cleopatra E III, f. 66a; this has the date '13 H6' (Sept. 1434–Aug. 1435) added. The English had applied unsuccessfully to be allowed to form a 'nation' in Nov. 1434. 'The Second English Delegation to the Council of Basel', *JEH*, XVII, no. 1, 49–50.

[4] *Foedera*, v. 1. 15. The only English named in this were the Bishop of London and the Abbot of York; the others were the Gascon Bishop of Dax, who had been included with the English members of the second delegation, and some Normans.

the lack of keen interest among English prelates in taking part in the Council and of the extent to which the English role there depended on a lead from the king.

The English at Basle outside the delegations are of interest. We can trace some of them from a variety of sources.[1] A lengthy list could be compiled of others who were intended to go and might have gone; the difficulty lies in proving their presence in the Council. The most useful single source ought to be the records edited by Haller and his collaborators in *Concilium Basiliense*, in particular the minutes of the general congregations and the deputation for general matters kept by the notary, Bruneti, during the earlier years of the Council when there were Englishmen present.[2] There has been controversy about the nature of these minutes— are they formal *acta* or something less? This need not delay us in the present context. But these minutes, although skilfully edited and indexed, are not an infallible record of proceedings. Incorporations are not always included; indeed, some Englishmen who are known to have been incorporated, are not mentioned. A few people were described as English probably in error in the first instance. There is also the problem of identifying those denoted by such descriptions as 'Robertus Anglicus' or 'Johannes doctor Anglicus'; furthermore, it is difficult to determine how consistently such vague descriptions were used to indicate the same person. We are indebted to Bruneti's minutes for knowledge of several Englishmen at the Council that might otherwise have been lost, but so far I have been able to identify with certainty only fourteen of the English recorded there; this figure is less than half the total of those we know were present. Any conclusions, analyses, or computerized results that were based on these minutes, without a good deal of preliminary work having been done and without the safeguard of some knowledge of the English ecclesiastical background, would be inaccurate and could be very misleading.

[1] 'The Second English Delegation to the Council of Basel', *JEH*, XVII, no. 1 45–7.

[2] *Concilium Basiliense*, II–VI. Lists of incorporations will also be found in Cardinal John of Segovia's history of the Council in *Monumenta Conciliorum Generalium XV Saeculi*, II and III; but these sometimes appear to be based on the minutes published by Haller; they also contain frequent mistakes in proper names.

English representation at Basle

There are many gaps in our knowledge, not all of which we can hope to fill. I venture to think, however, that much will come to light when it is possible to compare studies of England and other parts of Christendom and all the Councils of the fifteenth century. It is as a small contribution towards this end that I have offered these few further notes.

APPENDIX A

The following members of the first English delegation are known to have been in Basle in 1433:

Thomas Polton, Bishop of Worcester
Robert Fitzhugh, Bishop of London
William Worstede, Prior of Holy Trinity, Norwich
Thomas Brouns, Dean of Salisbury
Alexander Sparrow, Archdeacon of Berkshire
John Symondesburgh, Archdeacon of Wiltshire
John Salisbury, Sub-prior of Christchurch, Canterbury
Robert Burton, Precentor of Lincoln and Archdeacon of Northumberland
Peter Pertrich (Partriche), Chancellor of Lincoln
John Colvyle, knight

APPENDIX B

The following members of the second English delegation are known to have been in Basle during 1434–5:

Robert Fitzhugh, Bishop of London
John Langdon, Bishop of Rochester
Nicholas Frome, Abbot of Glastonbury
William Wells, Abbot of St Mary's, York
William Worstede, Prior of Norwich
Thomas Brouns, Dean of Salisbury
Edmund Beaufort, Count of Mortain
Henry Brounflete (Bromflete), knight
John Colvyle, knight
Thomas Launcelyn, Preceptor of the Knights of St John of Jerusalem (Knights Hospitallers) at Godsfield, Hants., Turcopolier of Rhodes

227   8-2

THE COUNCIL OF BASLE AND THE
SECOND VATICAN COUNCIL

by A. J. BLACK

MANY will have noticed how the renewal of the Church in modern times has drawn together strands of thought and behaviour that were in the past considered discordant. Thus the Second Vatican Council, it seems, in continuing the work of the First, would be likely to draw on that part of the Church's heritage which had previously been in apparent conflict with the doctrine of papal supremacy: namely, the notion of the supremacy of the Church as a body and of the council or the episcopate. In some ways there is a remarkable degree of continuity between the thought of the Council of Basle (1431–49) and of the Second Vatican Council.

One of the central ideas of the Council of Basle, an idea to which it consistently resorted as its final justification, was the corporate sovereignty of the church community taken as a whole. It used this as a basis for conciliar sovereignty, on the grounds that the council *was* this whole church community 'taken collectively', in the literal sense of being assembled in one place. (This somewhat arbitrary identification of the council with the Church was largely the result of exaggerating the analogy between the whole Church and a small college or corporation.) But it was on the idea of the ultimate sovereignty of the community as a whole that Basle frequently, and increasingly, fell back in justifying the sovereignty of the council over the pope. We find this in Panormitanus (citing Zabarella),[1] in Andrew of Escobar,[2] in several statements by universities, in particular by Cracow,[3] and most

---

[1] *Deutsche Reichstagsakten*, ed. H. Weigel and others, Stuttgart–Göttingen 1935–XVI, 483, 499, 506, 521. Cf. W. Ullmann, *The origins of the Great Schism*, London 1948, 211 f.; B. Tierney, *Foundations of conciliar theory*, Cambridge 1955, 225 f.
[2] H. v. Hardt, *Magnum oecumenicum Constantiense concilium*, Frankfurt–Leipzig 1697–1700, VI, 260.
[3] C. E. du Boulay, *Historia Universitatis Parisiensis*, v, Paris 1670, 489 f.

persistently in John of Segovia: 'supreme power...belongs to the Church continuously, permanently, invariably, and perpetually'.[1] Indeed, in both his ecclesiastical thought and his secular analogies, Segovia anticipates Rousseau's view that the community cannot alienate or delegate its supreme power any more than someone could alienate their own personal qualities: 'supreme power resides first of all in the community itself like a personal sense or inborn virtue'.[2] The difference between Segovia and Rousseau is that he speaks of the community as a whole, Rousseau of its individual members; hence, Segovia sees the council as comprising the community though many of its members are absent. Similarly, the decree of Vatican II *On the Church* (*Lumen Gentium*) speaks of the Church as a corporate entity (made 'into a single people', into which individual members are 'incorporated'),[3] and follows in the steps of conciliarist ecclesiology by asserting the infallibility of the Church as a whole:

The body of the faithful as a whole...cannot err in matters of belief. Thanks to a supernatural sense of the faith which characterizes the People as a whole, it manifests this unerring quality when, 'from the bishops down to the last member of the laity', it shows universal agreement in matters of faith and morals.[4]

We may notice, on the other hand, how Vatican II has gone far beyond Basle in elevating the position of the laity both in theory and practice.

The Council of Basle, in applying the collegiate model to the Church as a whole, and specifically to the Church-in-council, was largely, but not solely, concerned with legal and constitutional powers. As well as utilizing corporation-theory to assert the right of the community-in-assembly to supreme power (which included such important procedural details as the right to self-assembly, self-dissolution, and the equal standing of incorporated members in the council), the conciliarists of Basle, many of whom stemmed

[1] *Monumenta conciliorum generalium seculi decimi quinti*, ed. F. Palacky and others, Vienna–Basle 1857–1935, III, 802–3.
[2] *Loc. cit.*; cf. J.-J. Rousseau, *Du contrat social*, II, i.
[3] *The documents of Vatican II*, ed. J. Gallagher, London–Dublin 1966, 25, 29, 33.
[4] *Ibid.* 29; the quotation is from St Augustine, *loc. cit.*, n.

from those universities, monasteries, and the like where these principles were a matter of daily practice, sought also to reproduce in the central government of the Church that sense and spirit of communal self-administration with which they were familiar, and which formed their ideal in other spheres of activity (for example, the common mess, and the corporate ownership of property). Indeed, this may be said to link the Council of Basle with a widely felt concern, particularly in the North, to restore and promote 'the common life' in late medieval Church and society. Arguing for the equality of votes within the council, Escobar declares: 'Fraternity among Christians is based on charity... charity makes everything be held in common, and puts common things before private... Therefore also there must be one charity, one will, one intention in the council.'[1] The government of the Church, and to a lesser degree any government, is seen not merely as a matter of pursuing the best course, but as a communal and consultative activity which distils from the community its own self-awareness of what is just and true. (Here we may notice the confluence of the ideals of the Aristotelian *polis* and of the Germanic *Volk*.) One of the texts most often quoted in Baslean writings is that which asserts the communal nature of the Church: 'where two or three are gathered together.' And again Escobar says: 'The universal Church is a kind of unseen body, a kind of public possession of the Christian people... this most holy republic is the common property of the Christian people.'[2] Again, Cusa proclaims that 'the greater the unanimity, the more infallible the judgment'.[3] Segovia once more anticipates Rousseau, when he affirms that a truly communal decision is not arrived at simply by following the procedure of majority voting, but is the fruit of communal discourse: 'If all members of the city as individuals, or their greater part, perform some action, the city is not deemed to perform it... unless it is preceded by common discussion or common consent, tacit or explicit.'[4] This is an emphasis which seems

[1] Hardt, *Magnum oecumenicum Constantiense concilium*, VI, 265; cf. *ibid.* 195–6 on the need to restore 'vita communis'.   [2] *Ibid.* 328.
[3] Nicholas of Cusa, *De concordantia catholica*, II, iv.
[4] *Monumenta conciliorum generalium sec. XV*, III, 736; cf. Rousseau, *op. cit.*, II, iii.

to run through modern thinking on church government. Vatican II, for example, stresses that the sole aim of the church hierarchy is to 'work toward a common goal freely', and uses the fact of this 'common duty' as an argument for the corporate structure of the episcopate.[1]

Similarly, Vatican II consistently refers to the hierarchy as a 'ministry', and to church government as a service, quoting a text which was frequently on Segovia's lips, that 'he who is the greater should become as the lesser, and he who is the more distinguished, as the servant'.[2] Segovia generally referred to the pope as the 'prime minister', which was the topic of a pleasing exchange at the council:

The bishop of Ardjisch had happened to say that the Roman pontiff was the servant of the Church, which Panormitanus could not tolerate; and that day so far forgot his learning, which is very great, as not to shrink from claiming that the pope was ruler of the Church. John of Segovia replied, 'Watch what you are saying, Panormitanus. It is a very honourable title of the Roman pontiff when he calls himself "servant of the servants of God".'[3]

But, as well as these connections of a fairly general character, there is one more specific reason for linking the thought behind the Council of Basle with that behind the Second Vatican Council. In a work written after the council (*c.* 1450), called *On the great authority of Bishops in a general council,* John of Segovia took a remarkable step from the Baslean doctrine of the corporate sovereignty of the Church-in-council to an adumbration of the Vatican doctrine of the corporate sovereignty of the episcopate-in-council. He now bases the argument for conciliar sovereignty, no longer on the vague notion of the council as 'representing' the Church (which could only have been given real meaning in an electoral system), but on the fact that the council is essentially the bishops in assembly. Their supreme authority in turn he derives, as Vatican II derives it, from the fact that they succeed the apostles, to whom, as well as to Peter, the power of the keys was

[1] *Documents of Vatican II*, 27, 37, 47. [2] *Ibid.* 51.
[3] A. S. Piccolomini, *De gestis concilii Basiliensis commentariorum libri II*, ed. and trans. D. Hay and W. Smith, Oxford 1967, 27–9.

given—not only as individuals but as a jurisdictional group, or college.[1] Thus he seems to have been the first to have applied to the episcopate that notion of 'collegiality' which was so widespread in medieval political thought and ecclesiology, and which church thinkers of the Middle Ages had tended to apply in this form exclusively to the College of Cardinals. (Indeed, as Congar has pointed out, the 'cardinalist ideology' monopolized claims to a corporate sovereignty over against the pope's in the central government of the Church, during this period.)[2] Segovia, using the familiar conciliarist distinction between the members of a group taken singly and taken collectively, asserts, as Vatican II was to do, that in the latter though not in the former sense the episcopate holds supreme power in the Church, and is infallible when it teaches definitively on faith and morals.[3] Again, in this later tract, Segovia is less concerned with asserting conciliar supremacy against the pope, and more concerned with asserting it as a general principle. Indeed, just as his great opponent John of Turrecremata, in his *Summa on the Church* (1449), allowed that in certain cases a conciliar majority could override the pope,[4] so Segovia now maintained that the pope's fullness of power was in no way dependent on the council and could not be enhanced by it.[5] Thus we may find on both sides in the fifteenth-century dispute early traces of that reconciliation between the principles of papal and of conciliar authority, which seems to stand out as one of the great achievements of Vatican II, when it asserts the inseparability of papal and episcopal authority: 'Together with its head, the Roman pontiff, and never without this head, the episcopal order is the subject of supreme and full power over the universal church.'[6]

---

[1] *De magna auctoritate episcoporum in generali concilio*, in Basel Universitätsbibliothek, B.V. 15, f. 18 v, 36 v, 43 r, 75 r; *Documents of Vatican II*, 37–44.

[2] Y. Congar, 'La collégialité épiscopale, histoire et théologie', in *Unam Sanctam*, LII (Paris 1965), 118 f.

[3] *De magna auctoritate episcoporum*, f. 98 v, 200r ('tota multitudo episcoporum non potest simul deviare'), 201 v ('episcopi quorum status a fide et unitate ecclesie est indeclinabilis'), 203 v ('indeviabilitas episcopalis status ab ecclesia'); *Documents of Vatican II*, 48–9.

[4] *Summa de ecclesia*, Venice 1561, III, lxiv, f. 353 r.

[5] *De magna auctoritate episcoporum*, f. 182 r.   [6] *Documents of Vatican II*, 43.

Indeed, the aspiration towards unity in diversity, which formed one of the main elements in Nicholas of Cusa's ideal, and which was later also expressed by Turrecremata, may be found distinctly echoed in the Vatican decree *On the Church*:

It is definite...that the power of binding and loosing, which was given to Peter, was granted also to the college of apostles, joined with their head. This college, insofar as it is composed of many, expresses the variety and universality of the People of God, but insofar as it is assembled under one head, it expresses the unity of the flock of Christ.[1]

[1] *Ibid.* 43–4; Cusa, *De concordantia catholica*, II, xxxii; Turrecremata, *Summa de ecclesia*, II, i, f. 116v; cf. *Deutsche Reichstagsakten*, xv, 183: '(ut) vera concordia fieret et ex diversitate commixtio'.

THE COLLOQUIES BETWEEN
CATHOLICS AND PROTESTANTS,
1539–41

by BASIL HALL

RANKE, whose judgments always deserve respect, said of
the Colloquy of Regensburg.

If I am not mistaken this was a period of vital importance for Germany
and even for the world. For Germany… [came] at last the possibility
of reforming the ecclesiastical constitution of the nation, and, in relation
to the Pope, of giving it a freer and more independent position, exempt
from his temporal encroachments. The unity of the Church, and with
it that of the nation, would have been maintained, and even more
immense and enduring results would have emerged. If the moderate
party, by whom these attempts began and were guided, could have
maintained its ascendancy in Rome and in Italy, the Catholic world
must have assumed a very different aspect.[1]

While it is true that the 'might-have-beens' of history are un-
profitable speculations, yet the possibilities behind that Colloquy
of Regensburg have been too much neglected.

Has any Catholic scholar writing with authority spoken favourably and sympathetically of the Colloquies which took place
between Catholics and Protestants in Germany in the period
1539–41? From John Eck who took part in them down to Dr
Hubert Jedin, author of the magisterial history of the Council of
Trent, as far as I am aware, the Colloquies have been dismissed
as ill-grounded and irresponsible attempts at reconciling Catholic
truth with heresy by unauthorized means—a movement bound to
fail because it was undertaken by the wrong people, with the

[1] Leopold von Ranke, *Sämmtliche Werke* (3rd collected edition), vol. 37, *Die
Römischen Päpste in den letzen vier Iahrhunderten*, 1900, I, 107.

wrong methods, and with wrong ends in view. It is not that the Colloquies have been unduly neglected; Sleidan, Sarpi, and Seckendorf gave some desultory account of them long ago, and in the second half of the nineteenth century a number of books were written in Germany, especially by Catholics, which gave close attention to the Colloquies.[1] But the inevitable conclusion was, as Pastor exemplifies,[2] that they were an unfortunate interlude of political manoeuvring prior to the decisive and doctrinally sound purpose of holding a General Council under the Pope's authority. After the final session of the Council of Trent it was apparently psychologically impossible for Catholics to regard the Colloquies as having been a valid means for understanding and reunion. The Council had laid down a retrospective condemnation of Protestantism and its works. Perhaps since the coming of Pope John XXIII and the Council of the Vatican II, and since some relaxing of the grip that the Council of Trent laid on Catholicism, there are now Catholic scholars who are taking a more favourable look at that ecumenical failure at Regensburg in 1541 and what preceded it. Protestant scholars, while not so thorough in condemnation, have tended to ignore the Colloquies or to dismiss them in a summary account, offering no helpful analysis, as delusive gatherings hopeless from the beginning.

But judgments that may have seemed clearly demonstrated and final in, say, 1545, 1890, or 1950, may be reconsidered, for such judgments are made from within certain historical situations, under the pressure of particular convictions and particular apologetic trends, and with the course of time the situations change. Moreover, historians have oversimplified the issues with the certainties of hindsight. But it cannot be right that historians should continue to be content with over-simplifications where contemporaries felt torturing complexities. If good men of undoubted Catholic piety, learning and integrity like Cardinals Contarini, Sadoleto,

[1] For the nineteenth-century writers in Germany see the literature at the head of the article by Kolde, 'Regensburger Religionsgespräch und Regensburger Buch 1541', *Realencyklopädie für Protestantische Theologie und Kirche*, 3rd ed. 1905, vol. 16.

[2] This is a major theme of his book: Ludwig Pastor, *Die kirchlichen Reunionsbestrebungen während der Regierung Karls V*, Freiburg 1879.

and the Cologne theologian Gropper, to name but a few, believed
that it was worth while to try to reconcile Protestants on the
great question of grace, and from that basis come to an understanding on the nature of the Sacraments, the Church and the
Papacy, why dismiss their judgment with the easy hindsight of
four centuries of Tridentinism triumphant? Again, if Protestants
like Melanchthon and Bucer, for example, could discuss eirenically
with Catholics about the great question of grace, and after agreement there, go the second mile in seeking understanding on the
question of the Sacraments, the authority of the Church, and the
status of the Bishop of Rome, should they be dismissed as the weak
instruments of Imperial Chancellor Granvella's political manoeuvres, or as the earliest victims of the modern affliction called
'ecumania'? If those men of good-will on both sides could agree
on the very matter on which Luther had stormed out of the
Church of Rome in 1521 (or as some commentators wish to
affirm was thrust into a position which he had not originally
taken, and from thence compelled to act as he did after 1521), in
spite of the enormous pressures against such an agreement by
1541, is it not reasonable to look at the matter again, firmly setting
aside as far as possible the simplifications of either Catholic or
Protestant hindsight? The task will not be easy: it is not just a
matter of considering the theological texts which the theologians
of the Colloquies kept before them, or agreed upon, in 1539–41,
for that would be another form of over-simplification. Those
Colloquies were deeply involved in the oppositions of imperial,
papal and French politics; they were heavily compromised by the
intransigents who were not present, Martin Luther and the
Elector at Wittenberg and Pope Paul III at Rome, who showed
fervent mutual distrust; princes were changing sides during the
period of the meetings, the Elector of Brandenburg came into
Protestantism while continuing to attend Mass with cheerful
inconsistency at Regensburg, and the Landgrave Philip of Hesse
broke the Protestant alliance to support Charles V through fear
of the legal consequences of his own bigamous marriage; and
through all this the Catholic Bavarian dukes with beautiful simplicity explained to the Emperor that the answer to all these

problems of schism, heresy and political division was 'war, bloody war'.

Before entering upon an account of the Colloquies and of the political and partisan problems which were entangled with them, it would be well to ask whether the common assumption is valid that the Protestants were wholly opposed to Catholicism because of the basic principles on which they grounded their beliefs.[1] If we come forward from 1517 instead of going back through centuries of embittered antagonism we would find that the first reformers retained much of the Catholicism they are confidently assumed by Protestant controversialists to have opposed. It is significant that the Lutheran scholar, Jaroslav Pellikan, could write recently: 'Martin Luther was the first Protestant, and yet he was more Catholic than many of his Roman Catholic opponents.'[2] This apparent paradox contains a demonstrable and important truth which it has been possible to affirm only recently after centuries of holding Protestantism and Catholicism as self-evident terms of black and white opposition. This could lead us, of course, into a discussion of what meanings should be attached to these two words, but I do not propose to undertake this analysis, since it has so long been bound up with manoeuvring for positions suitable for defensive and offensive tactics characteristic of the controversy between Protestant and Catholic since Church History emerged as a specialist study in the sixteenth century precisely to enable both sides to demonstrate as fully as possible each other's fatal errors.[3] Let us rather look for common ground behind those two words which have been all too evocative of embattled fortresses.

Catholicism, in the form which challenged Luther to recant, can be understood as essentially consisting in the obedience of the faithful to papal and hierarchical absolutist authority, supported

[1] For example, *Dictionnaire de Théologie Catholique*, 1936, vol. 13, art. 'Réforme'.
[2] Jaroslav Pellikan, *Obedient Rebels*, 1964, p. 11.
[3] *The Historia Ecclesiae Christi*, 1559–74, edited by Flacius Illyricus with his collaborators ('the Magdeburg Centuriators'), was intended as a demonstration of the increasing domination of an earlier purer Christianity by the 'anti-Christian' Papacy. In spite of this partisan intention it initiated the modern study of Church History by its full use of sources. It was answered by the *Annales Ecclesiastici*, 1588–1607, of Cesare Baronius.

on the one hand by the all-embracing legal obligations of the
Canon Law, and on the other by scholasticism busily determining
heresies by a computerizing process of showing how new theological views might be placed in parallel with old condemnations,
and then using the overpowering bludgeon of canonical authority
to hammer down the proposers of such views into silence. Before
all those of good-will dismiss this description of sixteenth-century
Catholicism in terms of an intolerable tyranny, as an ill-drawn
caricature, let them remember that on that basis John Eck challenged Luther at the public debate at Leipzig. Eck was largely
indifferent to the great matter of grace raised by Luther as a
faithful Catholic seeking to re-establish sound doctrine against
decaying scholastic opinions and the development of superstitious
practices; in fact Eck avoided discussion with Luther, at bottom
he was possibly bored with the subject or, more probably,
realized how difficult it would be to refute Luther on it, and
preferred to spend his energies in demonstrating, by bludgeoning
authoritarianism, that Luther was really a Hussite, who had defied
the authority of the Pope and the laws of the Church, and who
should forthwith recant or be condemned out of hand. Even
Cardinal Cajetan, a distinguished Thomist, and competent in the
new biblical learning, who could have understood Luther's concern about grace, unfortunately (for this was a crucial interview)
irritably shifted the ground to that of authority with its requirement 'be silent and obey'.

Luther was bustled out of the Church under misleading
labels and by noisy demonstrations of authority: his whole
effort at repristinating the meaning of grace, and therefore
of the Sacraments, and the nature of the Church as the *corpus
mysticum* was ignored or overshadowed by insistence on papal
authority and its associated legalism. The theologically grounded
opposition from Latomus, Cochlaeus and Murner, among others,
did not get to close grips with Luther's profound analysis of the
nature of justification. Laymen of sound piety, of whom the
Elector Frederick the Wise may be taken as a significant example,
could not see where theologically on the basis of Scripture Luther
had been refuted—this was a major reason why Eck's debating

victory at Leipzig to his own surprise and irritation came to nothing. Even at the end of his life under what was tantamount to exile in an Austrian monastery Luther's former superior in religion and confessor, John Staupitz, was not convinced that Luther up to 1519 was theologically unsound on justification.[1]

Nor was Luther's position unique among those who were to become Protestants, in seeking to retain Catholic substance in his theological work of renewal. Melanchthon, in the Augsburg Confession, deliberately ignored what were later to become extremist Protestant positions, and intended the Confession as a basis for healing the growing schism. Bucer was prepared to go to greater lengths than other Protestants to find grounds for agreement on Catholic substance between Catholics and Protestants. Calvin wrote explicitly of his reluctance to break with the visible unity[2] of the Catholic Church, and throughout his career as a theologian thought of himself as restoring sound Catholicism rather than as creating a particular Protestant Church and society. Few realize, who have read little of Calvin, how very much more his writings are concerned with the Church and the Sacraments than with predestination. Archbishop Cranmer has suffered, like his continental contemporaries, from English writers whose Protestant zeal roused vigorous high-church counter-attack so that the Catholic substance in his work like that in the work of the men he so much admired and used, from Melanchthon and Bucer down to Justus Jonas, has been almost ignored by his English friends and foes in the last hundred and thirty years.

With the changes in historical and especially theological perspectives which have been taking place in the last decade (for example, the decline in the appeal to authority for its own sake, the shift away from traditional scholastic philosophy and theology; the raising again with fresh insights of the question of justification by Hans Küng) we can more easily see than could Joseph Lortz

---

[1] *Luther's Werke*, Weimar Ausgabe, *Briefwechsel*, III, No. 726.

[2] *Ioannis Calvini Opera quae supersunt omnia*, ed. Baum, Cunitz & Reuss, 1866, vol. v, col. 412. 'Una praesertim res animum ab illis meum avertebat, ecclesiae reverentia.'

or Hubert Jedin[1] or their Protestant contemporaries, that there was at least a measure of common ground that could make it sensible to try to bring Catholics and Protestants to discuss the possibility of reunion in the mid-sixteenth century.

A serious attempt at providing a last stand against taking those reunion talks seriously (other than by the method of authoritarian dismissal), which is insisted on by both Lortz and Jedin, is that the participants in and promoters of those Colloquies were the victims of Erasmianism. In his profound account of the German Reformation Lortz showed the strongest hostility to Erasmus: 'Erasmus constituted a threat to Christianity and to the Church.'[2] For him, before Erasmus can be interpreted, the definitive presupposition is required: one must believe in the necessity of a dogmatically fixed religion.[3] On that basis Erasmus and consequently the Erasmians are condemned with barely a hearing. 'He represented the threat to dogma by relativism, to the Kingdom of grace and redemption by ennobled stoic morality.'[4] Lortz also attacked Melanchthon for relativizing Luther's dogmatic principles by his humanist approach in the Augsburg Confession. He could even write: 'The timid, petty, sly dishonesty of Erasmus cast its shadow upon Melanchthon's image.'[5] After this it is not surprising that in his brief account of what he called 'the conciliatory theology' of the period of the Colloquies he described it as 'founded on Erasmus and his relativism'.[6]

Jedin went even further.[7] On Erasmus he makes the surprisingly pietistic statement that 'the circumstance that the *Praise of Folly* was written while Erasmus was staying in the house of a canonized saint does not alter the fact that...he had exposed to ridicule persons and institutions which up till then had been held in reverence'.[8] Again, Jedin prefaces his discussion of the Erasmianism of the Colloquies by showing that Erasmus was hopelessly at fault in 'coming to the conclusion that, given a measure of good-

---

[1] Joseph Lortz, *The Reformation of Germany*, 1968; Eng. trans. of *Die Reformation in Deutschland*, 3rd ed., 2 vols., Freiburg 1949; Hubert Jedin, *A History of the Council of Trent*, vol. I, Eng. trans. 1957, *Geschichte des Konzils von Trient*, 1949.
[2] Joseph Lortz, *The Reformation in Germany* I, 152.
[3] *Ibid.* 153.   [4] *Ibid.* 152–3.   [5] *Ibid.*   [6] *Ibid.* 245.
[7] Hubert Jedin, *A History of the Council of Trent*, I, 156 ff.   [8] *Ibid.* 160.

will, the sickness [of schism] was by no means incurable', and for adopting the attitude that 'after all both parties continued to believe in Christ!'.[1] He points to the large number of clergy, including some bishops, and also powerful laymen who were ecclesiastical politicians, influenced—apparently he only just stops at saying infected—by Erasmian ideas.[2] Then in one swingeing sentence Jedin condemns Erasmus by irrelevant association:

The Erasmians did not form a secret society as did the freemasons of the era of Enlightenment; they were linked together by the same community of thought as were the ecclesiastical rationalists two centuries later, and just as the ideas of the latter coincided largely with those of the Jansenists—hence with a current which at least in its beginnings ran directly counter to theirs—so did the Erasmian mentality coincide with that of the 'evangelicals'.[3]

Here freemasonry, the rationalism of the Enlightenment, and Jansenism are associated with Erasmus, not because they were directly relevant but because presumably they represent standard subjects of orthodox disapproval to make our flesh creep—and the wholly misleading word 'evangelical' is brought in to add another to its confusing usages. Thus the period of the Colloquies is condemned, before it is adequately discussed, as falsely grounded. But Erasmus was not responsible for Contarini discovering from his own studies something near to Luther's doctrine of justification in 1511. Nor was he responsible for the fact that across Europe there were many men who were deeply disturbed by the implications of merit-theology, with the lack of spiritual depth in teaching about the use of the Sacraments, and who were weary of those scholastic theologians who behaved as the swordsmen of dialectics rather than as pastors of the flock. His success as a writer was due at least in part to the fact that this situation existed—he did not create it, he addressed it, and roused with real insight fresh resources of the Christian spirit through his return to the sources in Scripture and the Fathers.

Few scholars at this time, including theologians, would agree with the attitude of Lortz and Jedin to Erasmus. In the generation

[1] *Ibid.* 359. [2] *Ibid.* 364. [3] *Ibid.* 364.

which has passed since they wrote there has emerged a sympathetic exposition of his work as one who sought to restore ancient piety, provide the basic principles for a new theological method, and provide a framework for these activities in the labour of editing the New Testament in Greek and scholarly editions of the Fathers.[1] From this more appreciative view of Erasmus's work as containing positive good, it is possible to see, more sympathetically than did Lortz or Jedin, the men who took part in the Colloquies. The Colloquies were not just politicians' devices or attempts by one religious party to put the other in a false position (though some on either side had hoped for this unscrupulous device) any more than they were examples of misleading Erasmianism; rather they contained within them sincere attempts at mutual understanding and even of reconciliation undertaken amid great difficulties from the opposition of extremists of both sides.

The religious condition within the German Empire was grave enough. Cardinal Aleandro after an Austrian journey wrote to the Pope in September 1538, with glum though pardonable exaggerations, that

divine worship and the administration of the Sacraments had for the most part ceased. The secular princes, with the exception of Ferdinand I, were either entirely Lutheran or full of hatred for the priesthood and greed of Church property; the prelates lived just as extravagantly as before and merely held positions in the Church. The religious orders had dwindled down to handfuls, the secular clergy were not much more numerous, and so immoral and ignorant that the few Catholics there were shunned them.[2]

This taken together with the political situation in the German Empire and the long procrastination in the past of Clement VII— who, fearing the consequences for himself,[3] had been opposed to calling a General Council of the Church anywhere at any time, in spite of his vague promises to the contrary—and the hesitations

---

[1] For example W. P. Eckert, *Erasmus von Rotterdam Werk und Werkung*, 2 vols., Cologne 1967; C. Bene, *Erasme et St Augustin*, Geneva 1969; J.-C. Margolin, *Recherches Erasmiennes*, Geneva 1969.

[2] Pastor, *The History of the Popes*, 1912, XI, 362.

[3] Among other problems for Clement VII was the fact of his illegitimate birth; Ranke, *Werke*, 37, 1.

about the timing and procedure of a Council by Paul III, who was nevertheless in favour of one being called, brought Charles V, who was sincerely concerned about the well-being of souls in his dominions, to feel that further delay in dealing with the Protestant schism would prove to be fatal. He determined to make an approach to the Protestant princes and in the Frankfurt Standstill of April 1539 provided that those who held to the Augsburg Confession should be free from attacks by the Catholic states for the sake of religion, and that all legal proceedings, for example, for the recovery of lands appropriated from the Church by Protestants, should be held over for a period (in the event six months). On the Protestant side no attacks should be made on Catholic states because of religion, no attempt should be made to draw hitherto Catholic or wavering princes into the Protestant defensive League of Schmalkald, and no further inroads upon Church property should be made. It was further agreed that a meeting should be held at Nürnberg in August to which both sides should send moderate-minded theologians to try to heal the divisions. There was from both sides, however, opposition to the Standstill: even the eirenic Bucer and the Landgrave Philip of Hesse (the leading Protestant prince in the League of Schmalkald) feared a political coup; and the Bavarian dukes exemplified extremist suspicion on the Catholic side. One significant, and remarkable, step in this decision, however, was the indifference shown to the position of Paul III; the papal legate had been excluded from the decision-making process, and religious discussions appeared to be about to take place without the Curia being represented.

But even this Standstill was ineffective, events were dissolving this uneasy compromise. Luther's old enemy, the Catholic Duke George the Bearded of Saxony, died that year, and his brother Henry, in spite of the terms of the Standstill, brought his territory into Lutheranism—and Leipzig, where Eck had defended the authority of the Papacy against Luther twenty years before, became a stronghold against that authority. Further, a very conservative form of Protestantism was adopted for his territory by the Elector of Brandenburg. At the same time the Emperor's hope of peace with France seemed about to fade, and the temporary truce with the Turks ceased: Charles greatly needed a settlement in the Empire, which meant a religious settlement, in order to meet these political challenges.

At this point some account is called for of the political environment of the Colloquies which Charles was about to call to establish this religious settlement. Imperial counsellors had urged upon Charles from the beginning that he was Emperor as though ordained by God himself: a ruler not acting immediately but mediately as the moral and political leader of the Christian West, one of whose functions was to challenge Islam and heresy after the tradition of the 'Catholic Kings' in Spain. Charles said at the Diet of Worms in 1521 that he was determined to hold fast the Catholic faith and defend it: he meant this and held to it all his life, and believed that his peculiar position as Emperor and, therefore, moral leader of the Christian West gave him the authority to initiate church reform, and to demand that the Pope should call a Council of the Church. These Ghibelline assumptions outraged the Curia, and an early attempt to challenge them in 1527 brought the Sack of Rome. Whatever steps Charles wished to take to heal the German schism were bound to produce counter-activity from the Curia, so that the Colloquies were held against the background of papal suspicion, a flurry of nuncios and the determined policy of the Pope to ensure that proposals and, even more so, decisions, concerning religious unity should be dependent on his assent. Alongside of this went the political rivalry with France. The French could not be content with the prospect of a massive power-complex from the Low Countries through to Germany, Italy and Spain on her borders, so Francis I would never let Charles rest. To Francis the healing of the religious schism in Germany could be disastrous, since it would increase enormously Charles' centralization of power. In fact he somewhat overrated this situation, since the source of Habsburg political, military and economic power was shifting from the Empire to Spain. Francis, though 'the Most Christian King', went so far as to make an alliance with the Turks to harass Charles when Charles invaded France in 1536 (Francis allied with them again in 1544), during the decade when Charles was exerting all his strength to halt the Turkish advance in Hungary and the Mediterranean. Francis was also willing to ally with the Protestant princes of Germany when the latter formed the Schmalkaldic League of defence against the Catholic princes. Charles not only faced difficulty from the Papacy, and from political relations with France and the Turks, but also his hope of mending the religious division, disappointed in 1530 at Augsburg, was made more difficult with the ten years' further delay which followed. Both sides had obtained martyrs, built up strong points of resistance on the dogmatic issues, created libraries of offence and defence which constituted a literary arms race over twenty years. Further, there was the determination to maintain opposition springing from such comparatively slighter matters as simple slander: for example, that the Protestants really wanted the Church's money, and cynically wished to use religious conferences as loud-hailers for their propaganda; that the Catholics were uninterested in religious truth and reform of abuses, and only concerned with imperial or papal politics; and that the Pope was wholly untrustworthy, and for some he was in any case the Antichrist. A study of the range of these problems in detail leads to surprise that the Colloquies ever took place, and achieved as much as they did.

Against this grim background and because the Standstill of 1539 appeared to be in danger of dissolving, Charles called for a conference on religious affairs for the Diet at Speyer in June 1540, and brushed aside papal indignation against laymen meeting to judge upon a discussion of theologians not authorized by the Holy See. Before the meeting arranged for June Charles had assumed that, like another Constantine, he could act as arbitrator; the Protestant princes suspiciously demanded that doctrinal decisions if made should be made on the basis of Scripture only; and the Curia made renewed efforts to turn the Emperor's policy aside by proposing a General Council, the only effective instrument for unity in faith and customs. But Charles admonished the legate that an Italian-based Council would not do, not only did the Protestants object to a Council outside of Germany itself, but also the Catholic princes were dubious, and three times he irritably remarked: 'His

Holiness had only to declare the Council open',[1] and concluded by stating that a religious conference was the only solution. Faced by this the Pope decided not to send the Cardinal Legate, Cervini, who remained with Charles in the Low Countries, but a nuncio, Morone, who was instructed to take no part in the forthcoming debate, and to offer no concessions. Bishop Morone was a friend of the Cardinals Pole and Contarini and sympathetic to their viewpoint on justification, and on Christian humanist views, but wholly committed, as they were, to the principle of papal authority.

Plague at Speyer, however, led to the conference being called to meet at Hagenau. Only a few princes and bishops arrived for the conference, the Elector of Saxony and the Landgrave of Hesse refused to attend because they held that the conference had not been called in terms of the Frankfurt Standstill, and Melanchthon, whose presence would have been of primary importance, took ill and failed to appear. King Ferdinand, on behalf of his brother Charles, was in charge of the proceedings, but because no adequate preparation had been made beforehand the meeting broke down on a discussion of procedure and of the matters to be debated. At the beginning the problem arose of the norm for the making of decisions; the Protestant theologians, of whom Bucer was the chief, together with some second-rank Wittenbergers, insisted that Scripture as interpreted by the Apostolic Church should be the standard of decision, and not the decrees of Fathers and Councils. The Catholic theologians, including Eck and Cochlaeus, suggested that the discussion should be based on the articles of compromise proposed at Augsburg in 1530—this was supported by Ferdinand.[2] But the Protestants insisted that those compromise articles had not been agreed upon in 1530, and demanded that the Augsburg Confession itself must be the basis for discussion since it contained the doctrine of 'the one ancient, true and Apostolic Church'. When Ferdinand reminded those present that the Pope would have to be consulted about any theological decisions taken, the Protestants true to their name protested. The conference had

[1] Pastor, *History of the Popes*, XI, 383.
[2] F. Lau and E. Bizer, *A History of the Reformation in Germany to 1555*, 1969, 162.

failed to get off the ground, and Ferdinand, since nothing effective could be done in the absence of the Elector of Saxony and the Landgrave of Hesse, postponed the conference, deciding that it should be convened again at Worms in October 1540.

The failure at Hagenau was due to wholly inadequate preparations beforehand: merely bringing men to a debate in the presence of members of the Diet, and hoping that something would emerge, had been shown to be useless. Before the meeting at Worms, a greater hope of something positive being achieved was possible because the Protestant demand that discussion should be on the basis of the Augsburg Confession was accepted, no doubt with some reservations, on the Catholic side. Certainly this was disapproved of at Rome, since once again a religious conference was to take place in the presence of laymen, and on the undesirable basis of a Protestant statement. Nevertheless, Paul III recognized that he must formally be represented at the conference for, as the nuncio to Charles, Poggio, said: 'If the Pope does not decide to send a legate and learned men to the conference, then the whole of Germany, indeed the whole of Christendom, will think that his Holiness does not trouble himself about religion and this nation, as many have already openly declared.'[1] The Pope appointed a canonist (hardly the most fruitful form of competence for a Colloquy), Bishop Tommaso Campeggi, not a cardinal, as his special nuncio; also four theologians to represent the Holy See; the nuncios to the Emperor, Morone and Poggio, were also to attend. Also present at the Colloquy of Worms was the Bishop of Capo d'Istria, Pietro Paolo Vergerio (later to be accused of Protestant heresy at Rome, and to end his days as an anti-papal polemicist, though not acceptable as a theologically sound Protestant), one of those curious cross-bench figures of the period, who was probably secretly representing the interests of the French.

Before the Colloquy at Worms opened, the Elector of Saxony had instructed his Wittenberg theologians to reject any decisions which would recognize the primacy of the Pope and the papal right

[1] Pastor, *History of the Popes*, XI, 403.

to make the final decision upon the conclusions of the Colloquy. The various theologians arrived in good time. On the Catholic side, Eck and Cochlaeus were present as well as the more eirenical Gropper and Pflug, who shared the old Erasmian hope of reunion on biblical and patristic rather than scholastic lines. For the Protestants there were Bucer and Capito from Strassburg (accompanying them as a representative for that city, though not commissioned as a debater, was Calvin); and there were Melanchthon, Osiander, Brenz and Amsdorf from among the Lutherans. But the Colloquy was held up for a month awaiting the arrival of Granvella, the Imperial Chancellor, representing Charles, who opened the meetings formally on 25 November, with a speech grumbling about the seditious evils Protestantism had created in the Empire.[1] The nuncio, Campeggi, did not appear until 8 December, and was given an inferior place by Granvella, who during Campeggi's rather flat speech about the Pope's zeal for unity did not uncover at the Pope's name, but did so when the Emperor's name was mentioned, a fact not lost on the Protestants present.[2] Granvella also permitted Protestant preaching in certain churches during the Colloquy. It is curious to learn that while the Protestants—frequently accused by their opponents of theological divisions among themselves—held a united front, as Bucer showed in a letter to Blaurer, 'Nostri ad unum consentiunt ut nihil remittatur quod per se Christi est',[3] the Catholics on the other hand were in some disarray. In this situation the nuncio Morone proposed, in what was his only positive effort at Worms, that the Catholic states should come to an understanding by presenting written statements of the viewpoint on the controverted issues. Four of these have been recovered, those from the Electors of Mainz, Trier, Cologne, the Bishops of Magdeburg, Salzburg and Strassburg, and the representatives of the Bavarians, a document projected by Eck himself; from the representatives of the Elector of Brandenburg; from the representatives of the Elector Palatine; and from the representatives of the Dukes of Jülich and

---

[1] *Ioannis Calvini Opera quae supersunt omnia*, XI, col. 136.
[2] Pastor, *History of the Popes*, XI, 410–11.
[3] *Ioannis Calvini Opera quae supersunt omnia*, XI, col. 103.

Cleves.[1] These statements are not remarkable theologically for either depth or insight, nor on the other hand do they show a narrow dogmatic intransigence. The comment of their editor that the theology does not go very deep is judicious, but we should not let it further persuade us to see weakness here through the eyes of Tridentine hindsight after the manner of Lortz and Jedin.[2]

Some comments of Calvin, whose letters from Worms provide one of our witnesses to those events, give some interesting sidelights. On worship at Worms he wrote that after Granvella's opening of the sessions on 25 November: 'Cecinerunt igitur missam suam de spiritu sancto ut auspicato aggrederentur. Nos etiam solennes supplicationes in templo nostro habuimus.'[3] His comment, in a letter to Farel, on Eck who was the dominating figure among the Catholic theologians is interesting though mordant: 'Propone tibi imaginem barbari sophistae inter illiteratos stolide exultantis, et habetis dimidiam partem Ecki.'[4] In fairness, an epigram on Calvin should be quoted, written with many others on the Protestant and Catholic theologians present by a humanist poet who observed both sides with shrewd irony:

Quaeso, quid indigne tot fundis inania verba?
Doctus es, at quid tum? Sis quoque porro pius![5]

In fact the making of verses seems to have been the only alleviation to the tedium of the long procedural discussions between 21 November and 14 January at Worms. Calvin records that he, Melanchthon, Sturm and others wrote verses on the Catholics present; Calvin's poem alone survives, *Epinicion Christo Cantatum*, a Juvenalian exercise in which Eck, Cochlaeus, Nausea and other Catholic theologians appear as captives chained to the triumph-car of Christ, victor over his enemies.[6]

---

[1] *Archiv für Reformationsgeschichte*, vol. 43. 1, 1952. W. Lipgens, 'Theologischer Standort fürstlicher Räte im sechzehnten Jahrhundert. Neue Quellen zum Wormser Verglichsgspräch, 1540/41'.   [2] *Ibid.* p. 44.

[3] *Ioannis Calvini opera quae supersunt omnia*, XI, col. 137.   [4] *Ibid.* XI, col. 146.

[5] *Zeitschrift für Kirchengeschichte*, vol. 50, 1931, *Epigramme auf Teilnehmer am Wormser Religionsgespräch*, 1540–1. O. Clemen, 449.

[6] Calvin, *Opera*, V, 427.
                 Eccius hesterno ruber atque inflatus Iaccho
                 Praebeat huc duris terga subacta flagris.

The outcome of the procedural wrangling—about methods of voting, who were to debate and who were to judge—was a decision to have one speaker from each side, and after further delay until 14 January 1541, Eck and Melanchthon, the appointed representatives, began a debate on original sin, and successfully reached an agreement in four days. But the Emperor commanded Granvella to close the Colloquy on the ground that no progress was being made, and Granvella referred the debate to the next Diet, which was to be at Regensburg in March 1541. Sleidan, the historian and an agent of the French crown in this period, wrote in an aside on the eve of the Colloquy of Worms: "This year was memorable for extraordinary heat and drought, however the wine was excellent.'[1] Much heat and aridity was to be felt at the Colloquy, but we should not overlook the excellent wine, since behind the official meetings there was a fruitful understanding of the first importance through secret meetings between Bucer and Gropper which led to the production of articles of agreement on many of the chief subjects of controversy between the two sides. Granvella, shrewd in judging men and situations, saw little use in holding public discussions upon subjects to be decided on publicly with consequent delays in manoeuvring for position amid mutual suspicion. He was aware that the Protestants were afraid that the Colloquies might be a cover behind which preparations were being made for war, since the attitude of the Bavarian dukes was well known, and Wauchope (a Scot, one of the four papal theologians at Worms) advocated in private that war was the only solution, a judgment in which he was certainly not alone at Rome.[2] Therefore Granvella was all the more anxious to promote these private discussions, for fear that the Protestant leaders might return home, or be too suspicious to agree to anything. Bucer and Capito

Huc caput indomitum subdat, verum ante recepta,
Qua semper caruit, fronte Cochlaeus iners.
Nausea verbosis generans fastidia libris
Occluso tacitus iam ferat ore iugum.

[1] *The General History of the Reformation of the Church, written in Latin by John Sleidan, and faithfully Englished*, by E. Bohun, 1689, 269.
[2] Calvin, *Opera*, XI, col. 66. Calvin here claimed that the Pope had offered 300,000 ducats to promote war.

had to inform Jacob Sturm, the able diplomatist and head of the Strassburg delegation at the Colloquy, of the possibility of private meetings with certain Catholics; the chancellor of Hesse, Feize, was also privately consulted. These two laymen were not attracted to the idea of secret meetings, since these would by-pass the public Colloquy, and they also feared that the Lutherans would be hostile to what would be produced because their representatives were not consulted; but after reflection they consented, since without the secret meetings there appeared to be no hope of progress.[1]

Veltwyk, an Imperial secretary and a Jewish convert to Catholicism was strongly attracted to Christian humanist studies. He was a friend of his fellow-Rhinelander Gropper and they held in common the Christian humanists' teachings on justification and original sin, and their emphasis on the centrality of Christ rather than on authoritarian legalism in the Church. Bucer had already met Gropper at the first Colloquy at Hagenau, and they found that they had many religious interests in common. During the wearying delays in November and December at Worms, Veltwyk, Gropper, Bucer and Capito found opportunities to talk together privately, and to discover how much ground they had in common, since all were influenced by the principles of Christian humanism, and none of them held the extremist views of, for example, Cochlaeus on the one side and Amsdorf on the other. Gropper had published his *Enchiridion Christianae Institutionis* in 1538: its very title was typical of the Christian humanist reform movement (*Enchiridion* and *Institutio* were Erasmian words, and the young Calvin, for example, had chosen the latter for his famous book first published in 1536). Gropper's book set out at some length his view of justification in which he hoped to reconcile the Protestant and Catholic positions. His interpretation resembles suggestions of Erasmus and is very close to the full statement of a similar development of justification in the writings of Contarini. Also Gropper had begun a reform in Cologne diocese on behalf of Archbishop Hermann von Wied, and he

---

[1] Hastings Eells, 'The Origins of the Regensburg Book', *Princeton Theological Review*, XXVI (1928), 359. This study was based on the materials in M. Lenz, *Briefwechsel Landgraf Philipps des Grossmütigen von Hessen mit Bucer*, 3 parts, Leipzig 1880, 1887, 1891.

feared that this movement might collapse through extremist Catholic reaction, or through being taken over by extremist Lutheranism. Therefore he was anxious to find a compromise between the extremes of both parties. Bucer had similar ends in view, and he had much in common theologically with Gropper, but he saw, if Sturm had not made it clear to him, that Granvella (on behalf of the Emperor) wished to gain political advantage from a Protestant–Catholic agreement.

Early in December, Veltwyk had urged Granvella to see Bucer privately, and Bucer called on Granvella at 6 a.m., by request, though he was happy to accept since he was always an aggressively early riser, and had to listen to a statement from him, characteristic in its pendulum swing between threats and assurances, concluding with the promise that no harm would come to Bucer and Capito by their sharing in a secret discussion with two Catholics, and that the public Colloquy would not be destroyed by these private meetings.[1] Bucer's deep and always sincere eirenical concern rose above this dubious presentation, and he agreed to bring Capito into a discussion with Gropper, not least because he was convinced by now that the public Colloquy would not prove to be fruitful. Whether Sturm had warned him, or whether he himself saw the danger of acting independently and secretly in discussion with Catholics, Bucer saw that he might bring on himself a disastrous and discreditable rejection by the Protestant leaders. Therefore, he urged the Landgrave Philip, with whom he had good relations, to provide him with a letter authorizing him by name to undertake this secret discussion beginning on 15 December, and to date it 10 December. The Landgrave said it should include the provision that Bucer was not to commit himself to anything to the detriment of the Protestant states. It is typical of the atmosphere of unease and political tension at the Colloquies that the Landgrave in turn tried to get Granvella to send him a letter so that he would not be thought of as acting independently of the Emperor, and clear himself too with the other Protestant leaders. At the same time Philip glumly reminded Bucer of the Scylla and Charybdis of Luther and the Pope.[2]

---

[1] *Ibid.* 359.   [2] *Ibid.* 363.

The secret meetings took place on several occasions in the second half of December. After various statements made by the four participants on doctrinal matters including justification, and on those aspects of discipline particularly emphasized by Bucer throughout his career, for example, a godly and hard-working priesthood, the purification of worship from superstition or inessential ceremonial, the revision of the liturgy, and the manner of dispensing the Sacraments, Gropper drew up articles based on the theological issues which had been debated. Bucer proposed some modifications of this draft prepared by Gropper, and, at the request of the Landgrave Philip, translated the articles into German, upon which Philip suggested some slight changes and sent them to the Elector of Brandenburg, asking the Elector after he had considered them to obtain Luther's opinion of them. Luther disliked the articles as too much of a compromise and because they would fail to satisfy the Lutheran theologians at a number of points. Melanchthon said cryptically of the articles: '*Politia Platonis*', and it should be remembered that he had not been aware of the secret meetings at Worms where they were prepared.[1] The articles were then sent to Granvella, who asked Gropper and some Catholic theologians to consider them, and after various emendations were made they were sent to the Emperor.

The next stage after the transfer of the Colloquy from Worms to Regensburg was the bringing of pressure to bear on Rome by Granvella for the Pope to send a cardinal legate with considerable authority to Regensburg. Contarini was mentioned among other names because he was highly regarded in Germany; and on 10 January 1541, the Pope appointed Contarini *legatus a latere* for Germany.[2] Meanwhile, Morone told the nuncio Campeggi sourly that he could advise Paul III, when he returned to Rome, that nothing would come of the proposed Colloquy at Regensburg; and the Bavarian dukes told Charles V that an attempt at reunion was a waste of time.[3] On 28 January the Pope sent instructions to Contarini in which full power to come to an agreement with the Protestants was not allowed, but which urged him to sound the

---

[1] Kolde, *Regensburger Religionsgespräch*, 548.
[2] Pastor, *History of the Popes*, XI, 421.   [3] *Ibid.* 425.

Protestant leaders to find what Catholic principles they had retained so that on this basis an understanding might be approached, for example, on the papal primacy, the seven Sacraments, and the long-authorized traditions of the Church—'you know what they are' ('tibi nota esse bene scimus'). This vagueness was deliberate, and if not helpful to Contarini it was helpful to the Pope.[1]

Cardinal Contarini is a most attractive figure among the participants at the Colloquy: he came to it with burning sincerity to achieve religious peace, and this was recognized gladly by Melanchthon, Bucer and other Protestants. Contarini had come near to Luther's position on justification as early as 1511:[2] he believed that this was the heart of the matter, and that once this could be decided favourably other matters, such as papal authority and the Sacraments, would fall into line. His doctrine of justification, as Ranke showed long ago, does not derive from the Cologne theologians, Pigghe and Gropper (though this has not prevented a number of writers from trying to establish that it does); it came to him through those Pauline and Augustinian studies in Italy which were prominent in the groups around Victoria Colonna, the Valdes brothers, and the author of that seminal work *Beneficio di Cristo*.[3] Contarini had written to his friend Giustiniani in February 1523: 'I have truly come to the firm conclusion...that no one can justify himself by his works...one must turn to the divine grace which can be obtained through faith in Jesus Christ as St Paul said...Wherefore I conclude that every living man is a thing of vanity and that one must justify oneself through another's righteousness, that is, through Christ's, and when one joins oneself to Him his righteousness becomes ours, nor must we then depend upon ourselves, even in the slightest degree.'[4] Again, in a treatise on Penance, Contarini wrote: 'Since therefore the

[1] *Ibid.* 429. For the written instructions of the Pope see Document 32 in Ranke, *Werke*, 37, III.
[2] *Archiv für Reformationsgeschichte*, 51, I, H. Mackensen, 'Contarini's Theological Role at Ratisbon in 1541', 50.
[3] Ranke, *Werke*, 37, I. 91, and n. 2, and Hans Rückert, *Die Theologische Entwicklung Casparo Contarinis*, Bonn 1926, 103.
[4] *Archiv für Reformationsgeschichte*, 51, I, Mackensen, 55.

foundation of the Lutheran edifice is true, we must say nothing against it but we must accept it as true and Catholic, indeed as the foundation of the Christian religion.'[1] He could write passages in which he reduces man's righteousness to almost nothing, and in which the righteousness of Christ is alone of value for salvation—passages which the Inquisition suppressed in the Venetian edition of his works in 1584. Nevertheless, he left open a possible merit of good works before God as a general principle. With the presence of such a man at the Colloquy the prospect of reunion had come closer than ever before.

On 23 February the Emperor came to Regensburg more than ever anxious to find religious peace for the Empire in view of the mounting threat of the renewal of war by the Turks and because he was aware of the diplomatic moves by Francis I to create an alliance with the Lutheran princes directed against himself. Contarini did not arrive until over two weeks after the Emperor, whom he told that he would aid him with all his strength to achieve religious peace in Germany. Gradually the other members of the Diet gathered together, and on 5 April 1541, the Colloquy —which was held within the setting of the Imperial Diet—was opened in the presence of the Emperor. A declaration of the Emperor's purpose was read in which the need for religious unity was strongly emphasized; it was affirmed that the debate was to be commenced on a new basis (that is, not starting from the Augsburg Confession, or from prolonged procedural discussions); and it was made known that he himself would select the theologians from both sides who should debate those matters wherein the two parties chiefly differed. On 21 April he chose Melanchthon, Bucer, and Pistorius (a theologian from the Landgrave's Church of Hesse) to represent the Protestants, and Gropper (now bishop-elect of Naumburg), Pflug, a theologian of similar interests, and Eck. The original purpose had been to keep Eck out of the debate but, on instructions from Rome, Contarini and Morone insisted on his being one of the Catholic speakers. The presidents of the Colloquy were to be the Count Palatine, and Granvella: there were also to be six observers present; among these were Burkhardt, Chan-

[1] *Ibid.* 41.

cellor of Saxony, Feize, Chancellor of Hesse, and Sturm of Strassburg. The balance between Catholic and Protestant authorities
will be seen here. Sealed copies of the Articles, the *Regensburg Book*,
as it came to be called later, but without title or other description,
were presented to the debaters, and taken up again each evening.
It is interesting to learn that Veltwyk introduced Bucer to
Cardinal Contarini on the opening of the Colloquy, and that
Contarini showed his zeal for reunion in the words: 'How great
will be the fruit of unity, and how profound the gratitude of all
mankind.' To which Bucer replied more explicitly: 'Both sides
have failed. Some of us have overemphasized unimportant points,
and others have not adequately reformed obvious abuses. With
God's will we shall ultimately find the truth.'[1]

At this point it would be well to examine, though inevitably
too briefly, the theological content of the *Regensburg Book*.[2]
The first five articles deal with the great issues relating to the doctrine of grace: 1. 'De conditione hominis et ante lapsum naturae
integritate'; 2. 'De libero arbitrio'; 3. 'De causa peccati'; 4. 'De
originali peccato'; 5. 'De restitutione regenerationis et justifica-
tione hominis gratia et merito, fide et operibus'. After alterations
had been made when the form in which Article 5 was presented
to the debaters was found unsuitable, the article as finally agreed
retained the characteristic marks of the mediating doctrine of
justification taught by Gropper and Contarini known since as
double justification because of the polarity of the terms used—
iustitia imputata and *iustitia inhaerens*.[3] Imputed justice is obtained
by faith, not only conceived of in the sense of accepting and appropriating to oneself doctrinal truths, but also in the sense Luther had

[1] Karl Brandi, *The Emperor Charles V*, trans. C. V. Wedgwood, 1954, 447.
[2] The Articles were published by Melanchthon and Bucer, and a French version
was issued by Calvin. *Philippi Melanthonis opera quae supersunt omnia*, ed. E. G.
Bretschneider, IV, 1836 ff.; Martin Bucer: *Acta Colloquii in comitiis imperii
Ratisponae habiti hoc est articuli de religione conciliati, et non conciliati omnes ut ab
Imperatore Ordinibus Imperii ad iudicandum, et deliberandum propositi sunt*. Strassburg
1541.
[3] *Melanthonis opera*, IV, col. 200: 'Iustitiam, quae est in Christo, sibi gratis impu-
tari, et quae simul pellicitationem Spiritus Sancti et charitatem accipit...Etsi
autem is, qui iustificatur, iustitiam accipit et habet per Christum, etiam
inhaerentem...'

urged long before, trust in the promises of God. This justification by faith is seen as the beginning of an inherent justice, since the faith which justifies is also seen as faith effective through love (*per charitatem*). Therefore, the Christian man is 'just' in a twofold way: he is reputed to be just by faith and by grace, and is actually just through his doing the works of love. However, the state of being just *per charitatem* is by nature imperfect; since it is derived from man, it cannot be said that the certainty of salvation rests in any way upon it: rather assurance of salvation always rests on being justified by faith and grace, that is, on *iustitia Christi nobis donata*.[1] Nevertheless, God does not ignore the inherent justice of those who seek diligently to fulfil the law of love: they have their reward, but the concept of *meritum* is not mentioned, and the dubious consequences of merit-theology which Luther had so passionately attacked are intended to be ruled out. Even the phrase which is the touchstone of Lutheran orthodoxy is commended, 'sola fide iustificamur', provided that penitence and the desire to fulfil the works of love are closely associated with it.[2]

There lie behind this concept of double justification ideas expressed by Gropper in his *Enchiridion* of 1538, and which Contarini had learned from his own experience and reflection in Italy after 1511. Gropper began from a position originally conceived of as opposing a Protestant error, when he insisted that justification must represent an inner reality, but he challenged that weakness in contemporary Catholic theology which Luther had challenged (in his doctrine of the enslaved will and in his assertion that the whole initiative of justifying grace lay in God alone) when he wrote of the distinction between the justice of man and the justice of God, from which he deduced that none of our acts can effectively be the cause of our justification. He affirmed as strongly as Luther that all our trust must rest on Christ. Faith justifies only because it makes us able to receive divine mercy. It turns us to God, and then calls us to follow good. So the efficient cause of our salvation is God alone, and the formal cause is his own grace which renews

---

[1] *Ibid.* col. 200: 'sed soli iustitiae Christi nobis donatae, sine qua omnino nulla est nec esse potest iustitia'.

[2] *Ibid.* col. 201, in the last paragraph of Article 5.

our hearts. The instrumental cause is faith in Christ, and the justification thus brought to us fills our hearts with love which we fulfil in works. These works are imperfect, but they become acceptable to God because of Christ in whom they are performed. It is characteristic of Gropper's position to affirm that our acts are only *causae dispositivae et susceptivae*. At this point it will suffice to add that Contarini agreed with the doctrine of double justification, and his position on this can be summed up thus: 'nos iustificari fide efficaci per charitatem'.[1]

Articles 6 to 9 deal with the Church and how it is to be recognized; article 6, 'De Ecclesia, et illius signis ac autoritate', begins with the definition: 'The Church is the assembly or congregation of men of all places, and of all times, who are called in the communion of the profession of the one same faith, doctrine and sacraments, according to the Catholic, true and Apostolic doctrine.' Article 7, 'De nota verbi', describes the first 'nota' or mark of the Church, the Word of God, though it does not set forth how this is to be developed, and adds that the true Church has the anointing of the Spirit which instructs us in all things. Article 8, 'De poenitentia post lapsum', which demonstrates that in this Catholic Church alone is there remission of sins, given to the penitent not only at baptism but also afterwards. Article 9, 'De autoritate Ecclesiae in discernanda et interpretanda Scriptura', in which it is asserted that the Church has the right to judge the Scriptures, and to discern what is canonical Scripture from what is not. Against this Article the Protestant collocutors were to present a criticism in writing closer to their view of the subject at the time it was debated. Article 10, 'De Sacramentis', is a very

---

[1] *Archiv für Reformationsgeschichte*, 1960, 51, 1, H. Mackensen, 'Contarini's Theological Role at Ratisbon in 1541', provides an analysis of Contarini's views on Justification. For a brief account of the views of Gropper on justification see W. van Gulik, *Johannes Gropper ein Beitrag zur Kirchengeschichte Deutschlands... im 16 Jahrhundert*, Freiburg im Breisgau 1906, 50 ff. Gulik cites the *Enchiridion* of Gropper, fol. 167b, 'Ob id tandum dicimus, fidem iustificare, non quia sit causa iustificationis, sed quia nulla alia re misericordiam et gratiam Dei... accipiamus'; fol. 171b, 'Constat enim in universum, operibus nostri causam iustificationis detrahi et recte ac vere dici nos sine operibus iustificari.' For the *causae* of justification see Gulik's citations from Gropper's *Antididagma*, fol. 13b, and his *Enchiridion*, fol. 129b; Gulik, 54.

brief statement on the Sacraments in general, declaring that they are effective visible signs of the invisible grace of God—the Word is joined to the element to make the Sacrament. Articles 11 to 17 take the Seven Sacraments in turn. Article 11 on the Sacrament of Order shows that Order is essential to prevent uncertainty on doctrine, and seven Orders are named. The element of this Sacrament is the imposition of hands by a bishop. Article 12, on Baptism, where the anxious mind is assured that Baptism conveys justification (Gal. iii. 27), and our baptism is to be remembered and exercised during the whole of our lives. Article 14 on the Eucharist contains these words, 'post consecrationem, verum corpus et verus sanguis domini, vere et substantialiter adsint, et fidelibus sub specie panis et vini' and in the original form they were followed immediately by the words, 'distribuuntur, qui habet in hunc modum. Accipite et manducati...Bibite'. But the following words were inserted between the two passages cited, probably by Contarini, or at his instigation, after the Worms text was prepared and prior to the debate at Regensburg: 'illis nimirum, hoc est, pane et vino in corpus et sanguinem transmutatis et transubstantiatis'—words which occasioned a sharp reaction from the Protestants. (Melanchthon added in the margin against these words in his published edition of the Articles: 'Hic collocutores protestantium exhibuerunt suum scriptum signatum B.' Calvin himself was to intervene in the debate at this point: 'Me quoque exponere latine oportuit quid sentirem...libere tamen sine timore offensionis, illam localem praesentiam damnavi: adorationem asserui mihi esse intolerabilem.' Further, alongside of Article 15, the Sacrament of Penance, the Protestants were to present at the debate two writings giving their point of view.) Article 18, 'De vinculo caritatis, quae est tertia Ecclesiae nota', represents the third sign of the presence of the Church after the Word and Sacraments set forth in Articles 7 and 10. Article 19, 'De Ecclesiae hierarchico ordine et in constituenda politia autoritate', shows that hierarchical order was also reckoned a note of the Church. (Alongside of this Article the Protestants were to present during the debate at Regensburg a statement on the unity of the Church, in which they do not oppose episcopacy but outline its duties while rejecting idle and ignorant prelates, and they grant primacy to the Roman see but not a final authority of jurisdiction to it.) Article 20, 'Dogmata quaedam quae ecclesiae autoritate declarata, firmata sunt', discusses such matters as invocation of saints (alongside of which the Protestants were to present a writing during the debate giving their view on this matter), relics, images and prayers for the dead. Article 21, 'De usu et administratione sacramentorum, et ceremoniis quibusdam speciatim', is on the ceremonial of the Mass and associated themes. (Once again the Protestants were to present a writing here on the sacrifice of the Mass, insisting that the sacrifice was offered by Christ Himself to the Father, and opposing the association of merit with it and the conception of it as an offering for the dead as well as the living. Further, they added another writing objecting to the concept of private Masses.) Article 22, 'De disciplina ecclesiastica', relates to celibacy, the condemnation of priestly concubinage, and reforms among monks. The last Article, 23, 'De disciplina populi', is on excommunication, public penance, and fasting.

Eck, well prepared on the Augsburg Confession since 1530, wished rather to discuss that document, and, as Morone noted, 'sought to assume a sort of sovereign and judicial authority in the deliberations and showed himself, to the disapproval of all men, more than necessarily contentious'.[1] But he was overruled, and had to accept as the basis of debate the secretly prepared articles of Worms handed to him with the other debaters under seal. As a further check on Eck, and also to maintain a united Catholic viewpoint, Gropper, Pflug and Eck met with Contarini every morning to discuss the subjects to be debated. The debates began on 27 April and lasted for a month. Contarini soon found that Eck needed careful handling, and at one stage he began to think that Eck, true to his old approach at Leipzig in 1519, brought forward much too early and too aggressively the highly divisive topic of papal authority and supremacy, and was trying to wreck the Colloquy. The first four Articles were soon accepted—agreement had already been reached on original sin at Worms—but the fifth Article on justification, which was much longer, was unacceptable

---

[1] Pastor, *History of the Popes*, 439.

because it was thought by both sides to be imprecise. An attempt was made to revise the Article, in which Contarini himself took part. Then, on 2 May, agreement was at last reached, through a reformulation by Gropper and Melanchthon, on this hitherto most divisive subject and which led to the astonishing hope that after all agreement could be possible between the two sides. Contarini had taken a vital part in this achievement, and the Article formulated showed close affinities with his own thought.

One of the most enthusiastic responses to Contarini's success over Article 5, which he himself described joyfully as miraculous, was that of his friend Cardinal Pole. 'When I observed this union of opinion I felt a delight such as no harmony of sounds could have inspired me with; not only because I see the approach of peace and concord, but because these Articles [that is, 1 to 5] are the foundation of the whole Christian faith.'[1] The reaction of Francis I, however, was predictably furious indignation in which he denounced the agreement to the papal nuncios in France, and wrote to the Protestant princes to dissuade them from supporting it. 'The advice of other princes [that is, from outside of Germany] should have been invited.'[2] Many of the German Catholic princes did not even attend the Diet, and an anonymous and indignant German wrote to the Pope about the Emperor, 'Nihil ordinabatur pro robore ecclesiae, quid timetur illi displicere.'[3] That the Colloquy was in danger was not yet immediately evident. There seems to have been little dispute on the Articles on the Sacraments until Article 14, 'De sacramento eucharistiae', when the Protestants led by Melanchthon challenged the concept of Transubstantiation and the veneration of the Reserved Sacrament. Contarini, who was not as well informed as he had thought on Protestantism, had not expected this, and was astonished and hurt. It was difficult if not impossible for Catholics, in the temper of the time, to reject the declared dogma of the Fourth Lateran Council, however much the Protestants argued that Councils of the Church could and would err. Granvella, however, was surprised at Contarini's

[1] Ranke, *Werke*, 37, I, 107, citing Quirini, *Epistolae Reginaldi Poli*, t. III, 25.
[2] Ranke, *Werke*, 37, I, 109 and n. I, citing Quirini, *Epistolae Reginaldi Poli*, t. III, ep. CCLV.   [3] Ranke, *Werke*, 37, I, 110, n. 2, citing Rainaldus.

indignation, since for him Transubstantiation was 'una cosa sottile e pertinente solo alli dotti, non toccata al popolo'[1]—for Jedin this is characteristic of the weak and betraying Erasmianism of the Imperial Chancellor. The Emperor would have been willing to be content with a declaration that Christ is really and truly present in the Eucharist, and to leave discussion of so scholastic a point as transubstantiation for a General Council to decide.

The Colloquy had now begun to drift back into the old antagonisms. The Protestants refused to accept the necessity of Penance, though they were willing to allow its practice. Even so, Bucer and Melanchthon (since Eck was ill and absent, Pistorius withdrew) accepted a Papal primacy—though not of jurisdiction —and debated amicably enough the Canon of the Mass, private Masses, and communion in both kinds. By the end of May, Granvella sensed that matters were reaching an impasse and he began to bring pressure on the Pope to call a General Council, and the Pope replied in June that he could tell the Emperor that a Council would be convened, since the Colloquy had broken down and no other solution remained. For all his great efforts Contarini, when he left Regensburg on 29 July, had won nothing of lasting value and he returned to Italy under the stigma of having turned Lutheran. His part in the final revision and acceptance of Article 5 on justification left him under the grave suspicion of having betrayed Catholic truth, and the last year of his life brought bitter difficulties for him in Italy, where the Inquisition was already attacking his friends and where the defence of his position at Regensburg in his last writing, *Epistola de iustificatione*, was received with hostility.

Contarini met the attacks on him with silent dignity, but the other participants in the Colloquy who were politically more vulnerable than a cardinal almost immediately began to publish explanations of their position at the Colloquy. The meeting of the Diet had barely closed before Eck was denouncing the *Regensburg Book*, as it was now being called, saying that he had not seen it beforehand, that its articles represented the views of

---

[1] Jedin, *History of the Council of Trent*, I, 381.

Lutherans, that the Book was unacceptable to Catholics, and that it 'Melanchthonized'. Bucer published at Strassburg promptly in 1541 the whole Book with the judgments as presented to the Diet by the Protestant and Catholic princes and cities, in which he inserted a short paragraph containing the reported view of Eck and his own comment.[1] To which Bucer added appended material in evidence.[2] This was a letter written by Pflug and Gropper in more graceful latinity than Bucer's own strangulated sentences usually attained, in which they indignantly reject Eck's report to 'Illustrissimi Principes Bavari' that he wished to have nothing to do with the Book.[3] They go on to show that Eck had shared with them in the discussions and the judgments arrived at together, and that they had acted with integrity throughout. One consequence of the secret preparation of the Regensburg Book at Worms was that doubt could be cast on its authenticity, and on who had prepared it and with what intentions. Bucer was indignant when Melanchthon began to spread the rumour that Bucer had written it, and said somewhat disingenuously that he knew of the preparation of it but had discussed it with its authors Gropper and Veltwyk. Melanchthon conceded he had made a mistake, and privately wrote later that Gropper had prepared it.[4] It is obvious that because the Colloquy had failed to achieve agreement, and because a vigorous opposition from Luther, the Pope, the Bavarian princes, Francis I and others had appeared, the participants tried to dissociate themselves from the probable consequences of condemnation or at least loss of prestige. Eck began this process of

[1] 'Neque placuit, neque placet, liber iste insulsus, neque placebit quo tot errores et vitia deprehendi: unde iudico, sicut semper iudicavi, eum a Catholicis nō recipiendū, qui relicto mō loquendi ecclesiae et patrū, Melanchthonizat.'

[2] 'Quā vane et impudenter haec Eccius scripserit, cognosces pie lector, ex supplicatione subiecta in qua nihil illi quod nō ita se habet, commemorarunt.'

[3] 'haec febricitans [Eck had recently recovered from the fever which had prevented him debating for a time at Regensburg] forsan impetu magis animi quam certo iudicio effuderit, comperimus tamen illum, hac sua suggestione evicisse... ad sic, ut ille vellet sentiendum sint [the princes and others] persuasi, et non persuasi tantum quod ad se attinet, sed etiam huc adducti, ut Caesariae quoque Maiestati haec quae Eccius effutivit, quam maxime approbata velint.'

[4] *Melanthonis opera*, v, 88.

Pilate-like repudiation, but the effect of Bucer's account of the proceedings and that of Melanchthon was to make the Protestants' position at Regensburg seem more positively Protestant than it was in fact. Eck followed up in 1542 with a little book in which he denounced what he called the calumnies of Bucer and offered a defence of Contarini as upholding the Church and papal authority.[1] Eck claimed that while Bucer considered the Articles to be reconciling and capable of being accepted by the Catholic princes, in fact the two Catholic debaters in the absence of Eck (he apparently wished to make it seem that he had hardly been more than present for a time, and then as a defender of Catholic truth against Protestant heresies) were 'non magni nominis in theologia', and yet, he wrote, all the 'Catholic Princes and Bishops were to cede to them!'.[2] In this climate of inglorious exculpation the impact of the Regensburg Book achieved little.

The more moderate or central group of princes, for example Brandenburg and Cologne, were willing to accept the Book at the end of the Colloquy, but the 'war party' headed by Bavaria opposed this. In the event the more extreme Catholic and Protestant positions won the day, since neither was prepared to compromise themselves by accepting the Book after the Colloquy had broken up. Contarini told the Emperor in July that he could not speak for the Pope, for the Book had to be judged by Paul III. On returning to Rome he tried to find a compromise whereby both sides could obtain a mutual toleration and find therein a better understanding, but the Curia rejected this outright—its mind could not grasp so eirenical a viewpoint. However, before leaving for Rome Contarini achieved the unique record of convoking the whole of the German episcopate before him and giving them a thorough dressing-down on their personal shortcomings and the need for effective reforms of abuses in their dioceses— this formal admonition of the legate sufficiently impressed the

---

[1] *Apologia pro reverendis et illustris Principibus Catholicis, ac aliis ordinibus Imperii adversus mucores et calumnias Buceri, super actis Comicorum Ratisponae. Apologia pro Reverendiss. se ap. Legato et Cardinale, Caspare Contareno. Iohan. Eckio Authore.* Cologne 1542. In the preface Eck accused Bucer of slandering the Catholic princes and Contarini in his account of the proceedings at Regensburg.

[2] *Ibid.* sig. B (the book is unpaginated).

Emperor, if not the bishops, for he obtained a copy and sent it to the Estates of the Diet.

For Jedin the failure of the Regensburg attempt at reunion could justify the drawing of the Tridentine line of demarcation.[1] But that Tridentine line for many today would seem to have resembled the Berlin Wall, an aggressive rejection of the possibility of union with the probability of death for reinfringement of it, even if it could be accepted that the failure of Regensburg necessarily demanded Tridentinism. Certainly the Emperor, and many others of Catholic mind, did not envisage that development but hoped for a Council which could approach the issues in the spirit represented by the Book. For Jedin, again, the rupture at Regensburg was caused essentially by 'the irreconcilable opposition of contradictory doctrines'.[2] In the light of what Gropper and Bucer sought to achieve and came near to achieving, this judgment is unduly harsh. Further, Tridentinism was not the only possible Catholic response, if theology alone was in question. But this was precisely the intolerable complexity of the problem: it was not theology alone, it was political intransigence that proved to be so harmful. The Bavarian dukes, Francis I, the Papacy in its political aspect, the Catholic League, the Schmalkaldic League, the Elector of Saxony, and after these the varying gradations of political colouring, used the Colloquies like the night battle at Jutland for manoeuvres and counter-manoeuvres. In those troubled waters the ark which Gropper and Bucer launched sank almost without trace. Some today might consider an attempt to raise it again to be a tiresome archaeological enterprise, on the ground that a new society like our own needs new theological methods. But Christianity is most intimately associated with the idea of the Church, and the Church is an historical reality. From that basis attempts at a better understanding between 'Catholic' and 'Protestant' might well find a starting-point in the themes which lay behind the *Regensburg Book*.

[1] Jedin, *History of the Council of Trent*, 408–9.   [2] *Ibid*. 409.

KING JAMES I'S CALL FOR AN ECUMENICAL COUNCIL

by W. B. PATTERSON

KING James I was not, in the commonly accepted view, a reconciler of religious differences. Yet there is considerable evidence from the first years of his reign in England—the very period of the Hampton Court Conference, which established for him a reputation of intolerance—that James was actively interested in reconciling religious differences. Surviving documents reveal, moreover, that he had a plan for attaining this objective, the essential feature of which was a proposal that an ecumenical council be convened, representing both Rome and the major Reformation traditions.[1]

James referred publicly to his plan in his speech to the first parliament of his reign, on 19 March 1604. In this speech, in which he expressed his gratitude for the friendly reception so far given him in England, he talked at length about the blessings of peace. His coming had brought outward peace, in that the war with Spain had been ended.[2] He had also brought inward peace, in that in him were combined the royal lines of Lancaster and York, and of England and Scotland, which circumstance, he hoped, would mean the end of internal wars in the island.[3] He also talked about religious peace. In the section dealing with Roman Catholics James expressed the wish that the differences between the churches might be reconciled, and he pledged his willingness to help effect such a reconciliation. 'I could wish from my heart', he said,

---

[1] Scattered references to this plan may be found in Samuel R. Gardiner, *History of England from the Accession of James I to the Outbreak of the Civil War, 1603–1642*, I, London 1883, 202–3, 220–1; Ludwig, Freiherr von Pastor, *The History of the Popes from the Close of the Middle Ages*, XXIV, St Louis 1952, 78; and D. Harris Willson, *King James VI and I*, London 1956, 219–20.

[2] Charles H. McIlwain, ed., *The Political Works of James I*, Cambridge, Mass. 1918, 270.　　　　[3] *Political Works of James I*, 271–3.

that it would please God to make me one of the members of such a generall Christian vnion in Religion, as laying wilfulnesse aside on both hands, wee might meete in the middest, which is the Center and perfection of all things. For if they would leaue, and be ashamed of such new and gross Corruptions of theirs, as themselues cannot maintaine, nor denie to bee worthy of reformation, I would for mine owne part be content to meete them in the mid-way, so that all nouelties might be renounced on either side. For as my faith is the Trew, Ancient Catholike and Apostolike faith, grounded vpon the Scriptures and expresse word of God: so will I euer yeeld all reuerence to antiquitie in the points of Ecclesiasticall pollicy; and by that meanes shall I euer with Gods grace keepe my selfe from either being an hereticke in Faith, or schismatick in matters of Pollicie.[1]

It was this 'generall Christian vnion' which James evidently hoped to effect by means of an ecumenical council. At the time he made this declaration to Parliament he had already communicated his desire for such a council through diplomatic channels which might be expected to lead to the papacy.

James had been proclaimed king on the death of Elizabeth on 24 March 1603, though his coronation had not taken place until 25 July. In the interval between these events, on 8 May 1603, the Venetian Secretary in England, Giovanni Carlo Scaramelli, had a conference with Lord Kinloss, a Scotsman who was a member of the Privy Council, which touched on religious affairs. Lord Kinloss informed Scaramelli that the king was deeply grateful to Pope Clement VIII, 'and spoke of him as truly Clement', because, though he had been urged to do so by other princes, the pope had not excommunicated him.[2] He added that the Catholics in England had little to fear from James: 'as long as the Catholics remain quiet and decently hidden they will neither be hunted nor persecuted'.[3] Scaramelli replied that many people expected much more from James, namely that 'his Majesty sooner or later would restore the Kingdom of England to the Roman cult'.[4] To this

---

[1] *Political Works of James I*, 275–6.
[2] Horatio F. Brown, ed., *Calendar of State Papers and Manuscripts, Relating to English Affairs, Existing in the Archives and Collections of Venice, and in Other Libraries of Northern Italy*, x, *1603–1607*, London 1900, 21.
[3] *Calendar of State Papers, Venetian*, x, 21–2.
[4] *Calendar of State Papers, Venetian*, x, 22.

Lord Kinloss answered emphatically, if not altogether unambiguously, 'No! beyond a doubt this will never happen; our bow which hitherto had two strings will have but one for the future, for he who wishes for the peaceable enjoyment of a kingdom must take care how he changes the religion of it, the smallest suspicion of such a thing is too serious a matter in a people firmly rooted in one faith.'[1] The reference to the bow and strings must mean, when considered along with the evidence of James's earlier negotiations with the papacy,[2] that whereas he had formerly played for the support of both Catholics and Protestants in England in his claim for the throne, he would henceforth rely upon the political support of the Protestants alone.

Lord Kinloss then disclosed James's plan for an ecumenical council, for which the king felt he could galvanize considerable support in northern Europe.

True it is that if the Pope wished to summon a General Council, which, according to the ancient usage, should be superior to all Churches, all doctrine, all Princes, secular and ecclesiastic, none excepted, my master, upon whom, as they will soon find out, depend in this and in other matters, Denmark, Sweden, Norway, the Free Cities of the Empire and the States as though upon an Emperor, would be extremely willing to take the lead and to prove himself the warm supporter of so great a benefit to Christendom. Beyond a doubt abuses would be removed on all hands, and a sound decision would put an end, perhaps for ever, to the discords in the Christian faith, nor would his Majesty think he could act more nobly than to be the first to offer complete obedience to Council's decrees.[3]

James thus proposed that the papacy take the initiative of calling a council which, it was hoped, would secure the religious peace of Christendom. At the end of September the Venetian Secretary found James wholeheartedly behind the plan, though there were aspects of the plan, as the Venetian understood it, about which the papacy might well have been apprehensive. Writing from Oxford on 28 September 1603, Scaramelli reported to the Doge

---

[1] *Calendar of State Papers, Venetian*, x, 22.
[2] See Arnold Oskar Meyer, 'Clemens VIII. und Jakob I. von England', *Quellen und Forschungen aus italienischen Archiven und Bibliotheken*, VII, 2 (1904), 268–306.
[3] *Calendar of State Papers, Venetian*, x, 22.

and Senate that the king showed 'a growing desire for the assembly of a free Council to discuss the basis of religion and the question of Papal authority'.[1]

James also approached the papacy more directly on the question of a council. In 1602 Pope Clement VIII, who had received a message from James's queen, a recent convert to Rome, assuring the pope of James's good will towards his Catholic subjects,[2] sent a letter and a verbal message to James. In the message, conveyed by Sir James Lindsay, a Scottish Catholic who was returning to his native land, the pope promised James support in his claim to the English throne, and even offered him a subsidy. In return James was to grant the request made in the letter, that the heir to the throne, Prince Henry, be brought up in the Roman Catholic faith.[3] Lindsay was, however, prevented for some time by illness from returning with James's answer. The king therefore undertook to send an answer by way of his ambassador in Paris, Sir Thomas Parry, who was to communicate it to the papal nuncio there. The letter was sent in November 1603,[4] by which time, of course, James had acceded to the English throne.

In his letter, James declined with some asperity the suggestion that the prince be brought up a Roman Catholic.[5] But he dealt seriously with the problem of the rival forms of Christianity in England. He wished justice, peace, and tranquillity for his Catholic subjects.

And would that (which has always been in our prayers) this course be entered upon, and care be taken, by means of a General Council, justly and legitimately declared and assembled, by which all contentions and controversies could be settled and composed: whence it would be clear

[1] *Calendar of State Papers, Venetian*, x, 98.
[2] Meyer, 'Clemens VIII. und Jakob I.', 279–80, 301–3.
[3] Meyer, 'Clemens VIII. und Jakob I.', 282–3, 304–5. See also Gardiner, *History of England*, I, 97–8.
[4] For the date and an English version of the letter, see M. S. Giuseppi, ed., *Calendar of the Manuscripts of the Most Hon. The Marquess of Salisbury, Preserved at Hatfield House, Hertfordshire*, Part xv, London 1930, 299–302.
[5] See the Latin version of the letter in M. A. Tierney, ed., *Dodd's Church History of England from the Commencement of the Sixteenth Century to the Revolution in 1688*, London 1841, IV, lxx.

in the case of each doctrine what would be agreeable to antiquity, to the first and purer times of the Christian Church, what was born from and sprang from the inventions of men not long ago.[1]

Just as he opposed the latter from an inner conviction, he favoured the former: 'whatever has been received from ancient times in the church, and confirmed by the authority of the divine word, these things we think ought to be preserved and observed most religiously'.[2] He added to the proposal an expression of his own desire for a common service of worship:

we think nothing is to be more earnestly wished for, and we should approve nothing more willingly than divine worship which is common and uniform in all things, not thoroughly defiled by the corruptions of men, nor repugnant to the divine laws; from which the church may receive the most joyful fruits of peace and tranquillity, and may acquire strength to repulse and carry the war to the finish against the common and most dangerous enemy of God and of all Christians.[3]

James's daring and visionary suggestion for a common service of worship was evidently intended to provide an experience through which Christians could enjoy a sense of unity.

Thus, by the spring of 1604, James had communicated his proposal for an ecumenical council to resolve the religious conflicts within Christendom to the papacy and had also communicated his desire for a 'generall Christian vnion' to Parliament. In the light of these developments it is interesting to note what was reported to the papacy from Catholic sources during the early months of 1604 concerning the atmosphere at the English court. As these reports indicate, James's receptiveness to a move towards a religious reconciliation was certainly not unknown there.

On 10 February 1604, Monsignor Innocenzo del Bufalo, Bishop of Camerino and Papal Nuncio to France, wrote to Cardinal Pietro Aldobrandino, a nephew of Pope Clement VIII, in Rome, and enclosed with his letter two recent letters to him from England reporting on affairs in that country. The author of the enclosed letters, the English Catholic Henry Constable, a Cambridge graduate and a friend of Sir Philip Sidney, had

---

[1] *Dodd's Church History*, IV, lxxi.   [2] *Ibid.*   [3] *Ibid.*

recently returned to England from France, where he had apparently become a pensioner of the French king. Whether or not he was on any kind of official mission is not clear, though he does profess his desire in the first letter to serve his Church, if he does not lack the means of being able to stay at the English court.[1] The first letter, dated 9 January 1604, at Hampton Court, expresses Constable's view that the king is 'most benign, and the enemy of persecution', but that nevertheless there cannot be any possibility of an official declaration of religious freedom for Catholics 'until such time as His Majesty is personally more convinced than he is at present of the authenticity and good grounds of the Catholic cause'.[2] For this purpose it would be highly desirable to send learned persons well versed in theological controversies to talk with the king. Constable had, furthermore, some advice for those sent to talk to James. 'In what follows', he wrote,

I am simply reporting to your Most Illustrious Lordship the opinion of those who are very well acquainted with the humour and disposition of the king at the present time and who desire, above all else, the good of the Catholic Religion, namely, that those who will speak with His Majesty on behalf of Our Master, His Holiness, should explain at once the intention which His Holiness has of negotiating with the King, in his capacity as the greatest and most able of those Princes who are today separated from the Apostolic See, about the ways and means of uniting the whole of Christendom in one faith and one single true religion.[3]

Since, he added, the king had a great opinion of his own knowledge of theology and deemed himself capable of great things, he would derive a great deal of satisfaction from discussing such a proposal which would, therefore, 'be of the utmost value in leading to the aim which we desire'.[4]

In a second letter, enclosed by del Bufalo with the first and sent to Cardinal Aldobrandino, Constable commented on what he saw as favourable opinion in England for such negotiations:

[1] PRO, MS 31/9/88 (Roman Transcripts), pp. 1–4. See also Sidney Lee, 'Henry Constable (1562–1613)', in *DNB*, IV, London (reprint of) 1937–8, 959–60.
[2] PRO, MS 31/9/88, p. 2.
[3] PRO, MS 31/9/88, pp. 2–3.
[4] PRO, MS 31/9/88, p. 3.

Meanwhile I have to inform your Lordship that the more I move in the court circle the more I become aware that the most important people at court, and the most learned amongst those who bear the title of Prelate in this kingdom, speak willingly and show themselves desirous of some move towards the reunion of England with the Apostolic See. Many of them have spoken about it with great emotion, and although the details that they have proposed are not such that they may be approved by a Catholic, nonetheless that feeling of contentment, nay of desire that negotiations for a reunion between His Holiness and the king, may be made, makes me hope well for the future.[1]

Del Bufalo's letters also give us a vivid picture of James describing aspects of his proposal to the representatives of a Catholic prince. On 21 September 1604, del Bufalo reported to Rome that the Duke of Lorraine had sent an embassy to England to treat with James about the status of the Catholics in his kingdom.[2] On their way back to Lorraine from England the duke's representatives had stopped off in Paris to report to the papal nuncio on their conversations. According to del Bufalo, they reported that James had repeated to them many times 'that he recognized the Roman Church as the Mother Church, and the Pope as the Universal Vicar of the whole Church, with spiritual authority over all, and that he himself would gladly be reunited with the Roman Church and would take three steps in that direction if only the Church would take one'.[3] They also reported that James appeared 'to believe all that which is revealed in the Scriptures and through the Holy Fathers of the three centuries after Christ, holding a different opinion of what St Augustine and St Bernard wrote from that expressed by Calvin and Luther'.[4] As for the treatment of the Catholics, he regretted that Parliament had confirmed the laws against them, but would himself see that no action was taken against Catholics on purely religious grounds.[5] The

---

[1] PRO, MS 31/9/88, p. 5. The letter is undated.
[2] PRO, MS 31/9/88, p. 121. The embassy from the Duke of Lorraine is mentioned in a communication from Dudley Carleton to John Chamberlain, from London, 27 August 1604. See Mary A. E. Green, ed., *Calendar of State Papers, Domestic Series, of the Reign of James I, 1603–1610*, London 1857, I, 146.
[3] PRO, MS 31/9/88, pp. 121–2.
[4] PRO, MS 31/9/88, p. 122.   [5] *Ibid.*

pope was not impressed by James's comments on religious matters. His cynical, even if amusing, observation written on the back of del Bufalo's letter reads: 'These are things which make me doubt that he believes anything.'[1]

Not surprisingly, in view of his reaction to the report of the embassy from Lorraine, Clement VIII did not move towards unity on the terms which James proposed in 1603–4. The king described the reception his proposal received in an interview with Zorzi Giustinian, the Venetian Ambassador in England, reported to the Doge and Senate on 14 June 1606:

Pope Clement VIII. invited me to join the Roman Church. I replied that if they would resolve the various difficulties in a general Council, legitimately convened, I would submit myself to its decisions. What do you think he answered?—just look at the zeal of the Vicar of Christ— why, he said, 'The King of England need not speak of Councils; I won't hear of one. If he will not come in by any other means things may stand as they are.'[2]

Judging from the tone of James's comments, the passage of time had not rendered him any the less outraged.

James's negotiations with the papacy on the subject of Christian unity, carried on through a variety of channels in the opening years of his reign, were thus without fruitful results. Indeed, they may even be said to have had a mischievous effect on Anglo-papal relations. James had given the impression that he viewed his Catholic subjects with benevolence and sympathetic understanding, yet those subjects observed that the laws against Catholics were not only not repealed, but were, in some cases, applied with increased severity.[3] A few Catholics were so exasperated as to seek a way out of their plight by blowing up King, Lords, and Commons when they were assembled for the opening of Parliament. The Gunpowder Plot,[4] planned for execution on 5 November 1605,

[1] PRO, MS 31/9/88, p. 122.
[2] *Calendar of State Papers, Venetian*, x, 360.
[3] Pastor, *History of the Popes*, xxiv, 79–80; Gardiner, *History of England*, i, 203, 222–4, 227–30.
[4] Gardiner, *History of England*, i, 234–64. For comments on the participants in the plot, see David Mathew, *James I*, London 1967, 141–50.

was fortunately exposed before any damage was done to its intended victims. But probably incalculable damage was done to the cause of good relations between Catholics and Protestants in England, and James's faith in Rome was shaken to the point that, though he did not give up his plan for unity, he elected to pursue it for the most part in other ways than by appealing to the papacy.

JOHN HALES AND THE SYNOD OF DORT

by ROBERT PETERS

O N 24 April 1619 the Synod of Dort sat for the 154th, and last, time. Ostensibly summoned to resolve differences between Dutch Remonstrants and Contra-Remonstrants within a context of Calvinist theology, in reality it pronounced predetermined decrees on unconditional election, a limited atonement, man's total depravity, the irresistibility of grace, and the perseverance of the elect.[1]

The Synod was national (sometimes, decidedly 'local') in nature; yet, because other states—Great Britain, France, Hesse, and the Palatinate among them—sent delegates, it assumed in the eyes of such men as James I and Du Plessis-Mornay an importance equal to that of Trent.[2]

Not all have so regarded it, however, and a contemporary, Richard Montague, soon to become Bishop of Chichester, was accused of casting a foul blot on Dort as early as 1626 (especially on James I's representatives there), by maintaining that the discipline of the Church of England differed fundamentally from that approved by Dort, and that the British delegates had been far from unanimous in their support of its decisions. For this, George Carleton, his predecessor at Chichester, and an English delegate,[3] took him to task as under-estimating the strength of the English opposition to the ruling by the Synod on the parity of ministers, and their other objections to the discipline it laid down; adding, nevertheless, that it was doctrine, not discipline, that was the chief concern.[4] Of this, Montague was well aware, as one of the articles

---

[1] As quoted by T. Fuller, *The Church History of Britain*, London 1837, x, 275.
[2] By some it is still so regarded. When the present writer began to work on the theology of James I, an eminent ecclesiastical historian pointed him to Dort as the touchstone of Calvinist orthodoxy.
[3] At the time of the Synod Carleton was Bishop of Llandaff.
[4] G. Carleton, *A Joynt Attestation Avowing that the Discipline of the Church of England was not Impeached at the Synod of Dort*, London 1626, esp. sig.: A3r.–C2.

in his 1628 visitation shows: 'Doth your Minister...fall upon those much disputed and little understood Doctrines of God's eternal Predestination, of Election precedaneous, of Reprobation irrespective without sin forseen, unfordable, untractable, at which the Great Apostle stood at a gaze?'[1]

Earlier still, even James I himself had forbidden sermons on matters allegedly authoritatively decided at Dort, on the grounds that they provoked unseemly questionings.[2] Not quite what might be expected after a decisive Synod!

It was the ardent Royalist, Peter Heylyn, who seems first to have grasped that James's support for Dort was dictated by political, not religious, motives and that the presence of his delegates there showed his support for the House of Orange.[3] At the end of the Dort century, Burnet shrewdly observed that when 'the point of State was no more mixed with [the dispute] the questions were handled with less heat'.[4] (A salutary caution to those who would dress James in ecumenical garb!) Two centuries later, von Ranke concluded that James found the burghers (amongst whom the Remonstrants had their strongest supporters) unfriendly towards England (compared with their warmth towards France) after the truce with Spain (1609), and that his mantle of Calvinist orthodoxy was also assumed because he had married his daughter, Elizabeth, to the Elector Frederick (related on his mother's side to the House of Orange) at the heat of the Dutch quarrel.[5] More recent historians, notably Huizinga, attribute very little significance at all to Dort.[6] Yet Dort remains one of the two ecclesiastical assemblies of the seventeenth century to produce credal statements. In one way or another, therefore, its effectiveness cannot be so lightly set aside. Certainly, it produced an effect on one, at least, of those who attended it: in later life, he

[1] Quoted by H. Hickman, *A Justification of the Fathers and the Schoolmen*, Oxford 1659, sig.: A2r.
[2] Printed, among other places, in Wilkins, IV, 465–7.
[3] P. Heylyn, *Cyprianus Anglicanus*, London 1688, 82.
[4] G. Burnet, *An Exposition of the Thirty-nine Articles of the Church of England*, London 1699, 12.
[5] L. von Ranke, *A History of England*, Oxford 1875, I, 426.
[6] J. Huizinga, *Dutch Civilization in the 17th Century*, London 1968, 52–3.

asserted that it was at Dort that he 'bade John Calvin "good-night"'.[1]

John Hales was not an official representative.[2] He was sent to Dort in his capacity of chaplain to the English Ambassador at The Hague, Sir Dudley Carleton, to whose service he was appointed in 1618. Like his master, Hales was then an ardent Calvinist in theology. His earlier career had been spent in Oxford: at Corpus Christi College first; afterwards at Merton under the Wardenship of Sir Henry Saville, who employed Hales in the production of his famous 'Eton' Chrysostom. In 1612 he was elected to the chair of Greek; in 1613 he delivered Sir Thomas Bodley's funeral oration.

Almost certainly the Synod explains his appointment to The Hague. His earliest printed biography tells us that 'as Sir Dudley was obliged to give the King an account of the Synod, he sent Mr Hales to Dort',[3] where he arrived on 24 November 1618, two weeks after the Synod's official opening. By the following 7 February, when he left Dort, he had furnished thirty-three reports on its proceedings. The unwillingness of the Contra-Remonstrants to allow the release of anything more than mere scraps of information of what was happening, which were all that the official delegates could legitimately report, necessitated some alternative means of obtaining information; although the reticence of the Contra-Remonstrants was not without reason. John Young, early in January 1619, complained that the 'contentions about those abstruse points [of doctrine] could come to be talked of so openly even by the vulgar of both sides':[4] unfortunately,

[1] Quoted by Des Maizeux, *An Historical and Critical Account of the Life and Writings of the Ever-Memorable Mr. John Hales*, London 1719, 69, also S. Brandt (trans. J. Chamberlayne), *The History of the Reformation in and about the Low Countries*, London 1721, III, 26.

[2] They were, in addition to George Carleton, Joseph Hall, then Dean of Worcester, later Bishop of Exeter and then of Norwich; John Davenant, then Lady Margaret Professor at Cambridge and subsequently Bishop of Salisbury; Samuel Ward, Master of Sidney Sussex College, Cambridge, and afterwards Lady Margaret Professor there; Walter Balcanqual, official (though far from acceptable) representative of the Church of Scotland; and Thomas Goad, chaplain to George Abbot, and replacement for Hall who returned to England on grounds of health. [3] Des Maizeux, *Hales*, p. 3.

[4] Bodleian Library, Tanner MSS, Vol. 74A, f. 180r.

this 'clamp-down' prevented information from reaching those most immediately interested in the Synod's proceedings. And curiosity was keen. In December 1618 William Bedell, former embassy chaplain at Venice and now Vicar of Bury St Edmunds, told Ward that the absence of news caused him no surprise, for he had

lately heard that [the] King hears nothing from those parts. An argument that nothing is yet done and the business proves difficulter than was thought it would after the discovery of the minds of the politicians of the one side, unless perhaps there be a general inhibition of intelligence till all be concluded. I pray God that or anything else may be the cause, rather than that nothing at all should be concluded.[1]

Bedell need not have feared! The Contra-Remonstrants had every intention of ensuring that 'all should be concluded'—to their satisfaction. Such a conclusion was clearly anticipated by much of the English correspondence of the period; but on the assumption that there would be some semblance, at least, of debate. The Archbishop of York, Tobie Matthew, for instance, hoped that the differences between the contestants 'would but serve to increase the union which could result from a settlement of their differences, in which the English delegates would be *fratres in unum*'.[2] Few perceived with John Lake, Bishop of Bath and Wells, that the

disquietness of...those provinces shows that politique heads set forward those ecclesiastical doubts, as religion is too commonly prophaned by malcontents, who think they shall move the more if their forge use that fire...I pray God that they that have been moved by others' wits abuse not themselves more...So ambitious are we of our conceit that we will rather harrow the Church than acknowledge that we are subject to error, especially in so high mysteries. And because the mysteries are so high, and the conscience is so choice the points should be soberly debated and the persons handled.[3]

Something of what Lake feared was experienced by Hales almost as soon as he presented his credentials to the clerical President, Bogermann, in an incident which indicates the diffi-

---

[1] *Ibid*. fol. 173r.   [2] *Ibid*. fol. 188r.   [3] *Ibid*. fol. 174r.

culties of his task. On 24 November he asked Bogermann for an account of the proceedings up to that time. But his evident optimism of obtaining it was not fulfilled. Four days later he had to report to Carleton that 'an index' was all he had been able to obtain. 'It is not that which I required', he apologized, 'but is as much as Festus Hominus [one of the assessors] could spare.' His request for an account of the whole proceedings was 'thought to be *nimis grande postulantem*'. Furthermore, he had been refused copies of two orations.[1]

Hales was surprised at this treatment—though nothing more— and resigned himself to relying on his own notes for his reports. In any event, it appeared to him that nothing of great moment had happened, since the Remonstrants had not yet appeared in the Synod. In that assumption he was mistaken. By legislating for an 'approved' translation of the Bible (under vigilant Contra-Remonstrant supervision, and with Dutch equivalents for such terms as Jehovah); preaching and catechizing (the latter leading up to the Heidelberg Catechism); the training and formation of the clergy ('the Church Regiment', whose duties the Synod clearly defined); and the baptism of the children of 'ethnic' parents (problems created by the beginnings of Dutch colonialism), the Synod, far from occupying itself with matters common to such gatherings, was in fact organizing an efficient propaganda machine through which to spread its theology.[2]

Some of the practices and procedures puzzled Hales. Why, for instance, were the opinions of the foreign theologians sought *after* the vote on an important issue had been taken, except when the baptism of the children of heathen parents was under discussion? He was particularly distressed when, following the long discussion on catechizing, and its obvious importance, his attempt to obtain copies of the forms on which Bogermann and the Assessors had agreed met with evasions amounting to a refusal.[3] He thought the rulings on 'ethnic' baptism—that intelligent adults might receive it if they so desired, but not infants until they reached years of discretion—'such as . . . no other Church either Ancient or Modern

[1] J. Hales, *Golden Remains*, London 1673, 373–4. [Hereafter *GR*.]
[2] *GR*, 368–403.   [3] *GR*, 369.

ever gave'. When his enquiry about what was to happen if the child's life were in danger was dismissed with the retort that 'want of baptism would not prejudice them with God, except we do determine as the Papists that Baptism is necessary to salvation', he reasonably observed that such a statement, coming from a country where Anabaptism had been rife, was almost beyond belief.[1] Nevertheless, these uneasinesses aside, there is as yet no evidence of any cracks in Hales's loyalty to Calvin or Dort. He was still fervent in his support of Bogermann, whose speech introducing the debate on catechizing particularly impressed him.

It was Joseph Hall at this point who appeared to show signs of uneasiness at the trend of events. He was one of the foreigners sufficiently learned (or rash?) to agree to preach, at very short notice, in Latin before the Synod, prior to the appearance of the Remonstrants. Taking as his text Eccles. 6. 17, he urged the need for righteousness to be balanced with wisdom: men can be too just—the magistrate, for example, who stands too strictly on the letter of the law. Next, he rounded on the theologians for 'presuming too far in prying into the judgments of God, and... the curious disputes which our age hath made concerning Predestination; that this dispute for all its endlessness was like the Mathematical Line, *divisibilis in semper divisibilia*'. To end it, he recommended that both parties should submit a short exposition of their understanding of the passage on predestination in Rom. 9. 24, observing, somewhat naïvely, that if the meaning of that discourse were once perfectly opened, the question were at an end.[2] Even so, Hall concluded by announcing that the English delegation had been specifically instructed by their king to 'exhort [the Synod] to keep unaltered the former confessions'. Hales's only recorded comment on this inflammable sermon was to question the wisdom of the public proclamation of this instruction, thus openly declaring opposition to the Remonstrants.[3] At a later stage, Davenant was to provide even more positive evidence of divergence from agreed doctrine (admittedly, in conformity with James's instructions not to deny entirely universal redemption),[4] and it is inconceivable that there were not private discussions

[1] GR, 400.   [2] GR, 382–3.   [3] GR, 383.   [4] GR, 586–91.

among the delegates of these problems, to which Hales would certainly be admitted and which may have influenced his later attitude.

Be that as it may, Hales's sympathies were not easily attracted towards the Remonstrants. For ten days after their first appearance in the Synod, on 6 December, he was highly critical of their conduct. He was astonished that Utrecht, 'the strength of the Remonstrants, could find no wiser men to handle their cause'.[1] He questioned their terminology: if the separation between themselves and their opponents was on dogmatic grounds, 'heresy' was the correct term, not 'schism' (that employed by the Remonstrants).[2] The able oration of Episcopius on 7 December evoked almost no comment from him: on the other hand, it may well have impressed him.[3] But ten days later, after hearing another of their discourses, he confessed surprise that they should produce such 'impertinent stuff' to support their claims.[4]

At the same time, the proceedings of the Synod also earned his irritation; especially its refusal to allow the Remonstrants to appear as a 'party', when they had been cited to appear corporately by the lay commissioners.[5]

Between 28 December and 21 January,[6] Hales's irritation gave place to disappointment and anger. On 28 December he complained to Carleton of the continued wrangling over whether or not the Remonstrants were a 'party', warning him that a crisis was imminent: either the Remonstrants must yield (an unlikely possibility) or the Synod must give in to them (an even more unlikely possibility).[7] Furthermore, his faith in the Synod's authority had been badly jolted by the ease with which it flouted in the evening decrees which it had solemnly passed the same morning: 'a pretty matter, in so grave a place'.[8]

Three days later, influenced almost certainly by the Synod's flouting of its authority as well as by his sense of reason, he voiced

---

[1] GR, 409. [2] GR, 433.
[3] Hales tends to be reticent when he is most impressed, and this was a most impressive address. (See F. Calder, *Memoirs of Simon Episcopius*, London 1835, 284–313, for fuller text than that in GR, 403–7.) [4] GR, 433.
[5] GR, 434 ff. [6] 'New Style'.
[7] GR, 437–42. [8] GR, 444.

his doubts on the capacity of the Synod to establish a uniform system of government among the Churches of the 'reformed' tradition, while he dismissed as wholly impracticable the possibility of its agreeing on a confession of faith acceptable both to 'Reformed' and Lutherans.[1]

By early January, he sympathized with the complaint of the Remonstrants that their opponents could not claim that their continued presence in Dort (following their refusal to have further dealings with the Synod, because of its refusal to treat them as a 'party' when considering their views on reprobation) constituted an embarrassment when the Contra-Remonstrants had expressly forbidden their departure.[2]

On Friday 11 January, after a series of night-time discussions as to how they were to be dealt with, the Remonstrants were expelled by the Synod, and informed that they would be judged on their writings. To the incredulity of Hales, Bogermann informed them that the Synod had 'dealt mildly, gently, and favourably with' them, but

with a lie you made your entrance into the Synod; with a lie you take your leave of it...Your actions have been full of fraud, equivocations, and deceit...But assure you the Synod shall make known your pertinacity to the world; and know that the Belgic churches want not *arma spiritualia*, with which in time convenient, they will proceed against you.[3]

Hales was certain that by the time his own report arrived, Carleton must have heard of 'this powdering speech with grief'. And 'grief', giving place to horror, best describes Hales's own attitude to this and the following sequence of events. An indignant outburst would not have been in keeping with his nature. All the more telling, therefore, is his observation that if the Remonstrants 'should write that the President produced a sentence not that of the Synod, they should not lie'.[4]

Two days after the Remonstrants' dismissal Hales was alarmed to learn that, not content with suppressing their opinions, their

[1] GR, 446–7.   [2] GR, 447–8.
[3] GR, 453–4.   [4] GR, 455.

very lives were endangered by their opponents. He recalled that on the day of their expulsion 'when they seemed to yield', the voices of the foreigners, urging that they be allowed to remain in the Synod, could not be heard, neither were their opinions sought, before the Remonstrants were expelled. He was compelled to conclude that the attack had all along been intended not only against their opinions but also against their very existence, and that the outcome had been predetermined.[1]

If Hales realized that 'reason' had been offended, he equally realized that 'reason' demanded compliance with the decision of the Synod for, as he told Carleton,

the errors of public actions...are with less inconvenience tolerated than amended. For the danger of alteration, of disgracing and disabling authority, makes that the fortune of such proceedings admits no regress, but being once...done, they must for ever after be upheld... The Synod therefore...must now go forward, and leave events to God, and for the continuance of their actions do the best they may.[2]

This is not an expression of hopelessness, but the balanced judgment of a man acutely alive to the realities of a situation.

It is clear that by now Hales had effectively bade John Calvin 'good-night', all the same. His sympathies with the 'moderates' in the Synod became more marked, as did his distaste for rigidity. He commended the moderation of Gomarus, but regretted his support of 'that extreme and rigid tenet [of predestination] which Beza and Perkins first aquainted the world with'.[3] Even more did he approve the moderation of Martinius of Bremen ('who goes in aequipace with Gomarus in learning, and before him in discretion') in his discourse on the manner in which Christ is *Fundamentum electionis*, even if it was favourably inclined towards the Remonstrants;[4] a position to which, despite his sympathies, Hales in no way inclined.

Nevertheless, this address by Martinius is almost certainly the last link in the chain of events which culminated in Hales's rejection of Calvinism. Brandt says that Martinius' address was largely exegesis of Jn. 3. 16.[5] It led to a series of conferences, held for the

---

[1] GR, 454.   [2] GR, 452-3.   [3] GR, 452.
[4] GR, 454-5.   [5] Brandt, III, 209.

most part in the Bishop of Llandaff's lodgings, between Martinius and the Bishop (possibly with other foreign theologians present), who, although unable to accept Martinius' opinions himself, yet promised moderation in the Synod. Hales conceded that the thoroughness with which Martinius expounded his proof-text was his strong point.[1]

When material for what was to be the first published 'Life' of Hales was being assembled, although the work itself was not published until 1719,[2] a friend of Hales named Farringdon maintained that Hales often declared that it was after hearing Episcopius expound Jn. 3. 16 that 'I bade John Calvin "good-night"',[3] and the story has been repeated. But no evidence exists that Episcopius based an address on this text at Dort.

On the other hand, Hales's younger contemporary and earlier potential biographer, William Fulman, Fellow of Corpus Christi College, Oxford, 1660–9, in his unfinished notes,[4] thought he could detect the influence of Martinius in two passages in Hales's letter-tracts. In the first, on Crellius and Grotius (December 1638), Hales argues that all controversialists fail to do justice to 'Satisfaction' and 'Pardon', 'Socinus maintaining Pardon denyes Satisfaction, and we maintaining Satisfaction take away Pardon, for when we teach, *Deum condonare quidem peccata, sed interveniente satisfactionis*, to my conceit we do in gentle English overthrow Pardon properly taken'.[5] At the end of the section, having gone on to discuss usury, he observes that 'John Calvin was the first good man...that maintained use to be lawfull: And I have often wished that whatever his conceit was he had been pleased to conceal it, for he hath done much hurt'.[6] Strong words for a once-devoted Calvinist!

The second passage occurs in the manuscript version of Hales's *Letter to an intimate Friend concerning the Eucharist—And the Churches Erring in Fundamentals*. Having described any form of the eucharistic 'Canon [as] a thing indifferent', Hales argues that 'Christians

[1] GR, 454.   [2] That of Des Maizeux.
[3] Des Maizeux, *Hales*, p. 69.
[4] Corpus Christi College MS 306, ff. 71r–106v.
[5] *Ibid*. fol. 82r.   [6] *Ibid*. fol. 87v.

have taken a greater libertie than they can well justifie...in forging sacraments more than God...did ever intend; and secondly, in adding to the Sacraments...many formalities'.[1] Having criticized the, for him, crudeness of the Lutheran view of the mode of the Eucharistic Presence as differing but little from the Roman, he considers whether the Words of Consecration are a mere 'trope', and whether Christ is received

after a secret and wonderful manner. From whence have proceeded those rude speeches of the learned of the Reformed parts...This conceit, besides the falsehood of it, is a mere novelty—neither is it to be found in the books of the Antients, till Martin Bucer arose...and from him it descended into the worship of Calvin and Beza...It is abused in Reformed Churches for many ends which Christ never thought of— as an arbitrator of civil business and...in ending civil business.[2]

The rest of the tract consists of an *apologia* for what (for purposes of brevity) may be described as 'Zwinglian rationalism'. At the end, Hales declares his faith to be built on 'Scripture and reason: beyond these two I have no ground for my religion'. The Remonstrants would have understood and, in a large measure, agreed.

To return to Dort, the sessions following Martinius' address were officially occupied in hurrying through the pre-arranged decrees, and the speed with which the delegates passed from one article to another alarmed Hales; particularly the indefensible practice of producing decrees in final form before discussion, let alone ratification, of their contents. His sense of justice compelled his admiration for the manner in which individuals handled this or that point, but his awareness that the final decisions were synodal in name only becomes apparent. No evidence exists of his request to Carleton to be relieved of his, by then, unpleasant task, but his relief at his recall to The Hague is evident. 'Our Synod goes on like a watch', he wrote on the day before he left Dort, 'the main wheels upon which the whole Business turns are least in sight. For all things of moment are acted in private sessions: what is done in public is only for show and entertainment.'[3]

---

[1] *Ibid.* fol. 92r.   [2] *Ibid.* fols. 92r–94r.   [3] GR, 460.

Years later, in the manuscript of the tract among Fulman's notes already quoted, he was to observe of Councils:

For what men are they of whom these great meetings do consist? Are they the best, the most learned, the most virtuous, the most likely to walk uprightly? No; the greatest, the most ambitious, and many times men neither of judgment or learning... And are these men in common equity likely to determine for truth? Again... their way to proceed to a conclusion, is not by weight of reason, but by multitude of votes... as if it were a maxim in Nature that the greater part must needs be the better. It was never heard in any profession that... truth went by plurality of voices, the Christian profession only excepted, and I have often mused how it comes to pass that the way which in all other sciences is not able to warrant the poorest conclusion should be thought sufficient... in Divinitie... It is given out that Christian meetings have such an assistance of God... that... they may assure themselves against all possibility of mistaking. And this... which to this way of ending controversies... in all other sciences is so contemptible, gives a determining to theological disputes of so great authority.[1]

Only experience could produce so deep a sense of disillusion: Hales gained that experience at Dort. His reason and tolerance spoke to an age unable to appreciate those qualities.

[1] Corpus Christi College MS 306, ff. 96r–96v.

ASSEMBLY AND ASSOCIATION IN DISSENT, 1689–1831

by GEOFFREY F. NUTTALL

PROBABLY the oldest existing institution of its kind in present-day Dissent, though now but a shadow of its former self, is that which has long gone under the name of 'The Exeter Assembly'. This body, composed of ministers only, and in the main of ministers of Presbyterian congregations in the county of Devon, first met at Tiverton on 17 and 18 March 1691, with fifteen ministers present. The inaugural meeting was followed by regular meetings held twice a year, usually in May and September. Save for three short breaks (1717–21, 1728–33, and 1753–63), the Assembly's minutes, or for the years 1691–1717 a contemporary copy transcribed by the Assembly's scribe and published in 1963 by the Devon and Cornwall Record Society,[1] have been preserved for the whole period from 1691 to the present time.

At their first meeting the ministers stated their purpose to be 'to advise together touching things pertaining to our office, the right ordering of our congregations, & the promoting of purity & unity in the churches of Christ'; and also to establish a fund 'to promote the preaching of the Gospel' and for the benefit of 'poor and aged Ministers & hopeful youths to be educated for the ministry'; such youths only 'as appear to the Ministers assembled to be poor, capable of learning & well inclin'd' to be assisted financially by being placed with 'Tutors that shall use their utmost care & diligence to bring them up in learning & ripen

---

[1] See *The Exeter Assembly: the minutes of the assemblies of the United Brethren of Devon and Cornwall, 1691–1717, as transcribed by the Reverend Isaac Gilling*, edited with an introduction by Allan Brockett (Devon & Cornwall Record Society, new series, vol. 6), Torquay 1963 [hereafter Brockett]; see also Priestley Paine, *Record of the United Brethren of Devon and Cornwall*, Manchester [1899]; and Allan Brockett, *Nonconformity in Exeter 1650–1875*, Manchester 1962, index, and for the whereabouts of the unpublished minutes, Appendix C.

them for so high an imploiment'. 'If the Fund will reach it the poor widdows & orphans of Dissenting Ministers' were also to be assisted. It was soon found that the Fund would not reach it: at the next meeting the reference to widows and orphans was to be 'at present expung'd'. Considerable sums of money, however, were raised for the increase of ministers' stipends and towards the training of candidates for the ministry. In May 1697, at the Assembly's fifteenth meeting, it was recorded that thirteen 'young scholars' were then being assisted with various amounts totalling payments of £34. 10. 0 quarterly or £138 for the year.[1]

At this fifteenth meeting twenty-two ministers were present. This is, in fact, the average number for attendance up to the end of the seventeenth century, i.e. for the fourteen meetings (out of the first twenty)[2] at which the names of those present are recorded. It is only a third of the total membership during the nine years, for this was sixty-six; but, since before the end of the period several members had died, some had left the county, and one, after falling into 'a notorious scandal',[3] had conformed to the Church of England, while others, including some not at first ordained, were not members at the outset, the number of those attending meetings was considerably more than a third of the actual membership at any one time. Those present at these first meetings were in charge of about thirty congregations.

By 1697 the Assembly was well established. Already at its second meeting, held in June 1691 at Topsham, the ministers had received a request for ordination from three candidates and had agreed that, after each had been examined, had preached on a stated text, and had defended a stated thesis, they 'be ordain'd'[4] at Exeter in the following August; and before 1697 ordination had taken place on a number of occasions. Although each ordination was by authority of the Assembly, and at the hands of some of its members, it was not a formal meeting of the Assembly and is thus not recorded in the minutes; but a certificate of ordination is sometimes mentioned,[5] and that ordination had taken place often

[1] Brockett, 2, 3, 5, 37.
[2] In 1691 and 1692 the Assembly met three times.
[3] Brockett, 28.   [4] Brockett, 6.   [5] Cf. Brockett, 53.

appears from the inclusion of the name of the former candidate in the subsequent attendance lists as now a member of the Assembly.

Needless to say, a sermon was preached at every meeting. In May 1699 Stephen Towgood[1] of Axminster, a troublesome Independent, 'having continu'd above two hours in sermon, all future preachers' were warned 'to keep to their hour'[2] with the help of the hourglass; but usually the preacher was thanked for his sermon and on occasion he was requested to print it and often did so.[3] The ministers often debated 'cases of conscience': such as 'Is it lawful to administer the Lords Supper at any other time than in the evening?'; 'What is to be done in case a person can't drink wine. Whether Beer or Cyder may not be receiv'd by such a one in the Lords Supper?'; or the perennial query 'Whether the Apostolical Office were essentially distinct from that of Presbyters?'. Though agreeing in 1691 not 'to intermeddle with state affairs', in 1707 they so far took notice of the Act of Settlement as to resolve 'tis fit that we should pray for the House of Hanover'. In May 1713, at a meeting exceptionally well attended, perhaps in honour of a distinguished visitor from London, Dr Edmund Calamy, thirty of the fifty-seven ministers present 'promis'd to give some books' to the 'new College being erected in Connecticut Colony',[4] now Yale University. More than once the Assembly 'caution'd' against encouraging vagrants'. On one occasion a

---

[1] For Towgood and others mentioned in the text of the first part of this paper for whom no further reference is given, see *Freedom after Ejection*, ed. Alexander Gordon, Manchester 1917, and/or *Calamy Revised*, ed. A. G. Matthews, Oxford 1934. [2] Brockett, 42.

[3] Cf. Samuel Stoddon, *The Pastor's Charge and the People's Duty*, 1693; John Enty, *The Ministry Secur'd from Contempt*, 1707; James Peirce, *An Useful Ministry a Valid one*, 1714; William Bartlet, *Barnabas's Character and Success*, 1716; Benjamin Wills, *Ministers set for the Defence of the Gospel*, 1720. For information concerning the preacher and his text at the meeting at Exeter on 4 May 1692, at a point where for two consecutive meetings the pages of the transcript of the minutes are left blank (Brockett, 13), see Edmund Calamy, *Continuation of the Account*, 1727, 217.

[4] Brockett, 25, 52, 54, 1, 62, 93. For Calamy's description of his visit, and of the sermon which despite 'some demur' (Brockett, 92) he preached and at the Assembly's request published as *The Prudence of the Serpent and Innocence of the Dove* (1713), see his *Historical Account of my own Life*, ed. J. T. Rutt, 2nd ed., 1830, II, 264–5.

10-2

member 'spake with much warmth against Ministers wearing long light powder'd wigs'. To doctrine there are surprisingly few references in the first twenty-five years—apart from the doctrine implicit in the theses defended or the (rhetorical) questions debated by ordinands; 'Arminianism and Socinianism' are mentioned once only. In September 1711 the Assembly drew up a paper condemning the antinomianism of a minister who was causing disturbance in Wales.[1] Apart from 'the Fund', the main business was twofold: the ordaining and settling of ministers; and arbitration in cases of disagreement between a minister and his congregation. The Assembly decided who should ordain as well as be ordained, and often when and where; and the decision was accepted as an 'order'. The ministers also agreed *nem. con.* 'that no person be licens'd to preach who is not in full communion'; and 'that no minister settled in any Congregation shall settle in another Congregation without offering his reasons to the Assembly'.[2]

Over ordinations difficulties soon arose, as they are apt to do. The Assembly not only assumed authority to ordain but exclusive authority to do so. Without its authority, moreover, no member of the Assembly was to take part in ordinations even outside the county. This was clearly laid down at its ninth meeting, in May 1694. Two years later, in September 1696, the Assembly received a letter from a Provincial Assembly met at Sherborne complaining that two of the Devon ministers had 'join'd in the Ordination of persons' who had 'not addressed themselves...to the Associated Brethren...when they might so have done'.[3] As might be expected, both the ministers involved, John Ashwood of Exeter and Stephen Towgood, were Independents. Ashwood

---

[1] Brockett, 47, 77, 17, 86. For reference to the Exeter Assembly by the minister disturbed, and for letters to him (translated by him into Welsh) from William Peard, Barnstaple, 7 August 1711, and from Jacob Bailies and William Bartlett, Bideford, 9 August 1711, members of the Assembly who were not present at its meeting in September 1711, see Jeremy Owen, *Golwg ar y Beiau* (1732–3),ed. R. T. Jenkins, Caerdydd 1950, 58, 60; and for elucidation of the disturbance, cf. my 'Northamptonshire and *The Modern Question*: a turning-point in eighteenth-century dissent', in *JTS*, new series, XVI. 1, 109.

[2] Brockett, 53, 75, 40.

[3] Brockett, 29.

admitted to having shared in an ordination at Bridport in Dorset,[1] but declared 'against an imposing spirit' and desired 'his liberty in things of this nature, & not to be oblig'd to acquaint Associations with such matters'.[2] He was 'earnestly importun'd for peace sake' not to repeat his misdemeanour; but at the next meeting both men expressed afresh 'much unwillingness to bring Ordinations to the Assembly'. A paper was further presented by Towgood, arguing that to refuse ordination to anyone on the ground that he would not acknowledge ecclesiastical jurisdiction 'superior to that in a Particular Church' was 'utterly unlawfull'.[3] This of course the Assembly rejected. The feeling aroused finds vent in a letter which at this point the scribe copied, a letter from himself to another member, in which he complains of the Independents' 'clubbing and caballing'. 'Why should we encourage others to play their old game, and teach them to undermine us?' he asks; ''Tis time to improve our method...We have 5 to 1.'[4]

According to Mr Brockett, whose acquaintance with the Assembly's history goes far beyond these early years about which, from his careful edition of its minutes, we can form our own conclusions, 'Congregationalists and Presbyterians continued to

---

[1] Ashwood stated in his defence 'That the neighbouring Ministers particularly Mr John Pinney had been sent to & desir'd to assist at the Ordination but came not' (Brockett, 29–30); for this invitation to Pinney, dated 10 June 1696 and signed by eleven members of the Bridport congregation, which is preserved in the Pinney family papers, see my *Letters of John Pinney 1679–1699*, 1939, 95–7, as Letter 55.

[2] Ashwood had been ordained at 'Excester' (Thomas Reynolds, *Sermon preach'd on the death of...John Ashwood*, 1707, 65), where he succeeded Lewis Stucley (d. 1687) as minister of Castle Lane Congregational church; unfortunately this church possesses 'no surviving records' (Brockett, *Nonconformity in Exeter*, 58).

[3] Brockett, 30, 38. Towgood had been ordained in '6th moneth' 1679 as minister of the Axminster Congregational church by Henry Butler of Yeovil, Robert Bartlet of Compton, Dorset, and Richard Down of Bridport, all three being Independents: cf. [Matthew Towgood] [Axminster 1874], *Ecclesiastica, or a Book of Remembrance*, 61.

[4] Brockett, 35–6. The phrase in this letter, dated '9bri 30, 1696', 'I wish there were more of your spirit to be found among those that are well-willers to these Mathematicks', indicates that its writer, Isaac Gilling, had been reading the words of John Owen when returning to Richard Baxter papers on 'our common Concord', 'I am still a well-wisher to those Mathematicks', as stated by Baxter in his autobiography, then newly published: cf. *Reliquiae Baxterianae*, ed. M. Sylvester, 1696 (preface, 13 May), Part III, p. 69, sect. 145.

join together in the Exeter Assembly until the middle of the eighteenth century'.[1] Participation by Congregationalists, however, was always slight—'5 to 1' against them is an understatement: during the Assembly's first nine years probably only seven members, including Ashwood and Towgood, were Independents.

One of the seven was the minister who served as Moderator of the Assembly at its second meeting, John Flavell. The reason for his election to this position of honour lay in part in the fact that, with others[2] who served as Moderator at some of these first meetings, he was of a select company who forty years earlier had been members of the Devon Association[3] of ministers formed in 1655 after the model of the better known Voluntary Association in Worcestershire sponsored by Richard Baxter. For a generation persecution and prosecution had been these men's lot. In 1672, shortly after Charles II's Declaration of Indulgence to Nonconformists, Flavell had been so bold as to join with other Devon ministers in a service of Nonconformist ordination;[4] but this was a singular and single occasion, and with the rescinding of the Declaration the liberty for it was soon passed. 'I am hurried hither out of Devonshire by the fury of the storme yt lyes hard upon me', Flavell wrote from London to the Earl of Bedford's chaplain in 1684; 'my estate is pursued as a prey by an Outlawry, my liberty by a Capias'.[5] Now at last, after the passing of the Act of Toleration in 1689, it was possible for Flavell and his friends freely and openly to meet not only for worship but in the kind of ordered

[1] Brockett, *Nonconformity in Exeter*, 65.
[2] E.g. John Berry (d. 1704) and Richard Saunders (d. 1694). Other members of the Exeter Assembly who had been members of the Devon Association were William Crompton (d. 1696), Robert Gaylard (d. 1697), Edward Hunt (d. 1695), and Michael Taylor (d. 1705). Another, who also served as Moderator, Samuel Tapper (d. 1709), had been a member of the Cornish Association.
[3] See Devon Association *Transactions*, IX (1877), 279–88.
[4] Dr Williams's Library, Quick MSS, 1.2.965; William Yeo of Wolborough is the only one of the other ministers who is named. In 1687, shortly after James II's Declaration of Indulgence, three other members of the Assembly, Benjamin Hooper, George Mortimer, who had been a member of the earlier Association, and George Trosse, who often served as Moderator of the Assembly, had similarly taken part in an ordination (Brockett, App. A2).
[5] *Calamy Revised*, 200, from Bodleian Library, Rawlinson Letters, 109.33.

ministerial gatherings which they had enjoyed during the Protectorate. These 'ancient' ministers hastened to associate while the
life was still in them. 'This is the Day I have often wished for':[1]
so opens the peroration of an Assembly sermon composed by
Flavell; but it was never preached. He died only two days after
the meeting at which he was Moderator.

Apart from the small but significant continuity in membership
between the Exeter Assembly and the earlier Devon Association,
the wording of the Assembly's Rules is often identical with that
of the Association's. In caring for ordination the Assembly was
also picking up the Association's work. Not all the Voluntary
Associations formed during the Commonwealth and Protectorate
had taken part in the work of ordaining[2]—Worcestershire had
not; but the Devon Association was one which had. So had the
Cornish Association.[3] Of six ministers in Cornwall whom in
1695 the Exeter Assembly requested to ordain, 'if they approve
him',[4] an assistant to the minister at Fowey, four had been
members of this earlier Cornish Association (one, indeed, had
received his own ordination from it), while a fifth was a younger
brother of one of its Moderators.

The Exeter Assembly was also like the Devon and Cornish
Associations in including Independents among its members. In
the strict sense it was thus not Presbyterian. It did not call itself
a presbytery or classis, nor was it one, for it contained no elders
(let alone other laymen). Its members were all ministers;[5] candidates for the ministry were permitted to be present, but their
names always appear at the end of attendance lists as a special
category. At the same time, the Assembly was clearly

[1] John Flavell, 'The Character of a Compleat Evangelical Pastor', in *Works*, 2nd
ed. 1716, II, 749. For the identification of this with the sermon which he had
prepared for preaching to a Provincial Assembly at Taunton following the
meeting of the Exeter Assembly at which he was Moderator, see Quick MSS
1.2.968.
[2] For this, cf. *From Uniformity to Unity 1662–1962*, ed. G. F. Nuttall and Owen
Chadwick, 1962, 172–3.
[3] For the Cornish Association, see Chetham Society, new series, xli, 175–88.
[4] Brockett, 26.
[5] There is evidence in some of the published sermons that laymen were present
when they were preached.

Presbyterian[1] in the broader sense which became usual during the eighteenth century. The division which soon arose over ordination —or more precisely over jurisdiction, over the claim to an exclusive right to ordain—is one which in Dissenting terms (it also appears beyond the borders of Dissent!) is a division between Presbyterianism and Independency. What Presbyterians regard as 'right ordering' is to Independents 'an imposing spirit'. The Assembly's express desire 'to act with the greatest uniformity'[2] is as typically Presbyterian as Ashwood's wish 'to be left to his liberty' is Independent.

In the notorious controversy over subscription to the doctrine of the Trinity, which in March 1719 led to the exclusion of a distinguished Exeter minister, James Peirce, from all the Exeter meeting-houses and trust funds, the Assembly was directly involved. In May it required subscription from its members and Peirce withdrew, together with eighteen others.[3] The tangled story—the correspondence between Exeter and London and the debate at Salters' Hall, where 'perished the good accord of English Dissent'[4]—has recently been unravelled by the Rev. Roger Thomas in an article in the *JEH*[5] and does not need telling again. Nor need I dwell on the 'Happy Union' of Presbyterian and Congregational ministers in London in March 1691. This also has been elucidated by Mr Thomas in his Hibbert Lecture[6] for 1962. I will only observe that the Exeter Assembly's first meeting took place within a few days of the London gathering and that at its second meeting all present 'consider'd, & assented to'[7] the *Heads of Agreement* adopted in London. I want rather to consider the evidence for the existence of Associations of ministers similar

[1] In 1711 a testator instructed his executrix to 'crave and follow the directions and advice of the Assembly of the Presbyterian Ministers that usually meet twice a year at Exon'; Brockett, 82.

[2] Brockett, 117.

[3] For the names of subscribers and non-subscribers, see F. J. Powicke, 'Arianism and the Exeter Assembly', in *Congregational Hist. Soc. Trans.*, VII (1916–18), 34–43.

[4] Alexander Gordon, in *DNB*, s.v. Thomas Bradbury.   [5] *JEH*, IV. 2.

[6] See Roger Thomas, 'The Break-up of Nonconformity' in G. F. Nuttall and others, *The Beginnings of Nonconformity*, 1964, 33–60.

[7] Brockett, 4.

to the Exeter Assembly in other parts of the country, and for their mutual awareness and support. The subject has not, I think, been previously investigated. Here also I shall often be following signposts provided by Mr Thomas.

To start where we are, in the South-West. The ministers in *Cornwall*, though invited in April 1693 by a Provincial Assembly of the 'United Brethren of the Counties of Devon, Somerset and Dorset' held at Exeter 'to unite, & associate themselves', did not revive the earlier Cornish Association. The Exeter Assembly acted for Cornwall. Launceston, Bodmin, St Ives, Looe, Liskeard, Truro, Falmouth, Penryn, and Penzance are among the congregations for which in its early years it accepted oversight; and from 1706 onwards its members commonly called themselves 'the United Brethren of Devon and Cornwall'.[1]

Somerset and *Dorset* we have just seen represented, with Devon, at a Provincial Assembly. Both counties sent delegates to the Exeter Assembly, though Dorset sent fewer and less regularly than did Somerset. Its representatives were present at other Provincial (or General) Assemblies: at Bristol and Taunton, for instance, in June and September 1690. In September 1696 Dorset was host to a Provincial Assembly at Sherborne. From the nature of correspondence between the Exeter Assembly and a congregation in Portsmouth in May 1716 it seems likely that in *Hampshire* there was then no Association; but that there had been one in 1691 appears from a sermon preached before it by a Portsmouth minister, Samuel Chandler, entitled *The Country's Concurrence with the London United Ministers in their late Heads of Agreement* (1691). An Association also existed in *Wiltshire*. In 1696 a Provincial Assembly was held in that county, at Bradford-on-Avon; and in 1690 it was reported in London that 'the ministers of Somerset-shire, Wiltshire and Glocestershire haue of late Sett up an association'.[2] This probably refers to a meeting held in Bristol in June 1690 and attended by thirty-six ministers from a number of counties, among them two from Wiltshire and two from Dorset.[3]

[1] Brockett, 13, 16, 60.
[2] *Freedom after Ejection*, ed. Alexander Gordon, Manchester 1917, 47.
[3] For their names, see Dr Williams's Library, Jollie MSS (cf. [Roger Thomas], *Thomas Jollie's Papers*, DWL Occasional Paper no. 3, [1956]), 12. 78.39, pr. by

At this meeting in Bristol more than half of those present were from *Somerset*, with John Moore of Bridgwater at their head. Of Moore Calamy relates that

he (together with Mr *Weeks* of *Bristol*, and Mr Alexander *Sinclare*, who fled thither from *Waterford* in *Ireland*, to escape the Rage of the *Papists* in the Reign of K. *James*), encourag'd the Ministers of *Somerset* first, and those of *Devon* afterwards, to assemble together, in stated Meetings, that they might maintain Order, Union, and Peace. He diligently attended the Assemblies in *Somerset* and sometimes even in his old-Age travell'd to those that were held in Exeter.[1]

Certainly for the Exeter Assembly's first ten years none of the numerous delegates from Somerset was more regular in attendance than Moore. Both the other men mentioned by Calamy, John Weeks of Bristol and Sinclair, who later returned to Ireland and became Moderator of the General Synod of Ulster, were also at this General Meeting in Bristol in June 1690; all three were at another General Meeting held at Taunton in September 1691, when Weeks was Moderator. Another Somerset leader present in Bristol was Robert Bartlet of Yeovil, of whom, though he did not go abroad as a delegate, Calamy says that he 'constantly attended the Associations of the Ministers in the County twice in the Year, and was of a very healing Spirit'.[2]

Calamy's statement that Somerset was the pioneer and associated even earlier than Devon can be substantiated. We have a number of letters about the movement for Association written to a friend in Lancashire, Thomas Jollie, by another of those present at the meeting in June 1690, Isaac Noble, the minister of the Congregational church at Castle Green, Bristol. In July 1690 Noble sent Jollie a document issued after a meeting of the Somerset ministers held on 24 June at Glastonbury; and in this document, which is signed by Sinclair as 'Register', it is stated that 'About 12 months agoe (alass! that it was soe late) wee began to consider,

Roger Thomas, *An Essay of Accommodation*, DWL Occasional Paper no. 6, 1957, 12, with identifications in n. 13; 'Will. Sloan, of Dorsetshire' died in 1716 as minister at Salisbury (DWL. Evans MS, 123).
[1] Edmund Calamy, *Continuation of the Account*, 1727, 412.
[2] *Ibid.* 431. This is the same Robert Bartlet as that mentioned above, p. 293, n. 3.

that our weak, shattered, and decaying condition required joynt counsell, and judged it our duty to Associate ourselves...Wee have meetings of whole, and half Countyes: and some of more Countyes, once a year.'[1] This puts the beginnings in Somerset as early as the summer of 1689. 'If we outrun London in this,' Noble writes proudly but generously, ''tis because they urged us not to stay for the precedence.' 'We all have cause to complain & be ashamd of a dull oscitancy [i.e. sluggishness] in our good M[aste]r's work.' In another letter he writes with equal magnanimity that the Devon ministers 'have far outgone us all, in a publick, catholick spirit'.[2]

From the single signature at the Bristol meeting of Daniel Higgs 'of Swanzey' it would be unwise to assume an Association in *South Wales*, especially since at this time Higgs was living in Worcestershire, where on 8 September 1691 he died.[3] For *Oxfordshire* there is also a solitary signature, that of Thomas Gilbert of Oxford; but in his case the words 'others absent' follow. For *Gloucestershire* there are six names, with that of James Forbes of Gloucester at their head. Like Flavell of Dartmouth and like Noble of Bristol, Forbes was an Independent; as a young man he had been present at the Congregational Savoy Conference of 1658. In September 1707, 'upon advice that the County of Gloucester hath not held Meetings of Ministers for several years,

[1] DWL MSS, 12.78.38. Somerset consisted of a Western and an Eastern Division; in September 1691 a Provincial Assembly attended by only two delegates from the Eastern Division 'resolv'd that they acquaint the Brethren of that Division that this Assembly is not well pleas'd that no more of them came hither, & that they desire more of them to attend such General Meetings, or greater Associations' (Brockett, 8).

[2] DWL MSS, 12.78.39 and 57. That the Somerset Association continued for some years is evident from the appearance of its fraternal delegates in the Exeter Assembly; from a reference to its meeting in 1711 at 'Siepton Malet' [Shepton Mallet] (Jeremy Owen, *Golwg ar y Beiau*, 58); and from sermons preached before it at Taunton by John Bowden, *Sermon*, 1714, and by John Davisson, *A Vindication of the Protestant Ministers Mission*, 1720. On 27 May 1708 Isaac Gilling preached before an Assembly of ministers from Somerset and Devon a sermon entitled *The Qualifications and Duties of Ministers* (Exeter 1708); this occasion is not noticed in his transcript of the Exeter Assembly's minutes.

[3] For Higgs's will, see R. T. Jones, 'Anghydffurfwyr Cymru, 1660–1662', in *Y Cofiadur*, XXXI (1962), 32–3.

that examinations of Candidates, & Ordinations are carried on by private hands, and that all things are in disorder', the Exeter Assembly wrote to Forbes desiring him 'to call upon your brethren in the Ministry of your neighbourhood and county to hold Assemblies at such times and places as shall be judged most convenient'. This letter, to which Forbes sent 'a thankful answer',[1] seems to have had an effect; at least we know that later, in 1711, the Gloucestershire Association was still meeting, for in that year Forbes preached before it at 'Stroudwater'[2] [Stroud] a sermon which after his death appeared in print.[3] Forbes also took part in the movement for Association beyond his own county. At a later General Assembly held in Bristol in May 1694 he served as Moderator; and from this meeting eleven articles, signed by him, desiring 'a General Correspondency betwixt all the United Ministers throughout the kingdom', were despatched not only to London but to Associations in various parts. They were copied by the scribe of the Exeter Assembly; they were also adopted by the ministers in Lancashire, one of them the Thomas Jollie of Altham on whose unpublished correspondence with Isaac Noble of Bristol I have been drawing, and among whose papers a copy of the articles has been preserved.[4]

Lancashire was well organized in four Divisions under the names Manchester, Warrington,[5] Bolton, and 'the North', the last of which covered an area from Lancaster and Preston, where meetings were held in 1691 and 1692, to Altham, near Whalley, where a meeting at Jollie's house was called in 1698.[6] General Meetings twice a year for the whole county were held now in one centre, now in another, Preston or Blackburn being chosen as a centre for 'the North'. The minutes of the fifteen General Meetings held

1 Brockett, 66, 68.
2 Edmund Calamy, *Continuation of the Account*, 1727, 500.
3 It precedes his funeral sermon by I[saac] N[oble] in the composite volume entitled *Pastoral Instruction*, 1713.
4 Brockett, 19–21; DWL MSS, 12.78.52; Chetham Society, new series, XXIV, 352.
5 For a transcript of the Minutes of eight meetings (1719–22) of the Warrington Division, made in 1888 from a manuscript at Renshaw Street (now Ullet Road) Unitarian Church, Liverpool, see DWL MSS 38.56. Cf. Chetham Society, n.s., XXXIII, 106–15.
6 DWL MSS, 12.78.40, 58, 10.

during the period from April 1693 to August 1700 are preserved in the Chetham Library at Manchester and have been published by the Chetham Society.[1]

Of the Association in the *West Riding of Yorkshire* little is known save that its meetings continued for a hundred years: in 1781 William Wood, Joseph Priestley's successor at Mill Hill Chapel, Leeds, preached before it at Bradford a sermon on *The Christian Duty of Cultivating a Spirit of Universal Benevolence* (Leeds 1781). We do, however, know who were the twenty ministers present at the inaugural meeting held at Wakefield on 2 September 1691.[2] All were from the West Riding. Since the prime mover in Yorkshire, with whom Jollie was in touch,[3] was Oliver Heywood of Northowram, Halifax, it is not surprising that a dozen others came from the Halifax–Leeds–Wakefield triangle. Six were from Sheffield or its neighbourhood. The twentieth, whose name stands first, was the eminent tutor of candidates for the ministry, Richard Frankland, whose academy circumstances had forced to be peripatetic but who since 1689 had returned to Yorkshire where he now lived comparatively free from prosecution at his own home at Rathmell, Giggleswick. Frankland, like Jollie, was in correspondence with Noble of Bristol; one of Noble's letters to Jollie also was to be 'imparted to good Mr Frankland'.[4]

The *Cheshire* Association (or Classis, as from soon after its formation it inexactly termed itself), in which an 'accumulating influence' was exercised by Matthew Henry, met twice a year, usually at Knutsford. It is like the Exeter Assembly in two ways. First, its earliest minutes (1691–1745) have been published, though they are far less full, being, as their editor remarks, 'in the nature of reminiscences rather than of records taken at the Meetings'.[5] Secondly, in amalgamation since 1765 with the Lancashire

---

[1] Chetham Society, new series, XXIV, 349–64.
[2] Cf. Joseph Hunter, *The Rise of the Old Dissent*, 1842, 373–5, from Heywood's manuscripts.   [3] Cf. DWL MSS, 12.78.8b.
[4] DWL MSS, 12.78.37, cf. 57. Noble was also in correspondence with Wales: for a letter of 28 July 1711 from him and his colleague George Fownes (here misprinted Townes), translated into Welsh, see Jeremy Owen, *Golwg ar y Beiau*, 59–60.
[5] *Cheshire Classis Minutes 1691–1745*, ed. Alexander Gordon, 1919, 178, 126.

Provincial Assembly, it is still in existence, though (again like the Exeter Assembly) it has for long consisted of Unitarians only.

Geographically speaking, these Northern Associations accepted a broader basis of membership than was permitted in Devon. Some ministers were members of both the Cheshire and the Lancashire Associations at one and the same time;[1] and the Cheshire Association welcomed ministers not only from other adjacent counties such as Derbyshire, Staffordshire, Shropshire and Denbighshire but from Warwickshire and Yorkshire. If a reason for this greater flexibility is to be sought, it may lie in the fact that some years earlier Jollie and others had taken part in an Association of ministers and 'messengers' from Congregational churches only, but (perhaps on that account) from a number of counties. Among the Jollie manuscripts is 'A brief account of the proceedings of the messengers of the Associated Churches in... Yorkshire, Lancashire and Cheshire' at meetings during 1674, which adopted the Congregational *Savoy Declaration* of 1658;[2] and also a 'Declaration of the sense of the associated Congregational Churches in the West Riding of Yorkshire, in Lancashire, Cheshire, Darbyshire and Nottinghamshire' issued at Sheffield as far back as September 1658, immediately before the conference at the Savoy, at which, like Forbes of Gloucester, Jollie was present.[3]

A comprehensive survey of published sermons[4] might be expected to reveal the existence of other Associations. To give one example: in a sermon by Joseph Dodson, *Moderation and*

[1] For four ministers with this double membership, *ibid.* 143.
[2] DWL MSS, 12.78.13. On 18 February 1677/8 Jollie wrote to Increase Mather, 'Wee kept up our Association-meetings for some time at two severall seasons, viz. before the change [i.e. 1660] and since, but it's now a long while since I could gett a meeting of the churches in these northern parts': *Massachusetts Hist. Soc. Collections*, 4th series, VIII, 321.
[3] DWL MSS, 12.78.1. Cf. Chetham Society, n.s. XXXIII, 129. Gordon remarks that in Cheshire in 1691 Matthew Henry's 'Chester flock was...the only one in the county distinctively Presbyterian': *Cheshire Classis*, 122–3.
[4] Much assistance may be gained from *Early Nonconformity 1566–1800: a catalogue of books in Dr Williams's Library, London*, Boston, Mass.: G. K. Hall, 1968, Subject Catalogue, *s.vv.* Associations and United Ministers.

Charity (1720), preached at Keswick, we learn of meetings of a *Cumberland & Westmorland* Association during 1718 and 1719; in 1769 a sermon entitled *Numbers no Criterion of Truth* (Whitehaven [1769]) was preached by Radcliffe Scholefield before a General Meeting for Cumberland held at Keswick; and as late as 1780 a *Sermon on the Nature of Christ's Kingdom* (Newcastle 1781) was preached by Robert Hood before a General Meeting held at Penrith.[1] There can be no doubt that these Associations of Dissenting ministers[2] were numerous and in close touch one with another, and that their influence was considerable. In every case their main concern was with ordination and good order.

To turn from the Associations of the 1690s to those of the 1790s is to step into another world. In 1790 Benjamin Francis, minister of the Baptist church at Horsley, Gloucestershire, and a leading member of the Baptist Western Association, published a poem entitled 'The Association' (who can imagine a member of the Exeter Assembly writing a poem on the Assembly?). Its definitions and repudiations tell as much as its more positive ideals.

> Not the vain tribe, assembled at the ball,
> Or glittering late, like glow-worms, at Vaux-hall,
> Or staring wild around the frantic stage,
> At mimic forms of mimic love and rage,...
> Nor the grave synod, grave in *garb* I mean,
> Where lords of conscience and her rights convene,
> Where superstition sanctifies old creeds,
> And priestcraft triumphs in oppressive deeds;...
> The sacred page thy only rule and guide,
> 'Thus saith the Lord' shall thy debates decide;
> While charity wide spreads her balmy wings
> O'er different notions, in indifferent things,
> And graceful order, walking hand in hand
> With cheerful freedom, leads her willing band...

[1] For a reference in 1752 to 'the friendly association of the two counties', see James Daye, *The Christian's Service, Compleated with Honour*, [1752], 19, and n.*.
[2] Since 1826 the Lancashire & Cheshire Assembly has admitted laymen to membership.

In thee, impartial discipline maintains
Harmonious order, but aloud disclaims
All human force to rule the human mind,
Impose opinions, and the conscience bind.[1]

In these 1790 Associations sermons are still preached, but almost everything else is different; and the sermons are evangelical, as are the circular letters issued under such titles as Christian Experience, Christian Patience, The Doctrines of Grace, The Work of the Spirit, or On Truth and Error, warning against 'two errors in particular, which in our day prevail', 'the leaven of Arminianism' and 'the baneful and pernicious poison of Antinomianism'.[2] The founders of the 1690 Associations, Flavell of Dartmouth, Forbes of Gloucester, Jollie of Altham, Heywood of Northowram, Frankland of Rathmell, and the rest, were elderly men seeking with a poignant nostalgia and incredulity to recover and to conserve the church order which they had practised when in the livings from which thirty years earlier they had been ejected. If they were on the defensive, who that knows what they suffered will blame them? They were seasoned timber, guarding their memories, dignified, quiet—there is something fine about a still December day. But in the 1790 Associations is the hopefulness and hidden excitement,

the first blushings and tender flushings of spring.

The ministers who are the leaders and who have additional meetings on their own (though in the churches' 'messengers', as those duly appointed as representatives were called, *these* Associations have lay members also) are often young men, outward-looking, adventurous, expectant, out to convert, not conserve. They believe in and practise church order, or discipline as they term it; they regularly take part in ordinations, though they claim no jurisdiction; but their prime concern is mission, to the dark corners of the land or of that more distant world on which William Carey looked out through his small cottage window at Moulton in Northamptonshire.

The oldest of these Baptist Associations were the Western,

[1] *Baptist Annual Register*, ed. John Rippon, I (1794), following p. 16. For Francis, see *Dict. of Welsh Biography* (1959).   [2] *Ibid.* I, 56.

comprising Gloucestershire, Wiltshire, Somerset, Devon, and Cornwall, which had met regularly since 1690 and in 1752 was the first to publish its minutes;[1] the Midland, comprising the West Midlands, also from 1690 but for long 'just an annual social meeting';[2] the small Northern from 1691, but with its 'documents lacking 1727–40';[3] and the York and Lancashire, which 'had first met in 1695, but its meetings were sporadic till 1786'.[4] The Northampton Association, which stretched from Nottingham-shire to Hertfordshire, was formed in 1765;[5] the Norfolk and Suffolk in 1769;[6] and the Kent and Sussex in 1779.[7] The successive meetings of the Northampton Association in June 1791 at Oak-ham, when 'Brother Carey (lately ordained at Leicester) con-cluded in prayer', and in May 1792 at Nottingham, when Carey preached from the text 'Enlarge the place of thy tent' and it was resolved to form a missionary society,[8] were thus long after the Association's foundation; but from its beginning, and especially after a sermon by Andrew Fuller of Kettering and an appeal by John Sutcliffe of Olney at a meeting at Nottingham in 1784,[9] the Northampton Association had issued calls to prayer for the revival of religion. By the 1790s the other Associations, including those founded earlier, were equally evangelical and were fully in sympathy with Northampton's missionary initiative. This is

[1] See J. G. Fuller, *Brief History of the Western Association*, Bristol 1845; *Baptist Bibliography*, ed. W. T. Whitley, 1916, I, 171, item 21–752. For its earlier history, see my 'The Baptist Western Association, 1653–1658', in *JEH*, XI. 2, 213–18; cf. also B. R. White, 'The Organisation of the Particular Baptists, 1644–1660', *ibid*. XVII. 2, 209–26.

[2] W. T. Whitley, *Baptist Association Life in Worcestershire, 1655–1926*, Worcester 1926, 6–7.

[3] W. T. Whitley, 'Association Life till 1815', in *Baptist Hist. Soc. Trans.*, v (1916–17), 29.

[4] A. C. Underwood, *History of the English Baptists*, 1947, 172.

[5] See T. S. H. Elwyn, *The Northamptonshire Baptist Association*, 1964.

[6] Cf. *Baptist Annual Register*, I. 62.

[7] W. T. Whitley, 'Association Life till 1815', 31. For Wales, see Joshua Thomas, *History of the Baptist Association in Wales, 1650–1790*, 1795; and app. 3 to the enlarged English translation of *Hanes y Bedyddwyr* by Thomas preserved in manuscript at Bristol Baptist College.

[8] Cf. *Baptist Annual Register*, I, 199, 419; for Carey's ordination, 519; for the form-ation of the missionary society, 375; for Carey's engaging to go to India, 485.

[9] Cf. E. A. Payne, *The Prayer Call of 1784*, 1941.

evident from the fact that they at once appointed representatives to receive subscriptions for the Baptist Missionary Society.[1]

Since 1719, and increasingly as the Presbyterians, content with the sobriquet 'Rational Dissenters', proved impervious to the Revival, the Independents had turned away from them towards the Baptists. In the later eighteenth century a Baptist minister may often be found taking part in an Independent ordination or preaching a funeral sermon for an Independent minister; an Independent meeting-house will be lent to the Baptists for baptisms, as at Northampton when Carey was baptized, or for the meeting of a Baptist Association, as at Ross-on-Wye in 1791.[2] In Bedfordshire relations had been close ever since Bunyan's day; and the Bedfordshire Union of Christians,[3] as it was ecumenically named, which was formed in 1797 by a company of Independents, was almost at once joined by a number of Baptists, among them John Sutcliffe of the Northampton Baptist Association. Evidently no objection was taken to membership of more than one Association at the same time—a thing so improper as to be impossible for the Exeter Assembly. The 1790s, just a century after the formation of the earlier Presbyterian Associations, saw a burst of fresh Independent Associations, formed on a narrower geographical base than the Baptists' but on the same pattern and with the same intent. In 1793 an Association was formed in Warwickshire; in 1795 in Dorset; in 1796 in Shropshire, Somerset and Derbyshire & Nottinghamshire; in 1797 in Bedfordshire, Wiltshire, and Surrey; in 1798 in Berkshire and Essex.[4] In every case their purpose was, in the words of the Somerset Association formed on 10 November 1796 at South Petherton, a 'missionary-design' for 'village-preaching'.[5] In the circular letter written by Dr Edward Williams,[6] then minister of the Congregational church at Carr's

[1] Cf. *Baptist Annual Register*, I, 531.   [2] *Ibid*. 206.
[3] For this, see John Brown and David Prothero, *History of the Bedfordshire Union of Christians*, 1946.
[4] See R. T. Jones, *Congregationalism in England 1662–1962*, 1962, 175, with n. 2; and for the Derbys. & Notts. Association, Maurice Phillips, *Family Instruction*, Doncaster 1799.
[5] *Evangelical Magazine*, 1797, 117–18.
[6] See W. T. Owen, *Edward Williams, D.D. 1750–1813*, Cardiff 1963.

Lane, Birmingham, and issued from the second meeting of the Warwickshire Association held on 6 August 1793 at Nuneaton, missionary work abroad was also urged; and from this letter, or the convictions which prompted it, came, much as had happened among the Baptists, the foundation two years later of the (London) Missionary Society.

Through the County Associations Williams also worked for a National Association; and on 18 May 1808 a 'General Congregational Union' was formed in London, Williams preaching before it a sermon published under the title *Christian Unanimity Recommended* (1808). 'Is it any thing similar to an episcopal or presbyterian government among independents?' Williams asked; 'nothing of the kind'. Two years later the Baptists followed with a 'General Union', still 'to encourage and support our missions'. Each Union expressly disclaimed 'all interference with, or control over, congregational discipline', 'all manner of superiority and superintendence over the churches; or any authority, or power, to impose'.[1] There seems some irony in the fact that the Baptists and Independents thus succeeded in organizing themselves nationally, when the Presbyterians had failed to do so. The two 'General Unions' served as models for the Congregational Union of England and Wales[2] and the Baptist Union of Great Britain and Ireland, each of which dates from 1831. With their formation, three years after the repeal of the Test and Corporation Acts, a new period in the history of Dissent may be held to begin.

The difference in character between the Associations of the 1690s and those of the 1790s is dramatic. The change did not, of course, come about suddenly. To show it actually taking place is made difficult both by the variations in its date and by discontinuity in the material so far discovered. For the most part the new Associations do not come into existence until after the old Associations have ceased to function. The congregations whose ministers and 'messengers' compose the new Associations are also

---

[1] Edward Williams, *Christian Unanimity Recommended*, 1808, 13–14; E. A. Payne, *The Baptist Union: a short history*, 1958, 24–5.

[2] See Albert Peel, *These Hundred Years: a history of the Congregational Union*, 1931.

rarely the same as those whose ministers (alone) compose the old; they are generally either Independent secessions from these or have suffered a Presbyterian secession or else are entirely new. Much might be learned from comparative study of the two Associations which in the same geographical area can claim a significant continuous existence, the Exeter Assembly and the Baptist Western Association. From 1719 the Western Association was in a state of 'storm for fourteen years'; 'in 1732 a division took place',[1] which left the orthodox in the majority. In the Exeter Assembly,which in 1719 had expelled James Peirce for declining doctrinal subscription, events worked the other way: in 1753 the Assembly itself resolved to abandon any doctrinal test before ordination. Unfortunately for the crucial decade 1753–63 the minutes have not survived; 'from then onwards', however, Mr Brockett writes, 'the impression gained from reading them is very different'.[2]

In few areas, it seems, were rival Associations in existence during the same period—perhaps only in Wales and in the North Midlands. In Wales after 1757, when they withdrew from the Academy at Carmarthen to found their own orthodox Academy at Brecon, the Independents also met separately in Association on a doctrinal basis. This was obnoxious to the older and continuing Association, and a pamphlet war ensued.[3] In the North Midlands a Presbyterian Association met at Nottingham in 1738, when a member of the Cheshire Classis, James Clegg, the minister at Chinley, near Chapel-en-le-Frith in Derbyshire, preached before

---

[1] W. T. Whitley, 'Association Life till 1815', in *Baptist Hist. Soc. Trans.*, v (1916–17), 28–9.

[2] Brockett, *Nonconformity in Exeter*, 131. Dr Edwin Welch kindly provides references to an orthodox, missionary, Plymouth Association in rivalry with the Exeter Assembly during the years 1798–1808: Batter Street, Plymouth, Congregational Church account book, fol. 14v, 18v, 19 and 24v (Plymouth Public Library, Acc. 168/9); and Diary of Thomas Almond of Devonport (Moravian Church House, London).

[3] See [Benjamin Davies], *Vindication of the Conduct of the Associated Ministers of Wales*, Carmarthen 1771; for elucidation of the issues, cf. R. T. Jones, 'Trefniadaeth Ryngeglwysig yr Annibynwyr' in *Y Cofiadur*, XXI (1951), 40–4, reprinting (in English) the Independents' 'Proposals' and the Presbyterians' 'Declaration and Protest', or more summarily his *Hanes Annibynwyr Cymru*, Abertawe 1966, 162–3.

it on *The Things That Make for Peace* (Nottingham 1738).[1] At this time meetings, usually at Bolsover, were also being held by a number of 'ministers and messengers' of Independent churches in Derbyshire, Nottinghamshire, and Sheffield who, after a series of secessions on doctrinal grounds *before* 1719, had formed their own Association, probably in 1720. In 1728 they were discussing the question 'What means are to be used for the Reviveing and Promoting Primitive Christianity?' and calling for 'Solemn Prayer to God in each Respective Church for the Poureing forth of the Spirit'.[2]

One does not quite expect this as early as 1728. We have not, in fact, done much more than climb two hills which look across to each other. In the 1790s another, lower, hill may be seen rising, a little apart, in 'the first Unitarian association in England',[3] formed in 1791; but the large and marshy plain between still calls to be explored.

[1] This Association may have been the one for whose formation on 27 November 1697 at Malcoffe, near Ford, Derbyshire, there is evidence in the manuscript diary of William Bagshaw preserved by his descendants at Ford Hall, Chapel-en-le-Frith: see Reginald Mansfield, 'The Development of Independency in Derbyshire', Manchester Ph.D. thesis, 1951, p. 120; but I have not discovered evidence of meetings in the intervening forty years.

[2] For this Association, which met regularly till at least 1767, see A. R. Henderson, *History of Castle Gate Congregational Church, Nottingham, 1655–1905*, 1905, ch. VIII; and Reginald Mansfield, 'The Development of Independency in Derbyshire', pp. 108–13. For a transcript of the material concerning the Association preserved in the church book at Castle Gate, which was a member of the Association, I have to thank Dr Mansfield.

[3] E. M. Wilbur, *History of Unitarianism*, Cambridge, Mass., 1946–52, II, 343.

THE CONVOCATION OF 1710:
AN ANGLICAN ATTEMPT AT
COUNTER-REVOLUTION

by G. V. BENNETT

THE Revolution of 1688 began for the clergy of the Church
of England an era of grave crisis. It was not merely that the
deposition of James II had posed for many of them a critical
question of conscience. More serious were the effects of the
Toleration Act of 1689 which quickly showed themselves in
diminished attendances at church, and in a marked decline in the
authority and status of the parish priest. By its literal provisions
the act permitted dissenters a bare liberty to worship in their own
way; but, as interpreted by successive administrations and by the
great majority of the laity, it effected an ecclesiastical revolution.[1]
Although various statutes required all Englishmen to attend their
parish-church each Sunday, and though the act merely permitted
them to go to a meeting-house instead, it was widely held after
1689 that church-attendance was voluntary. The ecclesiastical
courts continued to exercise their traditional jurisdiction in matri-
monial, probate, and faculty causes, and over the clergy; but their
coercive authority over the morals and religious duties of the laity
became virtually impossible to enforce. Likewise the Toleration
Act gave no permission for dissenting education, but bishops
found legal obstacles put in their way when they tried to assert
their right to license all schools and teachers. In 1695 the official
censorship of books was allowed to lapse and, though it remained
hazardous to libel ministers of the Crown, it became to all intents
allowable to defame the ministers of God and to deride orthodox
religious formulations. Amid the heavy taxation of the years of

[1] For a fuller account of the conditions of William's reign, see G. V. Bennett,
'Conflict in the Church', in *Britain after the Glorious Revolution* (ed. Geoffrey
Holmes), 1969.

King William's War the clergy seem to have fared very badly; and a decline in their economic position was generally noted.

By 1701 the Anglican clergy were possessed of a deep sense of betrayal at the hands of politicians and the bench of bishops. At the heart of the famous 'convocation controversy' was an attempt to revert to the conditions of the past by asserting their 'rights, powers, and privileges' according to the strictly legal terms of the Church's establishment. Led by Francis Atterbury, the stormy petrel of the High Church movement, a group of insistent propagandists began to agitate for a sitting and acting convocation to punish heretics and redefine the legal position of the national Church. Although the Convocation of Canterbury met in 1701 and in subsequent years down to 1708, its activities were clearly deeply embarrassing to the ministry of the Earl of Godolphin; and, by tacit agreement between the queen's ministers and Archbishop Tenison of Canterbury, the efforts of the High Church divines were tempered, thwarted, and brought to nothing.

But in the autumn of 1710 all this was changed, and there seemed a unique opportunity to use Convocation to put into effect a counter-revolution. The great Sacheverell trial had roused the Tories, both clerical and lay, to new heights of party feeling; and Godolphin's ministry, with its Whig and 'moderate' ecclesiastical support, had disintegrated. In November a 'country Tory' majority of overwhelming proportions was returned to the Commons and news came of considerable High Church successes in the proctorial elections for Convocation. In the weeks before the opening of the synod on 25 November there was on all sides expectation of a great ecclesiastical conflict. For Francis Atterbury in particular, this was a moment long awaited when he could put into effect a programme of measures designed to revive the Church's influence. He was not, of course, so sanguine as to imagine that this could be done by the authority of Convocation alone. Only statute had the binding force required, and thus he planned a working partnership between the prolocutor of the Lower House and the speaker of the House of Commons. The method was to be that employed at the Restoration. The Crown would license Convocation to discuss and draw up proposals for reform;

these in the form of draft bills would be embodied in a petition to the queen, and by her referred to the Commons who would initiate the legislative process. The whole procedure would require much management behind the scenes; it would need the co-operation of the queen and the ministry, and at least the acquiescence of the bishops. But Atterbury's prime cause of confidence lay in his friendship with William Bromley, the Tories' candidate for the speakership. Since the end of September they had been in close correspondence and in agreement that the lay and clerical campaigns must work in strict accord [1]

On the evening before the formal opening of Convocation on 25 November Atterbury held a meeting of his allies, and was delighted to learn not only that he would have under his command no less than sixty members against the archbishop's forty, but that they were unanimous that he should be prolocutor.[2] If what they had to do could be done peaceably, he would be content. 'There may be', he confided to a friend, 'some hopes of healing the breach, and compromising matters so far, as to proceed jointly on matters of public importance. A little time will show whether there be any grounds for these hopes.'[3] But in this he was clearly too optimistic. The archbishop's party was not against all reform; but they were deeply afraid of an all-out Tory regime in the Church, and many of them detested Atterbury personally. They were especially apprehensive that he might use Convocation to obtain a synodical endorsement of high-flying political theory. As the day drew near, Tenison, old and almost continually in pain, became more and more agitated. Urgent consultations took place with the Whig ex-ministers. 'God grant', groaned Bishop Wake of Lincoln, 'that things may go better than we fear.' On 11 November a meeting at Lambeth took the fateful decision to defy Atterbury and obstruct his programme: 'to set up a prolocutor;

---

[1] *The Epistolary Correspondence of Francis Atterbury* (ed. J. Nichols), 1789–99 [hereafter referred to as 'Atterbury *EC*'], I, 444–5: Bromley to Atterbury, 23 Sept. 1710.

[2] National Library of Wales, Ottley MSS 1534 and 1535: Atterbury to Adam Ottley, 2 and 24 Nov. 1710.

[3] Bodleian MS Eng. Th. c. 24, fo. 634: Atterbury to Thomas Brett, 7 Nov. 1710.

to get an address ready that shall meddle in no state affairs'.[1] On the 25th in St Paul's their fears were realized. Atterbury was elected to the chair by an overwhelming majority, and the triumphant Tory divines went to the length of trying to suppress all mention that there had been another candidate, Richard Willis, dean of Lincoln. On that evening Wake and other bishops drew up a formal Latin petition to the archbishop, praying him to quash the election of a man who was 'not only a disturber of the peace of the Church, but indeed the principal enemy of our order and authority'.[2] Although Tenison thought it the better part of valour to disregard his suffragans' request, he was deeply unhappy. When on 24 January the queen issued a Royal Licence which failed to acknowledge in full his position as president of the whole Convocation, his suspicions turned to determined resistance.[3] His supporters in the Lower House, led by White Kennett, dean of Peterborough, were commissioned to obstruct Atterbury's every step.

But it was not only the Whigs and their clerical adjutants who were thus fearful of an attempt at counter-revolution. Both the queen and her new chief minister, Robert Harley, were determined to avoid increased party conflict. Indeed Anne, who detested quarrels among the clergy, was at first unwilling to allow the Convocation to proceed to business at all. Harley, of course, knew that this was politically inexpedient, and he compromised with the queen by promising that the topics should be 'such as shall be first agreed upon, and they are to know that they are on their good behaviour; should they be extravagant, they can hurt none but themselves, and are easily sent going'.[4] Anne's friend and confessor, Archbishop Sharp of York, was called in to see that Atterbury did not go to extremes; and, though the Convocation

---

[1] Christ Church, Oxford, Wake MSS 17: Tenison to Wake, 10 Oct. 1710; Surrey County R.O., Somers MSS E/32: Sunderland to Somers, 6 Nov. 1710; Lambeth Palace MS 1770: the diary of William Wake, fo. 100, 8 Nov. 1710.

[2] Wake MSS 18, no foliation.

[3] On 28 Feb. the Upper House petitioned and obtained from the queen an 'explanation' of the licence which in some measure restored Tenison's position. See N. Sykes, *William Wake*, 1957, I, 125–30.

[4] *Hardwicke State Papers* (ed. Philip Yorke), 1778, II, 485: a memorandum for the queen, written by Harley and dated 30 Oct. 1710.

of Canterbury was no proper concern of his, he proceeded to hold meetings with leading Tory ministers and moderately minded Tory bishops. Atterbury was distinctly vexed to be summoned in and informed that the agenda were to be limited to a discussion of heretical books, the practice of excommunication in the church courts, and the project of a union with the Lutheran Church in Prussia. It is clear that he put up a spirited resistance and further meetings had to be held.[1] When at last on 13 January the royal letters of business were formally communicated to the Convocation they bore the mark of the prolocutor's success. Though the topics might at first have appeared innocuous, they provided an opportunity to build up a programme of draft bills on all the major subjects of clerical grievance. The queen proposed: 'the drawing up a Representation of the present state of religion among us, with regard to the late excessive growth of infidelity, heresy and profaneness'; regulating the practice of excommunication; preparing new 'occasional offices'; establishing the jurisdiction of rural deans; providing for 'more exact terriers and accounts of glebes, tithes and other possessions and profits belonging to benefices'; and regulating the issue of marriage licences. Before the lower clergy withdrew from the Upper House, Atterbury paused to address an urgent plea to the archbishop that there should be no delay in executing business which the queen had committed to them; and that joint-committees of both houses should at once be set up to consider separately each head of the royal proposals.[2]

The succeeding months, from February round to April, proved a time of the most wearisome labour. The committees met two or three times a week, and moved at a veritable snail's pace. Atterbury found himself sitting for hours in protracted discussion, and writing and rewriting the texts of reports. He seems to have

[1] T. Sharp, *The Life of John Sharp, Archbishop of York*, 2 vols., 1825, I, 531–3, for extracts from the archbishop's diary, now lost.
[2] The convocation sessions of 1710–11 are described in W. Pittis, *The History of the Present Parliament and Convocation*, 1711 [hereafter referred to as 'Pittis'], and in *The Proceedings of the Lower House of Convocation* (1713). A valuable and detailed record is to be found in the diary of White Kennett for 1710–14, British Museum Lansdowne MSS 1024.

savoured to the full the irrelevant verbosity of the lower clergy
and irritation with episcopal scruple over minor details. From
time to time deadlocked committees met at his house, and he
persuaded them to return to constructive work. But by the end
of March encouraging progress had been made. The joint-
committees had reached the point of composing draft parliamentary bills.[1] With regard to the church courts, detailed regulations
were drawn up as to their fees and procedures; and it was proposed
to increase their effectiveness by making it easier for the ecclesiastical judge to call in the assistance of the civil power. The
old draconic writ 'de excommunicato capiendo', which could
only be used against serious offenders who had first been
solemnly excommunicated, was to be replaced by a more
generally useful writ 'de contumaci capiendo' by which even
minor recalcitrants might be committed to prison until they
promised obedience. To protect the interests of the clergy from
the depredations of patrons and tithepayers, attested certificates
of the rights and revenues of each benefice were to be drawn up,
and these were to be admissible as evidence in the civil courts.
The issue of marriage (and by implication all other) licences was
to be regulated and put more firmly under episcopal control and
less in the hands of local legal functionaries. Reports were ready
containing recommendations about charity schools, new forms of
services, and the extent to which rural deans could be given a
disciplinary jurisdiction akin to that of an archdeacon. It was a not
unimpressive achievement, and Atterbury planned to have his
drafts and reports ready to be laid before the queen soon after
the Easter recess.[2]

The method by which this preparatory work was to be turned
into legislation was revealed on 28 February, when Atterbury
proposed to the Lower House that he, as prolocutor, should pay
a formal visit to Bromley, as speaker of the House of Commons.[3]
In the previous week, by Bromley's management, a Commons
committee had been set up to consider the shortage of church

[1] For copies of draft bills, see Lambeth Palace MSS 929, fos. 105–19.
[2] BM Lansdowne MSS 1013, fo. 150: Kennett to Blackwell, 17 Mar. 1710/11.
[3] Atterbury EC, IV, 304–6; Pittis, pp. 134–6, 166.

accommodation in the rapidly expanding areas of London and its suburbs. Accordingly on 1 March, accompanied by a body of leading Tory divines, Atterbury waited on the speaker to convey the thanks of 'the whole clergy of this province' for the gesture, and to offer any information or assistance which might be required. On being informed of the visit, the Commons proceeded to resolve that they would 'have a particular regard to such applications as shall at any time be made to them from the clergy in convocation assembled, according to ancient usage, together with this parliament'. On 10 March Bromley announced to the House that Atterbury had been with him the previous evening and had 'delivered to him a scheme of the number of churches and chapels and meeting-houses, within twenty-seven of those parishes in and near the cities of London and Westminster, and the suburbs thereof, where additional churches were judged to be most wanted'.[1] On the 26th the Convocation petitioned the queen to favour the project, and she graciously commended it to Parliament. Such was the origin of the famous act for the Fifty New Churches of 1711, which was to inaugurate the greatest church-building project of the Augustan age. Later, in September, Atterbury was to be one of the distinguished body of commissioners, Tories almost to a man, who were to convert the proceeds of a parliamentary tax on coal into the fabric of new churches. In the end only twelve of the fifty new churches were built, but even these, cool, classical, and ample structures by Vanbrugh, Hawksmoor, and Archer, stand as memorials to a brief moment when a great revival of the Church's influence seemed possible.

But after the Easter recess the situation suddenly looked much less favourable. All during the spring months the country gentlemen in the Commons had been agitating for their own version of Tory counter-revolution and for the expulsion of all known Whigs from public office. It was only by his characteristic methods of devious manoeuvre and feigned agreement that Harley could contain their attack. But on 8 March he suffered a seeming disaster

---

[1] On 20 March Atterbury received a reprimand from the secretary-of-state, Lord Dartmouth, for having acted without consulting the queen: Atterbury *EC*, IV, 304.

which proved to be a piece of amazing good fortune, when he was stabbed in the council chamber by a French spy under interrogation. A wave of sympathy re-established his political position, and (with the queen's aid) he felt strong enough to deal firmly with Tories like Henry St John and Francis Atterbury who aimed at radical measures. When convocation reassembled after Easter the life and heart had gone out of the High Church party. Perhaps Atterbury had driven his troops too hard, perhaps political events had unnerved them, but soon numbers diminished and were insufficient for the petitions to the queen.[1] Now to those wearied by the intricacies of reform, a new and exciting issue appeared in the person of William Whiston. In 1711 this controversial professor of mathematics at Cambridge had added to his reputation for colourful eccentricity by publishing a book, *An Historical Preface to Primitive Christianity Revived*, wherein he declared that the Christology of the pre-Nicene fathers was akin to that of Arius rather than to that of Athanasius. What could not be forgiven was his sheer effrontery in dedicating his heterodox work 'to the clergy of the province of Canterbury in convocation assembled'; and soon both bishops and presbyters were caught up in the heady excitement of a heresy hunt. Atterbury was as fierce as anyone in his anger against Whiston, but he looked on with dismay as time and energy were consumed. All other business fell away as the two Houses pored over copies of the book, and became entangled in the immensely complex question of how far a provincial convocation could conduct a trial for heresy.

At the end of May, as the town became hot and uncomfortable, Atterbury realized that his programme was doomed. In place of legislation he would have to be content with words. The queen's letter of business had authorized the drawing up of a 'Representation of the State of Religion', and he determined that this should be a comprehensive statement of the full Tory case. If possible it should accompany a similar 'Representation of the State of the Nation' from his friends in the Commons. All agree that the document which emerged from the joint-committee was of

---

[1] BM Lansdowne MSS 1013, fo. 146: Kennett to Blackwell, 22 May 1711; Hist. MSS Comm., *Portland MSS.*, VII, 30.

Atterbury's composition. It remains still the classic expression of Tory ecclesiastical doctrine, written in an emphatic and denunciatory style; and it may stand in place of the legislative programme which failed. The remedies, he wrote, were clear. 'The law, which makes those who abstain from all sorts of religious assemblies still obnoxious to punishment' must be 'exerted in its utmost force.' The press must be put under control, and 'the present excessive and scandalous liberty of printing wicked books at home, and importing them from abroad' must be ended. Convocation must be stirred up afresh so that 'some way might be found to restore the discipline of the Church, now so much relaxed and decayed, to its pristine life and vigour; and to strengthen the ordinary jurisdiction of the ecclesiastical courts'. Dissenters must be kept within the strict terms of the Toleration Act. Although Atterbury managed to obtain an enthusiastic acceptance of his draft in the Lower House, it was clear that the bishops as a whole would not co-operate. The *Representation* was never presented to Queen Anne and had to be printed as a private paper.

When Convocation was prorogued on 12 June, amid a display of bitter words and bad temper, it was clear that the High Church project had failed. Such were the internecine struggles of Tories and churchmen in later years that there was never again an opportunity as favourable as that of the session of 1710–11. The bid for counter-revolution had come to nothing, partly because of the covert opposition of queen and minister, and partly because the issue touched upon the party animosities of an embittered era. But in the long run it had no success because the Tory vision of a union of Church and State in a single authoritarian regime was itself a thing of the past. In the eighteenth-century age of reason and natural religion it could not endure.

LAYMEN IN SYNOD:
AN ASPECT OF THE BEGINNINGS
OF SYNODICAL GOVERNMENT
IN SOUTH AFRICA

by PETER HINCHLIFF

EVEN quite eminent Tractarians tended to think that, however impossible things might be in the Church of England,
the colonies provided the sort of field where they could
create the kind of Church in which they really believed. That
Church would follow patristic patterns, of course, would be free
from the nexus of establishment, and would be governed by
synods. As regards South Africa they nourished particularly high
hopes. Robert Gray, the first Bishop of Cape Town, was cam-
paigning for synodical government, the creation of ecclesiastical
courts to replace the Erastian Privy Council, and to check and
outlaw the heresy of Bishop Colenso. It looked so very much as
though this were a situation—heresiarchs and councils locked in
battle—straight out of the pages of early church history. So when
Gray lost his case against Colenso in the Privy Council in 1855,
Dr Pusey wrote in a letter to the *Churchman*, 'It is no loss to us
that it is discovered that the Queen had no power to give the
temporal powers which the former legal advisers of the Crown
thought she could...The Church in South Africa, then, is free.'[1]

Tractarians continued to support South Africa, to go and work
there and to lionize those who were there already. Some of them
called Gray 'the Athanasius of the South'.[2] James Green, Dean of
Colenso's cathedral and his bishop's arch-enemy, was presented
with a famous suit of vestments, supposedly the first to have been
worn in nineteenth-century England. And the new Bishop of the
Orange Free State, the most advanced Tractarian to have gone to

---

[1] C. N. Gray, *Life of Robert Gray*, 1876, II, 196.
[2] A. T. Wirgman, *Life of James Green*, 1909, I, viii.

South Africa, was given a chalice engraved with the names of the leaders of the movement. There were obviously many who believed that a Catholicism, primitive and Anglican, was being reborn in the southern tip of Africa. And it possessed synods.

It happens that the year of Pusey's letter to the *Churchman* was the very year in which the Convocation of Canterbury began again to conduct business. An enormous quantity of pamphlets flowed from the presses between 1830 and 1855, as the champions of synodical government pressed for the revival of Convocation. But these champions, as Dr Kemp has shown, were a rather different group of men from the Tractarians and had different ideals and aims.[1]

Because of the concurrence of dates and events it would be natural to suppose that the creation of synods in South Africa was a result either of the Tractarian veneration for the primitive or of the contemporaneous revival of Convocation in England. In fact, however, the sheer practical demands of the situation were the real cause. The reasons why the laity were included within the new synod reveal this.

It is true that Gray had read many of the pamphlets about Convocation[2] and in letters which he wrote to the Archbishop of Canterbury he had pleaded vigorously that parliament ought not to usurp Convocation's function as the Church's legislature.[3] But his real reasons for wanting synods in South Africa seem to have been essentially practical ones. An unestablished, unendowed Church needed money if it were to fulfil its vocation and mission. The laity would have to provide the bulk of that money. Moreover, the clergy needed to be welded together into a single task-force. They had become too used, in the colony, to living and working each in complete isolation, as parsons of the Church of England, temporarily occupying livings which happened to be abroad. Both laity and clergy needed to be drawn into consultation about the organization, expansion, and financing of the Church. Describing his first diocesan synod, Gray said that he

[1] E. W. Kemp, *Counsel and Consent*, 1961, 172.
[2] Diocesan Library, Cape Town: some of the pamphlets have Gray's name written on them.
[3] C. N. Gray, *Life*, I, 312 ff. and nn.

had challenged the Church to assume full responsibility for its own affairs, particularly in matters of finance.[1]

The question of lay representation in synod was crucial from the start. Many laymen and some clergy objected to synods on Erastian grounds and Gray was involved in public correspondence with a lawyer in the colony over the legality of his diocesan synod.[2] The lawyer argued that synods themselves were illegal unless summoned by the crown and that, even if a bishop could assemble his clergy for consultation, he had no right to require lay representation. Under these circumstances the whole matter of laymen in synod received much attention. It cannot be held that it was a matter of indifference or accident.

But Gray persisted in demanding that laymen be present not only in diocesan but also in provincial synod. In so far as the ancient tradition in the matter can be established at all, it seems to have leaned in the opposite direction. In the early Church 'diocesan' gatherings, no doubt, contained laymen. When Cyprian, for instance, wished to arrive at a decision about the discipline to be imposed on the lapsed, he promised to consult with the whole local Church.[3] The laity were also present when he discussed the matter with his fellow bishops at a 'provincial' level.[4] But the great synodical and conciliar gatherings, to which the Tractarians looked back in veneration, had been essentially gatherings of bishops. The concept of synods at a provincial level which had been formulated in the Middle Ages was also essentially episcopal.[5] It is never easy to be sure, of course, which early English assemblies are secular councils and which are ecclesiastical synods, and laymen and clerics seem to have been present at both.[6] Yet from the time that Convocation was established it is clear that it was an assembly which excluded laity.

---

[1] C. N. Gray, *Life*, I, 419 ff., but cf. Gray's letter to Keble (in the Keble Papers, Keble College, Oxford), 17 December 1863, 'I shall probably throw the responsibility very much on the laity themselves. If they are very anxious to come, I must invite them. If they are indifferent, they will forfeit their privilege.'

[2] *Correspondence between the Lord Bishop of Capetown and F. R. Surtees, Esq.*, Cape Town, 1857.   [3] Ep. XIV, 4 and cf. XXXIV, 13.   [4] Ep. XLV, 2.

[5] Cf. Benedict XIV, in *De Synodo Diocesana*, I, I, n.b. the final sentence.

[6] See M. Deanesly, *The Preconquest Church in England*, 1961, 212 ff.

Gray was, therefore, neither copying primitive precedent nor imitating the revived English Convocations when he insisted on full and formal representation of the laity in the South African provincial synod. His letters to the Archbishop of Canterbury, already referred to, are revealing on this point. Gray said he hoped that Convocation would become once more the Church's final legislative body. Sumner replied that it would be undesirable to persist with a clerical convocation since it would separate 'the Church' from the laity (i.e. the House of Commons). Gray's answer indicates that he cannot accept a definition of 'Church' which identifies it with the clergy, nor of 'the laity' which identifies it with a Commons who can be of any religion or none. This, he says, is his very reason for desiring to have laymen in South African synods. He is not prepared to claim for the laity a right to define doctrine but they must have the right to *assent* to it.[1]

It is true that there is some evidence to suggest that Gray and others did, on occasion, lean more towards the traditional or classical view of what constituted a synod. Great care was taken in both diocesan and provincial synods to make provision for voting by orders or houses. This, in effect, made it possible for the bishops or the clergy to exercise a veto. Dean Green and Colenso's other opponents in Natal objected strongly to a proposed Church Council, which Colenso intended to institute in place of a diocesan synod, because the clergy and laity were to form one single house in it. And Green did all he could to thwart Gray's plans to include laymen in the Provincial Synod.[2]

In the end the constitution of Provincial Synod was not the work of Gray. A draft constitution drawn up by the bishops and signed, clause by clause, by each of them (including Colenso) was begun in 1860. But at the first Lambeth Conference in 1867 Henry Cotterill, Bishop of Grahamstown, was secretary of the committee appointed to consider the government of independent provinces, of which Selwyn was chairman. Cotterill was a staunch Evangelical, alienated by Colenso's biblical criticism, and con-

[1] C. N. Gray, *Life*, I, 313 n.
[2] P. Hinchliff, *John Wilham Colenso*, 1964, 77.

sequently prepared to side with Gray in the attempt to create an independent, unestablished province in South Africa. What proportion of the detailed recommendations set out by the Lambeth Conference committee was actually contributed by Cotterill it is not possible to say. But he returned to South Africa a convinced supporter of synodical government, stumped the country to win the support of clergy and laity, and drafted a new proposed constitution. It is no surprise, then, to discover that the regulations adopted by the first Provincial Synod of 1870 faithfully reflects the 'Lambeth' pattern. And the Lambeth committee had said this about laymen in synod:

Your Committee consider that it is not at variance with the ancient principles of the Church that both Clergy and Laity should attend Diocesan Synod, and that it is expedient that the Synod should consist of the Bishop and clergy of the Diocese with Representatives of the Laity.

Without questioning the right of the Bishops of any Province to meet in Synod by themselves, and without affirming that the presence of others is essential to a Provincial Synod, your Committee recommend that, whenever no law or usage to the contrary already exists, it should consist of the Bishops of the Province, and of Representatives both of the Clergy and of the Laity in each Diocese.[1]

Laymen in synod were to prove something of an embarrassment to the infant province in its dealings with its friends elsewhere, some of whom were shocked at the thought that a layman might share in doctrinal decisions. The most determined of these was Prebendary J. W. Joyce. At the height of the controversy about the Judicial Committee of the Privy Council and its jurisdiction in ecclesiastical causes, he had written a scathing and sarcastic work, *The Sword and the Keys*, attacking everything that smelt in the least like Erastianism. Since the Colenso case was one of the most notorious of these issues and since the South African provincial constitution deliberately rejected the jurisdiction of the Privy Council, Joyce might have been reckoned as one of Gray's chief allies. But the presence of laymen in synod revolted his soul.

[1] R. T. Davidson, *The Six Lambeth Conferences*, 1929, 59 f.

He wrote a long and learned letter to Gray's successor, arguing that such a state of affairs vitiated the whole synodical principle; that whatever these South African assemblies were, they were not synods; and that it was highly dangerous to have the laity in an assembly that might have to decide doctrinal issues.[1] Joyce was too late. The laity had proved their worth, not only in financial and practical matters, but also in constitutional and even in quasi-doctrinal ones.[2] Nevertheless some South African churchmen remained sensitive on the point and as late as 1911 a priest of the S.S.J.E., who had spent a good deal of his ministry in South Africa, was to be found publicly defending the South African system before Anglicans in India. Part of his argument was that the provision for a vote by orders precluded the possibility of the laity deciding a doctrinal issue.[3]

In practice, of course, this danger has been found to be rather more remote than Prebendary Joyce anticipated. Synods do not normally find themselves 'defining doctrine' or discussing what might be called 'pure' theology—statements about the number of persons within the Trinity, for example. On the other hand, in a sense, almost every issue *can* have theological implications. Liturgical revision is an obvious case in point. And the procedure to be adopted for the election of a bishop says something about the nature of a bishop. A statement on racial or social issues is a statement about the doctrine of man. It has not been found necessary in South Africa to provide for the clergy to have a special doctrinal preserve in synods, nor would it be possible to define precisely how such a preserve could be maintained in practice. Even a vote by orders is a rare phenomenon, and is used as a procedural tactic rather than as a device for maintaining the purity of doctrine. And, indeed, the most common criticism of contemporary synods is that the laity seems less than enthusiastic about participating and that the clergy talk far too much.

To sum up, then, I think what I am really trying to say is this: that, if South Africa is in any sense typical, then modern Anglican

[1] Bishopscourt Archives, Cape Town. Letter dated 3/1/1888.
[2] See e.g. M. H. M. Wood, *A Father in God*, 1913, 234.
[3] F. W. Puller, *Synodical Government in the Church of the Province of South Africa*, Kolhapur 1911.

synods have owed much less to traditional patterns and theological justification than one might sometimes be led to suppose. It was the pressing need to legislate for and adapt to new situations which brought them into existence. And the laity are there, not as a result of theological or historical justification, but because they possessed the money and power which was needed and because by the nineteenth century a purely clerical gathering would have been not merely unthinkable but unworkable.

THE FIRST VATICAN COUNCIL

by E. E. Y. HALES

CENTENARIES are supposed to be occasions when we take stock of the event we are commemorating. In the light of developments in the last hundred years how does the work of the First Vatican Council look today? And since it so happens that the hundred years in question includes the Second Vatican Council, recently concluded, it is natural to put the question in this form: how does the work of Vatican I look today, in the light of Vatican II?

I think it would be fair to say that it is widely considered that the work of Vatican I was a little unfortunate, and has since proved embarrassing, because its definitions enhanced the authority of the papacy. Vatican II is supposed to have helped to redress that balance by disclosing the nature of the Church as a whole, from the bishops down to the People of God, or perhaps I should say from the bishops up to the People of God, in view of our preference nowadays for turning everything upside down. Such critics of Vatican I are not, of course, denying either the dogmatic infallibility or the juridical primacy of the Pope, which were defined at that Council; but they are saying that it is a distortion to stress the powers of the papacy and to neglect the powers of the college of bishops or the rights of the rest of the Church, and they are saying that the one-sided definitions of Vatican I tended to create such distortion in men's minds until they were balanced by the pronouncements of Vatican II.

There is a good deal about Vatican I about which we feel a little uncomfortable today. The preoccupation of that Council with the papal power seems to us now to reflect the attitude of an age when monarchy still mattered; our own democratic age prefers to place the emphasis rather differently. Again, to this ecumenical age, the definitions of Vatican I appear inopportune because they alarmed the non-Catholic world and upset sensitive people to an unnecessary extent. Much was said by critics at the time and has been written since about the arrogant and absolutist temper of a majority of the bishops, and especially of the Pope, Pius IX, in 1869–70. We are led to believe that it is really just as well that the Franco-Prussian war, which broke out in July 1870, and the Italian occupation of Rome, which followed as a consequence of that war, brought the Council to an end after it had lasted for only seven months. Had it continued to sit, it would have gone on to tackle the wider problems of the Church as a whole, and in particular the relations between Church and State, which were on its agenda, and would have done so in an intransigent spirit; so we are told we may see the finger of God in the armies of Bismarck and King Victor Emmanuel that cut short its work. I do not mean that those who express such views consider that any lasting harm was done by Vatican I, but rather that the achievement of Vatican I left us with a lop-sided and much too ultramontane attitude towards the Church, and that the temper of that Assembly made it unsuited to tackling those wider problems which have since been tackled with such vision and wisdom by Vatican II.

These judgements of Vatican I seem to me to be too patronizing and too complacent; nor are they quite consistent. And they assume a wisdom in the Second Vatican Council and a rash and ill-balanced impetuosity in the First which I do not think is fair to the First and may be over-flattering to the Second.

But let me concede, at the outset, one important point that lends substance to the criticisms of the work of Vatican I. It is this, that amongst the Minority at that Council, who were opposed to its defining the papal primacy and the papal infallibility, were to be found some of the ablest and most high-minded of the bishops present, such as Dupanloup of Orleans, Darboy of Paris, or Ketteler of Mainz, as well as some of the most intelligent of its scholars, such as Mgr Maret of the Sorbonne or the German historian of the Councils, Hefele of Rothenburg. I say nothing of distinguished critics outside the Council like Acton or Newman, who were also opposed. It should however be noted that what these critics were opposed to was the defining of these matters; they were not saying that the Pope did not possess these powers. They believed in the infallibility of the Church, resting on the promises of Christ, and that the Pope was supreme Head of the Church. But some of them, like Dupanloup, felt that it was very difficult to say when the Pope spoke infallibly, and therefore wiser not to try to do so; and others of them, like Darboy, or Ketteler, or Newman, felt that it was inopportune for the Council to do so; it might heighten the extravagances of fanatics and it might have an unfortunate effect on what today we call ecumenical understanding—it is noteworthy that most of the bishops of this Minority, who opposed the definitions, came from countries of mixed religion, where the Catholic Church was in a minority or at least, as in France, strongly challenged.

It seems to me that, although it is true that the definition of the papal primacy and the papal infallibility at Vatican I did make a very poor impression on the world at large, yet in the long run, after people had had time to consider matters soberly, they did not prove so disastrous. You cannot define without limiting, and because the Council defined the area within which the Pope was infallible it limited that area. And let us never forget that already in 1869 it had become extremely important to make it clear how very limited that area was, because the wildest things were already being said by fanatics about the Pope's absolutism and his infallibility. There existed already a strong neo-ultramontane tendency to accord sometimes grotesque and quasi-divine attributes to the Pope; it was less easy to do this after 1870 than it had been before because the Council had made it perfectly clear that hardly anything popes say is to be regarded as infallible. Catholics badly needed to be reminded of this in 1869, just as they still need to be reminded of it in 1969. The terms in which the definitions were drawn up in 1870 helped to remind them. And they still help to remind us. Thus it is because of the terms of those definitions that we can confidently say that *Humanae Vitae* is not an infallible document. I suspect that if this encyclical had been issued in the eighteen-sixties it would have been regarded by the ultramontane party, and especially by Louis Veuillot of the *Univers* and W. G. Ward of the *Dublin Review*, as infallible. That sort of misconception became impossible after Vatican I.

12-2

E. E. Y. HALES

Vatican I then limited because it defined the papal prerogatives. I sometimes wonder whether Vatican II, when it came to treat of the powers and characteristics of the rest of the Church in its decree *Lumen Gentium*, did so with as keen an eye to the practical implications of what it was talking about as was shown by the men of Vatican I. I am not, of course, questioning the truth or the wisdom or the value of *Lumen Gentium*, which undoubtedly constitutes a breakthrough and gives us a uniquely valuable picture of the nature of the Church as a whole. But the danger seems to exist that it may remain just that—a picture. How is the Church to be made to *work* in accordance with this admirable picture of what it *is*? Nobody seems quite to know, and everybody in this country is arguing about it from the columns of *The Times* and the *Tablet* downwards, or upwards; and the discussion is at least as lively in other countries. Cardinal Suenens tells us that it was a defect in the work of Vatican II that it failed to show how the concept of episcopal collegiality was to be made to work, as an effective power, in conjunction with the Papacy and the Curia. Surely it was. You can, if you like, say that the fault rests with Vatican I, for having defined the papal prerogatives in such a way as to make it very difficult for Vatican II to create, alongside those prerogatives, a viable collegiate power; but it seems to me you can only say that if you mean that Vatican I defined the papal prerogatives falsely. Even the most ardent liberal-progressive (if I may use emotive words) is not suggesting that. So it seems to me that the onus rested with Vatican II to show more precisely how the episcopal collegiality by which it set such store was to work. Bishop Butler has said in the *Tablet*, and the editor of *The Times* has followed him in saying, that a grave issue confronts the Church, namely how to give effect to Vatican II's teaching on collegiality; it certainly seems to me a pity that that Council did not show how it was to be done—as, for instance, the Council of Trent, which was so much preoccupied with heresy, showed how heresy was to be combated by the reorganization of seminary education.

However, I do not want to draw too many direct comparisons between Vatican I and Vatican II, which is not the purpose of

332

this paper. My main purpose is only to defend the work of Vatican I against the criticisms of those who have grown up in the heady atmosphere of Vatican II and who conceive that Vatican I led us astray. I don't think that, by tackling the matter of the papal authority, Vatican I distracted our attention from what matters even more, namely the Church as a whole; I think that it dealt with an isolated matter, of very great importance, which was the burning issue of that day in the Church, and dealt with it in a judicial and a practical way.

It would be hard to find circumstances in recent history more different than those in which these two councils met. In 1869, the prime objective, as at the Council of Trent, was to stop the rot (I speak here in Catholic terms) that was undermining the Church both from within and from without. In 1962 the prime objective was exactly the opposite, namely to bring the Church into closer *rapport* with the world, by renewing her interior life, and by extending her embrace to all elements in the modern world with which any fruitful contact could be made. It follows that at Vatican I, as at Trent, anathemas were the natural order of the day, whereas at Vatican II anathemas were themselves anathema. 'There have been enough anathemas', said Pope John.

The contrast extends, too, to the circumstances in which the two Councils assembled. 1962 was a year of relative *détente* in the struggle between the Church and the world, with a marked thaw in the icy hostility behind the iron curtain, and a sympathetic interest in what the Church was all about wonderfully awakened by Pope John. By contrast, 1869 was a year when a largely hostile world saw with satisfaction the Pope losing his temporal dominion and widely assumed he would lose his spiritual dominion along with it. Even an important part of the Catholic world, especially in the more democratic and advanced countries, had been turned against Rome by the provocative issue of the Pope's *Syllabus of Errors* in 1864, which appeared to condemn as erroneous most of the principles cherished by democrats everywhere.

It seemed almost incredible, when in 1867 the Pope first announced his proposal to hold a General Council, that he should contemplate summoning some 900 bishops to Rome at a time when he only survived in that city thanks to the French army, which Napoleon III was always threatening to withdraw. It has occasionally been said that he only summoned the Council in order to oblige the French army to stay at Rome to protect it. Fortunately the truth is rather different; his foreign policy was by this time entirely in the hands of his able Secretary of State, Cardinal Antonelli, who was strongly opposed to the summoning of the Council because he did not want to offend the French government, and the French government, like all other governments, was opposed to the idea.

Why were all governments, Catholic and Protestant alike, opposed? Why, indeed, were they interested? Nothing demonstrates more clearly the change in the public position of the Church between the two Vatican Councils than the intense interest of governments, and of the French, British, Austrian, and Bavarian governments in particular, in the work of Vatican I, and the benevolent indifference of governments to the work of Vatican II. It bears witness to the *de facto* (and beneficial) separation of Church from State in the twentieth century, which had come about although the *Syllabus of Errors* said it was an error to say the two should be separated. And why were the governments so hostile in 1869, especially the Catholic governments of Austria and Bavaria which made serious efforts to prevent a Council from being held? Why did that good Catholic, Lord Acton, use his influence with his friend Gladstone to try to get the British government to join with other governments to prevent the Council from discussing dangerous topics—which Gladstone might have done had he not been dissuaded by another of his friends, Cardinal Manning? Why did the French bishops, Dupanloup and Darboy, try to get Napoleon III to interfere—something he, too, might well have done, had he not been dissuaded by his Premier, Emile Ollivier, who was a Protestant? The Council was saved by the fact that the Protestant Prime Minister of England and the Protestant Premier of France decided it was wiser not to stop it. It was in greatest danger from the Catholic President of the Council of Ministers in Bavaria, Prince Hohenlohe, and the Protestant Chancellor Beust, of the Catholic Empire of Austria.

The reason for this hostility on the part of the governments was the issue by Rome of the *Syllabus of Errors* in December 1864. The shadow of that *Syllabus* hung heavy over the Council because it was widely supposed (and not without reason) that the Roman intention behind the summons of the Council was to give dogmatic force to the *Syllabus*. And the particular items amongst the eighty propositions of the *Syllabus* that gave rise to special alarm were those which reasserted the ancient claims of the Church in her centuries-old argument with the State. Thus the *Syllabus*, as we have seen, said it was an error to say that Church and State should be separated ('A free Church in a free State' was the phrase used by Cavour in Italy and by the Catholic liberal Montalembert in France); it was an error to say that all Christian Churches should be put on an equal footing by the State; it was an error to say that democratic majorities were free to do whatever they liked, irrespective of the rights of the Church—for instance in the field of marriage and education or the life of religious communities. The whole was summed up in a phrase that has become notorious, the eightieth and final proposition of the *Syllabus*, which stated that it was an error to say that the Pope should come to terms with progress, liberalism, and modern civilization.

Governments were alarmed by this *Syllabus*, and by the idea of a Council that might reinforce it, for two main reasons. They thought a Council might approve a Constitution on the rights of Church and State, conceived in the terms of the *Syllabus*, which would then become binding on Catholics everywhere and create immense difficulties for those governments which had many Catholic subjects. And they thought a Council might define the papal prerogatives in terms which would enable the Pope to count on the support of Catholics everywhere in his disputes with their governments and would effectively undermine their allegiance to those governments (and we may note that not only governments but bishops feared the likelihood of increased papal interference).

These were not idle fears. These things could have happened. A large number of the bishops at Vatican I would have liked to see them happen, and so would a great number of the faithful throughout the world whose enthusiasm was roused by journalists like Louis Veuillot and W. G. Ward. If the eighteen-fifties and -sixties were a time of scepticism among many intellectuals, they were also years of revival in religious faith and especially in the transcendental and miraculous element in religious faith (witness the progress of our own Oxford Movement) and there were plenty of people who, while they might not pine, as did W. G. Ward, to have a fresh papal bull to read every morning with their breakfast, yet were firmly convinced that it was only by papal bulls that the world would be saved. Moreover, it was not only the semi-popular Catholic press that invoked these dangerous ideas. The official organ of the Jesuits at Rome, the *Civiltà Cattolica*, was saying that it hoped the Council would proceed to give dogmatic force to the *Syllabus*. It also said it hoped the Council would declare the Pope infallible by acclamation; there was no need, the paper said, for the Council to debate this matter or to count heads; the Holy Ghost had no need to wait upon a debate; the Holy Ghost would descend upon the Assembly, like the tongues of fire at Pentecost, enabling it with a loud voice to proclaim the Pope infallible. Infallible when? In all his utterances? It seemed so.

Those were heady days. Better transport was making possible the holding of enormous Catholic congresses, and while some of the higher-level ones, like the famous congress of 1863 at Malines, where Montalembert made his great appeal for a free Church in a free State, reflected a liberal temper, and even foreshadowed the spirit of Vatican II, most of these great assemblies displayed a mounting devotion to the Pope, often expressed in extravagant terms. Meanwhile the Pope himself was adopting policies which were having the effect of centralizing the Church upon Rome. He was encouraging the bishops to make visits to Rome, *ad limina*; he was enlarging the ranks of the *Monsignori*—a papal appointment. He was encouraging the adoption everywhere of Roman rites, Roman vestments, the Roman liturgy.

By the later eighteen-sixties popular fanaticism about the Pope was being played upon by the journalists (and again one must give pride of place to Louis Veuillot), and leading to an emotional demand that the Pope be declared infallible by a General Council.

Not only governments but liberal and moderately minded Catholics everywhere were alarmed by this movement. For we have to remember that the fanatical neo-ultramontanes, as they are now called, enormously outnumbered the so-called liberal-Catholic movement. Montalembert's paper, the liberal *Correspondant*, was only a monthly, with a circulation of a mere 3,000 copies; Veuillot's *Univers* was the daily paper read by the French-reading parish priests, forming their outlook, and through them the outlook of the public at large, to the grief and concern of some of the French bishops, but to the satisfaction of more of them. We read, today, the protests of Lord Acton, or Döllinger, or Montalembert, who were demanding freedom from Roman interference for critical scholarship and a proper independence for local churches from the Curia, and we envisage a liberal-Catholic movement comparable to that which rallied behind Pope John and the majority of the bishops at Vatican II. There was nothing of the kind. Montalembert was the most distinguished and the most disinterested champion whom the Church had in the nineteenth century; but by the time the Council was getting down to its infallibility debates, in the spring of the year 1870, his had become a voice crying in the wilderness. In despair, he protested, in his last writing, that the ultramontanes at Rome were 'offering up justice and truth, reason and history as a holocaust to the idol they are erecting at the Vatican'. Pius IX didn't like that very much. He preferred the *Civiltà Cattolica*, which was now saying that the liberal-Catholics were not true Catholics.

'The idol they are erecting at the Vatican.' Well, some of them were trying to erect an idol. It had become *de mode* to refer to Pius IX as Pius the Great. No Pope had ever been the recipient of such vast assemblies of bishops and clergy and laity at Rome as were arriving in the eighteen-sixties, even before the Council itself brought the unprecedented number of 900 bishops in 1869. No less than 500 bishops attended the ceremonies for the eighteenth centenary of the martyrdom of Saints Peter and Paul on 29 June 1867, as well as 20,000 priests. At the canonization of the Japanese martyrs in 1862 there were 400 priests and 100,000 of the faithful. This was something quite new and, while we need not doubt that these crowds were filled with a true religious fervour, we should also note the beginning of papal publicity on a modern scale familiar to anybody who has attended a public papal audience. The Pope himself was glad to see them, and he was always a charming host; but at the time of the Council, when he domiciled many of the poorer bishops at his own expense, he remarked wryly: 'Non so se il Papa uscirà di questo Concilio fallibile od infallibile; ma questo è certo che sara fallito' ('I don't know whether the Pope will emerge from this Council fallible or infallible; but he will certainly be bankrupt').

The emotional build-up which, by the time the Council had been sitting for three months, seemed likely to result in its erecting an idol in the Vatican and declaring him infallible by acclamation, owed a great deal to the personality of Pius. He could be outrageous, as when he declared, to those who invoked the tradition of the Church that he himself was the Tradition ('la tradizione sono io!') or when he said that liberal Catholics were not true Catholics. But he said everything with a smile, and they loved him for it. And his behaviour was, in truth, a *tour de force*. How could he be so irrepressible after all that he had suffered, and the Church in Italy had suffered, at the hands of the Italian *Risorgimento*? The sheer audacity of his intransigence carried its own appeal. To tell the world, in the eighteen-sixties, that it was an error to say that the Pope should reconcile himself with progress, liberalism, and modern civilization required real courage. To hold a General Council at Rome in 1869–70, with the enemy literally at the gates of the city, required even more. To fasten public attention on the divine authority of the Church when everybody was saying that authority belonged to the People took men's breath away. I think that Pius IX's intransigence had much to do with his popular appeal, in much the same way as the uncompromising claims of Newman and Pusey kindled the devotion and self-sacrifice of the Oxford Movement.

But by the year 1869 the neo-ultramontane movement was becoming irresponsible and dangerous. It was wrong to say that the Pope was infallible by virtue of some sort of personal inspiration, a direct light from heaven—a most dangerous view, this—and it was absurd to say that his every utterance was infallibly true. There was a romantic element in all this, very characteristic of the nineteenth century. Yet before we dismiss the neo-ultramontanism of the eighteen-sixties as an altogether unhealthy excrescence, and give praise to Vatican I for putting it in its place (which is what I propose to do), we ought to remember that ultramontanism in the nineteenth century represented a necessary reaction against the appallingly low status to which the papacy had sunk in the eighteenth century, when even good popes, like Benedict XIV, thought of themselves as polite brothers in arms of the other enlightened despots, courtly princes preoccupied with the problems of their own states, and fighting, rather lethargically, a losing battle, outside Italy, for the rights of the Church. When Clement XIV suppressed the Jesuits in 1773, he betrayed the mission of the papacy because he did the deed to appease the governments of his time. Neo-ultramontanism was born when Pius VI resisted the French revolution and Pius VII resisted Napoleon and when Lamennais and Montalembert resisted Louis-Philippe. It was both useful and necessary; but by the end of the eighteen-sixties, with the *Syllabus*, with Veuillot, with the Jesuits of the *Civiltà Cattolica*, with the mass demonstrations at Rome and elsewhere, it was getting out of hand.

The great merit of Vatican I was that, despite the emotional pressures from within as well as from without, it arrived at well-balanced definitions that were the outcome of genuine and full debate, were in accordance with the tradition of the Church, and were ultimately accepted by all the bishops, and gave rise to no appreciable schismatic movement save the limited Old Catholic revolt in Germany, whose members followed Döllinger, a leader who was already estranged from Rome before the Council started. And although the mere fact that it did declare the pronouncements of the Pope, under certain special and rare conditions, to be infallible, sent a *frisson* of horror through Europe, adding impetus to anti-clericalism in France or to Bismarck's *Kulturkampf* in Germany, yet within a decade the crisis had passed, some of the steam had been taken out of the extravagances of the ultramontane movement, and men had learnt to live with the new definitions.

Let us look briefly at what the Council achieved in the brief seven months that it survived. It was not wholly preoccupied with the papal prerogatives. In its Constitution *Dei Filius* it isolated and anathematized some of the popular current heresies—notably rationalism, pantheism, and naturalism, affirming over against them the Catholic teaching on God, on Revelation, and on Faith. What is worth noting about this is that whereas the Council of Trent, in the sixteenth century, had been concerned with identifying and condemning erroneous interpretations of Christianity, Vatican I was concerned with identifying and condemning non-Christian beliefs which had emerged during the enlightenment of the eighteenth century. In other words the Church was no longer fighting against Luther and Calvin: it was fighting against Rousseau and the Encyclopaedists. But we must not delay over the Council's work on the contemporary heresies because the Council itself did not do so. It was in a hurry to get on to the matter of the papal prerogatives, because it was being pressed to do so by the ultramontane party, and the Pope himself was beginning, understandably, to show an impatient interest in the topic. So by March 1870 the Council turned its attention away from heresies and towards the papacy, taking the subject out of its turn from a *schema* that was concerned with the Church as a whole.

So began the struggle on the floor of the Council between the ultramontane or Majority party, organized by Archbishop Manning of Westminster, and the liberal or Minority party, organized by Bishop Dupanloup of Orleans. In some respects it was a little disedifying. One regrets, for example, the sharp practice of Manning, in packing with his own friends the important Deputation (or committee) *de fide*, which considered amendments to the *schemata*. One regrets the efforts of the Minority, behind the scenes, to persuade their governments to intervene and stop the work of the Council. One regrets the fact that Pius IX abandoned his neutral position and made it increasingly clear to everybody that he wanted a pronouncement that endorsed the concept of papal infallibility. But the important point, in the long run, was that the definitions, as they finally emerged, were a compromise, the result of a debate; and while they clearly expressed the juridical primacy of the Pope, and his dogmatic infallibility, they did so in terms that limited both concepts.

The definition of the pope's juridical primacy was the more sweeping of the two although, in effect, it only repeated the definition *Laetentur Coeli* reached at the Council of Florence in 1439. It affirmed the full and supreme jurisdiction of the Pope over the universal Church, and specifically anathematized anyone who said that the Pope had only the principal part but not the full plenitude of this supreme power, or that his universal power was not ordinary and immediate but exceptional. Some of the bishops were rather worried because they thought this might be taken to imply that their own ordinary and immediate jurisdiction, in their own dioceses, was only delegated to them by the Pope rather than coming direct to them from God; but in fact the Council was careful *not* to say that the power of the bishops came to them from the Pope. Thus at one and the same time the Council safeguarded the rights of bishops and yet killed finally the old Gallican tradition that the Pope had no ordinary juridical or administrative powers in certain countries, for instance France. His jurisdiction was universal.

Papal Infallibility proved more difficult to define than did the Primacy of the Pope. The final definition of it read:

The Roman Pontiff, when he speaks *ex cathedra*, that is when, exercising the office of pastor and teacher of all Christians, he defines with his supreme apostolic authority a doctrine concerning faith or morals to be held by the Universal Church, is possessed, through the divine assistance promised to him in St Peter, of that infallibility with which the divine Redeemer willed his Church to be endowed in defining doctrine concerning faith and morals: and therefore such definitions of the Roman Pontiff are irreformable of themselves and not from the consent of the Church.

We should note the following points:

First, what a long way this definition is from being a pronouncement 'by acclamation', or from being one which makes the Pope infallible whenever he happens to feel inspired. So far as I know the only occasion since 1870 on which the Pope has spoken infallibly, in the sense that Vatican I defined the matter, was when Pius XII in 1950 defined the dogma of the Assumption of the Blessed Virgin Mary into Heaven.

Second, there is a sting in the tail of the definition, in the last words: 'and therefore such definitions of the Roman Pontiff are irreformable of themselves and not from the consent of the Church'. (These words were added after the General Congregation had passed the text of the decree on 13 July; the Deputation *de fide* added them on 14 July and the General Congregation passed the amendment on 16 July. The Public Session and final vote were on 18 July.) The words mean that papal definitions do not *require* the formally expressed consent of the bishops; the words should not be taken to mean that the Pope has no need to take the advice of theologians, bishops, or other advisers, or that he is acting as other than head of, and therefore a part of, the Church.

Third, the decree *Pastor Aeternus*, which embraced these definitions of the primacy and the infallibility, was passed, at the final session of the Council, by 533 votes to 2, the two being the Bishop of Cajazzo, in Sicily, and the Bishop of Little Rock, in Arkansas. But many of the Minority had left Rome by then, led by Dupanloup, rather than remain and vote against the known wishes of the Pope. At the General Congregation which approved *Pastor Aeternus* as a whole, on 13 July, the voting was 451 *placet*, 88 *non-placet*, 62 *placet juxta modum*.

Fourth, the Minority bishops mostly made the outbreak of the Franco-Prussian war the excuse for their departure. All but a handful of them immediately wrote to the Pope expressing their acceptance of the definition, as finally adopted, and they had all done this before the end of the year 1872. If the Council did not achieve moral unanimity in the same measure as Vatican II did, it certainly expressed itself through the mouth of a large majority, and the minority yielded with a good grace after the event.

A word is necessary on the deplorable public relations aspect of Vatican I, an aspect in which a great improvement was effected at Vatican II. I know that the press and information departments at Vatican II came in for criticism; but at Vatican I no reliable news at all could be obtained most of the time; commentators depended for their information upon gossip and naturally preferred sensational gossip. The bishops at Vatican I took seriously their pledges of secrecy, and therefore failed to reply to the devastating attacks that were made by men like Acton or Döllinger, who conveyed the impression that the Council was fraudulent and intended to set up the despotism of a clique at Rome. Fortunately several of the bishops kept diaries, which later became the basis for interesting books, notably Bishop Ullathorne of Birmingham, whose diary became the basis for Abbot Butler's *Vatican Council* (published in 1930, now available as a Fontana paperback and the best account in English of the Council). But such books were only published much later. For thirty years the hostile press held the field, so that Bismarck in Germany and Gladstone in England had no difficulty in persuading a great proportion of their countrymen that the effect of the Council would be to make Catholics unreliable subjects. Yet all that had really happened was that the bishops had defined where, within the Church, authority ultimately lay, and, as Manning put it, in his reply to Gladstone, the decrees of the Council had 'in no jot or tittle changed either the obligations or the conditions of civil allegiance'.

But the rumours of fearful goings-on at Rome continued to circulate. And when the Vatican did at last allow the documents to be studied it gave them to a Jesuit historian, Father Granderath, who wrote an excellent five volumes on the subject, but was naturally suspected of having suppressed what was unpalatable to Rome. Only in the year 1927 did the full documentation become generally available in the Mansi records of the Councils. This secrecy was very bad policy and was wisely abandoned at Vatican II.

This contrast between the public relations of the two Councils reflects the utterly different atmosphere that came to prevail at Rome after the accession of Pope John. As I have said earlier, Vatican I was still defying and censuring the world, in the best traditional Roman manner, whereas Vatican II was moving outwards to meet the world. Pope John ushered in Vatican II with a note of optimism, castigating the 'prophets of doom'. This *volte-face* in the Roman attitude (because it was no less) was certainly timely and most welcome. But I don't think it was a turning of the back on the work of Vatican I; it was rather a turning of the back on neo-ultramontanism—curialism if you like—which survived Vatican I and was still evident during the reigns of the twentieth-century popes. This intransigent ultramontanism, of a triumphalist and dangerous kind, certainly existed at Rome in 1870; but it was not allowed to get into the decrees of the Council, which were well drawn up, soundly based, and expressed with moderation.

It is fitting, in conclusion, to notice the high regard that Pope John so often expressed for Pius IX and for the work of Vatican I. He hoped he might be able to canonize Pius IX, whose Cause had been entered long previously—while Vatican II was sitting. 'I am always thinking', he wrote in his Journal, 'of Pius IX, of saintly and glorious memory; and, imitating him in his sacrifices, I would like to be worthy of celebrating his canonization.' Well, he died too soon to have the chance of doing that. He also died too soon to see the outcome of his own Council, on which all his hopes were centred. Had he lived, one wonders whether he would have allowed that Council to be concluded without making proper provision of the *means* by which the bishops were to be enabled to play their proper part in a collegially controlled Church, of the *means* by which the Curia was to be kept in its proper place. However that may be, it is certain that Pope John did not see the decrees on the papal prerogatives promulgated by Vatican I as an obstacle to the development of responsible episcopal collegiality. Nor need they be. The real danger resides in the tendency, all too evident amongst Catholics over the last 150 years, to want to erect what Montalembert called an idol in the Vatican; and there is nothing in the decrees of Vatican I that warrants so irrational a procedure as the erecting of any idols anywhere.

KIKUYU AND EDINBURGH:
THE INTERACTION OF ATTITUDES TO
TWO CONFERENCES

by STUART P. MEWS

Two conferences of some significance took place shortly before the First World War: the World Missionary Conference at Edinburgh in 1910, and the Kikuyu Conference, held at a Church of Scotland mission station at an out-of-the-way place in East Africa in 1913. In an Ecumenical Age, the fame of the former is likely to endure, the notoriety of the latter to be forgotten. Yet it was the controversy raised by the second conference which caused Lord Morley to remark that the 'cacophonous' name of Kikuyu might one day rival in fame that of Trent.[1] Another grand claim was made for Kikuyu by the Bishop of Zanzibar—one with which *The Times* agreed—that 'there has not been a conference of such importance to the life of the *Ecclesia Anglicana* since the Reformation'.[2] And when the Kikuyu controversy was at its height in December 1913, Charles Gore, then Bishop of Oxford, recorded his conviction that the cohesion of the Church of England had never been more seriously threatened.[3] Admittedly Morley was too detached, and the two bishops too involved, for a correct reading of the temperature of the Church of England. But Kikuyu does seem to have brought to the boil discontents which had been simmering for a variety of reasons.[4] A. C. Headlam nicely distinguished between the actual proceedings at Kikuyu, and the agitation whipped up in England

[1] H. J. T. Johnson, *Anglicanism in Transition*, 1937, 127.
[2] *Ecclesia Anglicana. For What Does She Stand?*, 1913, 17; *The Times*, 4 December 1913. [3] *The Times*, 29 December 1913.
[4] For the use of the Kikuyu controversy as a rallying-point for an attack on liberal theology, see my unpublished Hulsean Prize Essay for 1968: Liberalism and Liberality in the Church of England, 1911–22 (University Library, Cambridge), ch. 4.

345

ostensibly on its account.[1] One aspect of that agitation, which is especially appropriate to the theme of this volume, is explored here, namely the relationship between two conferences, that at Kikuyu in 1913, and the great World Missionary Conference at Edinburgh in 1910. For even before Bishop Weston's dramatic intervention, a preliminary skirmish had been fought on the issue, 'What has Edinburgh to do with Kikuyu?'

Today it is widely recognized that 'Edinburgh 1910' was a major step in the modern quest for church unity. Missionary conferences had been held before, but Edinburgh was unique because of the carefully balanced representation of the different bodies, and the great influence and high positions of the participants. Yet, as Robert C. Mackie has observed, it was 'an event which has grown in importance in retrospect. At the time it was a notable concentration of foreign missionary interest and activity.'[2] Many of the participants may have hoped and believed that the final results of Edinburgh would go far beyond anything that was embodied in its carefully worded resolutions, but the wiser heads amongst them were alive to the dangers of exaggerating its achievements in advance.

Some contemporaries and some later historians have seen the Kikuyu Conference as one of the first fruits of Edinburgh. Bishop Stephen Neill, one of the foremost authorities on the history of missions and the ecumenical movement, in his widely circulated *History of Christian Missions*, writes:

The Edinburgh Conference of 1910 set in motion echoes throughout the whole of the Christian world, and the subject of unity, though not directly dealt with by the Conference, was one of those that inevitably came to the fore. One result was seen in the series of conferences held at Kikuyu in Kenya between missionaries of the Anglican, Presbyterian, and Methodist persuasions with a view to closer union. One of these conferences in 1913 let loose an explosion.[3]

---

[1] 'The Ecclesia Anglicana', CQR, April 1914, 141.
[2] *Layman Extraordinary, John R. Mott, 1865–1955*, 1956, 41. See also Hugh Martin, *Beginning at Edinburgh, A Jubilee Assessment of the World Missionary Conference, 1910–1960*, 1960, 3.
[3] Hodder and Stoughton edition, 1964, 550. I would like to acknowledge the kindness and help of Bishop Neill in several discussions on this and other topics,

Kikuyu and Edinburgh

Bishop Neill was not alone in making the connection between Kikuyu and Edinburgh. The first news of the Kikuyu Conference to reach Britain appeared in an article in *The Scotsman* of 9 August 1913. The Presbyterian author stated that, with a view to the ultimate union of the native churches, plans had been agreed upon for a federation of missionary societies. 'The missions in British East Africa', he reported, 'have solved the problem of how to coalesce Episcopacy and Presbyterianism.' The future native church was to consist of a Presbyterian structure completed by the use of the Episcopate as the coping stone. The account continued:

There was an hour in the World Missionary Conference at Edinburgh which those who were privileged to be present can never forget. It was the hour when that great assembly humbled itself before God because of the evils which have come upon the Church through the breaches of unity. And that hour in Edinburgh three years ago, is now transforming Christianity. Everywhere is the stirring of life—men groping to grasp each other's hands. It was at Kikuyu, in British East Africa, that I realized this in its fulness. There I found the first fruit being gathered of the World Missionary Conference.[1]

The article was written by the Rev. Norman Maclean, one of the more promising of the younger ministers of the Church of Scotland. He was already making his mark as a church leader (he was to be Moderator of the General Assembly in 1927), and as a popular writer (one of his books was called *Dwellers in the Mist*). Never a missionary, Maclean had been visiting Africa in 1913, attended the Kikuyu Conference, and actually preached at the famous Communion Service at its close.

The Scotsman report aroused much interest in British church circles, though little of the belligerence which was to be manifested later. A fortnight passed before a rejoinder was made by Edward Talbot, the High Church Bishop of Winchester, and a member of

and for introducing me to the relevant papers at Edinburgh House, Eaton Gate, London.
[1] 'A Great Day in British East Africa—The Problem of Church Union, a Contrast', *The Scotsman*, 9 August 1913. This crucial paragraph is repeated in Norman Maclean, *Africa in Transformation*, 1913, 164 f.

347

the Continuation Committee of the Edinburgh Conference. In a letter to *The Scotsman*, he sternly rebuked Maclean:

so far from these East African proceedings being upon 'Edinburgh lines', they precisely lack and contradict that which gave to 'Edinburgh' its distinctive character. 'Edinburgh' was made possible by the explicit condition that questions of union should not be brought before it. Its joy was that we could meet and confer and pray without any compromise of our general principles and convictions.[1]

Talbot was sure that the developments at Kikuyu, as described by Maclean, set back rather than advanced the grand design of Edinburgh. He was certain that the association of the two conferences would confuse and irritate those with reservations about Edinburgh, and jeopardize the possibilities opened up by this latter movement which 'faces all the facts of divided Christendom, and does not attempt hasty remedies which may only too easily increase instead of diminish our divisions'.

Talbot's position can be easily appreciated. More than anyone else, he had been responsible for High Church representation at Edinburgh. When the conference was first mooted, the S.P.G. had declined an invitation to take part. Tissington Tatlow and J. H. Oldham had then approached Talbot because they knew that his son, Neville, had interested him in the interdenominational approach of the S.C.M. When it was explained to him that the conference was to be held on *inter-* rather than *un*denominational lines, and that questions of faith and order were not to be touched upon, he agreed to attend, and with Bishop Gore persuaded the S.P.G. to reverse its previous decision.[2]

The Bishop of Winchester had been thrilled by Edinburgh. 'I think you know', he wrote in the *Chronicle*, 'how much importance I attached to that Conference as an event in Christian history; how I believed that in attending it we had been led more than we ourselves knew to take a step, responsible indeed in a high degree, but a true step in advance on a way of God's pre-

[1] 28 August 1913.
[2] Tissington Tatlow, 'The World Conference on Faith and Order', in Ruth Rouse and Stephen C. Neill, *A History of the Ecumenical Movement, 1517–1948*, 2nd ed., 1967, ch. 9, 406.

paring.'[1] He felt that closer contact would enable them to discern that which was most distinctive to each body: 'what we lack and need, what we have to learn and to receive'.[2]

Not without some misgivings on the part of the High Church representatives,[3] a Continuation Committee had been set up on which Talbot agreed to serve. The Committee sent its chairman, Dr John R. Mott, to visit the missions abroad, starting with India, where a series of regional conferences culminated in a National Conference for all India at Calcutta in December 1912. In addition to the conferences directly inaugurated by Mott, regional Continuation Committees, inspired by Edinburgh, were springing up in various parts of the globe, the first being in the Congo in 1911.[4]

Talbot seems to have regarded himself as the guardian of Catholic principles on the Continuation Committee. He felt that it was his duty to ensure that it did not go beyond the interdenominationalism which he called the 'Edinburgh lines'. He described the meeting of the 1912 Continuation Committee as ' a very happy and I hope very precious memory. I myself should find it difficult to express sufficiently how good the tone has been...not once through the whole time has there been a touch of friction, a sharp reply, or a flush of irritation. At the one or two places of some anxiety as to principle, the courtesy and even deference and desire to be loyal to our common ideal have been wonderful. So that the fear which I had that I might be in the anxious position of defending, with some help from Mrs Creighton and one or two more, lines for which the rest had neither understanding nor sympathy has *wholly* gone.'[5]

Recognizing the enormous potentialities of the movement begun in Edinburgh, Talbot knew only too well that its path was strewn with snares. Within his own camp, there were High Church

---

[1] Quoted in Gwendoline Stephenson, *Edward Stuart Talbot, 1844–1934*, 1936, 213.
[2] See his address to the Central Committee for Women's Church Work, *Guardian*, 5 December 1913, and his Preface to Herbert Kelly, *The Church and Religious Unity*, 1913, x.
[3] See Lord William Gascoyne-Cecil's speech, quoted in W. H. Temple Gairdner, '*Edinburgh 1910*', 1910, 193.
[4] C. P. Groves, *The Planting of Christianity in Africa*, III, 1955, 293.
[5] Stephenson, *Talbot*, 214.

Anglicans who were intensely suspicious of the whole movement. The decision of the S.P.G. to attend the Conference had resulted in a Formal Remonstrance being sent to the Standing Committee by 900 members of the Society. Edinburgh looked too much like a Pan-Protestant demonstration,[1] and if it were to result in any schemes of co-operation or unity which entailed a surrender by members of the Church of England of their Catholic inheritance, their worst suspicions would be confirmed.

This group received its first jolt early in 1913 when a report appeared in *The Times* about the National Conference for India, the very first national conference chaired by Mott. It came from the pen of Dr Robert F. Horton, the Hampstead Congregationalist minister, who, like Norman Maclean in the Kikuyu case, just happened to be on tour at the time, and at Mott's invitation had observed the proceedings. Horton had also been exhilarated by the Edinburgh Conference; he considered his participation in it to be 'the greatest privilege in my life'.[2] He was also well known for his strong anti-Catholic sentiments. Shortly after his return from Edinburgh, he had collaborated with Joseph Hocking in a book called *Shall Rome Reconquer England?* (1910). Describing the proceedings at Calcutta as 'the most significant sequel of the World's Missionary Conference of 1910 which has at present appeared', he reported that 'An Indian Church is coming into being. A National Missionary Society is winning the first victories. Before long the missionary forces may hand over to Indian Christians and an indigenous Church the task of winning India.' 'No important Church or Society was unrepresented except of course the Roman Church which declines to act with the other churches of Christendom.' He eulogized Mott: 'at his touch denominational rivalries or differences melt away. All churches act together. Unity is achieved.'[3]

The Anglo-Catholic old guard now knew that their instinctive antagonism to Edinburgh had been well founded. Mr Athelstan

[1] For this aspect of Edinburgh, see Eugene Stock, *The History of the Church Missionary Society*, IV, 1916, 560.
[2] R. F. Horton, *An Autobiography*, 1917, 296.
[3] 'India and Christianity', *The Times*, 24 January 1913; Stock, *Church Missionary Society*, 188.

Riley, the indefatigable watchdog of the interests of the English Church Union, felt vindicated by Horton's report, as he explained in the *Church Times*:

Some two or three years ago the Rev. D. T. W. Elsdale and I organized a remonstrance to the S.P.G. for its participation in the Edinburgh World's Missionary Conference. Many of those whose loyalty to the Church is beyond question, and whose opinion we very generally respect, including, if I remember right, the present Bishops of Winchester and Oxford and Dr Frere of Mirfield thought that we were unnecessarily apprehensive of the results which might flow from such participation. To all those who mistrusted our judgment I commend the letter from the Rev. R. F. Horton, the well-known Congregationalist minister in last Friday's *Times*.[1]

Only six months later, Maclean's misleading account of the Kikuyu Conference appeared in *The Scotsman*. If the *Church Times* is any guide, the Anglo-Catholic party was now becoming restless: India looked bad, but Kikuyu was far worse. If these were the fruits of Edinburgh, then by its fruits it would be known. Protests against both Kikuyu and Calcutta appeared in the *Church Times* of 22 August 1913. A leading article described the 'grotesque performance' at Kikuyu as the 'latest attempt at jerry-building', adding that 'the proceedings at Edinburgh were by no means free from its taint'. In the same issue, Archdeacon Wirgman voiced his misgivings about Dr Mott's journeys, and especially the National Conference at Calcutta, which he linked with 'the extraordinary pronouncements' of the Bishop of Madras upon the Historic Episcopate.[2] Against this background of rising Anglo-Catholic hostility, it is hardly surprising that the Bishop of Winchester wanted to sever any connection between Kikuyu and Edinburgh which might exist in the minds of High Churchmen, and in fact his letter repudiating Maclean was published just six days after the *Church Times* article had appeared. But Talbot's action did not mean, as Hensley Henson was to think, that

[1] 31 January 1913.
[2] For a discussion of the views of the Bishop of Madras in connection with Kikuyu, see A. C. Headlam, 'Notes on Reunion: The Kikuyu Conference', *CQR*, January 1914.

Talbot was opposed to all unity schemes. He urged support for the Indian Episcopate because it was genuinely acting on 'Edinburgh lines', unlike the bishops at Kikuyu, who seemed to him to have pledged themselves to a scheme of 'a strongly undenominational character'. Talbot warned a Church Congress audience not to suppose that 'the tendencies on the Mission fields to premature fusion with shallow estimates of the importance of doctrines or institutions, are due to Edinburgh or to any of its members as such'.[1]

The Bishop brought the matter before the Continuation Committee at its next meeting at The Hague in November, 1913.[2] Exactly what he said and the amount of support which he received is difficult to assess. However, the newspapers reported the passing of two motions which seemed to refer to Kikuyu. One of them deprecated the use of the name of the Edinburgh Conference in connection with proposals of a theological and ecclesiastical nature, though without passing judgment on any particular scheme. This motion seems to have been communicated to the press by Talbot. The other motion which was circulated to all the missions read:

In the judgment of the Continuation Committee, the only committees entitled to determine missionary policy are the Home Boards, the Missions, and the Churches concerned. It believes, however, that the missionary policy in any particular area can be rightly determined only in view of the situation of that area as a whole, and in relation to other work which is being carried on.

This resolution bears all the marks of a committee compromise. It gives the impression that an attempt had been made to condemn arrangements made at the local level. In the compromise resolution, the final word is left with the home body, but there is equal emphasis placed upon the local factors which must be considered.[3]

At this point, Talbot's behaviour was strongly challenged by

[1] *Guardian*, 5 December 1913.
[2] *Ibid.*
[3] Oldham later complained that though this resolution was the major topic of discussion at the Committee meeting, it had no connection with Kikuyu, *The Scotsman*, 20 December 1913.

Kikuyu and Edinburgh

the Dean of Durham, Dr Hensley Henson.[1] In a letter circulated to the clerical press and headed *Quo Tendimus?*, he argued that

a great error was made by the organisers of the Edinburgh Missionary Conference when they did not make intercommunion a condition of admission to their proceedings.[2] The inclusion of those who could not conscientiously own non-episcopalians at the Lord's Table as Christian brethren gave a delusive air of completeness to the Conference, limited unhappily the discussions...and committed the Conference to conditions of action which are really paralysing, and must lead finally to sterility. We are beginning to see the results of that initial blunder. The Bishop of Winchester—surely the strangest conceivable representative of the English Church at the Edinburgh Conference—is able to protest against the proceedings in East Africa as a breach of Edinburgh understandings! Mr Mott who is overwhelmed with lavish compliment by many who refuse religious fellowship with him at the Lord's Table, is in danger of being paraded before the Anglican world as the apologist of Anglican exclusiveness![3]

Henson concluded with a rousing appeal to the Evangelicals 'to guard the liberty of intercommunion in the Mission-field, a liberty which has long existed, but is now endangered'.

By this time, Frank Weston had published his 'Open Letter', and roused the Anglo-Catholic old guard. The stage was now set, if not for a full-scale battle, at least for a trial of strength between the High and Low Church parties. Weston believed that the time had come for 'the parting of the ways that we have so long dreaded and sought to avoid',[4] perhaps the only view which he shared with Henson. The latter's purpose in calling the Evangelicals to battle was fully set out in a private letter to the Archbishop of Canterbury:

[1] Henson was a persistent critic of Talbot. In 1911, for example, Henson supported J. M. Thompson when Talbot had withdrawn his licence to act as Dean of Divinity at Magdalen College, Oxford. See Mews, Liberalism and Liberality, 66.
[2] Temple Gairdner, an Anglican missionary in Cairo, and author of the popular report, also regretted that it was not possible to begin the Conference with the Eucharist, partly because he wanted to draw parallels with the great Ecumenical Councils of the past; *Edinburgh 1910*, 37.
[3] *Guardian*, 21 November 1913.
[4] *Ecclesia Anglicana*, 17.

I must needs think that this Kikuyu incident has great possibilities of good in it. An issue of the first importance, which could not be much longer postponed, has been raised in a form very favourable to its determination. The neo-Tractarians are now a purely Roman party, and they are out to wreck the Church of England. I do not mean, of course, the High Church Party which, albeit confused in its wits, is sound in its head, and quite honestly believes itself to be what it says it is. But I mean this new set, whose real leader is Gore (though they would probably disown him) and whose doughtiest champions are Knox, Figgis, Mackay, and their following. Personally I think there ought to be a secession of that section; and I should be disposed to interpret the task of statesmanship as being the making sure that the secession is secured in such circumstances that there is no disruption of the Church.

At present the Church of England is in danger of becoming 'an organized hypocrisy'. The attack of the Bishop of Zanzibar does but put into concrete form what the Neo-Tractarians are pressing continually. It is ceasing to be a question of intercommunion between us and Non-Anglicans: it is coming to be a question of intercommunion between dioceses of the Anglican Church.... Your Grace has the chance of your life. A clear, strong lead now would do a world of good, and, if it led to a secession of men whose *mentality* is Roman, and whole habit and method are anti-national, so much the better.

Incidentally, I hope this episode will put an end to the abuse of the Edinburgh Conference as a factor in the campaign against Protestantism. Few things have made me more indignant than the way in which the Bishop of Winchester tried to use the Continuation Committee to smother the action of Kikuyu. It was that more than anything else, which made me write the letter headed *Quo Tendimus?* and exert myself to get the Evangelicals to realize the potential gravity of the incident. The *Guardian* and *Church Times*, taking their cue from the Bishop of Winchester, boldly announced that the Edinburgh Committee *condemned* the action of the two Bishops, when, in point of fact, it warmly approved it, but only made it clear that it had no authority itself to take any action of this kind.[1]

Two comments might be made on Henson's letter. In the first place, it should be remembered that he had long been convinced

[1] H. H. Henson to R. T. Davidson, 31 December 1913 (Lambeth: Davidson Papers).

of the need for drastic action against the Anglo-Catholics. Fourteen years earlier, in 1899, he had written to William Sanday:

Personally I have a depressing sense, which grows over me increasingly, that things have gone too far for compromise; we must undergo a surgical operation which will either destroy us altogether, or badly maim us. The reckless ardour of Lord Halifax and his satellites offends and disgusts me in equal proportions.[1]

Henson's determination to drive out the Anglo-Catholics was evidently a long-held conviction, and not a sudden outburst of irritation. Now this long-awaited moment had come, and he was not going to let it pass. Though lest it might be thought that Henson was being over-dramatic in advocating the secession of that section championed by Knox, Figgis and Mackay, it is worth taking into account another private letter to the Archbishop on this issue—one pitched in a very different key: 'I do not detect in the situation the slightest cause for alarm. Beyond wishing that F. B. Mackay and R. A. Knox would go to Rome as soon as may be, I view the situation with almost unmingled hope.' That is the typically breezy opening of a letter from William Temple.[2]

Yet for all his indignation about the Anglo-Catholics and the behaviour of Dr Talbot, whom he obviously regarded as their representative on the Continuation Committee, it is clear from his letters to *The Times* that Henson was particularly disturbed by the attacks on the so-called 'Open Communion' service at Kikuyu. Perhaps this sensitivity was in part induced by an incident in his own Anglo-Catholic youth. In the last decade of the nineteenth century, Sir Henry Lunn, a prominent Wesleyan Methodist, had arranged a series of unofficial gatherings of church leaders at Grindelwald. In September 1892 the village had been badly burned in a fire; the English church had been severely damaged and the chaplain had left. In these circumstances (not unlike those

---

[1] H. H. Henson to W. Sanday, 25 October 1899 (Bodleian: Sanday Collection).
[2] W. Temple to R. T. Davidson, 11 April 1914 (Lambeth: Davidson Papers). In the event, only Ronald Knox was received into the Church of Rome: E. Waugh, *The Life of Ronald Knox*, 1959. F. B. Mackay was Vicar of All Saints, Margaret Street: Sidney Dark, *Mackay of All Saints*, 1937. J. N. Figgis was a member of the Community of the Resurrection, Mirfield: David Newsome, 'The Assault on Mammon: Charles Gore and John Neville Figgis', *JEH*, xii, October 1966.

prevailing on the last night of the Kikuyu Conference), Lunn had invited Dr J. J. Perowne, Bishop of Worcester, to conduct a communion service in the Zwinglian church. Among the non-Anglican communicants were Père Hyacinthe, Pastor Theodore Monod, Hugh Price Hughes, Dr T. B. Stephenson (the Wesleyan ex-President), Charles Berry of Wolverhampton, C. F. Aked, and Lunn himself. 'This incident', Lunn recalled, 'became the basis of a most cruel and sustained attack upon the Bishop of Worcester in *The Times*' by the young High Church Vicar of Barking, Hensley Henson.[1] On that occasion, Henson had written to *The Times*

because there are unconfirmed persons in this parish to whom I have refused the blessed sacrament on the specific ground that they are neither confirmed now nor, as the rubric has it, 'ready and desirous to be confirmed', and because these persons may be deluded into supposing that Dr Perowne is acting within the law when he admits to Holy Communion persons to whom the rubric notoriously does not apply.

It is because I reverence the Episcopate that I resent bitterly its degradation by those who have deliberately accepted it. Conduct does not change its character according to the dignity of individuals: and I have no other terms for the hypocrisy of prelates than those which have to do duty in the case of less important persons.[2]

In his denunciations of Grindelwald, Henson could rely on the staunch support of Athelstan Riley.

Henson's mental somersault on the Communion question does not, however, make him an unreliable witness of the events of 1913. His version of the verdict of the Edinburgh Committee seems to be correct. He was certainly right in saying that the *Church Times* and the *Guardian*[3] had reported that the Committee

[1] In his letter to the *Record*, 9 January 1914, Lunn has wrongly dated the incident as 1893 instead of 1892. Henson attacked the Grindelwald Conferences of both those years (in 1893, he wrote of the 'fantastic and disloyal pronouncements made at the so-called Reunion Conferences', *The Times*, 15 July 1893), but the Communion incident was in the former year. See also Sir Henry S. Lunn, *Chapters from my Life with special reference to Reunion*, 1918, 170 f.

[2] *The Times*, 17 September 1892.

[3] 'Unquestionably the Missionary Conference at Kikuyu travelled fast and far. It went, indeed, ahead even of the Edinburgh Conference, the Continuation Committee of which has already condemned its hasty action.' *Guardian*, 5 December 1913.

had condemned Kikuyu, which it certainly had not. Did the Bishop of Winchester attempt to get it condemned? J. H. Oldham, the secretary of the Committee, was notably reticent in his letters to the press—he wrote chiefly to correct the impression that the Committee had disapproved of Kikuyu. In a letter to *The Scotsman*, he simply repeated the resolution, and stated that it had not been moved by Talbot.[1] He did not reveal the name of the proposer. The silence of the officials of the Committee disturbed some of its strongest supporters. 'A Plain Churchman' complained that 'Strange to say, no mention of this minute is to be found in the report of the Continuation Committee in the *International Review of Missions*. Is Edinburgh then a brake on, instead of a stimulus to, union?...Is Edinburgh to be a synonym for talk?'[2]

The identity of the mysterious mover of the motion was never disclosed by Oldham, who seems to have found the whole episode painful and embarrassing. After a series of bitter attacks on the Bishop of Winchester in *The Scotsman*, Talbot's private secretary wrote to the paper pointing out that the motion had in fact been moved by the Rev. Arthur J. Brown, D.D., secretary of the Board of Foreign Missions of the Presbyterian Church in the United States.[3] But if Talbot had not moved the motion which was finally carried, he had, on his own admission,[4] raised the matter before the Committee. What had happened? In his diary, Hensley Henson records that in March 1914 he went to preach in Edinburgh, and at dinner met Sir Andrew Fraser, the father-in-law of J. H. Oldham, and himself a member of the Continuation Committee. Fraser had not attended The Hague meeting. 'But he told me', Henson writes, 'that the Bishop of Winchester endeavoured to secure a condemnation of the Kikuyu proceedings, and moved a resolution to that effect, but he received no support save from Mrs Creighton and another Anglican. Then was carried and drafted the ambiguous resolution which has lent itself to so much misunderstanding.'[5]

[1] *The Scotsman*, 20 December 1913.   [2] *Record*, 2 January 1914.
[3] *The Scotsman*, 22 December 1913.   [4] *Guardian*, 5 December 1913.
[5] *Retrospect of an Unimportant Life*, I, 1942, 164. The minutes of the Continuation Committee are kept at the World Council of Churches Headquarters at

But if Talbot had not got his condemnation, it is hard to believe that his stand did not have an effect on the Edinburgh movement. A week after the Hague meeting, Archbishop Davidson gave a long interview to J. R. Mott. The Archbishop wrote about it to Bishop Tugwell:

He [Mott] is profoundly convinced for the need of extreme caution as regards any action which appears to break down the distinctive differences between various forms of Christian faith and organisation. His instinct would be the other way. Personally he is an undenominational worker, but he has come to be convinced that our strength for going forward jointly will depend upon our not asking any body of Christians to water down their distinctive articles of belief into a common stock. This has been marked afresh in the Continuation Committee meeting at The Hague last week. They have re-affirmed the position taken at Edinburgh.[1]

The Archbishop thought that this marked 'undoubtedly a change of position from what used to be felt in such quarters'. He attributed it to a realization of the implications of the critical study of the Bible, which was a major theme in Talbot's argument against the undenominational position.[2] We would not be unjustified, therefore, in seeing something of Talbot's influence in Dr Mott's caution.

Geneva. I am indebted to the Rev. Philip A. Potter, Director of the Division of World Mission and Evangelism, for the following note: 'We have not been able to find either in the Minutes or in the correspondence of the time any reference to the motion of Dr A. J. Brown or to allegations which the Bishop of Winchester might have made. We do find that some of the background papers which form part of the Appendices to the meeting are missing. We do not know whether one of them might have been an account of Kikuyu plus a motion or proposed resolution. There is, of course, every likelihood that there was confidential correspondence on the matter, and quite possibly a long discussion which it was agreed not to minute. In those early ecumenical days there was a club atmosphere and very controversial matters tended to be kept under the counter and therefore quickly became part of folklore and hearsay.'

[1] R. T. Davidson to H. Tugwell, 25 November 1913 (Lambeth: Davidson Papers).
[2] A few days before meeting Mott, this point had been made to the Archbishop in a long letter about Kikuyu by Neville Talbot: Talbot to Davidson, 18 November 1913 (Lambeth: Davidson Papers). That E. S. Talbot held the same view can be seen from the *Guardian*, 5 December 1913.

358

Kikuyu and Edinburgh

The last word on the subject of this paper should surely rest, not with Edward Talbot or Randall Davidson, but with J. J. Willis, Bishop of Uganda, and the power behind the Kikuyu Conference of 1913. Long after Maclean's article in *The Scotsman*, and Talbot's initiative at The Hague, he wrote to the Bishop of Winchester:

I think it fair to point out that the recent Conference at Kikuyu in no sense *claimed* to be working under the guidance or inspiration of Edinburgh. No mention is made of Edinburgh in the printed memorandum of the Kikuyu Conference: no reference so far as I am aware was made to Edinburgh from beginning to end of the gathering: and the Resolutions passed were, in almost every detail, those already passed by a somewhat smaller Conference, at Nairobi in 1909. Certainly I myself had no thought of following or involving Edinburgh: the movement was entirely independent, the outcome of discussions dating back to 1907.[1]

So it would seem that Kikuyu owed nothing whatever to Edinburgh, but perhaps the movement begun at Edinburgh bore some marks of the controversy caused by the conference at Kikuyu.

[1] J. J. Willis to E. S. Talbot, 5 December 1913 (copy in Davidson Papers).